USAFE TACTICAL UNITS

IN THE UNITED KINGDOM IN THE COLD WAR 1950 TO 1992

USAFE TACTICAL UNITS

IN THE UNITED KINGDOM IN THE COLD WAR 1950 TO 1992

DOUG GORDON

FONTHILL

Fonthill Media Language Policy

Fonthill Media publishes in the international English language market. One language edition is published worldwide. As there are minor differences in spelling and presentation, especially with regard to American English and British English, a policy is necessary to define which form of English to use. The Fonthill Policy is to use the form of English native to the author. Doug Gordon was born and educated in Suffolk; therefore British English has been adopted in this publication.

Fonthill Media Limited
Fonthill Media LLC
www.fonthillmedia.com
office@fonthillmedia.com

First published in the United Kingdom and the United States of America 2022

British Library Cataloguing in Publication Data:
A catalogue record for this book is available from the British Library

ISBN 978-1-78155-860-7

Typeset in 10pt on13pt Sabon
Printed and bound in England

Foreword

I was born in 1945 in the Suffolk village of Orford. My earliest memories of aircraft dates back to those days, living as I did near the twin bases of Bentwaters and Woodbridge. My father worked with the Royal Aircraft Establishment on Orfordness, which I visited on several occasions as a child. Although I was fascinated by the collection of damaged German warplanes languishing on a dump on the 'island', I was increasingly distracted by the sound of the jet engines that emanated from the aircraft of the twin bases which seemed to be constantly overhead. First the F-86 Sabres of the 81st FIW at RAF Bentwaters and the F-84Es of the 79th FBS of the 20 FBW which were based at RAF Woodbridge. These were followed by the F-84F Thunderstreaks and the F-100 Super Sabres. We used have family picnics at Iken Cliffs on the River Alde, which was under the flight line for Bentwaters. Improvised games of cricket were, more often than not, interrupted by the sight of a pair of aircraft in the landing pattern passing overhead. A trip to Sudbourne Hall where my dad played cricket for the village was a good spot for 'spotting', when, on a summer's afternoon I would laze on my back in the sun watching the sky. I was never disappointed.

I recall one occasion when walking though the village in the direction of the church with a friend when we saw a parachute in the sky in the distance. This was exciting! We ran off in the direction of where the parachute was seen. Soon, however, we lost sight of it and were about to give up the chase when someone shouted that a 'plane had crashed near Sudbourne Hall'. Off we went and, sure enough, there in a field to the left of the road we were running down was a very broken and smoking Thunderstreak. Already the guards were there and standing around the crash site so we could not get very close. I recently did some research and, with difficulty, found out that the date was 25 April 1955 and the aircraft was F-84F 52-6557, piloted by Homer K. Hansen, assigned to the 91st FBS at RAF Bentwaters. He ejected safely when the aircraft stalled and then spun into the ground. Hansen, who was eventually promoted to major-general, was the operations officer of the 81st FBW.

Regular attendance at local air shows and a move to Farnborough reinforced my interest in military aviation throughout the remainder of the 1950s and the early 1960s, after which the demands of education and the obsessions of youth forced them into a back seat. Many years later, they were revived and I decided to write. The Cold War era has always had a particular fascination for me based on those childhood memories, and the United States Air Forces in Europe (USAFE) in particular. I had written about the aircraft and units of USAFE for some time before I decided, some couple of decades ago, to concentrate on those units of Tactical Air Command based in the United Kingdom. This book is the result.

I have focussed on the units that were permanently based in the UK during the Cold War. I have not included the tactical missile units. I have strived to include as much personal input into the narrative from people who were involved as possible. This has not always been easy and it has sometimes been difficult to locate and persuade folks to share their memories. I hope that those memories, stories, and anecdotes that are included help the reader to better appreciate the role that these people played in what were sometimes very worrying times.

I have included many photos to support the narrative. I note that many of these, particularly from the very early period, are not of the highest quality, but I do not apologise for their inclusion. In themselves they tell a unique story. Few people had cameras of the same sophistication that we enjoy nowadays, and even fewer people had the opportunity to photograph aircraft in what was a very security-conscious environment like a military airfield. Often air shows were the only opportunity to get close to modern jet aircraft. At a time when we did not have to suffer barriers at an air show and could wander around and underneath, and occasionally inside and on top, of these frontline aircraft, people were bound to get in the way of our photographs at the Armed Forces Days and the Open Houses.

There were many international events that encroached on all our lives to a greater or lesser degree throughout the period of the Cold War. I have brief accounts of these for the reader who may not be familiar with them. For those who are steeped in the story of the Cold War, they will perhaps serve to jog a memory or two. Some of these events prompted a very high alert status to be enacted on the bases. Some, not so serious, nevertheless demanded a response from USAFE, which led to the relocation of units both within Europe and into the UK, such as Red Richard. I have also included a section about the USAFE aerobatic team, the Skyblazers. Many people attending Armed Forces Days and Open Houses at the USAFE bases in the UK got to see the team during the period when it was active.

I have not dwelt at any length on the social and geopolitical aspects of life for the servicemen of the USAF who found themselves deployed to the UK, or indeed on their hosts who occupied the many small towns and villages that surrounded the bases. This book is unashamedly about the aircraft and the men who flew them in the Cold War that, thankfully, never got hot, but came close to it a few times!

Acknowledgements

This book has been many years in the writing, and there have been many people who have helped and supported my efforts during those years. I am particularly grateful to all those who were directly involved in the events and history that this work strives to tell. There are many who have shared their memories and 'war stories' with me via letters, emails, and telephone calls. Thanks to Fred Abrams, Marcus Anderson, Arlie Blood, Lee Bowden, Mike Briggs, 'Jiffy' Jerry Brown, Willi Bruenner, Richard Crandall, Jim Crumbliss, Rick Davis, Don Emigholz, George Fennell, Bob Fredette, Paul Fry, Larry Garrison, John 'Goldie' Goldenbaum, Bob Gould, Dick Grace, Jack Griffin, George Grill, Don Harding, Norman Harris, Robert Held, Jim Howard, George Howard, John Hugie, Ernst Janke, Richard Jarvis, Jim Jimenez, David Jones, Dick Johnson, Don Karges, Richard Kamm, Mike Kostelnik, David Kramer, Bill Landis, Gil Leimbach, Bruce MacLennen, Dean Maurer, Don McDonald, James McGorry, Fred Mills, Jim Morgan, Brad Mosher, Chuck Munroe, Robin Olds, 'Doc' Partridge, Don Pickard, Nick Pishvanov, Jim Preston, Ray Ramsey, Gordon Ranum, Kirk Ransome, Gerry Reponen, Bill Rial, Mike Robinson, Sandy Sanderson, Ed Satterfield, Gordon Scharnhorst, Scotty Schoolfield, Dick Sidak, Dave Skilling, Forrest Smith, John Summers, 'Smokey Sundell, Bob Sweet, Paul Taylor, Dale Thompson, Milton Torres, Peter Verney, Joe Williams, Jim Wilson, Jim Wisdom, Les Wood, and Robert Zaehringer. Sadly, many of these 'old warriors' have died during the last couple of decades it has taken to complete this work. I hope that this narrative will be a worthy tribute to them and their service.

There are many people who have helped me with photographs. A special thanks for this is due to Robbie Robinson, Art Sevigny, Duncan Curtis, the late Dave Menard, the late George Pennick, Mick Sudds, Simon Gladas of the Bentwaters Aviation Society, Neil Aird, Bob Ganci, Joe Williams, Kirk Ransome, George Fennell, Jim Stanitz, George Howard, the late Nick Pishvanov, Don Mikler, Gil Leimbach, Graham Gilbert, and Alan Scholefield. Thanks to John Bessette, historian of the Tac Tankers Association, and Walt Larimer of that organisation for helping me with my research into the story of the 420 AREFS and for helping with photos. There are many others, all of whose names appear in the credits to the photos. The Bob Gould and the Tac Recce Association have also been an invaluable help along with the Voodoo Association and the B-66 Destroyer Association. My research into the B-45A operations of the 47th BW would not have been as complete without the permission being given to quote aircrew from the video produced by Glenn Ludlow about the unit. Thanks to Carol Zimmerman and Glenn's daughter granting permission. Details of the video, *Cold War Remembered*, is included in the 'Bibliography and other Sources' at the end of this book. I am grateful to the Aircraft Engine Historical Society for permission to quote from the memoirs of Richard Kamm from their website.

Contents

Glossary of Abbreviations

AAA	Anti-Aircraft Artillery
AAF	Army Air Force
AB	Air Base
ACM	Air Combat Manoeuvring
ACMI	(Air Combat Manoeuvring Instrumentation)
AD	Air Division
ADC	Air Defence Command
ADIZ	Air Defence Identification Zone
AEC	Atomic Energy Commission
AFB	Air Force Base
AFRES	Air Refuelling Squadron
AGL	Above Ground Level
AMP	Aircraft Maintenance Programme
ANG	Air National Guard
APU	Auxiliary Power Unit
ATAF	Allied Tactical Air Force
ATC	Air Traffic Control
AWACS	Airborne Warning and Control System
A-X	Attack Experimental
BDA	Battle Damage Assessment
BW	Bombardment) Squadron
CAS	Close Air Support
CASF	Composite Air Strike Force
CCTG	Combat Crew Training Group
CCTS	Combat Crew Training Squadron
CENTO	Central Treaty Organisation
CONUS	Continental United States
CONAC	Continental Air Command

DACT	Dissimilar Air Combat Training
DMAS	Digital Modular Avionics System
DO	Director of Operations
DRC	Defensive Reaction Training
ECCM	Electronic Counter Countermeasures
ECM	Electronic Countermeasures
ECS	Electronic Combat Squadron
ECW	Electronic Combat Wing
ELINT	Electronic Intelligence
EW	Electronic Warfare.
EWO	Electronic Warfare Officer
FAC	Forward Air Controller
FBG	Fighter Bomber Group
FBW	Fighter Bomber wing
FBS	Fighter Bomber Squadron
FDS	Fighter Day Squadron
FEBA	Forward Edge of the Battle Area
FFAR	Folding Fin Aerial Rocket
FG	Fighter Group
FIW	Fighter Interceptor Wing
FIS	Fighter Interceptor Squadron
FLR	Forward Looking Radar
FMS	Foreign Military Sales
FOD	Foreign Object Damage
FOL	Forward Operating Location
FRL	Flight Refuelling Ltd
FW	Fighter Wing
FS	Fighter Squadron
GCA	Ground Control Approach
GCI	Ground Control Intercept
GDR	German Democratic Republic
GIB	Guy in the Back
GOR	General Operational Requirement
HARM	High-Speed Anti-radiation Missile
HF	High Frequency
HUD	Heads Up Display
HVAR	High-Velocity Aircraft Rockets
ICC	International Control Commission
IFR	Instrument Flight Rules
INS	Inertial Navigation System
IP	Instructor Pilot; Initial Point.
IR	Infrared
JAAT	Joint Air Attack Tactics
Kts	Knots

LABS	Low-Altitude Bombing System
LADD	Low-Altitude Drogue Delivery
LATN	Low-Altitude Tactical Navigation
LF	Low Frequency
LOC	Location
LORAN	Long-Range Aid to Navigation
LWF	Lightweight Fighter
MAP	Military Assistance Programme
MATS	Military Air Transport Service
MC	Mission Capable; Maintenance Costs
MDAP	Military Defence Acquisition Programme
MTD	Mobile Training Detachment
NATO	North Atlantic Treaty Organisation
NSC	National Security Council
ORI	Operational Readiness Inspection
PACAF	Pacific Air Forces
PI	Photo Interpreter
PPIF	Photo Processing and Interpretation Facility
PRS	Photographic Reconnaissance Squadron
RAD	Research and Development
RAE	Royal Aircraft Establishment
RHAW	Radar Homing and Warning
ROE	Rules of Engagement
RDT&E	Research Development Test and Evaluation
RTAFB	Royal Thai Air Force Base
SAC	Strategic Air Command
SALT	Strategic Arms Limitation Talks
SAM	Surface-to-Air Missile
SHORAN	Short-Range Navigation
SLAR	Side-Looking Airborne Radar
SLR	Side-Looking Radar
SIOP	Strategic Integrated Operations Plan
SOR	Specific Operational Requirements
TAC	Tactical Air Command
TACAN	Tactical Air Navigation
TARPS	Tactical Airborne Reconnaissance Pod System
TDY	Temporary Duty
TEREC	Tactical Electronic Reconnaissance System
TEWS	Tactical Electronic Warfare Squadron
TFR	Terrain-Following Radar
TFTS	Tactical Fighter Training Squadron
TFTAS	Tactical Fighter Training Aggressor Squadron
TFG	Tactical Fighter Group
TFS	Tactical Fighter Squadron

TFW	Tactical Fighter Wing
TGT	Target
TOT	Time Over Target
TRG(p)	Tactical Reconnaissance Group
TRS	Tactical Reconnaissance Squadron
TRTS	Tactical Reconnaissance Training Squadron
TRW	Tactical Reconnaissance Wing
TS	Tactical Squadron
TTW	Tactical Training Wing
UN	United Nations
USAF	United States Air Force
USAFE	United States Air Forces in Europe
VA	Victor Alert
VFR	Visual Flight Rules
WP	Warsaw Pact
WSO	Weapons Systems Officer
Wx	Weather

Introduction

Tactical Air Command

Tactical air warfare can be defined as providing support for surface forces in the battlefield environment. This would include firepower, aerial reconnaissance, and command and control facilities. It also includes an air defence role, intercepting and destroying enemy aircraft intent on attacking the ground forces and threatening the homeland. Over the years, it has also acquired and developed a significant battlefield electronic warfare (EW) mission. However, the mission of TAC was originally quite limited.

Tactical Air Command (TAC) was created by the War Department of the United States of America on 21 March 1946, in the immediate aftermath of the Second World War. The mission of the new command was to 'provide and operate that portion of the AAF [Army Air Forces] which is maintained in the United States, and in such other areas as may be designated from time to time, for co-operating with land and sea forces in the conduct of land and amphibious operations'. Attached to TAC were the Third Air Force, the Ninth Air Force, the Twelfth Air Force, the Nineteenth Tactical Air Command, and the Ninth Troop Carrier Command. Two other independent commands were also created at this time, Strategic Air Command (SAC) and Air Defence Command (ADC).

The role of TAC throughout the first four years of its existence was confined to the Continental United States (CONUS). During the period to the end of 1948, the command grew in stature and autonomy. Air power began to be seen in its own right and not simply as an extension to the army. Consequently, the development of tactics and roles could be developed independently, which is not to say that the surface support role was neglected, rather that the development of tactical capabilities improved that role. Korea had established that there had been inadequacies in the USAF's tactical air support role and this in itself stimulated a positive response from TAC.

However, in December 1948, after a year in which the command had grown in stature, confidence and independence, TAC had its wings and its aspirations severely clipped when it was downgraded to a subsidiary of the newly activated Continental Air Command (CONAC). Its mission now became to provide USAF cooperation with surface forces and operational training thereof. It was to be two years before TAC was restored to its major command status, on 1 December 1950.

The early 1950s saw a development in TAC's role and its expansion into a global entity. It was also a time when it was necessary to look closely at the missions of both SAC and TAC and begin differentiating the roles. Nuclear deterrence was a case in point. The acceptance of 'Massive Retaliation' as a first response to Soviet armed aggression in Europe prompted the US to proceed with the development of what came to be known as Tactical Nuclear Weapons (TNW).

In air force terms, a TNW can be defined as a relatively low-yield nuclear device capable of being delivered by a fighter aircraft or a tactical bomber to a target that could be described as within the battlefield arena. A philosophy of tactical nuclear strike was born and with it came the necessity to develop the weapon to be used. Tactical Air Command was given the task of developing the capability. Col. 'Mort' Lunsford was the director of materials in the 20th Fighter Bomber Wing (FBW) in the early 1950s and recalled in an article in *Air Force Magazine* in June 1978:

> The proposal to build a tactical atomic bomb, particularly one carried by fighters, met some opposition in those early days when SAC still had its hands full dealing with strategic nuclear weapons. But Col. John Stevenson and other proponents stumped the halls of the Pentagon and sold the idea. The Atomic Energy Commission (AEC) said that a tactical atomic bomb could be built. It would have something more than the yield of the Hiroshima bomb, and could be carried on the wing of a fighter or shaped to fit the bomb bay of a tactical bomber. The signal was given to go ahead. Along with it came the order to form the 49th Air Division (AD), composed of the North American B-45A Tornado equipped 47th Bomb Wing and the 20th Fighter Bomber Wing who Flew the Republic F-84G Thunderjet.

The end result was the design and development of the Mk 7 atomic bomb.

One of the roles for which TAC was responsible was that of tactical reconnaissance. The function of tactical reconnaissance is to gather intelligence about the enemy's disposition, strength, and technology in the confines of the battlefield and its environs. It differs from strategic reconnaissance, which embraces the finding and pinpointing of targets for intercontinental warfare and indications and warnings of possible surprise attack. The additional role 'to conduct weather reconnaissance over areas of Joint Air-Ground Operations' was added in 1952.

In the early 1950s, TAC gained control of several federalised Air National Guard reconnaissance and fighter units. Many of these units were assigned overseas, to Europe and Asia, such as, for example, the 117th Tactical Reconnaissance Wing, activated at Lawson AFB, Georgia, in November 1950 and deployed to Europe in January 1952. Another example was the 123rd Fighter Bomber Wing (FBW) assigned to the Kentucky ANG, which was deployed to the UK in November 1951.

The Lisbon Agreement on NATO force levels, which was endorsed by the North Atlantic Council in February 1952, prompted a further increase in the USAF's presence in Europe. The demands of NATO for an increase in forces to face the Soviet bloc, coupled with the policy demands of Massive Retaliation and the continuing development and production of ever faster, technologically advanced and capable second-generation tactical aircraft led the USAF and other western European nations to upgrade and augment their air forces. For the USAF, it meant the deployment of additional tactical wings: fighter, bomber, and reconnaissance.

The mission of the new tactical aircraft joining the TAC squadrons demanded that they be refuelled in-flight. In the early 1950s, these aircraft depended on SAC for this service. In 1954, TAC acquired the first of two refuelling squadrons equipped with Boeing KB-29P tankers, which were fitted with the Boeing-designed 'flying boom' system of air refuelling. The first two squadrons to be formed were the 429th Air Refuelling Squadron (AREFS) and the 420th AFRES. The 429th was activated at Langley AFB in July and the 420th at Alexandria AFB, Louisiana, in March. The flying boom system was matched to the Republic F-84G, F-84F, and RF-84F aircraft. It could also refuel TAC's North American B-45A Tornado bombers. When the Century series of fighters joined the inventory, the KB-29s were replaced by the KB-50 tankers, which used the hose and drogue system and could refuel three aircraft at the same time. In October 1954, the 420th AREFS was deployed to the UK and based at RAF Sculthorpe in Norfolk.

USAFE

The United States Air Forces in Europe (USAFE) was activated in August 1945 with the redesignation of the United States Strategic Air Forces in Europe. The headquarters of USAFE was established at Wiesbaden, Germany, on 28 September 1945. At its inception, the role of USAFE was concerned principally with disarming remnants of the German forces, the dismantling of the US presence in Europe, and the repatriation of personnel and materials to the United States. In addition, Operation Lusty involved the command in acquiring Luftwaffe aircraft of interest and dispatching them to the US to be evaluated. This included jet aircraft such as then Me 262 and the Heinkel He 162.

The rundown of USAF units in Europe reached a peak in 1947. At the end of this year, there was only one tactical unit in Europe: the 86th Composite Group comprised of three squadrons, the 525th, 526th, and 527th Fighter Squadrons each flying the Republic P-47D Thunderbolt from Neubiberg, Germany. Several events arrested the decline of the US forces in Europe. The first of these occurred in June 1948 when the Soviet Union blockaded West Berlin in an attempt to force the occupying forces out of the city. It was a strategy that failed because the airlift that was operated by the Allied forces succeeded in providing the food, fuel, and medical supplies that were needed. This event proved beyond any shadow of doubt that the Soviets and their allies in Eastern Europe were not to be trusted and this realisation led to establishment of the North Atlantic Treaty Organisation (NATO) in a treaty signed on 4 April 1949. Article 5 of the treaty states: 'The Parties agree that an armed attack against one or more of them in Europe or North America shall be considered an attack against them all…' This is the provision of the treaty that is most recalled in relation to the significance of the founding of the organisation. The provisions of Articles 2 and 3 were also important; Article 2 stating the principle of military cooperation between the signatories and Article 3 encouraged the principle of non-military cooperation. The explosion of an atomic bomb by the Soviet Union on 29 August 1949 also took the Western Allies by surprise. They had expected that the Soviets would not have an atomic capability for several years. The outbreak of the Korean War in 1950 gave further impetus to the necessity of developing the capabilities of the USAF and NATO and the role that USAFE would play in that development.

During the Berlin Airlift, on 23 August 1948, USAFE activated the 3rd Air Division (AD) in the UK to provide support to the airlift flights and the SAC bomber units on temporary deployment to the UK. Originally headquartered at RAF Marham, Norfolk, the 3rd AD moved to South Ruislip in April 1949.

The 3rd Air Force

Following the outbreak of the Korean War and the increasing animosity evident between NATO and the Soviet Union and its allies, the expansion of USAFE became a matter of some urgency. On 1 May 1951, USAFE deactivated the 3rd AD and activated the 3rd Air Force (AF) with the responsibility to oversee all tactical operations in the UK. SAC activated the 7th AD at this time to have control over its operations in the UK. Over the course of the next decade, the USAFE presence in the UK would increase dramatically.

In September 1951, the 81st Fighter Interceptor Wing (FIW) arrived in Suffolk, at the twin bases of RAF Bentwaters and RAF Shepherds Grove. Three months later, the 123rd Fighter Bomber Wing (FBW) arrived at RAF Manston. The year 1952 saw the arrival of the 49th AD with the 20th FBW deploying to RAF Wethersfield and Woodbridge and the 47th BW to RAF Sculthorpe.

1

The 81st FIW, FBW, TFW

The 81st started life as the 81st Pursuit Group on 9 February 1942 when it was activated at Morris Field, North Carolina. Three squadrons were assigned: the 91st, 92nd, and 93rd Pursuit Squadrons, flying the Bell P-39 Airacobra. In May 1942, the unit was redesignated as the 81st Fighter Group and moved to Dale Mabry Field, Florida. After a brief sojourn at Muroc Army Air Field (now Edwards Air Force Base), California, the 81st was assigned to the 12th Air Force and moved to the UK for training before detaching to Médiouna Airfield in French Morocco in January 1943.

The group supported ground operations and protected shipping in North Africa before covering the landings in Italy in Sicily and Anzio. While on patrol in the Mediterranean, the 81st FG also flew the Lockheed P-38 Lightning.

In early 1944, the group moved to Karachi in India, converting to Republic P-47 Thunderbolt and Curtiss P-40 Warhawk fighters. When combat ready in these aircraft, the 81st was attached to the 14th Air Force in China and moved to Kwangham Airfield in May 1944. The unit remained in China for the remainder of 1944 and all of 1945, flying from Fungwansham and Huhsien airfields. Its mission was primarily ground attack in support of friendly forces, targeting enemy airfields, Japanese troop concentrations, ammunition dumps, and communications. Escort missions were also flown in support of transport aircraft and parachute drops.

On 1 December 1945, the 81st Fighter Group was deactivated in China. On 15 October 1946, the 81st Fighter Group was reactivated in Hawaii at Wheeler Airfield taking over the assets of the deactivated 15th Fighter Group, flying the North American P-51D Mustang. It was attached to the 7th Fighter Wing. The primary mission of the group at this time was to conduct daylight patrols over the Hawaiian Islands. In 1948, the group's three squadrons converted to the P-47D. On 15 April 1948, the group became attached to the 81st Fighter Wing, which came under the direct control of the newly constituted Pacific Air Forces (PACAF).

In May, 1949, the 81st FW was returned to CONUS, to Kirtland AFB, New Mexico, and there began conversion to the North American F-86A Sabre. On 20 January 1950,

Badge of the 81st FIW.

the wing was redesignated the 81st Fighter Interceptor Wing and in April of that year Wing HQ and the 91st and 92nd Fighter Interceptor Squadrons moved to Moses Lake AFB (Larson), Washington, with the mission of air defence of the Washington area. The 93rd Squadron had remained at Kirtland and been reassigned. On 10 February 1951, the Washington Air National Guard was federalised and the 116th FIS was assigned to the 81st and converted to the F-86A. In May 1951, the 81st FIW received notice that they were to be assigned to USAFE's 3rd Air Force in the UK.

81st Fighter Interceptor Wing

North American F-86 Sabre

On 27 August 1951, Col. Robert Garrigan, commander of the 81st FIW, touched down at RAF Shepherds Grove. He was flying a North American F-86A Sabre. Second to land was Lt-Col. Frank Frost, commander of the 116th FIS.

RAF Shepherds Grove was situated near to the Suffolk town of Bury St Edmunds. It was originally opened in April 1944 for use by the USAAF; however, in the event, the first occupiers were 3 Group RAF, and in January 1945, it was taken over by 38 Group. Nos 196 and 299 Squadrons moved in with their Short Stirling transports. These squadrons remained at the Grove until March 1946, when the station came under the control of 60 Group as a satellite of RAF Watton. In 1950, it was put on care and maintenance until, in August 1951, it came under the control of the 81st FIW of the USAF.

The 116th FIS was an Air National Guard unit temporarily assigned to the 81st FIW. The headquarters of the 81st was to be RAF Bentwaters, but two of the wings squadrons were to be based at Shepherds Grove—the 116th and the 92nd FIS. The 81st was unique in that it was the only unit of a foreign air force that was tasked specifically with the air defence of the UK in peacetime. The wing worked closely with the RAF's 11 Group.

The 116th had the distinction of being the first unit of the USAF to bring the Sabre to Europe. They had left Spokane, Washington, at 4:50 a.m. on 13 August 1951 and had flown the northern route under the codename Fox Able 9. The flight was not without incident: bad weather, communications, and, at Bluie West One, water delaying the progress! Gil Leimbach made the crossing with the 116th FIS:

> When the Squadron pilots were preflighting their aircraft preparing to leave for Iceland, one pilot, Capt John R. Stevenson, noticed a peculiar liquid under his drop tank. The liquid did not appear smooth lying on the concrete as jet fuel would, but in droplets like water. Sure enough it was! Further opening up the gas caps revealed more water. Needless to say the whole operation came to a screeching halt. Seems the fuel farm had neglected to properly maintain their filters and they pumped a lot of H2O instead of Go-juice. All 25 aircraft were then checked for water and those that had it instead of jet fuel were immediately de-fuelled or, more accurately, de-watered![1]

Prior to their leaving the US, all the F-86s had been rotated to North American for modifications such as the A-1CM gunsights and AN/APG-30 radar. Every engine with over eighty hours was replaced. All the aircraft received new paint jobs, which comprised a lightning flash on the fuselage side in the squadron colour, and a blue tail on which were yellow lightning flashes. The squadron insignia was superimposed on the fuselage flash below the canopy. There was a profound awareness among those involved with the 81st FIW that this deployment was something special, not only because of the nature of the mission, but because the pilots were bringing with them one of the worlds paramount jet aircraft—the Sabre Jet.

On 5 September 1951, the 92nd FIS landed at Shepherds Grove, followed on 26 September by the 91st FIS. The 91st, however, did not linger, moving to RAF Bentwaters the following day. The 92nd had been delayed at Stornaway and so arrived a day later than scheduled.

Within a very short period of time, the Grove Sabres were involved in regular joint exercises with the RAF. One such, from 29 September to 7 October, was Exercise Pinnacle. In this exercise, the 116th FIS and 92nd FIS were tasked with defending the UK from simulated attacks by enemy aircraft. Pilots flew eighty-six sorties and achieved nineteen interceptions in sixteen scrambles. Gil Leimbach who was with the 116th FIS and flew in Pinnacle:

> We scrambled 16 aircraft from the 116th plus 16 from the 92nd and headed east to Bentwaters where 16 birds from the 91st joined up. We all climbed to altitude and with vectors from the GCI controller we levelled out at 35,000 feet, the 92nd at 30,000 feet and the 91st at 25,000 feet; all heading over the North Sea towards Belgium. Way in the distance contrails were visible at 12 o'clock. Lo and behold here came 48 Meteors and Vampires head on, almost 100 aircraft dogfighting. As we were top squadron at 35,000 with low airspeed of 230 knots; we immediately dived to pick up airspeed. We did a 180° turn and we had 10x10 mile hassle area. Later we were informed by RAF Fighter Command they expected two air-to-air accidents. Fortunately none occurred. Object of this was to actually test to see how unwieldy it was to vector big groups of aircraft to a certain area.[2]

Lt Alvin Post's F-86A at Keflavik, Iceland. Post was assigned to the 92nd FIS. From Iceland, the squadrons flew on to Stornoway and thence to Shepherds Grove. (*Alvin Post via Bill Knutzen*)

A photo call for these 116th FIS F-86s, which are joined by an aircraft of the 91st FIS, #8302, which arrived on 26 September. The Sabres of the 91st only lingered at Shepherds Grove for twenty-four hours, flying on to Bentwaters on 27 September. Note that the drop tanks of the 91st's aircraft carry the lightning bolt motif. (*via Robert Robinson*)

Their paint jobs looking in definite need of a retouch these F-86As of the 116th rest at the Grove. (*Chris Elliot*)

The Ace of Clubs' insignia of the 116th Fighter Interceptor Squadron. The 116th was the first of the squadrons of the 81st Fighter Interceptor Wing to touch down at Shepherds Grove and bring the F-86 Sabre to Europe. (*Chris Elliot*)

Aircraft 49-1096 gets a tow back to its ramp. Reason unknown! (*Chris Elliot*)

Joe Williams also flew with the 116th FIS and was involved in many of the air defence exercises with the RAF:

> We were the best airplane in Europe at the time and could out fly anything in England the whole time we were there. We would dog fight with the Gloster Meteor, the Venom, the Vampire and the Hawker Hunter; but the Venom, a spin off of the Vampire, could do some amazing things at high altitude that we could not touch. We had no trouble out-turning the USAF F-84G's stationed in England of the 20th Fighter Bomber Wing at Wethersfield.
>
> There was one problem our higher ups had with the British. A WWII left over, they would not scramble fighters until the enemy was in a particular sector, whereas the USAF wanted to go out and meet them before they got to the coast. A perfect example was one exercise we had with the RAF. We were the bad guys and were to strike London. There were three squadrons of F-86's. We were at 35,000 feet, so we went out to sea and came up the Thames Estuary heading for London on a beautiful clear day. They launched the Meteors after we coasted in and we met half way to London head on. By the time the Meteors got turned around, we had already hit London and so we turned around and had a great big dog fight. We flew many training missions with the RAF, but the Meteor was no match for the Sabre. Most of these training missions were a flight of four versus a flight of four. All control was from British radar. After the missions RAF would lead us on a high speed pass over their base. We would exchange gun camera film of our dog fights with the RAF. We'd put the film in the speed brake well, fly over the field and drop the film.[3]

In spite of the speed advantage, the dogfights with RAF Meteors were not always straightforward. Gil Leimbach:

> First day flying over there I was a wingman boring holes with my leader at 35,000 feet when I looked out and found a Meteor 8 locked on my wing! Hey! we're the fastest thing in the Area? So we poured on the coal and after a time made a turn and there he was right back in place! He merely cut us off in the turn. From that day on it was a dogfight every time after every take-off. We knew we had the speed and acceleration advantage but to slow down and gaggle with the Meteors in their speed range was more fun! If we were losing out we could accelerate past 400–450 knots and use our Aileron Boost to our advantage.[4]

There were two near accidents at about this time caused by hypoxia (loss of blood to the tissues), which was the direct result of the manoeuvring in dogfights with the Meteors and Vampires. Another problem associated with dogfighting was demonstrated on 5 May 1952 when the Sabres of the 92nd FIS acted as the attackers in a joint mission with the RAF. The 92nd Flight was intercepted by Meteors. In the course of the action, a collision occurred between an F-86 and a Meteor. Gil Leimbach recalls:

> They were the target aircraft. Two flights of 4 aircraft at 20,000′ at Mach 0.75 heading from the Continent towards London. It seems the RAF Meteors intercepted them over London. The Leader made a pass on the lead flight of four and forgot about the second flight directly behind. He crashed into the lead aircraft over London. Both pilots ejected safely, and both aircraft wound up in vacant fields! I talked to the F-86 pilot, Capt Whitford, afterwards. Evidently the whole front of his bird was missing and he could have stepped over the side. He ejected instead, floated down in his parachute and after landing was chased by a very irritated little old lady as he landed in her rose garden![5]

A considerable number of the pilots of the 116th and 92nd squadrons were combat experienced. Maj. Arlie Blood, who was 81st Wing operations officer in 1951, was himself a very experienced veteran of the Second World War and was of the view that, instead of locating to Europe, the squadrons should have gone to Korea instead of the 4th Fighter Wing. As a result of ongoing 'discussions' with the Pentagon, it was agreed that the 81st Wing should regularly detach pilots to Korea to ply their trade over the Yalu. Pilots of the 116th and 92nd FIS returned to the Grove, after they had completed their missions, many with MiG kills to their credit. Capt. Fred H. Barrett and 1Lt Robert E. Barnes returned to the 92nd FIS in September 1952. Both had one MiG-15 each to their credit. They returned to the squadron just in time to participate in the Battle of the Humber from 17–19 September. This exercise was set up to simulate Sabre *v.* MiG-15 in Korea. The Humber became a substitute Yalu River and a bomb line was set up approximately 40 nautical miles south of the river. Each day of the exercise, one of the squadrons would act as the enemy and the other two as UN forces. The 20th Fighter Bomber Wing flying F-84Gs and the 47th Bombardment Wing (BW) flying B-45 Tornados joined in the exercise as enemy bombers escorted by the 'MiG' F-86s. Gil Leimbach stated:

> Every Squadron had Black D-Day stripes painted on the wings; one stripe for the 91st, two for the 92nd, and 3 stripes for the 116th. We were to escort B-45's from Sculthorpe north to

> the Humber River. One squadron was bomber escort another was the 'enemy interceptors'. We found out that by following behind the B-45's was not the answer but by keeping our airspeed up to at least .9 mach doing figure eights behind we were able to provide more protection. One pilot in the 91st got into a hassle with another F-86, squadron unknown, and pulled so many 'G's' he broke the engine mounts; but he was able to return safely to Bentwaters. What a bird![6]

The exercise exposed some flaws in operational procedures. Difficulties were found in escorting high-altitude high-speed bombers and fighter bombers after the bomb drop. The smallness of the battle area posed problems for ground control.

In November 1952, the 116th FIS was returned to the US and its ANG status. Its pilots and aircraft were taken over by the newly activated 78th FIS: the 'Bushmasters'. All the pilots of the 116th were given the option of returning to Spokane and, all but one, the squadron commander, Lt-Col. Frost, opted to stay at the Grove. Arlie Blood became the commander of the 78th FIS, promoted to lieutenant-colonel.

One exercise regularly flown with the RAF was the Rat Terrier mission. This was a mission flown at low level, with the objective being to intercept intruders as they sneaked in over the coast from the continent. Royal Observer Corps and aircraft spotters on the coast were used to identify 'rats' and the information was relayed by phone to wing operations and thence to the interceptors. The Sabres were called upon on separate occasions to play both the defenders and the aggressors. In the early days, the missions were fraught for some of the more inexperienced pilots. The F-86 was basically a high-altitude interceptor and the pilots were often confused by flying low level over strange terrain where the density of towns and villages with strange sounding names merely added to their confusion. In time, when these initial difficulties were overcome, the Rat Terrier missions were looked forward to. The opportunity to fly low level was relished by the pilots whose experience and skills had developed markedly. Joe Williams now with the 78th FIS was one such:

> Another exercise we did that was real fun was the 'Rat Terrier' missions. These simulated the radar being out and ground observers would call in aircraft sightings to central control. These were single ship flights. We would fly out to sea about 50 miles, drop down on the deck and aim for a RAF field or town. We were limited to 350 knots airspeed and 500 foot altitude. We would do two hits and return to base, but the poor RAF was way behind and would catch us over Shepherds Grove where we were waiting for them. Then a great rat race would ensure until we ran out of fuel and had to land.[7]

The pilots of the 81st took their turn on alert status along with their RAF counterparts. Sometimes they were scrambled to identify unknown aircraft, but more often as part of regular, almost daily exercises with the RAF, and occasionally other NATO countries. The most regular missions were practice interceptions against RAF Meteors and Vampires. Pilots would stand by on alert until scrambled. They were given a heading to fly and a levelling altitude. After take-off, the section leader was given a radio contact on a certain channel. This contact would vector the flight on to the 'bogie'; if the flight

Capt. Jack Smith and Lt Joe Williams in front of F-86A 49-1095 at Shepherds Grove. (*Joe Williams*)

F-86As of the 116th FIS lined up on the ramp at Shepherds Grove during gunnery training. The Grove squadrons used the range at Dengie Flats, when not detached to Wheelus, Libya. (*Joe Williams*)

Lt-Col. Arlie Blood pre-flighting his F-86A. Lt-Col. Blood was the commanding officer of the 78th FIS. The 116th FIS was stood down from active duty in November 1952 and the aircraft and personnel absorbed into the newly activated 78th Fighter Interceptor Squadron: 'The Bushmasters'. The insignia of the squadron is seen to good effect in this photo. (*Joe Williams*)

got out of range, they were turned over to another contact for vectoring, and so it would proceed until the mission was complete.

The 92nd FIS was involved, on a number of occasions in supporting the RAF and the *Armée de L'Air* in the evaluation of their jet aircraft prototypes. For these purposes, the Sabre was ideally suited. Neither the RAF nor the French had anything to compare with it. Regular visits were made throughout 1952 to Hatfield and Orly. At Hatfield, both the Hunter and the DH.110 prototype programmes were supported by the 92nd.

Dan Scott was a technical sergeant with the 7519th Maintenance Squadron and accompanied one of these visits:

> I was there as Crew Chief of F-86 # 209 piloted by Maj. Jack B. Owens of the 92nd Fighter Squadron, We had three F-86's that we took to the Hawker base and also to de Havilland at Hatfield. We also got a ride on the first de Havilland Comet. There were only two Comets built at that time; the first was undergoing stress tests under water. We were fortunate enough to get about an hour's ride over the countryside.[8]

In 1952 the 116th also made an impromptu visit to the Farnborough Air Show, flying sixteen F-86s in 'V' formation over the airfield on the Friday of the show.

In addition to their forays to the gunnery range at Dengie Flats, the Shepherds Grove squadrons regularly detached to North Africa for gunnery training. All F-86 pilots were expected to remain proficient in ground gunnery, air-to-air gunnery, dive bombing, and rocketry.

In 1952, the 92nd FIS visited Hatfield on a number of occasions to support the development programme of the DH.110. USAF pilots were also allowed to fly the prototype. These two photos were taken in the course of such a visit on 30 April of that year. (*BAE SYSTEMS*)

Similar visits were made in support of the Hawker Hunter development. Here the prototype Hunter WB188 is in the company of Sabres 49-1197 and 49-1289. (*via Mick Stroud*)

It was essential for all USAFE units to have access to sunbases where they could hone their skills unhindered by the generally miserable North European weather. Gunnery training was undertaken at Wheelus in Libya. Arlie Blood noted:

> Shortly after assuming command of the 78th, it was our turn to go to Libya. We packed up all the needed equipment and together with maintenance and armament personnel, departed. We landed in Italy, refuelled and then flew across the Mediterranean to Libya. North Africa experiences wind storms which whip up the desert sands and after a time dust and fine sand can ascend to thirty or thirty five thousand feet. This was the situation as we approached Libya. There wasn't a cloud in the sky yet there was no horizon. It was like flying in a bowl of milk. Pilots were experiencing vertigo and I finally convinced them to go on instruments and fly as if there were in an overcast. Everyone landed safely.[9]

Joe Williams went to Wheelus with the 78th in 1953:

> At Wheelus, we had two altitudes we fired gunnery at: 10,000 and 20,000 feet. The lower altitude was so close to the base, you just about got your gear up and you were on the 'perch' where you started you gunnery run. We towed our own targets from another F-86 with the 'rag' attached to the speed brake. When the tow plane returned to Wheelus, all he had to do was open the speed brakes and the rag and 1,000 feet of tow cable fell from the plane. You had to stay below 150 knots or you would tear the target apart. The tow plane generally took-off at 05:30 and the first flight went at 06:00. We generally flew three missions as I recall. We had six guns in the 86, but only 90 rounds in two gun for a total of 180 rounds. Each airplane had the tips of the 50 calibre ammo dipped in a different colour paint so you knew who hit the target. To qualify, you needed 15% of your bullets to hit the target, or 72 holes. Since it was my first time firing gunnery, I was having trouble qualifying. One day the armament NCO told me, 'Lt, you have a full combat load, all guns fully charged', but I was still short, so they took me up in a T-33 and I found out I was firing way out of range. I was breaking off when I should have started firing. The next run I shot 26% and qualified, and everyone, including me was very happy.[10]

After returning to the UK, the squadrons selected a team of four gunners to take part in a group gunnery meet at Wheelus. Due to an unfortunate bout of infectious hepatitis, contracted in Wheelus, Arlie Blood was not able to lead the 78th's team, which came in second.

On 10 March 1953, two Czech pilots, Jaroslav Šrámek and Milan Forst, flying MiG-15s out of Pilsen, chanced upon two F-84s of the 36th FBW's 53rd FBS flying over their territory. They gave chase and were ordered to force the aircraft to land or, if they failed to comply, to shoot them down. The F-84s ran fast for the border but not fast enough. The lead aircraft flown by Lt W. G. Brown was hit with a burst of cannon fire from Šrámek's MiG. Brown baled out and fortunately came down safely on the right side of the border. The second F-84 escaped and returned to Bitburg. It was not the first incident of its kind and it would certainly not be the last, but coming when it did it galvanised all the Allied forces into action and prompted a great deal of thought about

Joe Williams returns from Wheelus sporting his fez while taxiing. (*Joe Williams*)

just how capable were their frontline air defence fighters. Re-equipment of crucial air defence units was moving forward with the F-86F and D eagerly awaited, but the only unit capable of making a significant reaction to the incursions of the MiGs into NATO airspace was the 81st FIW with its F-86As. The pilots were, in the main, experienced and contained by now a considerable number of Korean veterans. On 18 March, the order was received for the 92nd FIS to proceed from Shepherds Grove to Fürstenfeldbruck in Germany on a temporary detachment of three weeks. The mission was to identify unknown aircraft violating the US occupation zone of Germany. On arrival, the squadron was allowed one day of familiarisation flights. Twelve F-86s were kept on alert. Altogether thirty-six scrambles were performed. The 78th, in its turn, detached. None of the squadrons actually intercepted any bogies, their presence was deterrent enough; the closest they came was a sighting by a pilot of the 78th FIS of a contrail at 40,000 feet while he was patrolling the Czech border. Joe Williams detached to Fursty with the 78th:

> Our duty at Fursty was a 24 hour tour. Twelve noon to twelve noon, and then you were off for 24 hours. We flew a dawn patrol and a dusk patrol along the de-militarized Zone. The controllers would tell us we had company flying parallel to our route, but on the other side of the Zone; but we never saw any Migs. We carried a full combat load for our six fifty calibre guns. The crews that were off would party pretty good while the duty crews had to be in bed by 10 pm. The barracks at Fursty were great big buildings and when we came back from the club, we would get in line and everyone would slam the great doors. The first guys through would then run and ring the fire alarm. It was never peaceful there. One of the fun things about Fursty, was that after the first week, they let two 86's go back to Shepherds Grove for over night. We called this our 'Nooky Run'.[11]

The Sabres that had been brought over from the States were by the middle of 1953 beginning to show their age. Most of the aircraft had completed in excess of 1,000 hours. Corrosion was a major problem. The heavily salt-laden atmosphere and almost constant damp of Suffolk caused severe difficulties with the airframes. The F-86As were grounded in June 1953 for replacement of loose, cracked, and torn paddle assemblies on the elevators. Various problems had dogged the Sabres since their arrival at Shepherds Grove and Bentwaters. Gil Leimbach flew with the 78th FIS:

> I remember one thing we always did on preflight was to take a piece of emery cloth and clean the contact strips of the radio compass between the sliding canopy and the fuselage as the corrosion in England was so bad. Also we had to make sure the leading edge slats would come down freely because if one stuck, in a dog fight a noticeable SNAP roll would occur.[12]

There was a decision to be made on re-equipping the squadrons of the 81st. On 1 and 10 December 1953, the 78th FIS at Shepherds Grove received nine F-86F-25 aircraft. They transferred an equivalent number of F-86As to the other squadrons of the wing. The die seemed cast, and the assignment of more of these aircraft seemed imminent.

F-86A-5-NA 48-307, 91st FIS, crashed on the shingle of Orfordness on 4 December 1952. The pilot, Maj. Howard broke his back. (*Author's collection*)

F-86A-5-NA 49-1064, of the 92nd FIS, was at the Armed Forces Day at RAF Turnhouse in 1964. (*Author's collection*)

Lt Gil Leimbach flies his new F-86F, 51-13096. On 1 and 10 December 1953, the 78th FIS at Shepherds Grove received nine F-86F-25 aircraft. They transferred an equivalent number of F-86As to the other squadrons of the wing. (*Gil Leimbach*)

The 81st Fighter Bomber Wing

Republic F-84F Thunderstreak

In January 1954, General Order 27 was by published by HQ. The 3rd Air Force redesignating the 81st a Fighter Bomber Wing (FBW). It was to have a new mission and a new aircraft to carry out that mission, and this took effect on 1 April 1954. The primary mission of the wing became 'to destroy forces, resources and installations of the enemy'. To accomplish this mission, the 81st FBW was to fly the Republic F-84F Thunderstreak and carry tactical atomic weapons. However, the re-equipment was not to be realised for some months, and in the intervening period, the 78th FBS at Shepherds Grove continued to receive Sabres F-86E and F-86F, while the 91st and 92nd FBS' soldiered on with the F-86A.

The work of defending the UK was to continue into 1954, but an increasing amount of time was spent in training for the new mission. Training in bomb and 'Special Weapons' delivery had to be accomplished in the F-86. The bulk of the training took place in Nouasseur, Morocco, and consisted of dive and LABS (low-altitude bombing system) bombing. During one sojourn in North Africa in 1954, the 78th FBS flew 465 sorties and dropped 3,349 3-lb bombs.

The change of mission entailed not only a change in pilot training but also a revision of ground training and construction work to accommodate in total security the 'special weapons'. In the event, the first atomic weapons did not arrive at Shepherds Grove until 29 April 1955, carried by C-119 aircraft for the 78th Fighter Bomber Squadron.

The last F-86As were flown from Shepherds Grove to Prestwick on 26 February 1954 by Arnie Abrams and Joe Williams.

Conversion to the F-84F began in October 1954, with the first aircraft arriving by sea at Lisbon on 4 October. Not all the pilots of the 81st were initially enamoured of the F-84. Lt-Col. Arlie Blood was the CO of the 78th FBS based at Shepherds Grove:

> They took our beautiful F-86 away from us and equipped us with the F-84F fighter bomber. The F-84's were shipped to Lisbon, Portugal to a Republic Aviation crew that installed the wings and was then test hopped by a Republic test pilot. I flew down there and set up an 81st operation to 'buy' the airplanes after the test hop. I took off for England with the first F-84 airplane. I was requested to do a flyby at RAF Sculthorpe so all the Generals could see this 'great' nuclear carrier. I did and they asked what I thought of the new fighter. I said, 'It's no F-86.'[13]

Nouasseur, Morocco, was chosen as the venue for the squadrons to transition to the F-84F as well as for training. Fair weather made for a high mission rate and efficient training. During 1954, a considerable number of pilots qualified on the F-84 at the Moroccan base. Regrettably these training operations took their toll of men and machines. Capt. John T. Hale Jun of the 91st FBS and 1Lt William Garney were both killed while transitioning in Morocco. Arlie Blood noted: 'We lost a very skilled pilot at gunnery camp in Africa during a dive bomb run. Being used to the manoeuvrability of the F-86 he did not pull out of his dive in time and mushed into the ground'.

Joe Williams poses with his crew chief at the Grove beside his Thunderstreak. 'I was not overly fond of the F-84F or its mission. Going from Fighter Interceptor to Special missions was a big change for us all. But when you wear the uniform, you must go with the change'. (*Joe Williams*)

Four 91st FBS pilots. *From left to right*: Lt Bob Stone, Lt Sterling Lee, Lt Bob Russ, and Capt. Dick Schoenemann. Bob Stone was later shot down in Vietnam while flying an F-105, Sterling Lee was killed after ejecting from an F-101 at Bentwaters, Dick Schoenemann retired as a three-star general, and Bob Russ became a four-star general and commander of Tactical Air Command. (*Don Mikler*)

However, not all the pilots found the airplane as objectionable as Arlie. Maj. Bob Fredette was with the 78th FBS and described the transition from the F-86 to the F-84 as similar to converting from a sports car to a dump truck. However, he did warm to the Thunderstreak:

> Prior to flying the F-84F I flew the F-86A and F. Both had different missions and could not be compared objectively. You are basically talking apples and oranges. Our aircraft had wing spoilers and a slab stabilator. Its overall performance was very good and it had a tremendous rate of turn. It was an honest airplane. It had to outlive a prior bad name.[14]

In March 1955, the 92nd FBS moved from Shepherds Grove to RAF Manston. In May of that year, the last of the initial batch of F-84Fs arrived for the 81st FBW. All F-86As returned to the US, travelling by freighter from Belfast, Ireland.

The story of the service of the Thunderstreak with the 81st was characterised by a catalogue of problems, modifications, replacements, and frustrations on the one hand and outstanding success in completing the assigned mission on the other. The numerous problems associated with the aircraft's development inevitably followed it into service, and were compounded by new ones from time to time.

The primary offensive weapon of the F-84F was the Mk 7 atomic bomb, weighing approximately 2,000 lb and yielding in excess of 1 kiloton. For the carriage of this

Flying over France at approximately 190 knots, Al Broughton of the 91st FBS refuels from a Sculthorpe based KB-29 tanker *en route* to Nouasseur. (*Don Mikler*)

weapon, the aircraft was fitted with a specially designed pylon to be carried under the port wing. Special Weapons training, exercises, and security occupied much of both wing's time and energies. Training was hard and highly intensive. The bomb commanders, as the pilots were known, were used to much of the ethos that prevailed in an atomic strike unit, but it was a new experience for many of the pilots of the 81st, some of whom were new to the wing as well as the mission. With the change in role of the wing, many of the experienced personnel had returned home to be replaced by young pilots fresh from college, new to the air force and the wing.

Every bomb commander was obliged to attain a grade of at least 90 per cent every ninety days on knowledge of the weapon and the ramifications of its use. They would be monitored on a mock-up trainer and in flight, including the weapons loading, and pre- and post-flight procedures.

The F-84s delivered initially were the F-84F-35 and F-84F-40 series. These were powered by the unmodified J-65 engines, which brought its own problems, but they were also unsuited to LABS manoeuvres, being delivered with the MA-1 computer installed. This was the same system that had been used in the Thunderstreak's predecessor, the Thunderjet, and was not entirely satisfactory. For this reason, an alternative method of special weapon delivery was practiced. Lt Joe Williams stated:

January 1956 saw heavy snowfalls in Suffolk. It was not 'business as usual' for the 91st FBS! This photo was taken when the markings for the 91st FBS, in common with the other squadrons of the 81st FBW, were being changed. Some aircraft retained their factory numbers on the tail. Some had the 'new' US AIR FORCE on the nose, while some retained the buzz number on the nose. The aircraft in the centre right of the photo has no markings on the nose and is awaiting its US AIR FORCE logo. (*Don Mikler*)

'C' Flight of the 91st FBS fly a four-ship formation. Capt. Jack Bowman in the lead followed by Lt Don Hanto, Lt Jim Wilson, and Lt Harry Eckes. The blue lightning flashes were another example of the variety of markings carried by the 91st during the F-84F period. (*Don Mikler*)

> We used the 13,000 foot release in a high altitude dive bomb run. We would go into the dive at 24,000 feet and release at 13,000 feet. One time during practice dive bombing at the Dingy Flats in England, I forgot to pull the power off after climbing back up to the perch; and on the next dive, after bomb release, the air speed was 700 knots. Thank God for the 13,000 foot release. For bombing practice we had a small rotating rack that held 8 small 'Blue Boys' that were supposed to simulate the real thing with a shot gun charge that went off when the bomb hit the ground to show where it hit in relation to the target, and this was used to score the hits. When we flew with the big bomb shape, the aircraft had a tendency to roll as your speed built up in the dive run; but this was easily counted with aileron. We had one fellow in our squadron that went in at the Dengie Flats range, flew the airplane right into the ground. You have very poor depth perception over water so it is best to watch your altimeter.[15]

Later block 45 and 50 series aircraft were equipped with a spoiler to facilitate low-altitude bombing capability, and the MA-2 LABS computer which was to become standard throughout most of the service life of the F-84F.

When LABS was adopted as the standard method of Special Weapons delivery, it was practised primarily at Nouasseur, Morocco. Lt Gil Leimbach noted:

> The 78th went to Nouasseur Air Base near Casablanca in North Africa, to do LABS manoeuvres on a SAC bomber range. The LABS (Low Altitude Bombing System) was an all weather manoeuvre. The aircraft would come over the target visually at 500 feet at a very high speed and pull up at 4Gs in a loop manoeuvre. If it was cloudy or a VRF day, this would be on instruments. Roll out at the top using the Artificial Horizon Instrument. The practise bomb automatically releases, goes straight up loses velocity and goes straight down. This time allows the aircraft clearance to safely survive a nuclear explosion. Needless to say much better than high altitude bombing.[16]

The change in the primary mission and aircraft of the 81st FBW necessitated a change in the role that the wing was called upon to play in the many exercises in which they took part.

In March 1955, the 92nd FBS moved from Shepherds Grove to RAF Manston.

Exercise Carte Blanche occurred from 21–28 June 1955; this was arguably one of the first most significant exercises to take place in Cold War Europe at that time. It encompassed all NATO countries and a variety of tactical units and their aircraft, and its scenario was the outbreak of an atomic war. It was designed to test all current plans in dispersal, tactical control, and alert responses. Effectively the alliance went to war. The 81st was responsible for making simulated atomic bomb strikes on mainland Europe from dispersal points in the UK. The 91st FBS, 81st FBW, operated from Bentwaters and dispersed some aircraft to Manston. The exercise was a marked success and certainly for the F-84F bomb commanders it was a fitting reward for the intensive training. The 91st FBS for example launched twenty-six strikes on targets in Europe and all were successful! Gil Leimbach was with the 78th FBS and headed for France:

> I took off from Shepherd's Grove and headed for a French Aerodrome in the Lyon area. The weather was VFR, a beautiful day. Low level all the way (500 ft). I contacted the Airfield

Tower that I was coming. They acknowledged, and I made a LABS manoeuvre and headed back to the Grove. As far I can remember all of my real war targets were airfields in East Germany.[17]

Exercise Beware in September 1955 dispersed squadrons of the 81st FBW to bases in Europe to launch strikes against the UK in a test of air defences. The F-84s were more than a match for the Meteors and Venoms of RAF Fighter Command. The 92nd FBS was proud of its success in striking unhindered from its base in Germany. Success in penetration exercises such as Carte Blanche, Beware, and Fox Paw, the latter of which occurred in November 1955, were made in spite of the fact that facilities for training for the Thunderstreak wings were far from adequate. One of the principal problems was the lack of suitable range facilities. In England, the only range suitable for bomb delivery was Dengie Flats in Essex. Effective use of this range was dependent on the weather and the weather was the cause of the range being out of use for several months in every year. Operation Long Stride took the squadrons to North Africa on a regular basis for fair weather training, and it must be said that without this facility there would have been little chance of the bomb commanders being proficient enough to do the job should 'D-Day' ever happen.

In Exercise Brown Cow, the 91st FBS bomb commanders' navigation skills were tested as well as their aptitude in Special Weapons delivery. In the latter case, one 500-lb bomb was dropped by each of the bomb commanders. This took place on the Dengie Flats range. Predominant delivery method was by high-angle dive bombing. The 91st had only three dash 45 series F-84s at this time and only the pilots of these aircraft were allowed to use the over the shoulder LABS delivery, achieving marked success.

In May 1956 the 78th FIW moved from the Grove to RAF Sculthorpe.

The fact that the F-84F Thunderstreak was not a particularly popular aircraft can be put down to the many problems that were associated with its development and early service career. It is a tribute to the pilots who flew it and the ground crews who maintained it that they overcame many of the drawbacks and achieved some high degree of success. In July 1956, the 81st FBW flew down to Wheelus in Libya for a Special Weapons delivery meet. Pilots from each of the squadrons were representing their wing in what was to be a competition to determine the best in USAFE at Special Weapons delivery. The meet did include other aspects of the mission assigned but the atomic weapons delivery part was the most significant for the 81st. Pilots were selected for their skill and precision. They were the best the squadrons had to offer. Although they were competing against several other USAFE units flying aircraft such as the F-86F, the fact that they and the 20th FBW from Wethersfield were flying the F-84F Thunderstreak made the competition keener and also placed both of them in a position that made it important for their aircraft to prevail. The reputation of the F-84F had undoubtedly gone before it and this made victory or, at the very least, a respectable showing, imperative. Bob Fredette stated:

I have always been proud that the 81st TFW won the USAFE bombing meet and specifically the 78th Sq. At this time I was the commander of the 78th. The team representing the wing

> was composed of weapons loading crews and a total of six pilots. Two pilots from each of the 78th, 91st, and the 92nd. The material officer, Capt. Barrantine and the Fly Away Kit Section, parts and supplies, were all from the 78th.
>
> The meet was won by two 78th Sq. pilots: Capt. Dee McCarter and Capt. Raymond Kingston. We became the USAFE Special Weapons Delivery Champions. They ran away with it! As a result, in October, 1956 this team proceeded to Nellis AFB for the USAF Bombing Meet.
>
> The team departed England, the pilots flew our aircraft to Nellis AFB via Iceland and Goose Bay, Labrador. The maintenance team flew in a C-54 to Nellis. The entire team beat the favourites from the SAC team. The team was totally independent. They did not rely on any other support except for fuel! Again, Capt. Raymond Kingston and Capt. Dee McCarter won the meet on the final day by simply devastating the other teams on scoring. Upon return to England, the air-planes were painted with USAF CHAMPS on the fuselage. As far as the meet was concerned, even in publicity, SAC was supposed to be the 'shoe in.' Our team waxed them.
>
> Capt Raymond Kingston celebrated by stopping in Las Vegas and was showered with affection by Miss Candy Barr, Las Vegas Entertainer, famous in that period.[18]

It was fitting that the Thunderstreak should have been thrust into the limelight at such a time because it had been established at both these competitions that here was an aircraft that could do the job for which it had been designed in spite of the problems bedevilling it. By way of underlining this, the 81st FBW was awarded the USAFE Tactical Proficiency trophy for the first half of 1956. The Operational Readiness Inspection (ORT) team had considered the wing the best it had ever inspected!

The visit of the Bolshoi Ballet to the UK on 1 October 1956 should have been an occasion for cultural celebration but, coming as it did at a time of crisis, a considerable amount of consternation and confusion was evident in military circles on the day of arrival—not least at RAF Manston where the 92nd FBS resided alongside the 406th FIW. No warning had been given of the imminent arrival of the Tupolev Tu 104s, and hurried arrangements were made to cover up the sensitive special weapon practice stores slung under the wings of the F-84s of the 92nd.

The year 1956 also witnessed two international events that underlined the necessity of maintaining a high degree of readiness in all tactical strike units of NATO. During the Suez Crisis, there was no direct US involvement; the air force, however, placed its bases on alert and was ready to react if any Soviet moves were made against its allies, Britain and France. There was increased tension and the security of the bases had to be tightened considerably as long as the situation lasted. A twenty-four-hour alert condition was imposed with weapons loaded and bomb commanders on standby. The plutonium cores of the special weapons were beside the aircraft in their cages, guarded by an air police man and his German shepherd dog. The Soviet aggression in Hungary maintained the tension and readiness of the F-84F strike units. One thing that was imperative was that Wing Intelligence kept a watching brief on developments and a round the clock review of targets, charts, and maps. Briefings were given to personnel on the nature of the crisis. Security on the bases was tightened.

Tension eased towards the end of 1956. The F-84F was receiving further modifications at this time in the form of a selector switch to use with the MA-1 LABS computer, which enabled the pilot to select either conventional or 'over the shoulder' delivery. This was also used with the MA-2 system newly installed in some aircraft.

Although the F-84F had only been in service for less than two years, and was at the height of its mission success, moves were already in place to replace it in the 81st. The aircraft to do this was to be the North American F-100 Super Sabre. Some examples of this state-of-the-art fighter bomber were already in service with USAFE in mid- to late 1956, with the 36th Fighter Day Wing (FDW) and the 48th FBW, based in Germany and France respectively. The 81st FBW published its F-100D Conversion Plan 5-56 and was in regular contact with the 45th FDS at Sidi Slimane in French Morocco—a unit which was flying the F-100C and was tasked with converting USAFE pilots to the type. In the event, in publishing its conversion plan, the 81st was being unrealistically optimistic. The unit was destined never to fly the aircraft.

As the proficiency of the bomb commanders in Special Weapons delivery techniques increased, so did the frustrations with the F-84F and the nature of the exercises that were being undertaken. There was too great a restriction on low flying in the UK: 2,000 feet was just too high for an authentic mission to be flown. Exercise Vigilante flown in October 1956 against UK targets led to an appeal from the pilots to be allowed to drop their fuel tanks on approach to the target just as they would in wartime. The 81st flyers found that there was a dramatic increase in their target folders when they were required to take over those assigned to other US units while those units, such as the 20th FBW, converted to the F-100D. The 92nd FBS alone doubled its targets; unfortunately, many of these new targets had been designed for the F-100D. The efficient attacking of them required that aircraft's advanced performance. There was no question of the F-84s being unable to reach the targets, but they were limited by the necessity of flying that aircraft at optimum rather than maximum performance. In wartime, the consequences of this would be an increase in the number of aircraft that would be intercepted by the enemy. As 1957 progressed, these frustrations became more profound. Exercise Fog Cut in the latter part of the year when the 81st was attacking UK targets witnessed a number of intercepts, most of which, the pilots maintained, could have been avoided but for the restrictions placed upon the F-84F.

The F-84F was, in any event, proving problematic in meeting the requirements of the ever increasing developments in Special Weapons delivery. Several aircraft were destroyed while performing LABS delivery. Two aircraft hit the ground when they failed to recover from the manoeuvre. The 91st FBS instituted an indoctrination programme on Instrument Flight Conditions recovery from LABS manoeuvres. There was a lack of confidence in the altitude gyro. It was made mandatory that each mission contemplating IFR LABS recoveries must first obtain permission of the commander or operations officer. There were other accidents with the Thunderstreaks: 52-6707's main gear extended during a bombing run; another aircraft aborted during take-off and crashed and caught fire with pilot fatality; and yet another crashed on approach due to a hydraulic failure also killing the pilot. One common accident was loss of drag chute in flight due to excessive vibration causing the holding bolts to loosen.

In November 1957, 92nd FBS bomb commanders attended an F-100D training course at RAF Wethersfield. The dawning of 1958 saw a dramatic development. Moves were being made in the Pentagon to convert the 81st FBW not to the F-100D as everyone had supposed, but to an aircraft of which there was only one wing operating in the entire US Air Force: the McDonnell F-101 Voodoo. Not only was the Voodoo at the end of its production run, but it had been designed as an escort fighter for SAC bombers—not as a tactical atomic strike aircraft. Having just one wing of a particular aircraft type in the European theatre would seemingly pose considerable logistical problems. However, in spite of the apparently indisputable logistical reasons not to convert to the F-101 clearly and unequivocally stated by the commander of USAFE, Gen. Frank Everest, the conversion was to go ahead at the end of 1958. The 27th TFW was to move all its Voodoos and their pilots and support to re-equip the 81st TFW. Prior to this, on 28 July 1958, Maj. John 'JJ' Burns took four F-101Cs of the 522nd TFS to Europe, calling at Liege in Belgium and thence to Bentwaters, Soesterberg, and Nouasseur, by way of introduction to the type. Prior to the arrival of the new aircraft, there were other developments for the 81st. On 8 May 1958, the 92nd FBS moved to Bentwaters from Manston, heralding their arrival with a twenty-eight-ship flypast.

In the meantime, there was a mission to be performed with the Thunderstreak. The practising of the mission remained relentless. Cold Wind exercises were introduced, which were made up of regular exercises called by higher headquarters to test the wing's capabilities at performing atomic strikes. Missions were planned to hit friendly targets the same distance from base as the proposed enemy ones. The detachments to North Africa continued as regularly as ever. Lt Charles Taylor was sent to Iran to train Iranian pilots on the Thunderstreak. First Lieutenants Thomas Adams and Paul Baker detached

Both RAF Bentwaters and Shepherds Grove were fitted with arresting barriers when they acquired the 'Super Hog'. However, they were initially not very successful. Gil Leimbach was with the 78th FBS at the 'Grove'. On 16 March 1955, he experienced hydraulic problems while on check out in F-84F 52-6453. He requested the barrier be raised but, unfortunately, it did not stop him and he careered off the end of the runway. He was unhurt and back in the air the next day. (*Gil Leimbach*)

to Pakistan as members of a special squadron set up to be the aggressors in a Pakistan Air Force exercise. Could this have been one of the original Dissimilar Air Combat Training (DACT) exercises? The 78th FBS detached eight aircraft, accompanied by a C-130, to Sola in Norway for Exercise Full Play in July 1958.

On 8 July, the 81st Wing gained control of RAF Woodbridge from the 20th FBW. The day before, on 7 July, the wing became the 81st Tactical Fighter Wing. In December, the 78th Tactical Fighter Squadron moved from its temporary home at Sculthorpe into Woodbridge.

In July 1958, the F-101 Mobile Training Detachment was set up in the 92nd area at RAF Bentwaters and the simulator was received from Bergstrom. There had been a lot of contact with the 27th TFW during 1958. Pilots were detached to the Texas base for training on the Voodoo. By December, forty pilots had returned to the UK and the 81st had forty-eight F-101s on strength, as well as twenty-five F-84s. As the new aircraft arrived, so the Thunderstreaks were sent to Leeuwarden for the West German Air Force. The first to go were 52-6824 and 52-6792, and throughout the year, more and more filtered away. It required considerable skill and dedication for the squadrons to remain combat ready in the F-84F while quite significant changes were taking place, but it is a tribute to the men and machines that, in spite of the upheaval, this is what they did. In July 1958, Operation Blast Off was instigated; this required a number of aircraft and crews to be maintained on alert around the clock, ready to take-off at a moment's notice to strike key targets. During the Middle East crisis, centred on Lebanon, the number of crews on Blast Off was increased, but this was the only significant impact of the crisis on the 81st TFW.

It was during the latter part of 1958, when conversion to the Voodoo was well under way, that an F-84F of the 92nd TFS 'inadvertently' violated the East German Air Defence Zone (ADIZ). This rather disturbing navigational error resulted in an order going out from 81st HQ that no aircraft must proceed across the West German border without first receiving positive radar surveillance. In fact, this ruling was rescinded at the end of the year as it proved a handicap to realism in operational flying training because of the necessity of turning round at the border. During this period of the Cold War, this was but one of many hundreds of infringements of the borders by both sides in the interests of testing and exploring the air defence systems of the enemy, 'inadvertently' or otherwise.

At the end of 1958, all F-84Fs of the 81st TFW departed for service with the NATO allies or the Air National Guard. In all, the Thunderstreak had served but three short years as a frontline fighter bomber. Today, at a time when we measure the service life of a combat aircraft in decades rather than years, it is easy to view the F-84F as a failure. It had a difficult gestation and initially an equally difficult service career. It is highly probable that the pilots of the 81st TFW did not miss it one bit, but the memories of its successes, at Wheelus and Nellis in particular, have provided it, at the least, with a partial respectability as a competent strike aircraft.

F-84F 52-6780, 78th FBS. (*Robbie Robinson Collection*)

F-84F 52-6737, 92nd FBS. (*Robbie Robinson Collection*)

For a short period, the squadrons at Bentwaters detached to RAF Woodbridge while the runway at their home base was being repaired. Here they have just arrived back at the Bentwaters. Note the special weapons pylon on the nearest F-84F, left inboard on the left wing. (*Don Mikler*)

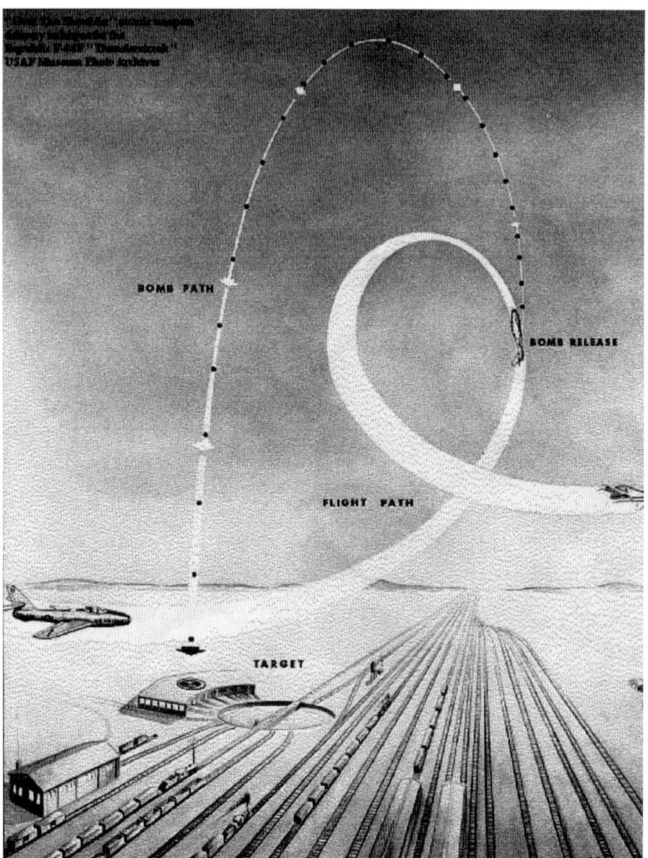

An illustration showing the 'over the shoulder' special weapons delivery technique practiced by the F-84Fs of the USAF. (*USAF*)

The 81st Tactical Fighter Wing

The McDonnell F-101 Voodoo

The wing's primary mission with the F-101 was to carry an atomic weapon to a predetermined target, release that weapon, and return home by whatever means possible. Most targets during the Voodoo's early days in Europe were well within its impressive range, thus allowing the 81st to operate independently of tanking assets. However, as the Cold War intensified, the list of identified targets also grew, as did their distance from Suffolk. This ultimately meant that the F-101s had to be modified to allow a retractable refuelling probe to be fitted immediately forward of the cockpit.

Initially, there were myriad problems in defining the mission parameters for an aircraft which was very much an unknown quantity. For much of its development the Voodoo had been an aircraft without a mission, but in the hands of the skilled pilots of the 81st TFW, the mission that was eventually defined for it was slowly, but surely, developed into a fine art.

One of the first stages in carving out a role for the big McDonnell fighter was the initiation of a radar improvement programme. The system fitted to the F-101A/C had been built for air-to-air work in its previous strategic fighter role with SAC, and following modification 'in the field', the radar became relatively effective in the air-to-ground mode—although low-level radar navigation remained a challenge for pilots up until the jets' retirement from USAFE.

In an effort to overcome the F-101's shortcomings at low-level, 'bomb commanders' spent much time pre-planning their various mission profiles and producing detailed target folders. Blast Off required a number of crews kept at a constant state of alert at RAF Bentwaters, and these pilots had to remain 'current' on folders for at least three to four targets at any one time. A regular squadron pilot was expected to know two. The codename for this alert duty had changed from Blast Off to Victor Alert by the end of December 1958.

The Voodoo had numerous design idiosyncrasies, some of which were rather hazardous. Arguably the most dangerous of these was its tendency to pitch up without any provocation from the pilot. This trait was blamed squarely on the big jet's T-tail configuration, for at high angles of attack and high-G manoeuvring, the wing blocked or disrupted the airflow over the rear flying surfaces, rendering the stabilators ineffective. This in turn caused the nose to pitch up at a high degree, creating a dramatic loss of air speed that eventually resulted in the jet stalling and spinning in. The pitch-up problem remained with the Voodoo throughout its service career, despite the fitting of an inhibiting system by McDonnell. Indeed, the company was so worried about the effects of this often fatal design flaw that in June 1960, Don Stuck, McDonnell's chief test pilot, conducted an indoctrination programme on pitch up recovery for the USAFE F-101/RF-101 community. Concurrent with this, safety personnel were constantly trying to develop procedures for calibrating the pitch up warning system.

The three squadrons of the 81st TFW spent a great deal of time at Wheelus AFB, in Libya, honing their special weapons delivery techniques on the vast El Outia range. This site consisted of two run-in lines and two huge black and white chequered targets, and

F-101C 54-1461 also belongs to the 92nd TFS and is seen here in 1960 in the company of one of the 81st TFW Lockheed T-33s and a couple of Spitfires at an open house in 1960. (*Alan Johnson*)

The second scheme in which the Voodoos were adorned was introduced in late 1960. The tails were painted in the squadron colours, on which were superimposed stars of differing sizes. Aircraft 56-0014 is a 78th TFS F-101C. At this time, the undercarriage doors were also painted in the squadron colours with a single star superimposed. (*Mick Stroud*)

The third and final change in the colour scheme occurred in 1962 when all individual squadron colours were replaced by the blue, yellow, and red colours applied to the tail and superimposed by stars, white for the 78th and 91st TFS, and black for the 92nd. F-101A-25-MC 54-1452 sits on the ramp at RAF Woodbridge alongside the forest. (*Author's collection*)

F-101A-35-MC 54-1469 is being prepared for flight. The aircraft is fitted with two 450-gallon fuel tanks on two fuselage hard-points. A central fuselage hard-point was used to carry a nuclear store. Although originally designed as an interceptor, the Voodoo was never used in this role. (*Author's collection*)

had been set up in 1956 by Col. Robin Olds when he had been assigned to Wheelus to convert the gunnery camp into a mini weapons centre. Robin Olds, who went on to command the 81st TFW in 1963, has fond memories of his numerous TDYs to the base, despite the fact that the flights to and from Libya were never straightforward, as he explains:

> Our course to Africa always took us down across central France, coasting out between Marseilles and Nice, over the Mediterranean past Malta and Pantelleria, and on to Tripoli. The French were always the French! Invariably, we would be given a lower altitude as we entered their airspace, and invariably we acknowledged, and then 'reported' arriving at the assigned lower height, when in fact we continued to cruise climb all the way in order to complete our journey.
>
> Their Mirage IIIs often intercepted us and they would regularly do arrogant barrel rolls around us as we plodded along, staying just ahead of stall speed, chasing the Mach. We rather enjoyed their antics, and always gave them the finger in the form of our air refuelling probe, which came up rudely out of the nose of the F-101.
>
> Once in Libya, all of us pilots truly enjoyed our times at Wheelus. We trained in 'nuke' strike delivery, as well as spending time on the conventional ranges.[19]

Operation Camel Saddle, as the regular detachments were called, was initially designed to qualify and re-qualify bomb commanders in LABS techniques with the Mk 28 atomic weapon, although it was also employed for later, more sophisticated, methods of delivery that were developed following the arrival of the F-101. One such technique was Low Altitude Drogue Delivery (LADD), which soon became popular for the delivery of special weapons following its introduction in 1960. Despite the adoption of LADD, LABS was still practised, and would have been used alongside the former in a 'hot' war. All crews had to be qualified in five delivery systems with no less than four special weapons. These were high-angle LABS using Mk 7 and Mk 28 bombs, visual laydown with the Mk 28 and Mk 43 device, visual or blind timed pull-up (both with the Mk 28RRE and the Mk 28RE), and blind level delivery with the Mk 28RE and the Mk 43. When it came to the varied methods of delivery practised by the 81st TFW, Col. Olds had his preferences:

> All methods were challenging and enjoyable to practice. However, I would have to say the laydown was probably the most accurate and the 'Over the Shoulder' the most fun, but what did it matter? Considering the strength of the object we were tasked with delivering, I don't suppose a few hundred feet this way or that would have made a hell of a lot of difference![20]

Aside from exercising over the vast deserts of Libya, the 81st TFW also used the Suippes range, in France, for special weapons delivery training. Missions to both sites were usually flown in four-ship formations, with each aircraft carrying a small pod housing six bomblets, which allowed the pilot to make an equal number of bomb runs.

The airspace over Suippes acquired a reputation for being rather hazardous from time to time, with unannounced aircraft often overflying the ranges. On 26 July 1963, two unidentified French aircraft did just that, crossing the training run-in line to the target while four 81st F-101s were using the range. Forty minutes later, a flight of four aircraft again dissected the line when a quartet of F-105s from the 36th TFW were making their bombing run. These were potentially fatal breaches of safety protocol for the pilots using the range, who were often fully preoccupied with their own bombing runs, and not looking out for other traffic.

Aside from the improvement in delivery techniques, the F-101 itself continued to be developed into a better strike aircraft thanks to programmes such as Project Lampshade, which oversaw the development of an all-weather target capability for the jet. This was also completed towards to the end of 1960, after which time the 81st TFW could boast the distinction of being the first tactical fighter wing in USAFE with a proven all-weather radar capability.

On 27 June 1961, the 81st TFW hosted an open house at RAF Bentwaters to celebrate a decade of service in the UK. This event proved very popular, and over 30,000 guests inspected the base. The open house came as a welcome distraction for the pilots, who were then engaged in intensive work-ups centred on mastering new bombing techniques that had been made available through the arrival of radar delivery. There were two methods of bombing which needed to be practised, the first of which saw the aircraft approach the target at a known altitude and airspeed. As the target passed through a fixed range marker, a timer was started using the aircraft's clock which eventually resulted in the bomb being released at a prescribed time, after which the pilot effected a level escape. This was the method used for a LADD delivery.

For a LABS run, however, newly developed MA-2 computer equipment was employed. As the target passed through a fixed range marker, a button was depressed, and at the end of the pre-computed time, a co-ordinated 3.5-G pull up was initiated. The moment the release angle was reached, the bomb left the aircraft, leaving the pilot to initiate his escape.

The pilots who flew the F-101s in USAFE were special men. They were working in the frontline of the Cold War, having been trained to fly first response missions from which they would almost certainly not return. The 78th TFS, for example, reported matter-of-factly, in December 1960, that with all aircraft taking off as soon as possible after H-Hour, and with all 81st TFW targets being clustered close together, some of its jets would be wiped out before they hit their targets because they would be flying directly into the atomic bursts of their predecessors.

In an effort to stop pilots being totally blinded by the glare given off by these detonations, they were each issued with an eye patch! It was hoped that by donning such a crude protective device, the wearer would retain the use of his sight in at least one eye, which he would uncover as he closed on his target.

In 1962, the Cuban Missile Crisis prompted alerts throughout the USAF. The 81st was no exception. Ray Ramsey noted:

> The Cuban Crisis was a huge highlight during this tour. It was obvious that the President was damn serious that the proposed withdrawal was going to happen or we were going to turn eastern Europe in to a 'big glow in the dark hog wallow'. Every bird in the wing was

F-101C-50-MC was assigned to the 78th TFS at RAF Woodbridge. Designed originally as a long-range fighter for SAC, the F-101A/C Voodoo carried enough internal fuel for a combat radius of some 700 nautical miles. The carriage of the 450-gallon tanks notably increased this range. It was also capable of being refuelled in flight, which extended it even further. (*Author's collection*)

Four F-101s fly in formation at an open house at RAF Bentwaters in 1964. It was at this time that Robin Olds commanded the 81st. He decided to form a four-ship F-101 demonstration team, which he did for the open house event in 1964. Unfortunately, the USAF hierarchy did not approve and Olds was reprimanded. These four Voodoos could be that team. (*Alan Johnson*)

F-101C-55-MC 56-0039 at RAF Bentwaters in May 1965. After service with the 81st, this Voodoo was converted to a reconnaissance RF-101H and assigned to the Nevada Air National Guard. (*Alan Johnson*)

> loaded and we went on constant alert for almost a week. Of course this required loaded planes to be guarded at all times under the prescribed access rules. We parked them on the usual hard spots all around the ops building and we lived and slept there until the USSR cargo ships turned around and went home! The tension of those days was in excess of any thing I experienced in my two tours in Vietnam. When all clear was announced, we simply went home and drank alone: totally uncharacteristic of fighter pilots![21]

Late in 1964, USAFE HQ announced to the 81st TFW that it would be converting to the all-new McDonnell F-4C Phantom II. The 78th TFS was to be the first squadron to receive the new aircraft, and by 1965, it was heavily involved in the conversion programme.

Despite this, the two remaining units within the 81st TFW still had to retain full mission readiness with their F-101s, and this meant that both aircraft and aircrew were still rotating through Wheelus for bomb commander training. Closer to home, the Suippes, Jurby (Isle of Man), and Holbeach (Lincolnshire) ranges were still extensively used although there was a reluctance among some pilots to target the latter site due to intermittent problems with bomb dispensers. They feared that ordnance could be accidentally dropped into the populated areas which surrounded the East Anglian facility should the dispenser malfunction.

Although Voodoos were being increasingly replaced in Suffolk by F-4Cs, pilots still flying the older McDonnell fighter continued to be engaged in an intensive round of close air support training exercises right up to the F-101's final demise. This had come about because

F-101C-55-MC is unique in that it was only one of two Voodoos, which were seen with no significant colour markings; the other was F-101A 54-1457. At RAF Wethersfield in 1964, the only unit marking carried is the wing badge on the port fuselage side below the rear canopy. (*Author's collection*)

F-101A-30-MC shares the ramp at Bentwaters with an English Electric Canberra at an open house in the early 1960s. (*Author's collection*)

of the re-emphasis by NATO on the conventional bombing and strafing mission, following the doctrine of 'Flexible Response', which had been adopted in the place of 'Massive Retaliation'. While fulfilling this new role, Voodoo pilots at last got to use the jet's integral M-39 20-mm cannon, which is rather ironic considering that the replacement F-4C variant of the Phantom II (dubbed by some the 'Super Voodoo') had no such internal weapon.

By the autumn of 1965, thirty F-4Cs had been delivered to Bentwaters, allowing the 91st to deploy to Wheelus in November with their new aircraft. By 3 January 1966, all F-101s had been replaced in the trio of units that comprised the 81st TFW, thus making it the first Phantom II-equipped fighter wing in USAFE.

A number of the redundant F-101A/Cs flown back to America were in turn issued to frontline and Air National Guard tactical reconnaissance squadrons, where they were used to train future RF-101 pilots. Going one step further, no less than twenty-nine A and 32 C models were converted into recce Voodoos to help offset attrition of the USAF's then-primary tactical reconnaissance platform.

For the majority of aircraft, however, the hot sunshine of Arizona awaited them, as they were deemed surplus to requirements. Stripped of their guns, the weary Cold War warriors were flown to Davis-Monthan AFB in Arizona and placed in the 'boneyard', the huge open-air storage facility on-base. All of these aircraft had been reduced to scrap by 1977. The Voodoo fighter bomber served with USAFE for almost eight years, and during this time, its contribution to maintaining the balance of power during the Cold War had been significant. Through sheer hard work and perseverance, the 'Bentwaters Bombers' had made McDonnell's once unwanted strategic fighter a credible deterrent in terms of its atomic weapons delivery capability—not bad for a makeshift combat aircraft.

The McDonnell F-4 Phantom

The first F-4C Phantoms arrived with the 81st TFW in October 1965. Of the three squadrons, the 78th, 91st, and 92nd TFS, the 78th was to be the first squadron to take the new aircraft and was heavily involved in the conversion programme, receiving its first Phantoms on 4 October 1965.

By the end of the year, thirty F-4Cs had been delivered to Bentwaters and the 91st TFS deployed to Wheelus in November with their new aircraft. By April 1966, conversion to the F-4C had been completed. The 81st TFW had become the first Phantom fighter wing in USAFE. In 1968, the wing commenced conversion to the F-4D.

The F-4 was much appreciated by all who flew in it; Lt-Col. James McGorry, who joined the 92nd TFS in May 1968 after flying combat in South-East Asia in the F-4D from August 1967 to April 1968, sums up the feelings of many: 'The F-4 was an excellent, multi-role fighter aircraft. Those roles included aircraft intercepts, air-to-air combat, very-low-altitude navigation, and air-to-ground weapons delivery, including nuclear weapons'. Lt-Col. John Hugie also flew with the 92nd TFS and heaps similar praise on the aircraft:

> As I flew B, C, D and E models of the F-4 for nearly 14 years, my opinion of the airplane may be biased. For me, the F-4 Phantom II in all of its different models and variations was the best airplane during its time as a front-line tactical fighter. It was, and still is, my

The buzz numbers soon disappeared from the 81st TFW Phantoms in accordance with a revised technical order published in 1965. F-4C-24-MC 64-0860 is seen here on the ramp at RAF Woodbridge. (*Author's collection*)

favourite aircraft that I had the privilege to fly in the USAF. It was easy to fly and was generally forgiving, even for the novice pilot. The F-4 was a 'beast' that could take a lot of punishment and still keep flying. It could be armed with a dizzying load of different armaments from air-to-air missiles, both heat-seeking and radar guided, to tactical nuclear weapons and everything in between.[22]

From the outset, the primary mission of the F-4s of the 81st TFW was nuclear strike in support of NATO; the secondary mission was conventional strike and ground support. The targets for the Phantom's 'special weapons' were those included in the US Strategic Integrated Operations Plan (SIOP). This plan, which was first instigated in 1960 and was reviewed and developed in subsequent years, identified targets specific to strategic bombers, tactical strike aircraft, and ballistic missiles.

Initially, the SIOP reflected the Eisenhower doctrine of 'Massive Retaliation'. SIOP 63 was published in 1963 under the Kennedy administration and introduced the doctrine of 'Flexible Response'. This doctrine was not adopted by NATO until 1967. It thus has a significant bearing on the development of the mission of the 81st Tactical Fighter Wing at this time.

Lt-Col. John Hugie recalls the nuclear mission:

The 81st, like all tactical fighter units in USAFE, was assigned a certain number of primary and secondary targets in the Warsaw Pact. The primary targets for the 81st were military and located in Poland and East Germany.

Considerable mission planning was done for all of the primary targets. This included preparing detailed maps for the ingress and egress routes. The maps included the route with headings, turn points with latitude and longitude, minimum altitudes, known defences, expected and distinctive airborne radar views, and, when possible, expected radar views of the route, turns and target.[23]

Victor Alert was maintained at both RAF Bentwaters and Woodbridge and the F-4s on alert were fully fuelled and armed with a nuclear weapon and AIM-7 Sparrow air-to-air missiles. The VA area maintained a tight security within a fenced enclosure. Each crew would be on alert for a period of forty-eight hours. During this time, it was necessary for alert aircrews to be within the VA area between 8 p.m. and 6 a.m. They could leave the area outside those hours, but they had to remain on base and in their flight gear. While on alert duty in the compound, the pilots and WSOs (Weapons Systems Officers) would spend their time in studying their target folders, playing cards, etc.

A photo call for the aircrew of the 92nd TFS in front of F-4C-25-MC 64-0925 at RAF Bentwaters in 1968. (*John Hugie*)

'C' Flight of the 92nd TFS at RAF Bentwaters in 1968. *Standing, from left to right*: Mike Dowell, Robert Sun, John Hugie, Arnie Weber, Ray Zavislak, Steve Leisge, and Tom Slemons. *Kneeling, from left to right*: Floyd Gutowski, John Perdue, Mike Sharp, Manny Maza, and Tom Amos. (*John Hugie*)

During the times that John Hugie was with the 92nd TFS, the 81st TFW had a visit from Second World War RAF ace Douglas Bader. This photo was taken at an 81st TFW Dining-in where Bader was the speaker. *Those in the photo, from left to right*: unknown (81st TFW public affairs officer), Steve Leisge, Lynn Nofziger (92nd TFS intelligence officer), Douglas Bader, John Hugie, and Devol 'Rocky' Brett (81st TFW Commander). (*John Hugie*)

During its service with the 81st TFW, the F-4 had considerable upgrades to its weapons systems, not least being the 'special weapons' that it carried on its centreline station. The Mk 28 and Mk 43 thermonuclear bombs were replaced in due course by the Mk 57 and eventually the Mk 61. The principle methods of delivery of the bombs were LADD and Laydown. The LABS was practiced in the F-4C, but not in the F-4D.

Lt-Col. James McGorry describes the LADD and Laydown deliveries:

> We used two delivery methods/profiles: laydown and LADD. Laydown was simple and straight-forward: Come whistling in at 100' and 500 knots (575 mph) and hit the pickle button (bomb-release button) when the pipper (illuminated dot on the heads-up display) hits the target. Then streak straight through at maximum power (lest your trailing control surfaces on your wings and tail get melted off by the blast).
>
> The LADD was much more involved. You would come streaking in as before, but you would hit the pickle button when flying over an initial point somewhat short of the target. Steering bars would jump into place on your attitude indicator, and preset timers would start. After so many seconds, the steering bars would call for a rapid pull up to, say, 40 degrees nose high. Then hold that until another timer released the weapon. At weapon release, the steering bars would jump out of sight, and you would roll over, pull down, roll upright, and streak through at maximum power.
>
> If you were doing the deliveries at night or in bad weather (or practising doing so), you would go in using radar at a slightly higher altitude, same speed, and start the timers for the laydown or LADD (using different timer settings, of course) at certain ranges from radar-identifiable points near the target.[24]

Practice for nuclear delivery was carried out regularly on a variety of ranges, both in the UK and overseas.

In common with other USAF units, the 81st was regularly subjected to Operational Readiness Inspections. These many faceted inspections were rigorous and demanding, test exercises often requiring an immediate response. John Hugie was involved in a nuclear delivery mission in one of his inspections:

> One exercise I remember quite well tasked a few of us to simulate a nuclear weapons delivery on a target located on a bombing range in the Netherlands. Our mission task was to fly a 200 mile low level route, but not below 200 or over 500 feet, and drop a 1,000 pound simulated nuclear weapon on the target within a 30 second time window. Very realistic even to the part about nearly panicking as we finally located the target 2 miles out, just in time to initiate the programmed climb to release altitude. Never did get a report about where the 1,000 pound concrete training bomb impacted in the target area. Then again, miss distances weren't as critical with a nuclear bomb![25]

Every six months, pilots had to give a briefing to a colonel detailing how they were planning to approach one of their targets if required to do so immediately in response to a surprise attack by Warsaw Pact forces. These briefings would include tactics, navigation to the target, and identification of the target in all kinds of weather. Normally,

The F-4Cs were regularly modified and served alongside the F-4Ds at the twin bases for some years. F-4C-20-MC 63-7620 wears the dragon badge of the 81st TFW on the port side of the fuselage. (*Author's collection*)

F-4C-25-MC 63-7582 wears the tail code WT. Tail codes were introduced for all USAF tactical aircraft commencing in 1968, reaching USAFE based aircraft in 1970. Three codes were used by the 81st TFW: WR for the 78th TFS; WS for the 91st TFS; and WT for the 92nd TFS. (*Author's collection*)

Capt. James McGorry of the 92nd TFS at RAF Bentwaters in 1971. James McGorry retired from the USAF in 1986 as a lieutenant-colonel with twenty-one years of commissioned service. (*James McGorry*)

the weather question could be answered by a visit to the weather office just prior to the briefing. Lt-Col. Lee Bowden recalled one such briefing when another method of weather forecasting was used:

> When squadron pilot of polish descent came to the weather part of his certification briefing, he went into all sorts of crazy detail about the weather. 'There is low mist in the east with heavy clouds out west and rain is falling on the hills ... it's a bit chilly, but should be warmer in the afternoon' ... stuff like that instead of the usual aviation weather forecast. After the briefing was complete, the colonel asked: 'That was an excellent briefing captain, but your weather forecast was unusual. Could you explain?'
>
> The pilot looked at him with a straight face and said: 'Sir, before my briefing I called my grandmother who lives in Poland right next to the airfield I'm going to drop a nuclear bomb on. She gave me the current weather by looking outside her window.'[26]

During the time that the Phantom served with the 81st TFW, the emphasis on the conventional air-to-ground mission of the wing gained in importance in response to the doctrine of flexible response. The visits to the ranges for training with various types of weaponry combined simulated practice with conventional as well as nuclear weapons.

The overseas ranges used by the 81st aircrews regularly were Vliehors, The Netherlands; Incirlik AB, Turkey; Maniago, Aviano AB, Italy; Bardenas Reales, Zaragoza AB, Spain; and Decimomannu AB, Sardinia. In the early days of the F-4 at the twin bases, Wheelus AB in Libya had been a regular venue with its excellent ranges. The revolution and the rise of Gaddafi forced the USAF to close this base in 1970.

Lt-Col. Mike Robinson joined the 92nd Tactical Fighter Squadron in 1974 and recalls a typical routine F-4D mission to the ranges:

> Often we would fly a mission to one of the bombing ranges in the U.K. This was generally a two-ship or four-ship flight. We would do individual take-offs with five second spacing, or formation take-offs with one and two going first. I loved to do formation take-offs and I think I was pretty good at it. We would join up at medium altitude and cruise to the bombing range, usually Wainfleet or Holbeach. Generally we were loaded with two 370-gallon external wing tanks, two bomb dispensers on the inboard pylons and a SUU-23 Gatling gun on the centreline. The practice bomb load out was either all 'blue' bombs, which flew like a Mark 82 (a 500-pound slick with no retardation) or 'blue' and 'orange' bombs. The 'orange' bombs were shaped to fly like they were retarded with a parachute, which is the way the special weapon was designed. The idea was that the first two bombs out of a mixed load-out were supposed to be the orange bombs. Our first bomb runs simulated special weapon delivery.
>
> We would approach the range once the wing tanks were empty and get ready to bomb. The jets would fly over the range in echelon and then pitch out with 10 second or so spacing. We would fly a rectangular pattern keeping the briefed distance between jets and set up our switches. The WSO usually read the checklist and the last switch was the red Master Arm switch. Each aircraft made its run and we would usually drop two orange bombs. Often the target was just off shore and it was sometimes difficult to see it as you approached at low altitude. The WSO could help if the target had a radar reflector, but in close you had to see the target and get your timer started. When the practice bomb hit the ground it would give off a white puff of smoke and you could score it yourself before the official score came from the range officer over the radio. Of course we bet on every bomb, usually 25 cents. After delivering the orange bombs we would climb up for conventional deliveries, starting with 30-degree dive bomb if the ceiling was high enough. Two each, then 15-degree, then 10-degree (simulating napalm), and finally strafe. You usually had only 100 rounds of ball (TP or Target Practice ammunition) you could shoot. A rounds limiter was set by the load crew.
>
> The guns were notorious for being badly sighted, so your first run was a very short 'sighter' burst (the gun shoots 100 rounds per second). You had to see where the bullets were going so you could adjust on the second and last pass. The bullets were supersonic and left a sonic trail that you could see. You remembered where the gun was really shooting relative to the gun sight and adjusted on the last pass. Strafe bet was 50 cents. Then we joined up, looked each over for any damage and headed for home.[27]

Conventional bomb delivery employed a number of different techniques, skip bombing and dive bombing being practised regularly at the ranges. Skip bombing was a technique

Zaragoza in Spain was a regular deployment base for the 81st TFW Phantoms for weapons training over the Bardenas Reales ranges. F-4Ds of the 78th TFS prepare for another busy day. (*via Graham Gilbert*)

A pair of Phantoms of the 81st TFW fly a two-ship mission. Before transfer to the 81st TFW, 66-7511 was assigned to the 36th TFW at Bitburg, Germany. The aircraft on the right of the photo is carrying an SUU-21 practice bomb dispenser on its inboard pylons. (*via Graham Gilbert*)

F-4D in flight over Spain during a weapons training deployment to Zaragoza. (*Capt. Rocky McCutcheon via Graham Gilbert*)

developed during the Second World War primarily to attack shipping where the bomb would be released at low level and skip over the water to strike the target. After the war, it was refined to be used against ground targets. James McGorry remembers practising this at Holbeach and Wheelus:

> You would come in very low, go into a shallow dive, 5 to 10 degrees, as you would for strafing, and try to drop the 20-pound practice bomb into a narrow rectangle marked on the ground, perhaps 10′ by 30′, to have the bomb bounce or 'skip' ahead and up to hit a vertical panel just beyond the rectangle. It didn't seem very practical, but it was pretty sporty. You were going 460 mph (400 knots) a few feet above the ground and descending when you released the bomb.[28]

James also enjoyed what he described as the Disney 'E' Ticket ride that 45-degree dive bombing afforded the crew of the Phantom:

> At 10,000' and 300 knots (345 mph), you make a 90-degree turn by pulling the nose up and rolling toward the target, going inverted, pulling the nose down, rolling out with the nose pointed below the target. All you can see out the windscreen is the Earth, and you're accelerating from 300 to 450 knots. You have a maximum of 7 seconds to make one, two, or, if you're really good, three corrections in that time before you release the bomb and

> pull. Pull to save your life. Pull with at least 4 Gs, usually 5 Gs: You don't want to hit the ground. Sometimes 6 Gs. if you delayed half a second past your planned 'pickle' altitude.[29]

One new bombing system that was tested by the 81st TFW was the HOBO (Homing Bomb System). This involved a television camera and steering computer mounted on the front end of a 2,000-lb bomb. 'Steering fins' would fly the munition towards the target.

A small TV receiver was fixed in the rear cockpit. Compared to today's 'smart bombs', HOBO was very primitive, but it was innovative and would eventually lead on to greater things. Mike Robinson was on the team which evaluated the system:

> Here's how we employed the HOBO: *En route* to the target the pilot would dial the computed depression in the gunsight and select the bomb (which turned on the TV camera), and the WSO would fire up his little television. The pilot would find an object in the sky ahead of him and fly the reticle onto the 'target'. The WSO would look at the image in the TV receiver and give the pilot corrections up and down. The depression was adjusted until the WSO was happy. We would fly out over the English Channel looking for a 'target' somewhere on the water, like a nice white boat. We set up an orbit at medium altitude over the unsuspecting vessel. When it was our turn to deliver, we would roll into a dive, 25 to 30 degrees comes to mind, and the pilot would put his reticle on the target. The WSO would call out corrections up and down, and he would use the rudder pedals in the back seat to steer left and right. When the target was centred the WSO would lock on, call it, and the pilot would simulate release of the bomb using the pickle button. Obviously this delivery profile left the jet vulnerable to AAA (Anti-Aircraft Artillery) and surface-to-air missiles, so it would work only on targets that were lightly defended. HOBO was an early version of a 'smart bomb', and portended new tactics for attacking ground targets.[30]

The role of Close Air Support (CAS) was one with which the 81st was tasked as part of its secondary mission. There were issues. The large turning radius of the F-4 made it difficult to identify the target and to differentiate friend and foe. However, some exercises did take place in Germany in cooperation with the NATO armies on manoeuvre.

Col. Jim Crumbliss flew with the 92 TFS as a GIB joining the squadron on 19 October 1969. He had previously flown with the 497th TFS, which was the only dedicated night-flying fighter squadron in SE Asia. In one year, he had completed 256 'night owl' missions. He recalls an exercise in the German Buffer Zone:

> We refuelled in air on these flights and were assigned a Forward Air Controller [FAC] to work with otherwise we could not enter the Buffer Zone. These were CAS type missions in support of an army exercise and the CAS targets were often 'notional' although sometimes other NATO units acted as aggressors. BDA was at the FAC's discretion depending how he graded our weapons delivery passes. These were lots of fun and sometimes we landed at Ramstein to refuel if a tanker wasn't available.[31]

In February 1972, Jim detached to McDill AFB in Florida for upgrade training and later returned to Bentwaters as a new aircraft commander.

The F-4C and F-4D acquitted themselves well in the war in SE Asia, achieving several kills with air-to-air missiles, and also with its centreline mounted SUU-23 gun pod. The mission of the 81st TFW did not include an air-to-air role, but the aircrews still needed to defend themselves and their aircraft if they encountered enemy interceptors when engaged in their primary and secondary missions. Both aircraft could carry the Sidewinder and Falcon air-to air-missiles and the SUU-23. Routine air-to-air exercises were flown over the North Sea under strict safety regulations as no one wanted to have to eject into the icy cold waters.

Impromptu air-to-air encounters occurred often and sometimes spontaneously. Perhaps another NATO aircraft would be spotted by a pair or single F-4 and the latter would attempt to get into the six o'clock position to simulate a kill. From this chance encounter, a brief dogfight might occur which would serve to help to hone each pilots skills. John Hugie recalled a memorable encounter with the RAF:

> One 'air-to-air' engagement really got my attention, and respect. We were flying two-ship air-to-air training mission over the North Sea when radar control advised us to be on the lookout for a Vulcan bomber transiting the area. We located the bomber slightly below of our altitude of 25,000 or so and immediately decided that here was an easy pickings target. Lowering the aircraft nose and increasing power to gain more airspeed we started toward the Vulcan. As we approached the 'kill zone' at 6 o'clock, the Vulcan rolled and turned into our path of attack. The next thing I saw was that the Vulcan, with that huge wing area, had turned well inside us and at that altitude we were unable to match his turn and maintain any attack position. The only face saving grace we had was that the Vulcan didn't turn to position himself at our 6 o'clock![32]

An encounter over the Wash with BAC Lightnings from the 226 OCU (Operational Conversion Unit) at RAF Coltishall engaged Jim Crumbliss's attention:

> Our configuration was less than optimum for engaging other aircraft, three fuel tanks! Nevertheless we had a great time going round and round with them. The only 'shot' I got was on a TF model [Lightning T.5]. The side-by-side cockpit arrangement was certainly strange looking and I think it gave me an advantage because of his impaired cockpit visibility.[33]

In common with other NATO units, the squadrons of the 81st TFW took part in exchange visits with other units. These exchanges were designed to develop co-operation and camaraderie between units, often with dissimilar missions, and to share tactics and expertise. In August 1972, Jim Crumbliss took part in an exchange visit to Bodo in Norway with 334 Squadron of the Royal Norwegian Air Force (RNAF), which was equipped with Northrop F-5s. The mission of the 334 Squadron was maritime defence and anti-shipping. In addition to having a very rewarding time flying low level through the Norwegian fjords, Jim had to get used to wearing sunglasses at 3 a.m.

NATO also endorsed a programme of interoperability, which involved aircraft flying from one base to another and being serviced by personnel on the base: refuelling,

Two F-4Ds line up for take-off with an F-5E of the 527th Tactical Fighter Training Aggressor Squadron (TFTAS) based at RAF Alconbury on 6 June 1978. Most of the air-to-air training for the 81st TFW was carried out over the North Sea. (*via Graham Gilbert*)

On 6 June 1978, F-4Ds 66-7754 and 66-7694 were in the secure area at RAF Bentwaters. F-4D 66-7754 carries an ALQ/119 jamming pod and an AGM-65 Maverick missile. (*USAF Archives*)

F-4D-28-MC 65-0702 carries an ALQ/AN-119 ECM pod on its missile recess on the port side. It was assigned to the 78th TFS based at RAF Woodbridge. (*Bentwaters Cold War Museum via Simon Gladas*)

drag-chute replacement, and launch procedures. Once again, this was not necessarily a visit to a base which flew the same aircraft. Col. Crumbliss recalled three visits: to Karup in Denmark which flew the Saab Draken, Gilze-Rijen with Northrop NF-5s, and Grosseto in Italy which was equipped with Lockheed F-104S Starfighters.

Regular cross-country flights were made by the aircrews of the 81st. Because the weather in Northern Europe was abysmally bad for much of the time, such flights were very important for the purposes of logging flying hours.

Approval for such flights had to be requested and were subject to several conditions. The F-4 needed to be available and not required for any scheduled operations. Visits could only be made to bases that could service an F-4 and the total flight time must be for a minimum of six hours. The bases chosen for the visits had to have a runway of 8,000 feet or more and have a cable-type barrier capable of stopping an F-4 if necessary. John Hugie recalls that, during his four years at Bentwaters, he averaged one cross-country every five or six weeks. These flights were usually taken at the weekend, ideally taking off on a Friday:

> My typical cross country plan was to have two legs of two-plus hours flying time on Friday ending at a base where we would park the plane and stay, usually in a nearby city, until Sunday. The final two required hours would be logged on the return to Bentwaters to complete required flying time minimum. Favourite places to visit were Torrejón AB, Spain; Aalborg, Denmark; Fürstenfeldbruck AB, Germany; Bitburg AB, Germany; Hahn AB, Germany.[34]

In 1978, there were radical changes in store for the 81st TFW. The F-4D was to be replaced by the Fairchild A-10 Thunderbolt II. The F-4Ds were passed over to the 401st TFW at Torrejón, Spain.

The Republic A-10A Thunderbolt II

On 25 January 1979, fifteen A-10As landed at a very snowbound Bentwaters. They were the first aircraft assigned to the 92nd TFS. The 81st was destined to become the largest fighter wing in the USAF, eventually comprising six squadrons: the 78th TFS, 91st TFS, 92nd TFS, 509th TFS, 510th TFS, and 511th TFS.

Training for the close air support mission had begun, for the initial cadre of A-10 pilots of the 81st, at Davis-Monthan AFB in Tucson, Arizona, with the 355th TTW. This wing had been established as the A-10 training wing in 1976. The first 355th TTW A-10 pilots converting to the A-10 at Davis-Monthan came mainly from the McDonnell Douglas F-4 Phantom and the Ling Tempo Vought A-7 Corsair community. Later trainees came from a wider field of experience.

Low-altitude tactical navigation was but one aspect of training in the A-10 which was directly related to the aircraft's mission. Attack profiles were practised and developed. These included terrain masking approaches to the targets and live firings of weapons at real tanks. First Lieutenant Jim Preston commenced his A-10 training in June 1980 and remembers the weapons training:

> Dropping bombs and shooting the 30mm gun were always fun, but very challenging for new pilots. The gun made a lot of noise, but it was simple to employ. Put the gun cross on the target (allowing for the wind, especially at the longer ranges) and pull the trigger. Our bursts were no more than a second, firing 50-80 rounds per burst. We had to cease-fire by 2,000 feet from the target, and misjudging that range meant a foul—and two of those meant you went home.[35]

It was in Europe that the training for their wartime mission began in earnest for the pilots of the 81st TFW. The first few weeks were spent in local orientation flights and getting used to the very different air traffic control procedures used in the UK and the rest of Europe. First Lieutenant Matt Modleski recalls those early days with the 81st TFW:

> There was a very structured syllabus to introduce all the nuances of flying in the UK. After completing a Mission Ready (MR) check ride in the jet, there was a graduation exercise. It was to plan a simulated war-time mission with a certified flight lead, present that plan to the entire squadron and then answer any and all questions about contingencies that might come up in exercising that mission. It was stressful and yet once complete, you were considered a mission ready member of the Squadron.[36]

There was necessarily, a good deal of low-level flying. In specially designated areas, the permitted low-level altitude was 250 feet, but generally, outside these areas, the A-10s operated at a minimum of 500 feet. LATN flying was a lot different in Europe compared to Arizona. Jim Preston noted:

The first of the 81st TFW squadrons to receive the A-10A was the 92nd Tactical Fighter Squadron. Fifteen of the aircraft touched down at a snowy Bentwaters on 25 January 1979. A-10A 77-248 was one of those early arrivals. (*USAF*)

The A-10 was introduced to the local population on 7 July 1979 at an open house. One of the most striking features of the aircraft, the GAU-8 Gatling gun is displayed here. (*Author's collection*)

> We probably had five flights to regain our instrument currency and get used to operations around Bentwaters, then we had a check ride. Once past that we began our mission training, where we began our LATN and weapons delivery training. I can remember being absolutely lost on my first few low level flights. The forests, towns and rivers all looked the same. There were no mountains.[37]

One particular aspect of flying in Northern Europe which could have a significant effect on mission capability was the weather. Regular rain and mist with accompanying low ceilings is commonplace, particularly in the three months from December through to February. During such periods, there is bound to be a degradation of the support that the air force can offer the army on the ground. The original USAF specifications for the close air support aircraft required the capability of operating under a ceiling of 1,000 feet with 1-mile visibility. The A-10 met this criteria and the aircraft has demonstrated a capability to perform the visual ground attack mission in reduced visibilities down to 1.5 miles. The ability of the A-10 to operate at very low levels meant that it could stay under a low ceiling if the visibility was reasonable. Therefore, although it could not operate in all weathers, it could certainly do so effectively in adverse weather conditions.

The 81st TFW utilised a number of ranges in the UK for weapons training, including RAF Holbeach, Lincolnshire; RAF Donna Nook, Lincolnshire; RAF Wainfleet, Lincolnshire; and RAF Cowden, East Yorkshire. The disadvantage with the UK ranges was that there was no opportunity to drop live bombs, although there was the opportunity to drop the BDU-33, which was a blue 25-lb steel shape that was supposed to be similar in ballistics to the Mk 82, the widely available 500-lb bomb most likely to be carried in combat. The A-10s would go to the range with six or more BDU-33s, which had smoke charges at the aft end for helping to score their accuracy.

Unfortunately, there was not a facility where the pilots could fire Maverick missiles. RAE Aberporth, Ceredigion, was made available by the Ministry of Defence for the purpose of live missile firing, but it was not entirely satisfactory. Lt Les Wood stated:

> It took a lot of coordination with good weather, range clearance of boats, weapons loading, and pilot study to get a successful mission. I believe the first couple of tries were unsuccessful because of wave heights. The target buoys swung to and fro and prevented the Maverick seeker from getting a proper lock on. As I departed BTW/WDB in 1984, I believe we had only one successful firing.[38]

The opportunities to fire the formidable GAU-8 Avenger, however, were available at all the ranges. Only RAF Holbeach was equipped with acoustical scoring using the DelMar Acoustiscore system. The other ranges relied on the controllers calling the scores to the pilots.

The A-10s also used Salisbury plain and RAF Otterburn, Northumberland, tactics ranges for live firings.

In the late 1970s it was estimated that there were forty-eight Warsaw Pact armoured divisions in Eastern Europe and the number of main battle tanks in operational service in Poland, Czechoslovakia, and East Germany was 16,200. Facing this force in the west were 6,500 NATO main battle tanks. It was against this armour that the A-10 was aimed. In order to be effective, it could not, of course, operate from the UK. It was vital that the aircraft and crews were on the ground to deal quickly and efficiently with any incursion. Four Forward Operating Locations (FOL) were established in Germany. Detachment 1 was at Sembach AB in the Central region; Detachment 2, at Leipheim AB in the south; Detachment 3 at Ahlhorn AB in the North; and Detachment 4 at Nörvenich AB in the North Central region. Nörvenich and Ahlhorn were attached to the 2nd Allied Tactical Air Force (ATAF) and Sembach and Leipheim to the 4th ATAF.

Each of the six squadrons of the 81st TFW was divided into three flights, A, B, and C Flights. Each flight would deploy to a forward operating base for a period of two weeks at a time. Detachments to one of the FOLs were welcomed by the pilots. Jim Preston noted:

> We were able to focus on wartime training. We spent a lot of time getting familiar with our wartime target areas. Each squadron had an area where they'd be tasked, so they could spend lots of time figuring out the terrain, looking for good attack avenues, discerning possible enemy approach routes, etc. We'd arrive on a Monday and generally fly one sortie that afternoon, then fly twice each day thereafter until the Friday almost two weeks later. The exercises were as close to real war as we could make them. We did real go-to-war tasking orders. We sat cockpit alert where we'd have to launch within five minutes of receiving the order. We'd get our target assignments after launch, so you had to be prepared for any target area.[39]

One of the most important aspects of the A-10s mission in Europe was collaboration with the armies of the NATO allies. In the close air support role, the importance of this cannot be over emphasised. For this reason, the A-10 flights based at the FOLs spent a lot of their time working in concert with ground based forward air controllers and the Bell AH-1 Cobra helicopter gunships of the army. Such manoeuvres were designed to develop Joint Air Attack Tactics (JAAT) and were invaluable not only in this regard, but also in cementing relationships between the troops on the ground and the close air support A-10 aircrews. One of the regiments with which the 81st TFW A-10s trained extensively was the 7th Cavalry Regiment based at Giebelstadt in Bavaria. Cooperation with the US Army extended to other areas. Jim Preston noted:

> Sometimes the Army would let us ride in their Hueys (Bell UH-1)as they flew along the border. It was invaluable to work with them on that level. We got to know them as people, and I hope they came to respect what we brought to the fight. We also did what we called 'terrain walks' where we'd drive to our wartime target sectors and see what they looked like from the ground. We'd get right up to the East German border and watch the guards in the towers take pictures of us. We removed our squadron insignia and name tags, but if we'd been taken prisoner, they'd have had those pictures.[40]

In order for the A-10 to perform its mission, it was important that the allies had air superiority. The altitude at which the A-10 plied its trade was not, in itself, a guarantee of immunity from attack from enemy interceptors. This was brought home dramatically to 1Lt Matt Modleski while on exercise in Germany: 'I will say that while in Germany

This 'Hog is sitting outside its hardened Shelter at Norvenich in the Federal Republic of Germany. Norvenich was one of four forward operating locations (FOL) in Germany. It is carrying two 600-gallon fuel tanks. The A-10 did not carry external fuel into combat. The tanks were used for the ferry trips from the UK to the FOL. (*USAF*)

Loading the GAU-8 Avenger at the FOL of Ahlhorn in Germany. The detached flights were able to conduct live fire exercises at the Grafenwöhr or Hohenfels ranges in Bavaria. (*USAF*)

Four A-10s taxi at Sembach AB in the Rhineland-Palatinate near Kaiserslautern. Sembach was also one of the FOLs for the 81st TFW in Germany. This photograph was taken during Exercise

Reforger 1986. A-10A 80-0144 takes on fuel from a KC-135. This A-10 is equipped with an AN/ALQ-119 jamming pod on its outer port pylon, and on its inner starboard pylon, an SUU-30 bomblet dispenser. (*USAF*)

Some of the A-10 flights detached to Ahlhorn used the A-29 autobahn nearby during operations in 'Exercise Highway 84'. (*USAF*)

On 'Exercise Highway 84', refuelling facilities were on site for a fast turn round of the aircraft. (*USAF*)

conducting LATN at 250 feet I was surprised to be attacked/intercepted by a Tornado from below! He made his intercept at 100 feet and I never forgot the lesson that just because I was low that an air threat couldn't be lower'.

The pilots of the Thunderbolts did take part in DACT (Dissimilar Air Combat Training) with other units. The specialist unit for DACT in USAFE was the 527th TFTAS based at RAF Alconbury, Huntingdonshire, in the UK. The 527th F-5E Tiger 11s usually deployed to RAF Bentwaters when working with the A-10s at what they referred to as Defensive Reaction Training. (DRT) Jeff Brown flew with the 527th:

> I do remember deploying for a week to RAF Bentwaters to fly with the A-10 guys. We tried to teach them a basic move to escape the air-to-air guys. They didn't have AIM-9's like they have now; all they had was their 30 mm cannon. Our focus was to be able to get them to intimidate us with their gun. Their gun, inside 6–7000 feet, had very little bullet drop, so it was very intimidating.[41]

DRT could also be dangerous business. Capt. Paul Taylor detached to Bentwaters from Alconbury on 12 December 1983:

> I was the DETCO (Detachment Commander) of our three pilot, eight maintenance technicians, three jet detachment. On the very first mission of the two week deployment the two A-10's I was flying against ran into each other right in front of me. Not a good mission to start the deployment off. One of the A-10 pilots was killed and the other was rescued from the North Sea by an RAF helicopter out of RAF Coltishall.[42]

When the 527th TFTAS converted to the F-16, they were based at RAF Bentwaters alongside the A-10s. There was ample opportunity for the two aircraft to fly DACT missions together. Col. Jim Wisdom was the CO of the 527th at Bentwaters:

> They were truly dissimilar air combat sorties! In spite of the A-10's lack of speed and power, it could turn very well and always stayed in the low block optimizing their performance. The key for their success was visual look out and situational awareness gathered from their Radar Warning System and ability to visually acquire that fast moving F-16 soon enough before weapons were employed.[43]

It was evident that, within reasonable limits, the A-10 could survive in a hostile air-to-air environment. However, it was also apparent that NATO air superiority over the battlefield was essential in ensuring that the close support role of the aircraft was allowed to proceed without too much hindrance.

Throughout the years of service with the 81st at Bentwaters and Woodbridge, the A-10 underwent modifications which enhanced its role and its survivability on the battlefield; the emphasis in these developments being protection against hostile aircraft and missiles. These included the ability to carry the AIM-9L Sidewinder air-to-air missile for defence, and a series of electronic countermeasure pods including the Westinghouse AN/ALQ-119 'self-protection' jammer pod.

Back at RAF Bentwaters, an A-10 awaits the mounting of four Maverick missiles. (*USAF*)

Flanked by an F-4E of the 52nd TFW and an RF-4C of the 1st TRS, 10th TRW; this A-10A, 81-0955, belongs to the 511th TFS of the 81st TFW. (*USAF*)

Ground crewmen, in chemical warfare gear, load a Mk 82 bombs on to the pylon of an 81st TFW A-10 Thunderbolt II aircraft during Exercise UREX 82 on 22 April 1982. (*USAF*)

There is no doubt that it would have been a formidable weapon when wielded against the plethora of Warsaw Pact armour that would have been ranged against it. Of all the aircraft in the NATO inventory, it was uniquely suited to the close support role. It was not fancy and it was not fast but the ability to fly at low speed could be a distinct advantage in target acquisition and destruction. Unlike its faster contemporaries the A-10 rarely overflew the target when searching for it and having acquired it, one short burst with the GAU-8 usually negated the necessity to try again when the enemy might be waiting. The 'Hog' was designed to be survivable. It could take a lot of hits and get back to base for repairs, or, at worst, make it to friendly territory before it failed. It could, if necessary, hold its own in an air-to-air encounter. The power of its gun would have made many a would-be assassin think twice about taking it on. There were drawbacks of course: the A-10 was a large aircraft with a large radar signature, and in tight turns it would bleed a lot of speed, increasing its vulnerability.

In 1988, two squadrons, the 509th TFS and the 511th TFS, left the 81st to join the newly activated 10th TFW at RAF Alconbury, Huntingdonshire.

On 6 April 1991, a joint task force including the air forces of the France, the US, the UK, and Turkey initiated Operation Provide Comfort. This operation was designed to support the Kurds of northern Iraq and protect them from persecution by Saddam Hussein's forces. Apart from providing much needed food and other supplies to the besieged Kurds, the role of the air forces was to create and maintain a 'no fly zone' over north Iraq, and to retaliate with force if this zone was violated. Among the units detached to Incirlik AB in Turkey was the 78th TFS with their Warthogs. The responsibilities of the 78th detachment to Turkey were twofold. Initially it was necessary to supply the Kurds with airdrops. A-10s preceded the cargo planes into the designated areas to quell any hostile reactions by the Iraqi army. During these operations, McDonnell Douglas F-15s and General Dynamics F-16s provided air combat patrols to ensure that there was no interference from the air. Once an effective no fly zone had been established and the Iraqi ground forces had been encouraged to retreat to an acceptable distance from the zone of operations; the role of the A-10s was to maintain regular patrols to ensure the safety of all the ground forces in the area and serve as a further reminder to Iraq to keep its distance.

It was on one of these regular patrols that the commander of the 78th TFS, Bill Rial, flew one of his most memorable sorties:

> While deployed to Incirlik AB, Turkey, it was brought to my attention that myself and my squadron weapons officer were both approaching the '2,000 hour' mark in the A-10 with almost identical total flying hours. It was suggested that we go over that '2,000 hour' mark together, at the same time, on a Provide Comfort mission. We did! I led the 2-ship out of Incirlik and to the KC-135 orbiting just north of Iraq. We conducted our refuelling and 'dropped down' into our assigned patrol area in Iraq. Approximately halfway during the patrol, we both went over 2,000hrs. At that point, I gave my weapons officer the lead. He

After flying a memorable mission, during which they flew though the 2,000-hour barrier, 78th Cdr Bill Rial and his squadron weapons officer, John Mott, were awarded with a traditional bottle of champagne each and a good soaking. (*Bill Rial*)

In the spring of 1991, a detachment of the 78th TFS went to Incirlik in Turkey to support Operation Provide Comfort in Northern Iraq. Prior to leaving RAF Woodbridge, the detachment posed in front of A-10A 80-233. Sqn Cdr Col. Bill Rial is in the front row, sixth from the right. (*Bill Rial*)

> led us back to the tanker for top-off before returning to Incirlik. I still get excited about that memory today. That particular [approximately 5hr] sortie was topped off with fire trucks spraying a water arch for us to taxi beneath on the way back into our parking ramp where the entire squadron and base VIPs met us with a hose-down and Champagne.[44]

It was shortly after the 78th's return from Turkey that the squadron and the 81st Tactical Fighter Wing was deactivated, its mission in Europe completed after forty years. However, in spite of many attempts to retire the A-10 since its removal from the European theatre, it is still flies with the USAF. Jim Preston stated:

> There is no airplane that can do what the Hog does, and it's still cheap to operate and maintain. How many squadrons of A-10s might be still be operated for the cost of one or two F-35s? I don't mean to malign the F-35. Rather, I just think it's ludicrous to believe that the aircraft can do the Close Air Support mission as effectively and efficiently as an A-10.[45]

2

The 406th FBW, FIW

The 406th Bombardment Group was activated at Key Field, Mississippi, as a dive-bombing unit in March 1943. In August 1943, the group was redesignated as the 406th Fighter Bomber Group and equipped with Republic P-47 Thunderbolts. It prepared for service in the European theatre of operations, where it deployed in March 1944, assigned to the 9th Air Force. The group had three squadrons assigned: the 512th, 513th, and 514th Fighter Bomber Squadrons. Operating from RAF Ashford in Kent, the group supported the Normandy landings and the advance into France, their P-47s attacking railroads and other supply routes, ammunition dumps, gun emplacements, and bridges.

In August 1944, the group moved to France and for the next four months followed the allies advance from Normandy, the Loire, and eventually into Belgium and Germany. During this advance, the unit received Distinguished Unit Citations; the first came in September for frustrating the retreat and escape of a large a large German armoured column. The unit operated in the Ardennes region during December and earned its second Distinguished Unit Citation when it defended the town of Bastogne against the German advance during the Battle of the Bulge, destroying many tanks and gun emplacements in addition to providing close air support to the Allied counterattack. Following the Allied advance through Belgium and into Germany, the 406th eventually based at Nordholz Airfield.

With the cessation of hostilities and the end of the war, the group was assigned to USAFE, and in August 1946 was deactivated, its personnel and equipment being taken over by the newly activated 86th Fighter Group.

The 406th FBW was reactivated on 10 July 1952 at RAF Manston in Kent, taking over the assets of the federalised 123rd FBW which returned to the control of the Kentucky Air National Guard. The 123rd had arrived in the UK the previous November, having been activated at Godman AFB, Fort Knox, the previous year, manned by National Guardsmen. Three squadrons were attached: the 156th FBS, the 165th FBS, and the 167th FBS. On activation of the 406th FBW, these squadrons became the 512th FBS, the 513th FBS, and the 514th FBS respectively. They were equipped with the Republic F-84E Thunderjet.

406th Fighter Bomber Wing

The Republic F-84E Thunderjet

The primary mission of the 406th was to 'conduct fighter bomber operations under the operational control of the 3rd Air Force, and to retard and stabilize any aggressor forces in Northern and Western Europe'. The secondary mission of the wing was to conduct air defence operations under the operational control of the RAF.

The F-84Es of the 406th were troublesome and in-commission rate was comparatively low. On some aircraft, cracked right wing spars were sent for replacement to the 85th Air Depot, who carelessly or forgetfully sent one aircraft back the Manston without the replacement being carried out. There were also moves to reduce the vibratory stresses in the rotor blades of the J35-GE-17B engines. Morale among the personnel, although not low, was not as high as would have been liked. This was probably due to a number of factors, including the aircraft problems, a shortage of pilots, and a shortage of field ranges over which to practice their fighter bomber skills. One of the means by which wing HQ sought to raise morale was a squadron of the month competition.

A spate of accidents in the summer of 1952 cannot have done much to raise morale. On 29 July, a 513th FBS F-84 on dive-bombing practice over Dengie Flats flew into the ground and disintegrated. The pilot, 1Lt James Sims, was killed. On 22 July, a pilot shot off a tow target and collided with it. He did manage to get his F-84 home but with major damage and a dead engine. This was 512th's last accident at Manston. On

In November 1951, the 123rd FBW of the Kentucky ANG arrived at RAF Manston in Kent. The 123rd had three squadrons assigned: the 156th, 165th, and 167th FBS. These aircraft, parked on the temporary steel planking surface, wear the blue colours of the 167th FBS. (*via Duncan Curtis*)

In July 1952, the 123rd FBS was returned on paper to the US, and the aircraft were taken over by the newly activated 406th FBW. The 156th FBS was renamed the 512th FBS, the 165th the 513th FBS, and the 167th the 514th FBS. FS-328 was assigned to the 512th FBS and wears that unit's badge on the nose. (*via Duncan Curtis*)

F-84E-1-RE 49-2054 is parked on the bare earth on Manston's loop dispersal in 1952. Concrete dispersals were completed by March 1953. (*Merle Omsted via Dave McLaren*)

the same day while the 514th FBS were at Wheelus, an explosion occurred in an F-84 shortly after take-off. The pilot jettisoned the canopy and ditched the aircraft in the sea. The impact of the plane with the water caused the seat to fire and the pilot was catapulted into the sea where he managed to disentangle himself and inflate his life raft. On 13 August, at 8,000 feet, an F-84E exploded. The fortunate pilot ejected safely. On 1 September, however, another pilot, Capt. Roscoe Nemer of 513th FBS, was killed when his F-84 crashed into the sea off Margate. On 30 November 1952, Capt. Raymond L. Dennany of the 513th FBS was returning to Manston from RAF Sculthorpe, home of the 47th Bombardment Wing; as dusk began to fall, the flight arrived over Thanet and it was decided to practice a let-down and penetration through the winter's murk that was overhanging the countryside. After the let-down, and in a straight and level climb, Capt. Dennany flying F-84E 49-2071 experienced an explosion and his wingman informed him that the aircraft was on fire in the vicinity of the under fuselage dive break. Dennany ejected safely and the aircraft fell burning through the overcast. Lt Forrest Smith, another F-84E pilot, was enjoying a day off at his house in Deal and takes up the story:

> Hearing a roaring sound, I looked up and saw an F-84 aircraft arcing across the sky at about 500 feet [153m] above the ground, one wing gone but a red tip tank plainly visible. It pitched over the edge of the cliff just a few hundred yards away and plunged into the sea. Tiny pieces of metal came down from the sky like falling leaves. I grabbed my camera and ran to the edge of the cliff and took a photograph of the burning spot in the sea and a few minutes later, took another of the area, but this time there was a tanker in the background.
>
> All the while, I looked for a parachute but saw none. The base of the overcast was around 1,000 feet [305m]. Due to the rising terrain south towards St. Margarets Bay, and the overcast, I could not see Denanny's parachute as he landed in the Channel. He got into his dinghy and was picked up by the tanker that had appeared in my second photograph! Soon, a helicopter bearing Capt. Strich, MD, flew over and picked up Capt. Denanny from the deck of the tanker.[1]

Two significant exercises took place in 1952. Exercise Kentucky in July involved the 406th in a variety of missions: gunnery, interdiction, ground control intercept, and reconnaissance. Blue Alliance in September took the 406th to Neubiberg in Germany in an exercise to test their ability to move aircraft and equipment to a base on the continent. Thirty-six F-84Es flew out on 14 September with ground crews following in Fairchild C-119s. The missions flown included close support, fighter intercept, interdiction, reconnaissance, and high-altitude bombing. They were flying against the RB-26s of the 1st TRS, 10th TRW, out of Toul-Rosières, France; the 53rd FBS flying F-84s out of Bitburg, Germany; the 526th and 527th FBS based at Ramstein Landstuhl, Germany; and the B-26s of the 136th and 108th Bomb Squadrons from Laon, France. Exercise Ardent in October saw 406th FBW Thunderjets acting as escorts for 'attacking' bombers in the UK's annual air defence exercise.

Routine operations for the 406th FBW included air weapons demonstrations, aerial attacks on targets in England, gunnery, and interception exercises in conjunction with Metropolitan sector of RAF Fighter Command. Air weapons demonstrations were not always successful for a variety of reasons. In a demo at Old Sarum in 1952 only strafing took place. Some components for the rockets were not available and the use of napalm was discouraged by the English authorities.

In early 1953, the wing received notice that it was to convert to the North American F-86F Sabre in fiscal year 1954, and the response to this was highly positive; the very prospect sent morale soaring, and in anticipation, a request was put immediately forward to USAFE command to include 406th personnel on the Mobile Training detachment scheduled for the 36th and 86th FBW and for personnel to visit RAF Bentwaters for on the job training with the 81st FIW currently flying the F-86A. Representation was also requested from North American and General Electric.

Meanwhile, life with the F-84E went on. Regular trips to North Africa were by now very much part of the routine for all USAFE tactical units in Northern Europe; how else could they guarantee even a minimum of training in the face of the weather which regularly frustrated operations? Preparations for a detachment to Wheelus near Tripoli always required a trip to RAF Bentwaters where there were facilities for bore sighting and firing in the aircraft. Personnel and equipment were transported by C-119 transports. The squadrons usually spent some six weeks away practising their gunnery and bombing skills beginning in May 1953.

Back in the UK, one of the most significant events of 1953 was the severe flooding all along the East Coast. The personnel of the 406th, like those of the other USAF units based in this part of the UK, were very active in supporting and helping the victims and the authorities at this traumatic time. An air-sea rescue (ASR) was loaned to stockmen

Corrosion of the F-84 airframe was a serious problem for the 406th FBW. Manston was very close to the sea, and the salt water was not kind to the aluminium. This Thunderjet has been thoroughly washed and stripped off prior to repainting. (*Dick Grace*)

desperate to save some of their stricken herd. Pumps were provided to flooded homes. Collections were organised for toys and clothes, and in a period of a few hours, 1 ton of goods was collected. Personnel were among the rescuers, including two men who rescued a seventy-four-year-old lady and to this day are still only identified by the names of Hank and Mike. Alas, tragedy also struck the 406th on 6 February 1953 when two 514th FBS F-84Es collided over Deal in Kent, killing both pilots: Capt. Philip Conserva and Lt Clyde Jones.

Exercise Coronet, which started on 23 July and ended on the 31st detached the 406th FBW to Wiesbaden in Germany. For the purposes of this exercise, the wing was attached to the 4th ATAF and flew a variety of missions against targets in Germany. The wing did not remain at Wiesbaden, however. Dick Grace flew with the 512th FBS:

> After several days, we were told our make-believe enemy was overtaking the base, and we hastily evacuated our aircraft, loaded our equipment into some C-119s that were brought in, climbed on board and departed for a destination unknown. We ended up at a base that was just being completed, which was Sembach AB, near Kaiserslautern, Germany.
>
> We continued to operate out of Sembach until 'Coronet' was completed. As usual, at the end of these TDY trips we sent off our aircraft, then loaded and boarded the C-119s for the flight back to Manston. As I recall, the weather wasn't the best and we waited around for quite a while before the decision was made to depart. Upon our return to Manston, as it turned out, the weather had gotten worse and blanket fog covered the base. All of the C-119s were placed in a holding pattern and were brought in, one at a time by the GCA people. Because of the number of planes, this took a long time.[2]

The F-86F Sabre

In August 1953, the F-86Fs began to arrive for the 406th. By March 1954, all pilots had completed transition training and all F-84s had returned to the US. Exercise Magna Flux in March was designed to test the air defences of the UK. For the purposes of the exercise, the 512th and 513th FBS operated from Bitburg in Germany. The mission of the 406th in Magna Flux was to make fighter sweeps of sixteen aircraft over areas of England, using Manston as a post-strike staging base. Two missions were to be flown daily, but in the event, inclement weather cut the number of missions down to a total of three over the five-day period. Manston was used as a staging base for other aircraft and units during the exercise, playing host to twelve RF-80As and thirty-two F-86s. Paul Fry flew the F-86F with the 513th FBS: 'Somewhere in the late Summer or Fall of 1953, we received F-86Fs. In February 1954, we were in Bitburg, Germany with them, probably for NATO exercises. The Sabre was a breeze to maintain and keep in-commission. Its low wing design made refuelling and servicing easy'.

While Magna Flux was being played out over the fields of England, the 514th FBS was at Nouasseur in Morocco for gunnery practise. Sixteen aircraft flew down via Bordeaux where they were held up in bad weather, arriving in Morocco on 27 March. During the course of the detachment, eighteen pilots were qualified in both high- and low-altitude gunnery. Unfortunately, two major accidents marred the period. On 19 April, Lt Joseph DeBlock of 514th FIS in F-86F 51-13510 made two dry passes at an aerial target towed

In April 1954, the 406th FBW was redesignated the 406th FIW and its primary mission became air defence. The squadrons detached regularly to Nouasseur in Morocco for gunnery practice. This F-86F is being rearmed ready for its next mission in May 1954. Note that the 512th Squadron's bulldog on the badge backed by an F-86 silhouette. (*Dick Grace via Duncan Curtis*)

The arrival of the F-86F was welcomed by the squadrons of the 406th. It compared favourably to the F-84E in almost every aspect—a joy to fly and a joy to maintain. (*via Duncan Curtis*)

by an F-86. On the third pass, he developed 'target fixation' and collided with it. He was fortunate indeed in managing to land his damaged aircraft back at Nouasseur safely. On 23 April, Capt. Thomas J. Fox, Jnr, of 514th FIS flying F-86F 51-13465 apparently stalled on take-off and hit the ground, catching fire immediately. In spite of escaping from the wreckage, Capt. Fox later died as a result of damage to his lungs.

Another fatality occurred on the afternoon of 2 December 1953 when Capt. Lee Barrows of the 514th FBS, flying F-86F 51-13509, crashed on landing. His aircraft went out of control. Fellow 514th pilot Don Sidak recalls the incident:

> Captain Barrows ... crashed his F-86 [which] spun in on finals and [he] was killed. Capt. Barrows had some previous F-86 time, but it was in an earlier F-86 model that had leading-edge slats. Our F-86F models did not have the leading-edge slat on the wings and would stall without warning, and were more sensitive to stalling.[3]

406th Fighter Interceptor Wing

In April 1954, the 406th was redesignated Fighter Interceptor Wing. The effect of this was virtually to reverse the primary and secondary missions of the wing, although initially it did not significantly alter the operations the wing participated in and the roles flown in those operations. It was also planned that the 513th and 514th FIS should convert to the F-86D Sabre. These squadrons began to receive pilots with experience

F-86F-25-NA 52-5274 was assigned to the 512th FIS and was the aircraft of Lt William T. Grace. In November 1954, the 512th Fighter Day Squadron (solely redesignated thus during August) moved out of Manston for a new home at Soesterberg in the Netherlands to be committed to the air defence of that country, while still being managed by the 406th. (*Dick Grace via Duncan Curtis*)

of the 'Dog' from mid-1954 onwards. The 512th FIS was not to re-equip with the new aircraft. There were other plans for this squadron which were to have long term effects for its future.

Meanwhile, operations with the F-86F continued. In June 1954, the wing flew a variety of low-level missions against Metropolitan targets, operating at 500 feet (152 metres). The object of the exercise was to provide low-level interception practice for the 'Terriers' of Fighter Command, with the F-86s being the 'Rats'. This provided good practice at low-level navigation for the pilots, but successful intercepts were made by the RAF Meteors. Operations Order 9/54 called upon the 514th FIS to provide four aircraft to dive bomb Fairford, four aircraft to dive bomb Sculthorpe, and four aircraft to strafe Tangmere. All three of these bases had been occupied by the forces of the 'aggressor'. Order 11/54 required the 406th to support the air shows at Yeadon and Hucknall and to combine this support with raids on these airfields to attack enemy troops landed in an amphibious attack between Cleethorpes and Skegness. Order 15/54 required the 406th to provide rat aircraft to attack London, avoiding Heathrow and Windsor Castle by 5 miles. Going into July's Exercise Dividend, the annual test of home defences, many of 406th's Sabre crews were less than fully trained on the new machine. When the exercise finished, only 30 per cent of intercepts had been successful, and even less against high-flying B-47s.

Such was the nature of the weather that contingency plans were laid in the autumn of 1954 in the event of a hurricane striking RAF Manston! Part of this plan entailed being prepared to evacuate all flyable aircraft to dispersal bases and ensuring that there were always pilots to fly them; being prepared to tie all tactical aircraft down; and provide covers for all parts of the aircraft that could suffer damage from heavy rain.

In November 1954, 512th Fighter Day Squadron (solely redesignated thus during August) moved out of Manston for a new home at Soesterberg in the Netherlands to be committed to the air defence of that country, while still being managed by the 406th. First F-86Ds for the remaining Manston squadrons arrived during October, and in December 1954, the 87th FIS arrived at RAF Bentwaters. Flying F-86Ds, 87th FIS was assigned to 3rd AF, but briefly attached to 406th FIW for administrative purposes. The conversion to the Sabre Dog got under way, and during the period January to June 1955, the wing was relieved of its operational commitments due to the urgency of its conversion. As a result, the Manston Sabre squadrons did not deploy for their annual overseas weapon firing during the year. Meanwhile, the 512th FDS at Soesterberg continued its operations in the F-86F.

The F-86D Sabre Dog

The F-86D was radically different from any other interceptor that had gone before, with the possible exception of the F-89 Scorpion and, to a lesser extent, the F-94 Starfire. The 'Dog', as it was known, was not armed with guns, but with rockets—twenty-four FFAR (folding fin aircraft rockets)—and it was the first single-seat fighter to use lead collision course interception. The F-89 and the F-94 were two seaters. The collision course interception was the system whereby the pilot was vectored to the target in the traditional way. When the aircraft was near enough for its own radar to make contact, then that radar locked on. Both pilot and radar were from that moment single minded in their purpose. Bob Archibald flew the 'Dog' with the 406th:

> Our computer would give us a steering dot in a circle, centre and it as soon as possible. As the range decreased the circle would shrink. Rockets would have been selected hot when committed to a hostile target (or tow target on the range) and the trigger depressed as the circle shrunk. In the final seconds (hopefully with the dot in the centre of a very small circle, the circle would turn to a very short line so you could now only steer in pitch mode with wings level. The rockets would then fire at the proper 'F Pole' automatically at which time the scope signal would become an X (F Pole is an imaginary pole directly ahead of the nose and as long as the flight time of the rocket. When that imaginary pole touched the predicted future location of the target at the same flight time ... it would fire). Our word would then be 'Splash______!' naming the target or simply 'Splash!' The rocket dispersion pattern was designed to cover the silhouette of a TU-4 Bull from a 90 degree angle to its flight path.[4]

The advantages of the lead collision interception were that the intercept was quicker, radar contact was constant, and a successful intercept was not necessarily dependent on the interceptor being fast enough to overhaul its quarry. However, most lead collision interceptors were two seaters and so there was always someone on the lookout for enemy aircraft and any other hazards. In the case of the single-seat F-86D, the pilot would be heads down to the scope for the majority of the mission. The majority of Sabre Dogs were received by the 513th and 514th FIS during the first months of 1955. The 512th at Soesterberg continued with the F-86F and was the only unit of the 406th to participate in Exercise Carte Blanche in June 1955. The squadron flew 249 interception missions for the 2nd ATAF.

On 8 September 1955, the 512th FDS at Soesterberg was redesignated the 32nd FDS and assigned to the 36th FDW at Bitburg in West Germany. Simultaneously, the 87th FIS was redesignated the 512nd FIS and permanently assigned its F-86Ds to 406th FIW. The loss of the Dutch-based unit was a boon for the 406th. It removed the distraction and frustration of managing a squadron in another country, with different aircraft operationally controlled by a different agency.

With the conversion to the F-86D completed, the 406th came under the operational control of RAF Fighter Command. The 512th operated under the control of eastern sector, 12 Group, and the 513th and 514th under the control of metropolitan sector, 1 Group. The first major exercise to include the F-86s was Beware from 23 September to 2 October 1955, and it proved problematic for the wing. The object of the exercise was to test the air defences of the UK and the 406th was tasked with the role of intercepting, within its area of operations, all incursions into UK airspace made by the aggressors be they from the RAF or USAF.

Unfortunately, the RAF would not allow the F-86D to use its lead collision intercepts against its aircraft in the exercise. This resulted in a distinct lack of co-operation which had to be passed to higher authorities to resolve. Both USAFE and the RAF had to draw up a rules of engagement that would be mutually satisfactory, and develop a clear tactical doctrine for the F-86D. Fortunately, the issue was resolved and the aircraft was allowed to perform its mission as designed. At a press conference held at RAF Fighter

F-86D 52-10086 of the 87th FIS. This unit was based at RAF Bentwaters where it arrived in December 1954 from Sioux City, Iowa. The 87th was initially assigned to the 3rd Air Force, but attached to the 406th FIW for administration purposes. (*George Pennick*)

F-86D 51-6187 of the 87th FIS at a Bentwaters' open house in 1955. In September 1955, the 512th FIS of the 406th FIW, based at Soesterberg in the Netherlands, was redesignated the 32nd Fighter Defence Squadron, and the 87th became the 512th FIS and was permanently assigned to the 406th FIW. (*Author's collection*)

Under a glowering East Anglian sky, this all-weather fighter is in its element. (*George Pennick*)

Command HQ soon after Beware finished, the air officer commanding-in-chief, AM Sir Dermot Boyle, declared the exercise an 'undoubted success. What we stood up to is tougher than anything they could do to us now, either in quantity or quality.'

Rocket firing deployments to Wheelus AB in Libya began during April 1956, one squadron at a time, and became an annual event.

The year 1956 saw several significant events implications for the 406th FIW. The visit of the Bolshoi Ballet to the UK on 1 October 1956 should have been an occasion for cultural celebration, but, coming as it did at a time of crisis, a considerable amount of consternation and confusion was evident in military circles on the day of arrival, not least at RAF Manston. Milt Torres was doing his shopping at the base commissary when he heard the announcement that the base was being placed on red alert and he should report to his squadron at once:

> I left the cart and ran to my car and immediately went back to my squadron and checked in to operations. In turn they gave me a tail number and told to pick up my gear and check in on Sq common as soon as I was ready to fly. I was in the aircraft within a couple of minutes and did a walk around with my crew chief at a running pace. Not more than 10 minutes had passed and with the APU on I checked in on the radio. I was facing the runway in the aircraft when I looked up and saw a TU-104 with Soviet markings landing directly in front of me. When I talked to ops they advised me to shut down and recover to ops. I was particularly miffed as I was eager to get into the fight when I looked up and saw yet another TU 104 and the comment I made to ops was why are we quitting without firing a single shot. I thought the Russians had a lot of cheek to invade by landing planes on our

> field. At any rate how they caught us off guard was the 92nd FBS had their F-84F's flying around with the shape hanging on the wings of the aircraft. The shape (atomic bomb) was classified top secret and the base went crazy running around covering the shape with tarps as they taxied in.[5]

The end of October saw events unfold in Hungary which were to have considerable implications for NATO and its air forces. All air force units were put on varying stages of alert, not least the interceptors of the 406th. Milt Torres noted:

> We were put on full alert and they scheduled us for duty 18 hours on and six hours off. All the in commission F-86D's were on alert and we were scheduled by time increments: 5 minute alert were on the ramps with APU's running and pilots in the cockpit ready for scramble; 30 minute alert (less stringent) pilots gear in aircraft cleared by pre-flights and the pilot would stay in the flight shacks. The remainder were on one hour alert, assigned to pilots physically present in the squadron ready room. All the aircraft were loaded with hot rockets and ready to go. Flight meals were provided for all of us in case we got hungry. The 5 minute alert would keep pilots in the cockpit for two hours and they would be relieved by the pilots in the 30 minute alert and we would be released to go to squadron ops. The guys in squadron ops would take the aircraft being released from the 5 minute alert and go on 30 minute alert and so forth. A quarter of the pilots would take off for the six hour release of duty and go home to eat or sleep or whatever to be back in 6 hours. At the end of two weeks we were all dead tired. We had a couple of practice scrambles during the two weeks but nothing to speak of as far as incidents. We really had no idea what was going on at headquarters but we were given timely notices of the political situation.[6]

Over time, the 406th became, debatably, one of the most efficient interceptor units in the entire USAF. In October 1956, they represented USAFE at the Worldwide Rocketry Meet at Yuma, and 1957 was the year in which the 512th FIS was declared the best fighter interceptor squadron in the air force, winning the Hughes Achievement Award. This prestigious award was presented in Washington and seven members of the squadron went there to receive it in August of that year.

Also in 1957, USAFE Weapons Centre devised a new interceptor training programme over the ranges of Wheelus. The unit chosen to be the guinea pigs for this programme were the 514th FIS. For the first time, B-57E aircraft were used to tow the targets and intercepts were practised at high altitude, 31,400 feet; medium altitude, 20,000 to 29,000 feet; and low altitude, below 10,000 feet. The 514th expended 4,943 Mighty Mouse rockets during 94.5 hours of range time. The targets towed by the B-57s were more difficult to hit than those towed by the old B-29s. The only thing to mar what was a very successful detachment for the 514th FIS was the malfunction that occurred in the wing cameras of some of the F-86Ds.

It was in the spring of 1957 that Milt Torres and Dave Robertson, both of the 514th FIS experienced an intercept that can best be described as unusual. They were standing alert at Manston on the night of 20 May, a dismal and overcast night. They were ordered to scramble and vectored by metropolitan sector to a point over the North Sea where a GCI site directed them to an initial point at 32,000 feet. Afterburners were selected and

F-86D 52-10035 of the 512th FIS. This aircraft was displayed at RAF Burtonwood's open day on 17 May 1958. (*Robert Robinson collection*)

This beautiful photo shows off a 512th 'Dog' resplendent in its unit colours and natural metal finish. F-86D-45-NA 52-4151 served with all three squadrons of the 406th FIW. It is seen here in the colours of the 512th FIS. (*USAF via Robert Robinson*)

The squadrons of the 406th regularly detached to the ranges at Wheelus in Libya. F-86D-50-NA 52-10045 has just returned from a mission. (*via George Pennick*)

the F-86Ds proceeded at maximum speed to intercept the 'bogey', an unidentified flying object. It was impossible for either of the pilots to make any visual contact whatsoever, so bad was the visibility. Torres, however, recalls the order, which was authenticated, to fire a salvo of rockets at the target. Radar contact was made:

> The final turn was given, and the instructions were given to look 30 degrees to port for my bogey. I did not have a hard time at all. There it was exactly where I was told it would be, at 30 degrees and at 15 miles (24km). The blip was burning a hole in the radar with its incredible intensity. It was similar to a blip I had received from B-52s, and seemed to be a magnet of light. These things I remember clearly. I ran the range gate marker over the blip, and the jizzle band faded as the marker superimposed over the blip. I had a lock on that had the proportions of a flying aircraft carrier. By that, I mean the return on the radar was so strong that it could not be overlooked by the fire control system on the F-86D. I called to the GCI. 'Judy', which signified that I would take all further steering information from my radar computer [rather than the GCI site]
>
> I had an overtake of 800 knots and my radar was rock stable. The dot was centred and only the slightest corrections were necessary. This was a very fast intercept, and the circle started to shrink. I called '20 seconds', and the GCI indicated he was standing by. The overtake was still indicating in the 7 or 8 o'clock position. At about 10 seconds to go, I noticed that the overtake position was changing its position. It moved rapidly to the 6 o'clock, then 3 o'clock, then 12 o'clock and finally rested about the 11 o'clock position.

> This indicated a negative overtake of 200 knots (the maximum negative overtake displayed). There was no way of knowing of what the actual speed of the UFO was, as he [could have been] travelling at very high Mach numbers, and I would only see the 200 knot negative overtake. The circle, which was down to about an inch-and-a-half in diameter, started to open up rapidly. Within seconds, it was back to 3 inches in diameter, and the blip was visible in the blackened jizzle band moving up the scope. This meant that it was going away from me. I reported this to the GCI site, and they replied by asking, 'Do you have a Tally Ho?' I reported that I was still in the soup and could see nothing. By this time the UFO had broken lock and I saw him leaving my 30 mile range. Again, I reported that he was gone, only to be told that he was now off their scope as well. With the loss of the blip off their scope, the mission was over. We were vectored back to home plate (Manston) and secured our switches.[7]

In common with most USAF units through the 1950s and '60s, the 406th has its fair share of UFO stories, and it would not be appropriate to comment further on this one. Suffice to say that pilots like Milt Torres were successful in their jobs because of their sound judgement and professionalism.

In early 1958, the decision was made to deactivate the 406th FIW. There were a number of factors which led to this. Primarily, the RAF was introducing its own all-weather interceptors into service, and there was subsequently no need for the USAF to retain a unit dedicated to the air defence of the UK. The Gloster Javelin in particular undertook the 'immediate readiness' role, previously the responsibility of the 406th FIW and before them, the 81st FIW.

The three squadrons of the wing, however, were not to be deactivated. Between March and May, all three joined the 86th Fighter Wing on Mainland Europe. The 512th went to Sembach, the 513th to Phalsbourg, and the 514th to Ramstein Landstuhl. Prior to the departure of the squadrons from Manston, a community event was held on 29 March to thank local people for their support over the years. The event culminated in a flyby of sixteen aircraft.

Aircraft 52-4203 is here being prepared for a rocket-firing practice mission at Wheelus. The armament crew are loading the 2.75-inch (70-mm) Mighty Mouse FFARs for the sortie. (*via George Pennick*)

In this publicity photo, three F-86Ds of the 513th FIS fly in formation over an unknown town. (*USAF*)

3

The 47th Bombardment Wing

The 47th Bombardment Wing was activated at Biggs Field, Texas, in August 1947, with the prospect of receiving the USAF's new jet bomber, the North American B-45 Tornado. The wing relocated to Bergstrom AFB in November 1948 and began to receive their B-45s. Three squadrons were attached to the unit: the 84th, 85th, and 86th Bombardment Squadrons. In October 1949, the USAF decided to deactivate the 47th. The two Tornado-equipped squadrons, the 84th and 85th BS, moved to Langley AFB with their new aircraft and were assigned to the 363rd Tactical Reconnaissance Wing. In March 1951, the 47th was reactivated at Langley, the 84th and 85th BS reassigned, and the unit attached to Tactical Air Command.

In mid-1951, the decision was taken to modify all existing B-45As to carry and deliver the atomic bomb. This programme of modifications was called Project Back Breaker. Modifications included installation of the AN/APQ-24 radar, structural changes to the bomb bay to accommodate three types of special weapons, and installation of new aircraft defence systems, including chaff dispensers and additional fuel storage to increase range.

The 47th BW was to be TACs first tactical nuclear strike unit. During the period from March 1951, it intensively practised the nuclear delivery role. When the 49th Air Division was reactivated in 1951, the 47th BW was assigned to it together with the 20th Fighter Bomber Wing. In 1952, both units detached to the UK.

The North American B-45 Tornado

In December 1951, the 47th BW was alerted that it would be detaching overseas to RAF Sculthorpe in the UK. The mission of the 47th as part of the 49th Air Division was nuclear deterrence. Their mission, in support of NATO, was to carry 'special weapons' to the enemy's airfields, communications, and other military installations in the event of war breaking out. It was considered unlikely that NATO could resist a Soviet advance across Europe by conventional means. The Tornados of the 47th would 'break the back' of any Soviet incursion with their atomic bombs. At that time they

North American B-45As on the ramp at Langley AFB, Virginia, USA. On its activation in 1951, two squadrons were assigned: the 84th BS and the 85th BS. (*Tom Cress via Dave Menard*)

were, together with the 20th Fighter Bomber Wing, the only units in NATO with this capability. The principal special weapon carried by the Tornados was the Mk 5 atomic bomb.

The 47th had its problems in the early days at Sculthorpe. Accommodation was very substandard and the USAF was unable to do any renovation or development of the facilities without the permission of the British government department responsible, and then the work was to go to locally based contractors. Eventually these problems were ironed out and were alleviated because they were a unit with a very unique mission. Col. 'Davy' Jones was the CO, and he noted: 'We had high priority which was one of the reasons we were in pretty good shape because of our mission had been given a high priority, equivalent of SAC priority'

Training for the squadrons of the 47th were designed to reinforce the skills needed in the execution of their primary mission. This involved exercises in the UK and in Europe as a whole. Bomb practice was carried out over the Wash with inert concrete shapes simulating the Mk 5 'special weapon' which was carried by the aircraft. These White Elephant missions were performed over the sea for the simple reason that there was a desire to keep the nuclear mission of the 47th as secret as possible, for as long as possible, from the local populace.

In spite of its having had a troublesome gestation, the B-45A was accident free during the first months of its time at Sculthorpe. However, on 14 December 1952, aircraft 47-070 was taking off from Munich and had climbed to approximately 18,000 feet when both wings came off simultaneously. Only the tail gunner, Sgt Dave Hamilton, and the pilot, Maj. Grovert, survived the crash. Both the co-pilot and a passenger were

The bombardier/navigator's position did not have an ejector seat. In the event of an emergency, he was to exit through the side hatch. (*Robert Ashby*)

Aircraft 47-083, photographed at an open house in 1957, crashed on 20 September 1957 while on a routine training flight near West Raynham. The crew of three were killed. (*APN*)

A fine study of two B-45As belonging to the 85th BS. (*Courtesy of the Schrecengost Archives—Col. Ray W. Schrecengost, Jnr, USAF*)

The gunner entered the aircraft through a hatch under the rear fuselage and would make his way through the cramped fuselage to his position. Having no ejector seat, he was expected to exit in the same way. The defensive armament of the B-45 consisted of two 12.7-mm M.3 machine guns. (*Robert Ashby*)

killed. The subsequent investigation concluded the crash had been caused by stress in the main wing spars caused by fatigue. In addition, there was a suggestion that wash and eddies from the fuel tanks that the aircraft was carrying at the time under its engine nacelles exacerbated the stress to the already fatigued spars. All the B-45s were grounded for some months while checks took place and metal plates were fitted to the wings to strengthen them.

This grounding had a profound effect on the mission effectiveness of the 47th BW in carrying out its primary mission. However, if hostilities had broken out then, undoubtedly, the Tornados would have carried their lethal loads to their targets as planned. Since before leaving the US, the crews of the 47th BW had had their target folders.

Exercises over Europe involved the B-45s flying to targets and simulating their wartime mission though on the right side of the Soviet ADIZ Some missions also entailed the B-45s flying along the borders of Warsaw Pact countries, which often attracted unwanted attention. Col. Sandy Sanderson was with the 84th BS and noted: 'We used to fly right up to the border and then turn parallel; and, just opposite us, on the other side was a Mig, and we became quite friendly'. On one occasion, a pilot strayed over the buffer zone and so USAFE issued new orders instructing aircraft to fly no closer to the zone than 50 miles (81 km). The purpose of these flights and the presence of the B-45s throughout Europe was a constant reminder to the Soviets that the B-45s were there and they had a particular nuclear mission.

The 86th BS joined the 47th in March 1954 and was initially based at RAF Alconbury. Routine missions and alerts at Sculthorpe were not always so fraught, but the much-despised British weather did play a significant part in operations. Bill McDonald was a navigator/bomber in the B-45 with the 86th BS:

> I do recall one instance when the weather played a major role in one of our ground operations. Aircrews were required to oversee (and assist) the loading of the Mark 5 A-bomb in the B-45. The overall loading sequence took approximately three hours because the bomb and its cradle was extremely large in girth and could not be positioned under the bomb bay without completely removing one of the clam-shell bomb doors from its hinge and hydraulics, a procedure that took considerable time and effort. Then the bomb would be rolled in from the side and hoisted up to the shackles. The bomb door would then be reinstalled and tested. Downloading the ordinance required the reverse procedure and equal time. Because of the frequent squalls and occasional gale force winds that could occur almost without warning, the aircraft on the ramp were normally tied down with chains from the landing gear to eye hooks on the tarmac. Following a particularly virulent gale-like storm, it was discovered that either the ground crew had not secured the nose gear properly or the chain/hook had failed and the B-45 was left sitting back on its tail skid with the nose pointing skyward. Maintenance personnel discovered that they could walk upright under the entire front portion of the fuselage when the airplane was in that position. It was a light-bulb moment as someone obviously noted how simple it might be to open the bomb-bay doors and roll the Mark 5 in from the front with the plane in that position (tipped up) and avoid the extensive time it took to remove and replace a door during loading. A

> quick experiment revealed that with a strap slung over the tail section, just forward of the vertical stabilizer and the downward weight of four or five men (perhaps crew members felt more useful now) was all that was needed to raise the nose and lower the tail onto its skid. A simple locally devised nose gear prop provided the safety and the rest was history loading the nuke became just over a one-hour operation due to the English weather.[1]

Because of its unique and singularly important mission, the 47th BW was subject to regular scheduled and unscheduled inspections. The purpose of these was to test the readiness of the wing to respond to an alert order, get airborne, and *en route* to the targets. Don Felts was with the 85th BS and recalls one such alert inspection which was unexpected:

> One Friday when the 'wing weenies' as we called them, from London were visiting, the 85th Bomb Squadron hosted a party in their honour at the O Club (Officers Club). Along about 10:30 or so when the party was rolling along and the 'adult beverages' were flowing rather freely, the alert bell rang.
>
> We couldn't believe they would do that, since they knew what we had been doing, but decided we'd better look like we heard it, so after making arrangements for car pools to get the wives home, we headed for the flight line. After one opportunity for the alert to be cancelled, we changed into flight suits and when targets were called in went out to preflight the planes. When we called for taxi instructions, another opportunity to call the alert off was missed because we were given taxi instructions. By this time, the officers on the crew had been up for about 20 hours, so we couldn't believe they would let us fly. In addition to no sleep, the drinks we had had further convinced us that when we called number one for take-off, we would be told to return to the hard-stand.
>
> I called number one and the tower said 'Cleared for take-off.' There was nothing to do but to 'pour the coal on' and take-off. The targets being mostly in Germany, we headed into the rising sun, headaches and all. I don't know what the gunner thought, because he knew what shape the three up front were in. If I had been in his spot, I would have been praying very hard, I know that.
>
> Somehow we made it around the course, and arrived back at Sculthorpe where the weather, fortunately, was not up to usual English standards, in other words was pretty good. After landing were got through debriefing and were told to go get some sleep and report back to Operations later.
>
> When we got back, we assembled in the briefing room, with the Londoners in the front row. Our Ops Officer who was the living breathing personification of a Prussian Officer, and I mean that as a compliment, got up and said to our visitors, 'See, I told you my boys could do the job even if they were drunk on their a****!'[2]

Regular exercises were flown in conjunction with the RAF and other NATO air forces. One such in 1955 was Carte Blanche. The role of the 47th BW and its Tornados in this exercise was to disperse to alternative airfields and launch attacks on the facilities of the 'enemy'. Other exercises such as Dividend and Beware were designed to test the air defences of the UK. In these exercises, aircraft of the 47th dispersed to the continent and simulated bombing attacks on the UK. On one such occasion things did not go quite according to plan. Davy Jones was to lead the whole squadron with a mission to attack the UK:

> We were flying from Frankfurt, all 18 of us. We were going to attack England. The weather was not very good. In fact it was miserable. We got airborne. We were all strung out. I was the last one off and we found we were one hour ahead of our time. Here we are, airborne at 35,000 feet, going north roughly; so I said 'Okay everyone make 90 degree turn to the right and in 30 minutes make a 180 and come back.

Unfortunately the right turn headed all eighteen aircraft towards the East German border: 'I'm sure some controller in East Germany whose hair must have stood on end! They must have known something was going to happen, then we all turned round and left. We got home. We all made it'.[3]

There was undoubtedly great consternation in the Soviet camp, as well there should have been.

However, the role of the B-45s in these UK air defence exercises was invaluable to the RAF. In the early years, the opposition to the B-45s were the Meteors, Vampires, and Venoms in their different guises of day- and night-fighter variants. The B-45s provided these fighters with a formidable target, very similar to the Ilyushin Il-28, which the Soviets would undoubtedly send in the first wave of attacks against the country. The B-45s were difficult to catch. Later on after the Hunters and Javelins came into service, it was a different story. Their superior performance placed the, by then, venerable B-45s at a disadvantage. It was a sobering fact acknowledged by the crews of the B-45s that, in the event of war breaking out, they would probably not be returning from their bombing missions. Theirs was to be a one way trip.

Bill MacDonald noted:

> We were quite aware that the reality was a one-way mission into East Germany or beyond with scant chance to make it back to base. In-flight refuelling over the English Channel was part of the return plan but the Gods were not with the odds that a KB-29 (later KB-50) would be actually on station like we sometimes practised in training missions.[4]

The year 1956 proved to be a stressful year for the crews of the 47th BW B-45s. Two main events were to dominate the international headlines and the mission of the wing. During the Hungarian uprising, Frank Riggs was the CO of the 84th Bombardment Squadron:

> We loaded up the aeroplanes. We brought out the nuclear core, and we kept the crews around the aeroplane for several days. We were ready to go. We had the target folders and the flight crews had done their flight planning. But this happened in the middle of an inspection. We excluded the inspection team from the briefing. They were a little upset about this. 'We just want to see how you operate'. I said, 'Look, I got instructions that nobody sees these target folders, except the flight crews and that's it. You're not getting in!'[5]

Two B-45A Tornados 49-065 and 49-067 belong to the 85th BS. (*Robert Robinson collection*)

B-45A 47-057 belongs to the 86th BS. (*Robert Robinson collection*)

Although the US was not directly involved in the events in Egypt at the time of the Suez Crisis, there was uncertainty about how the Soviet Union would react to the unfolding events, and the US Armed Forces responded accordingly. The B-45s of the 47th BW were again put on alert. Bill Slattery was a pilot with the 86th BS which at the time had moved temporarily from Alconbury to Molesworth. His story underlined a significant problem with a long standing alert posture:

> We were at Molesworth at the time of Suez and we went on alert and, of course, loaded nuclear weapons on the aircraft. We had a problem almost immediately because no one expected that we would load weapons and sit them on the ground for days waiting for take off. As a result the silicone gel inside the weapon was beginning to soak up water and we had to start replenishing them twice a day; and in rapid order we ran out of it, and they had to fly in more of the material from the States to keep us going.[6]

Almost exactly a year later, the squadrons of the 47th BW began conversion to the B-66. The Tornados were scrapped, flying out to bases all over Europe to exercise fire crews and Battle Damage Repair units.

Fortunately, the Tornados of the 47th BW never had to go to war. It is perhaps a measure of their effectiveness that this was so. Even their routine operations over the continent of Europe served notice on the Soviet Union and its allies that, should they attempt any aggressive moves against Western Europe, the reaction would be swift and devastating. The contribution of these aircraft and the crews that flew

RB-45C 48-014 in the colours of the 84th BS. When the 19th TRS began to re-equip with the B-66, some of the RB-45s were sent to other squadrons of the 47th BW for a short period. (*Dave Menard collection*)

On Friday 13 June 1958, Vernon Morgan, an airman second class, climbed into the cockpit of B-45A 47-046 and took off. Approximately three minutes later, the Tornado came down straddling the London to Edinburgh railway line. (*Richard Liley*)

Wreckage from 47-046 was scattered over a wide area. Morgan's bizarre and fatal behaviour has been attributed to an extra-marital affair gone wrong. Paradoxically, his was the last crash of a B-45. (*Richard Lilley*)

The fate of all 47th BW Tornadoes was to be distributed to USAFE bases in Europe and North Africa for fire practice. Aircraft 47-056 rests on the Alconbury dump where it remained until it was sold for scrap in the mid-1960s. (*Author's collection*)

them to the maintenance of the, sometimes fragile, peace in Europe cannot be over-emphasised.

The Douglas B-66 Destroyer

The origin of the B-66 goes back to the development of the A-3 Skywarrior for the US Navy. The USAF decided to use the design of the A-3 to develop a light bomber to replace the Douglas A-26 Invader and the North American B-45 Tornado. In reality, the B-66 turned out to be a very different aircraft to the Skywarrior. The first of seventy-two B-66Bs produced flew on 4 January 1955 and the first aircraft entered service with TAC in 1956, equipping the 17th Bombardment Wing at Hulbert Field AFB in Florida.

The 17th BW was deactivated in 1958 and its B-66Bs were transferred to the 47th BW at RAF Sculthorpe. The first sixteen aircraft were delivered to the 84th BS at Sculthorpe in January 1958. In May, the 86th BS which was based at RAF Alconbury at the time received its B-66s, and the 85th completed the conversion of the wing in July. Pilot conversion and training for the B-66B took place at Shaw AFB in South Carolina. Shaw was the principle Tactical Reconnaissance base in TAC and was responsible for training crews for the RB-66 recce variant of the aircraft. B-66 bomber crews had to follow the same syllabus as the recce crews. Don Harding followed the course before travelling to Sculthorpe in April 1959:

> Early in 1959 there was a fairly large influx of new crew members into the three bomb squadrons, 84th, 85th and 86th that made up the 47th Bomb Wing under the command of Colonel K.C. Dempster at RAF Sculthorpe, England. I went to the basic school for the B-66

B-66B-DL 53-483 was assigned to the 86th BS in May 1958, which was based at RAF Alconbury at that time, moving to Sculthorpe in 1959. The B-66 was a considerable improvement on the B-45 Tornadoes and carried the variable yield Mk 28 nuclear bomb. (*Robert Robinson collection*)

> at Shaw AFB, S.C. It was actually a Photo Recce course. We flew the RB-66B and learned how to take pictures with quite an array of cameras. We grumbled a lot about having to learn the Photo Recce business since we were going to the bomber. However; it all came back to me when I was assigned to a Photo Recce outfit at Chambley AB, France in 1965![7]

For those who had flown the B-45, the Destroyer was definitely a step up. Bill MacDonald was a navigator/bombardier at Sculthorpe from 1957 to 1961 and recalls:

> The B-66 Destroyer was pretty cool and was fairly new to the USAF inventory so it represented a step up from the B-45. The K-5 bomb system was far superior to the antiquated and cantankerous one in the B-45. I do no longer recall the exact name of the B-45 system but it was not at all easy to manipulate and required considerable manual dexterity to deal with all the necessary knobs and wheels and mechanical readouts. I also recall that it was not very reliable a la maintenance and apparently very time-consuming to repair. From the nav/bomb (my) position in the nose of the Tornado, the change to B-66 was a considerable upgrade in potential survivability in the event of a bailout. The B-66 upward-powered ejection seat was a huge improvement over the egress procedure for a B-45 nav/bomb. In the B-45, the nav's 'emergency' lever merely blew out the side door and swivelled the seat 90 degrees left. Then the poor soul had to unbuckle and do a forward somersault out of the opening in the fuselage while praying that the gear wasn't extended or he didn't get sucked through the jet engine in the process. As I recall, the pilot and co-pilot were supposed to wait patiently to make sure the nav/bomb was out before blowing their canopy, a circumstance that would have created a serious wind tunnel experience for the

> exiting nav/bomb. The only advantage I note for the B-45 was that it did not require special equipment to start the engines like the B-66 did. The Tornado had starter generators and only required an electrical unit which was common to most bases. It could land and take-off anywhere. As such, the range of fields visited through Europe and Africa was greater and more fun. As far as the B-66 shortcomings, the puny engines would have to stand out, the aircraft was definitely underpowered.[8]

With the arrival of the B-66B, the mission of the 47th BW remained the same, that of a rapid first response to an attack on NATO by the Soviet Union and its allies in the east. With the B-66, the 47th maintained a Victor Alert. Bill MacDonald noted:

> After the transition to B-66, we pulled that duty; two crews and two loaded aircraft from each of the three squadrons, for seven day periods, staying the entire week in a secured compound near the aircraft and subjected to periodic practice 'scrambles', most often in the dead of night. We would exercise our launch routine right up to engine start. The living quarters were quite primitive as I recall and it was sometimes easiest to simply live in a flight suit day and night. It was a good time for card games, reading or catching up on correspondence courses. Other than that, and our awareness that our assigned aircraft had nukes aboard, it was a very boring week.[9]

The 47th BW Destroyers were regular attenders at the annual open house events at USAF bases in the UK. B-66B-DL 53-484 served with the 85th BS and is seen here at RAF Alconbury's open house in 1959. (*Robert Robinson collection*)

Don Harding takes up the story:

> Victor Alert was a big part of our lives. The 47th Bomb Wing was one of the foremost deterrents of the 'cold war' with just over 50 bombers available.
>
> When we signed in through the gate, names were verified and the crews on duty notified. We all met at the aircraft as we had to personally meet the point guard before he would let you inside a 50 foot circle around the bird. This done we went to our quarters about a 100 yds from the A/C to stow our gear, etc. We then opened our target folders to review any changes that might have taken place since our last visit. We, pilot, navigator/bombardier and gunner, went back to the aircraft and went through preflight procedures, which in this case all switches were set for an immediate scramble. We then went through a special check list to make sure the two nuclear weapons were functional and were set for the nuclear yield for your targets. The MK-28 weapon was the most powerful in the inventory at the time and had 4 different yields from 4KT to 1.1 Megaton. They were called Y settings and were set through a small door in the tail of the bomb. Both my targets called for Y-1 settings.
>
> The wing command post up base just loved to set off the VA alert bell all hours of the day or night, mostly about 3am; and scare the wits out of us. We ran to the A/C, started the APU and called the command post on the radio to check in. It was then that you received a coded message which you asked for authentication from a secret table in your target folder. Thank heaven it always turned out to be just a drill![10]

Bomb commanders, as the pilots were known, had a responsibility to keep up to date with their target folders. Targets for the 47th BW were mostly in Northeastern Europe and included the Baltic States, East Germany, and Poland. Two of Don Harding's targets were in this area:

> Both the targets I was responsible for required the MK-28 and a Y-1 setting. The weapon on my primary target, however, was set for a 3000ft. airburst and my secondary target was a Y-1 ground burst. Number one target was the Russian Naval HQs, Baltic. It was located in a big building in the city of Riga, Latvia. My bombing altitude in those days was 38,500 ft. At 480 mph and, believe it or not there was no safe 'fly-over' or you would have been blown out of the sky! I planned a hard right-hand break of about 135 degrees, diving at full throttle, even then the book said you might get your 'tail feathers singed'. The 'Trail Time' for the bomb was 45 seconds so if you dove immediately upon release chances are you would be OK. This manoeuvre was also performed on instruments as there was a 'Blast Curtain' you zipped up prior to release of the weapon. I practised this manoeuvre often and was no problem. Also, the aircraft could exceed the speed of sound which it was built to do, but the best I could get out of it was Mach .98. I had an aerial photo of the Russian HQ building taken by a U-2 in my target folder. It was a big perfectly round building. My next target, if I survived the first, was Katowice Airbase, Poland; a Russian fighter base at the time. I had doubts about reaching this target. The saving grace here was if the bell went off there would be so many aircraft in the air and bombs going off, you may be lucky enough to get through. Fighters were our biggest worry, there were only a few missile sites around

Displayed beside the B-45A it was replacing, this Douglas B-66B is at RAF Alconbury for their open house on 17 May 1958. (*Author's collection*)

> in those days so they were easily avoided. Another big worry was we didn't know where the other outfits target were located or their time of release. Big screw-up in the planning![11]

Once a month, the crews of the B-66Bs were stringently tested. When the test was initiated each of the three squadrons had an hour to identify ten crews who would have to fly an exercise the following day. The ten crews would go the 47th briefing room where they would have to sit a written test comprising twenty questions. These questions were related to the target, route, the bomb being carried, and its management. On the following day, the crews would man their ten B-66s and take off at ten-minute intervals. Only two spares were permitted to fill any aborted take-offs. The ten aircraft would the fly to the Jurby gunnery range on the Isle of Man. There they would have to drop a 200-lb inert concrete bomb at a 60 by 90-foot metal-covered raft anchored just off shore. From Jurby, they would proceed to three radar bomb scoring sites located in Scotland and England before locating and a tanker and refuelling in complete radio silence. Finally, in order to check the guns and allow the gunner some relaxation, they would fly low level over the sea and fire their load of fifty rounds into the water.

The B-66B did not serve long with the 47th BW as that unit was deactivated on 22 June 1961, when Sculthorpe became a standby base administered by the 7375 Support Group.

The Reconnaissance RB-45C

In addition to the B-45A bombers, Sculthorpe also played host to the RB-45Cs of the 19th Tactical Reconnaissance Squadron.

The RB-45Cs of the 19th TRS arrived at Sculthorpe from May 1954. The assigned mission of the 19th TRS RB-45Cs was to support the operations of the units of the 49th AD with visual and photographic reconnaissance, primarily by night. (*Courtesy of the Schrecengost Archives—Col. Ray W. Schrecengost, Jnr, USAF*)

RB-45C 48-036 was one of the aircraft used to train the RAF crews at RAF Sculthorpe in 1952. The aircraft returned to Sculthorpe wearing the colours of the 19th TRS in 1954. (*Author's collection*)

The RB-45Cs of the 19th TRS had originally been assigned to 91st Strategic Reconnaissance Wing at Barksdale. When SAC began to receive the RB-47 Stratojet, the Tornados were turned over to TAC and the 19th TRS.

The 19th TRS arrived at Sculthorpe in May 1954. The reconnaissance aircraft were not an unfamiliar sight at the Norfolk base; having deployed there in 1952 when three of the aircraft had undertaken clandestine flights over the Soviet Union on 17 April of that year. Just prior to the arrival of the 19th TRS, three RB-45Cs had also deployed to Sculthorpe and had undertaken a further RAF mission over the Soviet Union.

One of the outcomes of that particular mission was the realisation that the RB-45C was no longer a suitable aircraft to conduct overflights. Because of its relatively low operating ceiling, it had become too vulnerable to flak, and its relatively low speed made it prey to interceptors. Although the RAF Special Duty Flight flew no more overflights, the 19th TRS did.

On 29 March 1955, Maj. John B. Anderson, the 19th TRS squadron commander, took off from RAF Sculthorpe with three RB-45s. Their mission was to obtain radar scope photographs of targets in Hungary, Yugoslavia, and East Germany. They were not to overfly the Soviet Union. The photographs thus obtained would, as they had in previous such flights, provide valuable information to include in the target folders of the crews flying offensive atomic bomb missions against those targets in the event of war.

The three RB-45s were piloted by Anderson, Capt. Bert Grigsby, and Capt. Robert A. Schambers. Maj. Anderson flew into Hungary and photographed targets in and around Budapest. Capt. Schambers flew over East Berlin and Capt. Grigsby's overflight took him to Yugoslavia. Attempts were made to intercept the RB-45s of Anderson and Schambers, but Grigsby's mission passed off without incident. Because his evasive tactics against MiGs necessitated him climbing, Anderson's RB-45 had to land at Fürstenfeldbruck in Germany to refuel after the mission. Grigsby and Schambers made it home to Sculthorpe. For their participation in this mission, all aircrew members received the DFC.

The main mission of the 19th TRS RB-45s was to support the 49th AD with visual and photographic reconnaissance of targets and BDA.

Routine missions included involvement in a number of NATO exercises. During Carte Blanche, the 49th AD was responsible for launching simulated atomic strikes against the forces of the 2nd ATAF. Prior to the onset of hostilities the 19th TRS was responsible for obtaining target and radar scope photographs for use by the bomber crews. Subsequent to a simulated strike, it would undertake post-strike recce and BDA. Operation Brown Cow in August 1955 was another full-scale NATO exercise in which the 19th TRS excelled.

On 1 January 1957, the 19th TRS was assigned to the 66th TRW at Sembach Germany but remained at RAF Sculthorpe instead of moving to Sembach. Commensurate with this reassignment, the squadron began conversion to the Douglas RB-66 Destroyer. On 1 February, three RB-66Bs arrived. By 31 March 1957, twelve of the new aircraft had been received and the squadron had transferred five of its Tornados to the 84th BS. In December 1957, General Order 88 form USAFE HQ assigned the 19th TRS to the 10th TRW. The 10th TRW was based at Spangdahlem in Germany, but the 19th remained at Sculthorpe for the time being.

4

The 20th FBW, TFW

The 20th Fighter Wing was originally activated at Shaw AFB on 28 July 1947. Three squadrons were attached: the 55th, 77th, and 79th Fighter Squadrons flying the North American P-51 Mustang. The 20th Fighter Wing equipped for the jet age in February 1948 when it converted to the Republic P(F)-84B Thunderjet. On 20 January 1950, the wing was redesignated the 20th Fighter Bomber Wing. At this time the unit began to replace its F-84Bs with the F-84D Thunderjet.

Commensurate with the start of the Korean War and the build-up of US forces in Europe, the 20th was ordered to the UK on temporary duty in July 1950 and flew the northern route via Dow AFB; Goose bay, Labrador; Bluie West One, Greenland; Keflavik, Iceland; and Kinloss, Scotland, eventually reaching their temporary home at RAF Manston. This trip was historically significant as it marked the first mass deployment of fighters from the USA to Europe. The F-84Ds had flown the route with 'hot guns', fearing possible interference with the flight by the Soviets. The crossing was made with only one mishap, albeit, sadly, a fatal one. One of the F-84Ds, 48-0726, experienced a flame out. The pilot exited the aircraft but, unfortunately, died of exposure in the cold waters of the North Atlantic before he could be rescued.

The deployment to Manston lasted for five months. During that time, the aircraft were involved in numerous exercises. Regrettably, they also lost five Thunderjets. The wing returned to their home at Shaw in December 1950.

In 1952, the 20th returned to the UK with a different aircraft and a very different role.

20th Fighter Bomber Wing

The Republic F-84G Thunderjet

In mid-1952, when the 49th AD deployed to the UK, the 20th FBW, deployed to RAF Wethersfield and RAF Bentwaters. The 55th and 77th FBS' deployed to Wethersfield and the 79th FBS to Bentwaters because facilities and space at Wethersfield were inadequate.

The first Cold War detachment of the 20th Fighter Bomber Wing to the UK took place between July and December 1950. At that time, the 20th flew the F-84D variant of the Thunderjet in the conventional fighter bomber role. The 20th FBW received its first F-84Ds in January 1950 at Shaw AFB. The F-84D was the first of the Thunderjets to see service in Korea. (*via Dave Menard*)

In November 1951, the 20th FBW moved to Langley AFB, sharing that base with the 47th Bombardment Wing. Both units formed the 49th Air Division. At Langley, the 20th FBW converted to the nuclear capable F-84G and began training for the new and unique role. This F-84G wears the yellow colours of the 79th Fighter Bomber Squadron. B-45s of the 47th BW can be seen in the background. (*20th FW Historical Office via Art Sevigny*)

The 20th FBW began the Atlantic Crossing with their F-84Gs on 20 May 1952. They travelled by the northern route, the first stop being Goose Bay, Labrador. The flight was delayed at Goose Bay for five days due to bad weather over Greenland, their next stop. (*20th FW Historical Office via Art Sevigny*)

On arrival in the UK, the 55th and 77th FBS became based at RAF Wethersfield and the 79th at RAF Woodbridge. Unfortunately, Wethersfield had no perimeter fences at this time and guards had to be posted around the parked aircraft around the clock. (*20th FW Historical Office via Art Sevigny*)

The mission directive of the 49th AD was to halt any Soviet land invasion of Western Europe using tactical nuclear weapons. This weapon had to be modified for the Thunderjet. In order to provide proper ground clearance, the lower fin was stowed in a retracted position on the ground and extended once the fighter was airborne.

On arrival in the UK, the initial tasks of the pilots of the pilots of the 20th FBW were practising inflight refuelling, an exercise with which many of them were unfamiliar; long-range navigation flights; and, both in the UK and in North Africa, dive bombing, rocketry, and ground gunnery. Practising for the atomic delivery role with the Mk 7 bomb was, of course, paramount.

Regular deployments to bases in North Africa were essential for most USAFE units operating out of Northern Europe. The weather around their bases and the ranges they used was generally so unreliable as to prove hugely detrimental to general day to day operations and mission success. The squadrons of the 20th FBW deployed to Sidi Slimane in Morocco and spent a considerable amount of time there. Initially, the base was used for dive bombing training. Dengie Flats in Essex was used, when weather permitted, for ground rocketry and gunnery. The first of the squadrons to deploy to Morocco was the 77th FBS in October 1952, followed by the 55th, which in turn was replaced by the 79th. The 55th FBS deployed for thirty days in all and pioneered a new pattern of movement. Each pilot flew down in one day, bombed for the next two days and flew home on the fourth day. This means of deployment ensured, not only that the bombing practice took place, but also met the requirements for long range navigation flights. Bill Landis flew with the 55th FBS in 1952 and recalls the TDYs to Sidi:

> The 20th FBW had exclusive use of the bombing range in the Atlas Mts, as far as I know. We did not have in-flight refuelling. We refuelled at Marseilles going south and Algiers going north. This gave us a full fuel load over the Med in case we had to go to an alternative base. Another 55th Sqdn pilot and myself were the advance party at Sidi for our first missions there to drop practice bombs from high altitudes. The so-called bombing range was merely a very large circle by the Atlas mountains. We did our own scheduling, one aircraft at a time over the range, dropping practice bombs at about 10000 ft. It was about 30 min flight time, as I recall. No one was on the ground, at least there was not supposed to be. The area was pretty remote. We did our own bomb accuracy assessment by looking to see where the smoke was from where the practice bomb hit; not the best procedure, but that was all we had; and as you might expect sometimes we didn't hit in the circle!!
>
> It was not easy to hit the target with practice bombs because of various unknowns: upper level winds were difficult to forecast and the slightest error in the bomb run would throw the bomb any where but in the target area.[1]

The methods of delivery of the Mk 7 special weapon as practised by the squadrons of the 20th in the early days were inefficient for a number of reasons. The accuracy of the high-altitude delivery was dependant on favourable weather conditions. Dive bombing was reasonably accurate but, bearing in mind the 20-kiloton yield of the bomb, was tantamount to a suicide mission. Both methods of delivery rendered the aircraft extremely susceptible to anti-aircraft defences. It was of paramount importance

The F-84G was the first of the Thunderjets able to be refuelled in the air. This was essential to the aircraft's nuclear strike mission and was practised regularly. Here, a 77th FBS Thunderjet takes on fuel from a KC-97G tanker somewhere over the UK. (*20th FW Historical Office via Art Sevigny*)

At an open house in 1953 at RAF Wethersfield, ground crew demonstrate how to remove an engine from the F-84G while visitors look on in rapt attention. The weather does not appear to have improved much in the last sixty years. (*20th FW Historical Office via Art Sevigny*)

that a method of delivery be found that was accurate and gave the pilots an element of protection from anti-aircraft defences and the best chance of avoiding the nuclear blast when their bomb detonated. In the US, the LABS was being developed and tested, but it would be a little while before it reached the 20th FBW standing on the frontline in Europe.

Meanwhile, back in the UK, settling in to their new home was not coming easily at Wethersfield. Facilities at the base were far from adequate. There was a lack of runway overruns and poor night-lighting facilities. The LF Beacon was unreliable over 15 to 20 miles. Worst of all was the interminably bad weather. Runways were invariably wet and slippery and there was a problem with mud. Special weapons programmes were compromised because there was no adequate shelter from the inclement weather, which included high winds, for loading practice to take place. Even the F-84Gs systems were subject to interference from the almost constant damp and fog. The ARC-3 radio and ARN-6 radio compass were often rendered unreliable due to moisture seeping into relay ports and cannon plugs.

In spite of the difficulties, it was essential that the wing developed its war plans as soon as possible. Capt. (later Brig.-Gen.) Richard Baughn was with the wing at this time and recalls in his paper '20th Fighter Wing first in nucs & bare bones over-the-shoulder bombing'.

F-84G 51-980 under tow at Wethersfield. Even the tow truck carries the blue squadron lightning flash! (*20th FW Historical Office via Art Sevigny*)

Formation flying also practised on a regular basis. In this photograph, the 77th FBS are put through their paces. (*20th FW Historical Office via Art Sevigny*)

Not to be outdone, the 55th FBS fly four F-84Gs in Box Formation. (*USAF*)

While the 20th FBW continued their aggressive flight training program and the married airmen searched for a place to live, the wing and 49th Air Division staffs finalized the war plan. US policy at the time didn't permit the wing to possess all the critical components for their MK-7's. These components had to be flown in from the US on C-124's and the plan called for them to be in place within 24-36 hours after the wing had begun posturing for nuclear strikes.

Since the wing couldn't go to war until the critical components arrived, no part of the force was on alert. If tensions rose and war time posturing became necessary during off duty periods, a carefully prepared, frequently tested and revised pyramid phone notification plan had to be activated by the 'Officer and NCO of the Day' to assemble the wing's widely scattered personnel.

As people reported for duty, the wing's next step was to disperse its personnel, weapons and aircraft to avoid having all its eggs in one basket. The three fighter squadrons had been divided in half to form six task forces. Each task force was assigned at least 15 aircraft, along with their share of support equipment and personnel. Four of the task forces dispersed to active airfields, one task force remained at Wethersfield and one at Bentwaters.

Since I was one of the four task force commanders that had to disperse, I'll add my recollections. When first assigned the job, I took the supervisors for aircraft maintenance, weapons, supply, security police, intelligence, communications, transportation and other base support people with me to survey our dispersal base and determine the configuration and extent of the support requirements. Once the support package was sized, we calculated the number and types of convoy vehicles that were necessary to move the package to the dispersal base. As part of the planning, the convoy commander took his assistant and key support personnel and drove the narrow and twisting British roads leading to the dispersal base to ensure there were no obstacles that would hinder the passage of the convoy's vehicles and equipment. At the dispersal base, the key supervisors also determined the best on base routing to their function's operating location. After the routes to and on base were proofed, maps were annotated and given each supervisor whenever the dispersal plan was activated. Most task forces had to use some tents, because of the shortage of building space at their dispersal base. For example, my task force required four tents, one of which was used as our mess hall.

During the dispersal phase, the aircraft were dispatched singularly or in pairs as the aircraft were readied and pilots became available. Spare pilots came with the convoy. The squadron intelligence section monitored the pilot assignments to make certain each pilot's target folders were included in the task force's intelligence package.

Simultaneously with aircraft dispersal, the convoys began to form. I can't recall the exact number of personnel and vehicles in the convoy, but there were well over a hundred people and probably at least 40 vehicles. Due to extensive planning and coordination, every support function maintained a listing of the number, types and status of equipment/vehicles that each dispersing task force required. There was a lot of equipment to assemble, load, move, then unload and made ready for use; and the job had to be done safely and rapidly, under tight security.

As soon as the convoy arrived at the dispersal base, the aircraft were configured for combat and we waited for the C-124's to deliver the critical MK-7 components. Two man security and closely monitored certification was maintained throughout the transfer weapons components and the loading process. After the critical components were installed, we waited for the launch order.[2]

F-84G 51-964 comes in to land at RAF Woodbridge. This aircraft ended its days at the AMARC boneyard at Davis-Monthan in 1957. (*Author's collection*)

F-84G-1-RE 51-945 of the 77th FBS pictured at Wethersfield on 21 May 1955. (*George Pennick*)

F-84G-1-RE 51-948 wears the red trim of the 77th FBS at Wethersfield in 1955. (*Mick Sudds*)

However, in spite of these problems, a variety of missions were flown. On 1, 4, and 12 December 1952, the 79th FBS flew a series of missions in conjunction with RAF Trimley Heath GCI Centre. The purpose of these was to evaluate the tracking qualities of its radar on jet aircraft. Various formations of various numbers of aircraft were used during these operations, which included simulated attacks on a defended area in order to detect early warning and intercept capabilities. On 11 December 1952, the 55th FBS flew some simulated attacks on London after first flying a long-range navigation sortie. The attacking flights were flown at different altitudes, different speeds, and in different formations, the better to test radar response and identify, which methods of attack offered the least chance of radar detection and subsequent interception.

There was a significant shortage of pilots in these early days. Between them, the squadrons needed some twenty-two pilots to bring them up to strength, the most urgent need being with the 79th FBS at RAF Bentwaters. One of the principle reasons for this was the release of National Guard officers from active service and their return home.

Early 1953 saw continuous bad weather having a very adverse effect on operations. The East Coast floods, though providing an opportunity for good public relations work with their English hosts, put Dengie Flats out of commission for dive bombing for thirty days.

The excursions to North Africa continued apace with the 55th FBS spending a month at Sidi Slimane from 10 January to 13 February. The 77th went in March and conducted some joint operations with SAC B-29s on intercept and camera gunnery missions. The exercise was not deemed to have been of a great deal of value to the twenty pilots of the squadron, as they became more and more exasperated by continuous requests from the bomber jockeys for them to slow down, as they were having difficulty getting pictures.

On 10 March, the first fatal accident with the F-84G in the UK occurred when Lt Reynolds of the 77th FBS flying aircraft 51-917 experienced engine compressor failure. He attempted to land the Thunderjet in a ploughed field, but hit the bank of a sunken road and the aircraft disintegrated. His death prompted a recommendation from wing HQ that it was always best to bale out than risk a forced landed in open country.

In May 1953, the 20th FBW had to face an ORT from the 18th to the 21st of that month. All crews and aircraft in North Africa were recalled for the test which was held in conjunction with Operation Prophecy. The ORT revealed shortcomings in both the aircraft and the practices of the 20th. The limitations of the A-7 gunsight on the F-84G when used for atomic delivery was established. There was a significant lack of aircraft spares and inadequate electronic equipment, which, in turn, led to poor combat readiness of the F-84s. A total 103 sorties were flown, of which eighty-seven were deemed to have been successful or effective. Operation One Run also formed part of the ORT. This was carried out on the Nordheim range in Germany. This bombing exercise achieved only a 59-per cent effectiveness rating. However, the participants were vocal in protesting that the very rules of the test precluded the effectiveness that should have been expected. For example, all aircraft were assigned to one target area where bad weather and faulty forecasts led to a high number of aborts for lack of fuel. In a true wartime scenario, this would simply not have occurred.

The decidedly poor score for dive bombing in the ORT clearly underlined the need for the 20th to adopt a more efficient method of special weapons delivery. The development of the LABS bombing system had been proceeding apace back in the USA, and in late 1952, four LABS computers had been delivered to the wing for evaluation. Various problems were encountered with these computers and they were returned state-side for further development.

Meanwhile, 20th FBW pilots had been busy developing and perfecting their own system of non-computer-aided low-altitude bombing. The LABS system involved approaching the target at 500 feet. The pilot would instigate a 4-G pull up and release the bomb when the flight indicator showed an altitude of 6,000 feet at an attitude of 110 degrees to the horizontal. Immediately following bomb release, the pilot would execute an Immelmann turn and depart the area. The bomb would arc to 12,000 feet before descent. One major difficulty to be overcome was the identification of the IP (or Initial Point), at which the aircraft would climb prior to bomb delivery. Dick Baughn noted:

> Since they had been coping with the European weather and had months of extensive target study, most 20th FBW pilots were convinced that good IP's were not easy to find, especially in marginal weather. Many of the targets were airfields and were much easier to spot than most IP's. As a result, there was a consensus that the target would be a highly desirable option as pull up point for low altitude bombing. Pilots concluded that if you're going to toss the bomb, why not toss it straight up from the target and let it fall back. Some people jokingly referred to it as 'upside down dive bombing', but eventually it became known as 'over-the-shoulder' bomb delivery.[3]

F-84G of the 79th FBS at RAF Sculthorpe. (*Mick Sudds*)

This 79th FBS F-84G is under tow at RAF Wethersfield. (*20th FW Historical Office via Art Sevigny*)

The atomic mission of the wing was undoubtedly developing apace. Forty-three F-84Gs had undergone the necessary LABS modifications at Burtonwood and Brize Norton. Earlier, in April, special weapons storage was completed at Bentwaters, while at Wethersfield, tests were conducted for adapting C-119s to carry a larger payload of atomic bombs by storing tails and main bomb separately. This did in fact increase the carrying capacity of these transports, which were the subject of many loading and unloading practice exercises at Wethersfield and Bentwaters. Concurrent with these developments, the 49th AD devised a new form of target allocation. Task forces were assigned a primary and secondary target area. Each area included a number of individual targets with which all pilots in the task force would have to become familiar. The feasibility of this form of target allocation was tried out in Operation Prophecy and the general consensus was favourable, but it did require the retraining of bomb commanders and certainly increased the workload of the squadron intelligence sections.

The decision to convert the 20th FBW from the Republic F-84G to the Republic F-84F Thunderstreak was confirmed in 1954, but it was to be some time before the changeover was finalised. A maintenance school was set up jointly with the 81st FBW at RAF Bentwaters. That unit was also to convert to the F-84F. The Mobile Training detachment (MTD) was set up at RAF Shepherds Grove, home of the 78th FBS of the 81st FBW.

This 7th FBS F-84G-1-RE is undergoing maintenance at RAF Woodbridge. On 11 February 1954, this aircraft crashed near Nouasseur, Morocco, while on a practice bombing run. (*20th FW Historical Office via Art Sevigny*)

Modification of the F-84Gs, however, did not slow down, in spite of their imminent replacement. It was, of course, vital for the 20th to remain combat ready, and the atomic mission retained its priority status. The modified LABS computers arrived with the wing and began to be installed in the F-84Gs. This increased the means of delivery of special weapons by the F-84G to three: dive bombing, LABS toss bombing, and 'over the shoulder'. MA-1 LABS equipment was fitted to all F-84G-1RE aircraft. It transpired, however, that the system was not entirely satisfactory for the 'over the shoulder' delivery. A further modification was required to the gyro, which involved mounting it an angle of 45 degrees to provide the pilot with roll information from 45 degrees to 135 degrees, instead of 0 to 90 degrees. This modification was made pending the delivery and testing of the MA-2 system. Unfortunately, when the MA-2 was installed in an F-84G, the aircraft crashed near Marseilles in France. The equipment, however, was undamaged and was subsequently reserved for testing in an F-84F.

Exercises, operations, and deployments continued apace during 1954. One of the most significant of these was Operation Dividend, which took place from 16–26 July. This exercise was a test of Britain's air defences and the 20th F-84Gs flew out of Bitburg and Spangdahlem in Germany. Altogether, 328 sorties were flown. In Exercise Falling Leaf in August the F-84Gs were tasked with attacking 12th Air Force bases in Germany as a test of that units defence systems. From 13–20 September, another ORT took place, testing the operational war plans of the 49th Air Division and the individual skills of the bomb commanders. A total of 577 hours were flown by 20th pilots during this test. Directly after the ORT, the wing was involved in Operation Battle Star designed to test the support tactics of the 2nd and 4th ATAFs in Germany. Operation Longbridge took the 77th FBS to Elevsis in Greece for dive bombing exercises and the 55th FBS to Balıkesir in Turkey in August. A return visit was made to mainland Greece and Crete in December 1954 when a detachment of the wing undertook an examination of the possibility of mounting atomic strikes from these areas against targets in the Soviet Union, which could not be reached from elsewhere.

On 16 July 1954, the 20th detached some F-84Gs to the gunnery range at Indian Springs, Nevada, for a conventional gunnery competition. The exercises included ground strafing, dive bombing, skip bombing, and rocketry. The 20th FBW came out on top place. Maj. John J. Kropenick won first place in high level and dive bombing.

Towards the end of 1954, a number of aircraft crashes took place, some fatal, which underlined the need for conversion to the Thunderstreak. Capt. Robert L. Fair safely ejected when from 51-936 after an engine fire started. Captains James Tedder and Louis Nonetta of the 55th FBS unfortunately died when their F-84Gs 51-581 and 51-892 collided with the ground on approach to Wethersfield in bad weather. On 6 July, two aircraft of the 77th FBS collided while practising for a flyby in Germany. F-84G 51-925 suffered an engine explosion and debris hit aircraft 51-931. Capt. Frederick E. Detling succeeded in belly landing 51-925 and Capt. Robert E. Bordern landed 51-931 at Spangdahlem. On 2 November another 79th pilot was killed when his aircraft, 51-923, crashed while on a bombing run at Nouasseur. F-84G 51-933 was destroyed when it suffered a bird strike while taking off from Sculthorpe on 3 December. The pilot, 1Lt Jerold B. Weller, was thankfully unhurt.

On 1 October 1954, the 79 FBS moved into RAF Woodbridge. Although other units subsequently adopted the tactical special weapons mission, the 20th FBW remains unique in that it was the first wing in the USAF to be assigned this significant task. For over three years, it alone among the tactical fighter units of USAFE faced down the might of the Soviet Union and its allies, when, together with the 47th Bombardment Wing, its mission loudly stated: 'We are here and we will stop you. Thus far and no further!'

The F-84F Thunderstreak

As 1955 dawned, conversion to the F-84F commenced. The first two aircraft arrived at RAF Wethersfield on 10 February. These were not in fact new machines, but were on loan from the 81st FBW which had received a considerable number at the end of the previous year. The MTD for the F-84F had been established at Wethersfield just two days prior to the arrival of the two aircraft. The plan was to transition the 55th and 77th FBS at Nouasseur. The aircraft were received at Alvena at Lisbon in Portugal and from there flown to the Moroccan base for acceptance inspection and transition training. Fair weather and an 11,000-foot runway were ideal. The 79th FBS was not expected to transition until late spring when it was expected the weather in the UK might be more conducive to intensive training. By the end of July 1955, all squadrons had converted to the new aircraft, but not without some problems. The F-84Fs were delivered with the MA-1 LABS equipment fitted and had to receive the same modification to the gyro that had been applied to the F-84Gs previously. There were also problems with the special weapons pylons on the Thunderstreaks which required modification before they could be used satisfactorily. Rough runway take-offs with Mk 7 special weapons attached produced an unpleasant lateral sway. This was not a safety issue as the weapons were secured to the pylon and it was not a phenomenon which occurred when the aircraft was in flight. The problem was alleviated by the replacement of the pylon pull-out electrical cables, but the pylon remained problematic.

One of the most significant exercises to take place involving USAFE and other NATO countries occurred from 21 to 28 June 1955—this was Exercise Carte Blanche. The 20th FBW took an active part in the exercise, flying simulated bombing missions over mainland Europe from dispersal bases in the UK. The 55th FBS, for example, operated from RAF Woodbridge. Both F-84G and F-84Fs were used in the exercise; both the 55th and the 77th FBS having received a large complement of the latter aircraft. There was considerable practice in special weapons dispersal proficiency before and during Carte Blanche. Dispersal of weapons to strike aircraft was accomplished in fifty-two minutes following alert notification during the exercise.

Bombing and other range work remained problematic. Dengie Flats was constantly out of use because of bad weather. A conservative estimate placed the range out of bounds for at least seven months a year. In addition to this, a number of pilots had to remain on standby daily and weekly in the hope of being able to use it for bombing. The imposition of the secondary gunnery mission placed a considerable burden on the wing, its pilots and its ability to satisfactorily do its job if 'D' day did come round. There were difficulties in working with the French at Cazaux and Nouasseur, not least

F-84F-40-GE 52-6570 at Wethersfield. This aircraft is the mount of the wing commander, Col. Arthur G. Salisbury. Col. Salisbury was commander of the 20th from June 1955 to April 1997. (*Author's collection*)

Belonging to the 77th FBS, F-84F-35-RE 52-6440 was present at an open day at RAF Wethersfield. (*Mike Hooks*)

Wearing the blue colours of the 55th FBS, this F-84F-45-RE, 52-6667, was photographed in 1956, and it carries the buzz number on the forward fuselage. The inboard pylon on the port wing was designed to carry the special weapon, the Mk 7 atomic bomb. (*Mick Sudds*)

On the ramp at Nouasseur, F-84F-45-RE awaits its next training flight. The aircraft were received at Alvena, Lisbon, Portugal, and from there flown to the Moroccan base for acceptance inspection and transition training. Fair weather and an 11,000-foot runway were ideal. (*via Art Sevigny, 20th FBW Historian*)

First Lieutenant F. G. Jones of the 55th FBS rests for a photo before taking to the cockpit for another training flight at Nouasseur in 1955 in F-84F. (*via Art Sevigny, 20th FBW Historian*)

because they only worked a five and a half day week! In fact, Nouasseur threw up another impediment to mission success when, in January 1955, the 55th FBS did no LABS practice because of swarms of locusts over the range.

The F-84F was also not without its own problems. There was no autopilot in the aircraft on delivery. The installation of the MB-2 autopilot did not take place until mid-1956, when the drag chutes also began to be fitted. This extensive modification programme in itself raised difficulties. At the height of it, the squadrons found themselves with insufficient aircraft to fulfil mission requirements. The range and modification problems were further compounded in early 1956 when Dengie was put out of bounds, not because of bad weather, but because of local complaints of noise and some incidences of accidental release of practice bombs. The latter problem was solved when the Thunderstreaks were fitted with the Royal Navy 25-lb bomb racks.

The year 1956 was significant for the 20th Fighter Bomber Wing, not least because, when they had barely got their hands on their new Thunderstreaks, the news broke in September that the wing was to convert to the North American F-100D Super Sabre. It was also the year when the pilots of this and other bombing units in NATO faced the real possibility of going to war, when they sat alert in their aircraft with weapons loaded at the height of the Suez and Hungary crises.

Two important exercises took place early in the year with Rejuvenate and Quickshot. The former exercise was designed as a test of the UK's air defence systems. Pilots would fly from their bases to the south of Ireland, drop their outboard tanks, and return

Shrouded against the wind and rain, F-84F-45-RE 52-6752 was the aircraft of the squadron commander, Maj. Peter Peters, and was photographed at RAF Wethersfield in June 1957. (*Mick Sudds*)

Yellow colours of the Tiger Squadron of the 20th, the 79th FBS, adorn this F-84F-40-GE in 1957. The 79th was based at RAF Woodbridge. This F-84F is carrying a fuel tank pylon instead of the special weapon pylon on the port wing inner station. (*Mick Sudds*)

Photographed at RAF Bentwaters in 1957, F-84F-45-RE belongs to the 79th FBS. (*Alan Johnson*)

while the RAF attempted to intercept them. The exercise was a marked success for the squadrons of the 20th FBW in that, out of a total of fifteen sorties flown, there was only one intercept. Whether the RAF was quite so pleased with the results is not so certain. Operation Quickshot took place in May and was a test of low-level navigation and LABS 'over the shoulder' delivery. The participating aircraft made maximum load assisted take-offs, navigated to Luce Bay in Scotland where they dropped their outboard tanks. They then made a low-level return to Dengie Flats to drop a T-63 and their inboard 450-gallon tanks in a LABS manoeuvre. Twenty-five aircraft of the wing delivered twenty-two bombs.

Exercise Stopwatch was started. This involved telling any bomb commander, without warning, to hit one of his targets. Subsequent to this the individual must then do all flight planning, draw all required equipment, proceed to his aircraft, and complete the check on his weapons. All this to be done under the stopwatch. After the exercise, the pilot was critiqued. Stopwatch was an ongoing exercise and could happen to any pilot at any time without warning.

In September 1956, one pilot from each squadron was sent TDY to Sidi Slimane to qualify on the F-100 in anticipation of the wings conversion to the type. They returned with a good deal of enthusiasm and to the envy of those they had left behind.

From 7–21 November, all units of the 20th FBW were placed on alert and atomic bombs were loaded; this was done in direct response to the dramatic increase in tension brought about by the Soviet aggression in Hungary and the conflict in the Middle East. The US was not directly involved in the latter hostilities, but the potential for escalation

F-84F-40-GE 52-6534 of the 55th FBS is at RAF Bentwaters' open house in 1957. (*Author's collection*)

On the hardstanding at Wethersfield is F-84F-45-RE assigned to the 55th FBS. (*via Art Sevigny, 20th FBW Historian*)

of the conflict was all too clear. Fortunately, the pilots were stood down from the alert condition when international tensions eased.

Sadly, the year was a bad one for accidents in the wing. In February, F-84F 52-6719 was engaged in a dogfight with an RAF Hunter, which culminated in a collision and damage to the vertical stabiliser of the aircraft. The Hunter was undamaged. In April, in a three-ship formation, the number three aircraft pulled back after losing the leader in the sun. While pulling back into position in a climbing turn, the pilot realised he had only one aircraft in sight. He broke right and collided with the left wing of the number two. Both aircraft succeeded in landing. In May, two F-84Fs collided while on a bombing run. Aircraft 52-7100 crashed, killing the pilot and a civilian. Also, during May, aircraft 52-6678 of the 55th FBS landed wheels up at Wethersfield. In June, there were five major accidents; thankfully only one of them resulting in death to the pilot. This occurred when aircraft 52-7106 rolled to the left and nosed down when taking off at Woodbridge. There were two ejections during June. Both F-84Fs, 52-6742 and 52-6711, were abandoned by their pilots. Significantly, of the five June accidents, three were caused by materiel failure. The F-84Fs were not the only aircraft involved in crashes. F-84G 51-965 piloted by 1Lt James D. Goggins crashed into the North Sea in April. No trace of the pilot or the aircraft was ever found. Later, in November, 1Lt Warrington G. Lent crashed his F-84F into the North Sea after piloting the flamed-out aircraft clear of all populated areas. For this, he was posthumously awarded the DFC.

The early part of 1957 was characterised by finding out more about the F-100. There were visits to various continental bases which were already homes to the 'Hun'. One such was Chaumont where the 48th FBW was based. Several pilots went to this French

Helen of Troy is the name given to this F-84F-45-RE forming as a backdrop to all the 77th FBS pilots in 1956. *From left to right, standing*: unknown, Chaffee, George Branch, Howard Farr, Walter H. Baxter, William F. Harris, Herman A. Meyer, William C. Barnes, Anatole A. Semenov, Wesley B. Collins, James R. Brown, Robert Perkins, and James Barnes. *From left to right, kneeling*: Bill Busking, Dugan, Robert S. Fogg, James A. Garroitt, Gerald F. Punteney, Sherrell W. Wylie, Robert W. Bazley, Cammeron, unknown, Russell Scott, and Chuck Crittenden. (*via Art Sevigny, 20th FW Historical Office*)

base in March and April, both to convert to the type and to gain first-hand experience of problems associated with special weapons delivery by the Super Sabre.

While conversion to the new aircraft went ahead, the wing was, of course, required to maintain combat readiness with the F-84F. Stopwatch was temporarily suspended during the changeover, but otherwise exercises continued as intensively as ever. Detachments to Nouasseur for bombing practice took place regularly. Exercise Southern Exposure required pilots to fly two missions per month simulating actual attacks on wartime targets. These missions required the dumping of external fuel tanks, but the 20th obtained an exception to this rule owing to a shortage of these. Capt. Stuart L. Jackson, an air force intelligence officer, visited Wethersfield in April to brief senior officers on the Soviet order of battle in Eastern Europe and the implications of this for route planning and target assignation.

The F-100 Super Sabre

During 1957, conversion to the F-100 was well under way with transition training taking place at the sun base of Nouasseur in Morocco. Pilots who had been with the 48th at Chaumont in France were appointed instructors, and sent extended TDY to Nouasseur to initiate all squadron pilots. The mobile training detachment for the F-100 was set up at Wethersfield in January and the simulator at Woodbridge in April. On 15 June 1957, the 20th FBW hosted an open house at RAF Wethersfield to introduce the new aircraft to the British public. Some 46,000 people attended the base to witness an impressive static and flying display by NATO aircraft, the highlight of which was a display by the Skyblazers aerobatic team from the 36th FBW flying F-100Cs. The leader of the team, Capt. Wilbur L. Creech, gave an impromptu encore solo performance. F-100F 56-5730 The Spirit of St Louis, fresh from the Paris Air Show, was on static display together with F-100Ds 54-2161 and 54-2173 for the press and public to admire. In a press briefing, Capt. Tolliver, commanding the 20th, went to great pains to stress the awareness felt by the air force about noise and the effect on the local environment. He acknowledged that the F-100 was a noisy aeroplane, but reassured all present that noise would be kept to a minimum. The approach to the base would be from the east, disturbing as few people as possible. Engine tests on the afterburning J-57s would only be conducted during daylight hours. As with all new aeroplanes, there was a sharp learning curve for the pilots when first encountering the F-100.

Mike Briggs was with the 55th FBS:

> The F-100 was a good aircraft for both nuclear and conventional weapons delivery. It had several idiosyncrasies, however, of which the pilot had to be aware. First, under high g-loads the moving the stick to the side caused the aircraft to roll in the opposite direction intended. In the early days of the airplane before its characteristics were clearly understood this was particularly problematic when pilots rolled to line up on a ground target for a strafing pass. Rolling into the turn worked fine but when trying to roll out the plane would roll down towards the ground rather than rolling out to level flight. Second, another idiosyncrasy was its flight characteristics at low speeds most noticeable when landing. As the plane neared landing speeds, the ailerons became ineffective and picking a wing up or small turns had to

The Spirit of St Louis arrived at Wethersfield on 15 June 1957 from the Paris Air Show for an open house held at the base to show off the new aircraft. This F-100D was assigned to the 77th Tactical Fighter Squadron. The pilots of the 77th are here posing for a group photograph in the autumn of 1957. *The Spirit of St Louis* went on to serve in the 50th TFW and the Colorado and New Jersey Air National Guard. (*Ray Rider via Art Sevigny, 20th FW Historical Office*)

At an open house at RAF Bentwaters in 1959, F-100D 56-3006 is being closely examined by an admiring public. The 20th TFW F-100s carried this scheme in individual squadron colours from 1957 through to 1960. (*Author's collection*)

be made with the rudders. Both of these characteristics became second nature after flying the plane for some time and not a particular problem.[4]

Conversion to the F-100 was completed by the end of July 1957 and mission training began. In July 1958, the 20th Fighter Bomber Wing was redesignated the 20th Tactical Fighter Wing (TFW). The primary mission of the wing remained special weapon delivery, with a secondary role of conventional delivery of napalm, rockets, and bombs.

20th Tactical Fighter Wing

The nuclear mission was of paramount importance in a Cold War scenario where hostilities could break out at any time. Special weapons training, exercises, and security occupied much of both wing's time and energies. A team from Lowry AFB was set up to train 120 selected ground crew in the handling of the Mk 28 Special Weapon. In June 1958, an alert procedure was adopted which required two bomb commanders, one duty officer, and support crews to be on alert from midnight to 7 p.m. the following day. This was the precursor of Operation Blast Off which commenced in July 1958 and was later renamed Victor Alert in December 1958. At this time, the number of pilots standing alert was four per squadron seven times a month for twenty-four hours each day.

Training was hard and highly intensive. Pilots were tested two to four times a month on their knowledge of assigned targets. They had to make a sketch map of the target and the final approach to it, and draw from memory the route to and return from the target. When a new target was assigned pilots were tested within forty-eight hours of receiving the assignment. Other tests from Intelligence posed such questions as 'In your last 50 nautical miles to your target, what is the highest elevation encountered along your route and 10 miles either side of it? Give the number and type of aircraft presently stationed at your target. What anti-aircraft weapons are located within a 5 mile radius of your target?' Nothing less than a 100-per cent positive response to these and other questions was acceptable.

In the event that a nuclear conflict broke out, each of the F-100s would take-off and fly solo to their targets to deliver their nuclear weapons. However, there were exceptions to this rule. George Grill flew with the 77th TFS:

If the balloon went up, we had one set of two Huns that were planned to take off together. This was unique. In this one case, however, it happened that the IP of one attacker (#1) was the target of the other (#2). Therefore, they would have flown together to the IP of the nearest target, whereupon the jock whose IP that was (#2) would make a lazy 360, leaving the other guy (#1) to proceed to his IP (#2's TGT). Number 1 would turn on his IP and push it up to 500K on the way to his target. At the conclusion of his 360, #2 pushed up to 500K and a very few minutes later would obliterate #1's IP. The timing of the thing would have both bombs detonating at very nearly the same time at places fairly close to one another.[5]

F-100D, 55-3668, was assigned to the 55th TFS. It was the aircraft of the deputy commander of the 20th, Col. J. T. Robbins, and carries all three squadron badges on the fuselage side and the three squadron colours on the tail flash. (*Robert Robinson collection*)

Aircraft colours changed again in 1961 when all squadron insignia ware removed and the tail flash now carried the three squadron colours. (*Author's collection*)

Three Huns of the Woodbridge-based 79th TFS fly over snow-covered mountains in this photograph. (*Raymond Toliver via Art Sevigny, 20th FW Historical Office*)

Targets were many and diverse. A bomb commander 'sat' his targets. Sometimes the assigned target was obviously of significant and primary importance, an airfield perhaps. Sometimes, however, it seemed insignificant. George Grill stated:

> I do clearly remember that one of the targets I 'sat' was a small wooden bridge near the border with East Germany. Now, there was nothing with vertical development anywhere within miles of that country bridge. I assumed that the Army wanted it struck in anticipation of Red troops massing in that area or using it as a location for attack. Mine was not to question why. The point is, The United States of America was prepared to drop an atomic bomb on this nondescript little wooden bridge! Seemed like a waste to me then, and I still wonder at it.
>
> On the other hand on Victor Alert I sat a target of obviously more military value, a Soviet airfield in the Ukraine. It, too was unique it a totally different way. The 20th only had a couple of these long distance targets. I'm not sure what units on the continent had, but I'll tell you, the Ukraine is a far piece from Wethersfield.
>
> The only way to reach it was the high, low high, profile. In other words I would have been cruising at a very reachable altitude through hostile skies for an appreciable time before letting down to attack. Following that, after staying low for a few miles to exit the USSR I would have climbed back to a 'high' return leg, but not for long, as my fuel ran out over western Czechoslovakia. In theory, should I make it to the banks of a certain lake I might find partisans to get me home. Hah! Even if everything worked perfectly, it was doubtful there would be a base to get 'home' to or any transportation to get me there.[6]

Bearing in mind that not only were the F-100s proceeding to their targets within a few minutes of the commencement of hostilities, but also strikes were being made by, initially, short-range missiles (Mace and Matador) and latterly, long-range missiles (IRBMs and ICBMs), and the nuclear bombers of NATO (B-47, B-52, V Bombers)—the devastation would have been enormous. In addition to this, the pilots of the aircraft delivering the nuclear weapons had to be protected from the flashes of the bombs exploding around them. 'Huns' on Victor Alert were fitted with a canvas 'flash hood'. George Grill noted: 'The canvas came in two flavours. One was silvered on the outside, the other was bone white. There were rather more of the latter, as I recall. When deployed, the hood folded forward from behind the ejection headrest and cut off all peripheral sight lines forward to the canopy bow'.

This effectively blocked the side views from the cockpit and the pilot's eyesight was not adversely affected by the nuclear detonations. In common with all bomb commanders, the pilots were issued with the eye patch to avoid being blinded by the flashes of the nuclear detonations directly in front of them.

The dawning of the 1960s brought with it an intensification of the Cold War and the subsequent imperative for faster and faster technological progress. The secondary mission of the wing was maintained, but the special weapons delivery role once more grew in importance. In addition to the Mk 7 and the Mk 28, the Mk 43 weapon was accepted into the inventory. Detachments to Wheelus in North Africa for special weapons training became more regular and intensive. The 20th maintained a permanent presence of twelve aircraft at the Libyan base. Each fighter squadron had five pilots there at any one time: two TDYs for each pilot in each six-month time period. While at Wheelus they had to fly at least ten special weapons sorties every day.

Air-to-air photo of the El Outia range used by the units operating out of Wheelus. The concentric circles had a particular purpose. George Grill noted: 'Our nuclear training consisted of dropping practice bombs on limed concentric circles, the outermost being 1,500 feet in diameter. The bombs were a simple cast iron tear drop shape, with cruciform fins, weighing 25 pounds. The nose held a shotgun shell size charge of black powder which gave off a puff of white smoke upon impact. We usually carried six o these practice bombs in a white, streamlined container on the centre line pylon. How many bombs we dropped in what mode depended on mission qualification requirements. A representative sortie might be two or three Low Altitude Bombing System (LABS) manoeuvres and two or three 40 degree dive bomb attacks. A qualifying dive attack was a bomb hit within an inner circle of 300′ diameter. Most dive attacks were within 100'. A qualifying LABS attack was a hit within the outer circle'. (*Harv Segrest via Art Sevigny, 20th FW Historical Office*)

Opposite page: This F-100D is set for a long haul to Wheelus in Libya. Mike Briggs recalled: 'The trip was about the maximum range and if the winds were against us we would have to stop over to refuel, generally at Aviano, Italy; which was not that bad since the Italian food at a little restaurant near the base was always great. Going into Wheelus with low fuel was not a particular problem since the weather was always good'. (*Harv Segrest via Art Sevigny, 20th FW Historical Office*)

Above and below: The 20th TFW Huns at the Wheelus bore-sighting range. The range was where the weapons specialists ensured the path of bullets shot from the aircraft's 20-mm Pontiac M-39 cannons was aligned with pilots' targeting systems in the cockpit's heads-up display, or HUD. (*via Art Sevigny, 20th FW Historical Office*)

Flights to and from Wheelus were flown in formation. These four Huns are returning from the Libyan base and are heading out over the Mediterranean in 1964. (*Glenn Ramsden via Art Sevigny, 20th FW Historical Office*)

The primary method of nuclear delivery practised by the pilots of the 20th was LABS 'over the shoulder'. The F-100D was fitted with the AN/AJB-1B computer. For many, this was the favoured method of delivery. Dave Skilling was with the 20th from 1965 to 1968:

> I personally enjoyed LABS most, and was the Wing accuracy champ with that very inaccurate delivery for a while. Run-in was at minimum altitude, to avoid defences. Holbeach, Wainfleet and Jurby were all water ranges, so we could practice low run-ins without noise complaints. During the pull-up, the weapon was released automatically at a climb angle set by the pilot into a gyro in the top of the fuselage behind the cockpit. The release angle would be calculated using the conditions of the day, such as wind, temperature and altitude of the target. The dial of the gyro did not face the outside of the airplane, and the pilot had to use a dental mirror to see and adjust the setting![7]

The wing also practised visual laydown and LADD.

Training at home through exercises and operations became more demanding. Razor's Edge was the wings plan to exercise and test their capability to react to war plans. Local exercises were regularly held and tested personnel reaction in a wide range of wartime scenarios: nuclear fallout procedures, breakout and delivery of wartime readiness materials, and dealing with contaminated aircraft and simulated aircraft were but a few of these. The wing also added loss of communication and sabotage to give added realism.

Exercise Grand Slam which occurred from 9–13 April 1962 was an example of the type of regular stringent testing that the 20th TFW and many other NATO units had to go through. The exercise was divided into two phases: Phase One began with a simulated conventional attack on certain NATO bases. In Phase Two, the aggressor launched a nuclear attack. This was followed by a nuclear exchange. The 20th TFW was confined to Phase Two of the exercise. At 11 a.m. on 10 April, all bases went on alert status. An additional twenty-five aircraft were loaded, but at this stage no target assignments were made by 4th ATAF control. At 1 p.m., Wethersfield and Woodbridge experienced a conventional attack. Pre-planned losses of aircraft and aircrew were injected into the scenario by base controls on a regular basis. At 3:35 p.m., all available aircraft were launched on their atomic strikes, but just as the last of these was recovering, Wethersfield was put out of action by a nearby 200-kt airburst. The dead were tagged with armbands and separated from the living. Live personnel were fed from a tent, and umpires spent a great deal of time observing each section to see how they were coping under such heavy losses. The base recovered sufficiently to be able to launch some aircraft at 5:30 a.m. on 11 April. Phase Two finished at 4 p.m. on this day.

In addition to its atomic role, it was necessary for the 20th TFW to practice and maintain its conventional capability. To this end, regular gunnery and conventional bombing skills and tactics were practised at a variety of ranges. The wing, in common with other USAFE fighter bomber units used Wheelus in Libya regularly, but also used Holbeach in the Wash and Jurby located on the north-west coast of the Isle of Man. Suippes in France was also used.

In the latter half of the 1960s, regular detachments were made to Çiğli in Turkey and Aviano in Italy, and when, in 1970, Wheelus closed after Gaddafi's coup, the ranges at Zaragoza in Spain were made available. The 20th set up a weapons training detachment at Torrejón AB in November 1969, the first squadrons, detaching there in January 1970.

At Holbeach, the F-100 pilots practised dive bombing, rocketry, and strafing, in addition to their nuclear LABS and LADD delivery. Trips to Wheelus were primarily for gunnery and bombing practice, but there was time also for air-to-air combat practice, though this was not the Hun's forte. George Grill noted:

> How it would have performed as a pure air superiority fighter against Soviet air was never plumbed as far as I know. We had no RED FLAG. We never encountered an opponent using Soviet tactics. We never trained in dissimilar ACM. It was always Hun *vs.* Hun. I thought it was a pretty good ACM bird, but my experience in that arena was limited and by the time I got to it the Hun had been altered into the 'D', a specialized attack version. When I flew 'one on one' I found the 'D' could be moved around pretty effectively with liberal application of rudder. I remember chasing a guy around the skies of Libya one day. I was on his tail and I saw his rudder come over hard and his entire vertical stabilizer curled into an arc. That

Above and next page: This 55th TFS Hun is under a thorough periodic maintenance check. (*Paul Boncz via Art Sevigny, 20th FW Historical Office*)

URC
F
CAUTION

> was amazing, and a lesson to me in the tremendous strength of the assembly. From then on I used that knowledge and my confidence in the airframe to advantage.
>
> I think the principal air-to-air strength of the bird was its high degree of inherent instability. The Hun was a bowling ball on a stick. It had to be juggled to fly straight. One flew the Hun with one's thumb, constantly working the trim button to maintain stable flight. Ask any Hun jock. Two fingers on the stick, thumb energetically working the trim button to keep the bird upright. Though the J-57 was state of the art, it lacked enough power to fight in the vertical, as the F-4 did so well.[8]

Air-to-ground gunnery using the four 20-mm Pontaic M-39 cannons was a regular feature of the Wheelus TDYs. The 20th TFW also took part in regular gunnery meets with other USAFE and NATO forces.

In October 1960, the wing represented USAFE in the annual weapons meet William Tell at Nellis AFB. The team was based at Williams AFB for the preliminary training which entailed twenty sorties a day. The competition included conventional and nuclear bombing and gunnery, consisting of strafing, dive bombing, napalm, skip bombing, and air-to-air dart firing.

In July 1964, the 20th took part in the 3rd AF Gunnery Meet based at Chaumont AB in France. The meet was designed to test the training and operational capability of pilots and crews assigned to Allied Air Forces Central Europe. The competition was between the forces of the 2nd Allied Tactical Air Force and the 4th ATAF. The 2nd ATAF was represented by the RAF, Royal Netherlands Air Force, and Belgium. The 4th ATAF was represented by the USAF, Canada, Germany, and France. Representing the 20th TFW at the meet was 1Lt Howard 'Tick' Loitwood of the 55th TFS. The pilots were tested in the following areas: rocketry, strafing, skip bombing, and simulated nuclear strike combing. All the missions were flown over the Suippes range in France, located between Reims and Metz. 'Tick' Loitwood won the strafing part of the competition. The 20th TFW journal, *The Wingman*, reported:

> 'Tick' as he is known by fellow pilots and Wethersfielders, flew a total of three missions in the strafing category, each time outscoring other pilots. The targets he shot at consisted of a 20 by 20 feet white cloth. Method of strafing used was a 10 degree dive angle at a speed of about 400 knots and a minimum altitude of 50 feet. Score was totalled for one pass with four cannons fired simultaneously.[9]

In July 1961, the 79th TFS at RAF Woodbridge hosted the first ever Tiger Meet at the base. All NATO squadrons featuring the tiger in their unit badge were invited to participate. The event was great success and led to a tradition for the Tiger squadrons that has endured to this day.

The pilots of the 20th TFW undertook a great deal of low flying. It was an essential part of their mission and often took them away from Wethersfield and the UK. Bob Pahl stated:

> For low level practice France was the option used for check rides. The real benefit of our rotations to Turkey and Spain was the ability to fly long low levels. Turkey had one range

The advent of camouflage signalled the end of the bright colour schemes worn, not only by the 20th TFW Huns, but for all USAF aircraft. (*via Art Sevigny, 20th FW Historical Office*)

A close-up of a thirsty Hun taking a drink from the boom of a KC-135. When the Huns first arrived in the UK, they were refuelled by the probe and drogue method by the KB-50Js of the 420th AREFS. When the Boeing KC-135s came into the theatre, they used the flying boom system. (*via Art Sevigny, 20th FW Historical Office*)

As well as flying the F-100D, the 20th TFW had a number of F-100Fs. These were particularly useful when on squadron exchange with NATO allies as it gave the opportunity for rides to be given to other pilots with no knowledge of the aircraft. (*Author's collection*)

F-100D 56-2963 trails its drag chute after landing at Wethersfield. (*Author's collection*)

> we could use. However, Konya was so far from Çiğli on the west coast north of Izmir, that we could only make a few passes. Aviano, Italy, offered low level opportunities and a range, Maniago, which was just a few miles from the base.[10]

Because the wing also had a role of close support for the Army, it was the practice to detach pilots as forward air controllers to frontline army units based in Germany. Dave Skilling was one such:

> We also trained for Close Air Support, and had occasional practice missions on the continent. Those were the days when squadron-based Forward Air Controllers were promised to German-based US Army units. In my mind, it was questionable how we would get to those units on the ground in an emergency, or even whether the squadrons would let us go. The system was drastically changed in future years. Nevertheless, most of us young pilots spent a month on the continent with the Army. I went to Baumholder initially. Great fun, actually. Ten years later I got to do the same thing again for three years, not so voluntarily, with the 82nd Airborne Division![11]

In common with many other squadrons in the NATO Air Arms, the 20th regularly exchanged with other units in Europe and the US. Mike Briggs recalls such a TDY to the *Jagdbombergeschwader* 22 based at Lechfield in Germany:

> I participated in an exchange with the German Air Force and spent 2 weeks flying with the Germans out of Lechfeld AB near Munich. We had a great time. We had one F-100F and took the Germans for rides on some of our missions. They did the same in their 2 seated F-104. That was a real hoot riding in the 104 since it was so much faster than the 100. The German pilots were very friendly and we went in with them at least once to one of the Munich beer halls and had a get-together on base sharing a keg of beer from one of the local monasteries.[12]

Exchanges were also held with the Royal Danish Air Force and others.

The 20th TFW flew the F-100 in the UK for a period of thirteen years. In June 1970, the unit moved to RAF Upper Heyford and began conversion to the General Dynamics F-111. At Heyford, the three squadrons of the wing were united for the first time since their arrival in the England.

The General Dynamics F-111E Aardvark

The first F-111Es arrived at Upper Heyford on 12 September 1970. The F-111Es were similar to the F-111As and were fitted with the Radar Homing and Warning (RHAW) and ECM, which were badly needed in Europe. The all-weather and night capability and the TFR were also crucial to their primary mission which was nuclear delivery. They would also have a secondary conventional role. The last F-100s left Upper Heyford in February 1971 and in November of that year the wing was declared operational on the F-111E.

If the F-111 had one problem, it was the difficulty experienced by the ground crews in maintaining the aircraft to the standard required for the mission.

F-111E 68-025 assigned to the 79th TFS. Shortly after the F-111Es first arrived with the 20th TFW in September 1970, tail codes were introduced for all USAF wings. The 20th adopted UR for the 79th TFS, US for the 55th TFS, and UT for the 77th TFS. These tail codes did not last long, however, being changed to JR, JS, and JT in early 1971. (*Author's collection*)

F-111E 68-021 was assigned to the 77th TFS and wears the tail code assigned to that unit in January 1970. The dark areas on the nose centred on the circle are the antenna covers for the AN/APS-109 RHAW of the aircraft. At this time, they were not painted over. There were more such antennae on the wing root and towards the front edge of the stabilator. (*Author's collection*)

Seen at RAF Upper Heyford armed forces day in August 1972 was F-111E 68-016 belonging to the 55th TFS. (*Author's collection*)

The F-111Es at Upper Heyford experienced problems with maintenance, spares, and conventional weapons from the outset of their deployment to Upper Heyford. The primary reason for this was the dramatic cut in government funding, which became acute in the mid- to late 1970s. In commission of the aircraft rates were below 50 per cent. It was difficult to maintain aircrew proficiencies and the maintenance crews worked overtime canning parts off aircraft to repair others. It was a very unsatisfactory state of affairs.

The nuclear mission was the only one that the wing was capable of sustaining in the early days at Heyford. However, throughout the 1980s, the situation did improve, not least because of the extra money provided for the air force and navy when Ronald Reagan assumed the presidency in 1981. By 1985, for example, 20th TFW was achieving an 85-per cent MC rate and by the early 1990s the wing was winning awards for its high maintenance statistics, achieving an MC rate of 88.8 per cent in 1993.

For the 20th TFW, the 1980s were characterised by a renewed accent on training for conventional war. Aircrew typically flew from twenty-five to thirty-five hours per month—perhaps an average of three flights per week. Missions were planned from scratch. Regular four ship missions were flown. Planning for such missions occupied five hours before the aircraft took off. It was necessary to pick a target which would be attacked from four different directions. These would of necessity have been flexible, the notorious weather in the UK being a constantly influencing factor. Missions took on average two and a half hours. The range of the F-111E was formidable, but if a tanker became available a mission might be extended. When the mission had been completed

F-111E 68-047 of the 79th TFS, 1972. The top of the tail was painted with the squadron colours, in this case yellow. (*Author's collection*)

Languishing on a particularly wet and grey day at Upper Heyford is F-111E 68-031. It was because of the regularity of days like this in the UK that even the all-weather day and night Aardvark had to fly to more sunny climes in order to enable the pilots to accomplish weapons delivery qualifications. (*Author's collection*)

debriefing took anything up to a couple of hours. Hence, with all the other duties required, the average F-111E aircrew day could extend to as much as twelve hours. Ranges used were generally in England and Scotland. The problem was that majority of these ranges were approached over water. This did not make for realistic training for the aircrews of the F-111. In the event of war, the mission of the aircraft would be to fly TFR, low level overland in Europe to targets in East Germany, Poland, and the Baltic States. To overcome this discrepancy in TFR training, the 20th TFW began to regularly deploy to Incirlik in Turkey to practice their low-level mission.

Two events were imminent which were to test the effectiveness of the conventional training: the 20th TFW did not participate directly in the raid on Libya, Operation Eldorado Canyon, but they did play a very significant role in the development and planning of the mission.

In 1985, the 20th TFW was tasked with a very special training mission. The commander of the wing at that time was Col. Thompson. Col. Dale W. Thompson was director of operations with the 20th TFW at Upper Heyford. Col. Thompson was a highly experienced pilot, having flown the North American F-100 Super Sabre and the Republic F-105 Thunderchief prior to the F-111E. As a major, he had first been assigned to the 20th TFW at Upper Heyford in 1973 as executive officer and later, in 1979, as director of operations. Col. Thompson returned to the wing in June 1981 as deputy commander and was appointed commander in February 1984. On the morning of 16

F-111E 68-057 crashed at Mapperton Farm Estate, Almer, Dorset, on 29 April 1980. Both pilot Capt. Jack A. Hines and WSO Capt. Richard J. Franks were killed. The aircraft was one of a pair on a training flight. (*Author's collection*)

October 1985, he received a call to personally meet a plane that would be arriving at 6 a.m.; he takes up the story of Operation Ghost Rider:

> When the team of 5 officers got off their aircraft, they handed me a letter which directed the 20th Tactical Fighter Wing to bomb a simulated runway target at geographical coordinates 52-31.5N, 61-47.3W at 1016 ZULU on 18 October with 10 F-111Es loaded with 8 Mk 82 retarded 500 pound inert bombs, and then return to Upper Heyford. The mission was to be accomplished in the strictest secrecy and the team was there to assist in coordinating outside help as required.
>
> I did not know where those coordinates were, so Bill LaTulipe [Col. Bill LaTulipe, operations officer] and I walked into Base Operations and plotted them on the world-wide map on the wall. To my surprise, the target was in Eastern Canada about 100 miles south west of Goose Bay, Labrador, a remote wilderness area nearly 3,000 miles away. 1016 ZULU was just about sunrise in the target area. After a bit of calculating, Bill and I concluded that it was about a six hour flight one way, and that we had less than 46 hours to plan the mission and to generate the aircrews and aircraft before we had to launch. To my knowledge, no fighter wing had ever been tasked to perform a mission of this magnitude before on a no-notice basis. It sounded like an enormous task, and it was. The 3 of us went back to the Command Post, and I selectively recalled some of the senior battle staff.[13]

It was, indeed, a formidable task and had to be accomplished in two days. Colonel Thompson continued:

> In maintenance we had to identify our best night, TFR, low-level aircraft, get them in top shape, configure them to carry the munitions, get the bombs out of the munitions storage area and loaded on the aircraft, and plan for complete aircraft systems checks before take off.
>
> In operations we had to identify the aircrews, plan the route, arrange for aerial refuelling, accomplish detailed low-level flight planning, build strip maps, develop radar predictions of the target, work up defensive tactics for the simulated enemy defence, develop a minimum communications plan, define pre-take off and post-take off abort procedures, ground and air spare procedures, and build a night taxi plan. To meet out TOT, our aircraft would need to launch several hours before dawn from Upper Heyford.
>
> In the support area we had to refine our base security plan, develop an air traffic control plan for comm-out operations, and arrange for base quarters, meals, and transportation for our aircrews. It was obvious that it was going to be a base-wide effort, ultimately requiring the assistance of virtually every squadron and agency in the wing.[14]

In the event, the planning over the two-day period before the operation went according to schedule and on the morning of 18 Friday October at 4.25 a.m., fourteen F-111Es took off from Upper Heyford, ten mission aircraft and four spares. Seven tankers took off from Mildenhall to conduct the first in-flight refuelling of the Aardvarks. Dale Thompson takes up the story:

The fighter formation was initially in 2 ship elements separated by one minute or about 8 miles in trail. That made the fighter string about 40 miles long. We were using comm. out procedures and in and out of the weather so the rejoin was difficult and complicated. I came very close to terminating the mission during that rejoin, but I finally broke radio silence and told the crews where we were. Finally after about 40 minutes we got all 14 F-111s on their assigned tankers and cycled each one through for a refuelling check of the aircraft systems. Our 10 primary aircraft were all OK at this point, so I sent the four airborne spares home.

Two aerial refuellings were conducted over the ocean on the 6 hour flight to the target, and our F-111s had to change tankers after the first refuelling. We used 17 tankers in all, with 6 meeting us in mid-Atlantic from the U.S. on the way over and 4 coming out of Mildenhall, England, on the way home. Each F-111 required about 70,000 pounds of jet fuel during the mission in four refuellings.

The F-111s made their last refuelling and descended to low-level 150 miles east of their first land check point at Bell Island, Newfoundland, where they went into a low-level timing orbit. Each aircraft left the orbit point separated by 1 minute from the aircraft ahead and flew their night, low-level route as a single ship. The route was flown at 400 feet above the ground and 480 knots on their automatic TFR systems. Total communications-out procedures were followed all the way to the target which was about 350 miles from the coast in point. The terrain in the target area was mountainous, covered by dense forests, and had many lakes and rivers throughout the area a low level radar navigation nightmare. The target was a simulated runway outlined by 5 pairs of radar reflectors 250 feet apart and spaced at 2,000 foot intervals. Each aircraft had a distinct aiming point, as we were trying to simulate cutting the runway into segments of less than 2,000 feet. A special support team had erected the reflectors on the day before the flight, and had to rebuild 2 of them that were torn down by brown bears that night. The team remained on site and observed each aircraft's bombing run, checked our timing, and scored each bomb that dropped. They videotaped each aircraft's bomb run, but unfortunately it was too dark to get good video pictures.

Colonel Bill LaTulipe was first across the target. He was within five seconds of his scheduled TOT. As I recall, all eight of his bombs impacted with the simulated runway area for a perfect score. The following crews were all close to being on time the worst was about 15 seconds late after a six hour flight. Timing was critical because the bomb runs were 1 minute apart and fragmentation patterns from previously dropped bombs last about 35 seconds. Even though our bombs were inert, we treated them as actual weapons. Of the 80 bombs dropped, over 50% impacted the simulated runway for a pretty good record. It was still nearly dark at TOT and the bombing runs were made on radar only. A couple of the 500 pound bomb retarding devices failed and those bombs went long of the target. One aircraft could only get one bomb off on the first pass because of a release malfunction, so he had to make a couple of jettison passes in the area since our aircraft didn't have the fuel to make it back to the United Kingdom with bombs on board the aircraft. In the final analysis, however, the control team determined that we had cut the runway at each designated point. The first nine aircraft got joined back up with our tankers on schedule, but I had to turn the entire string around and go back to pick up the last aircraft with the release problem. He was pretty low on gas when he got joined up, and I'm certain you can appreciate the pilots voice when he reported, 'I'm taking on fuel.'[15]

The F-111Es returned to Upper Heyford without mishap, the first touching down at approximately 4 p.m. The mission was deemed a success. It had taken a great deal of hard work under considerable pressure to plan and execute. Many lessons were learnt which would later prove of inestimable value in undertaking similar missions. Indeed, it was later revealed that 'Ghostrider', as the operation was named, was a dress rehearsal for the raid on Libya which took place in April 1986.

Although much of the training for both the nuclear and conventional missions was carried out in the UK, the 20th TFW deployed regularly to Europe, North Africa, and the Middle East, on exchange visits and for weapons training. The 20th TFW deployed a detachment of F-111Es to Karachi in Pakistan in 1976 for Exercise Midlink 76. This was a CENTO air defence and anti-shipping exercise. Prior to this, a detachment from the 20th had deployed to Shiraz in Iran for another CENTO exercise. Closer to home the Aardvarks took part in a variety of exercises. 'Display Determination' was an annual NATO southern region exercise which was designed to develop and rehearse the tactics that would be used to support and reinforce the countries of NATO in the event that they were threatened by Soviet naval activities in the Mediterranean and eastern Atlantic.

In 1990, some F-111Es were returned to the US for the Aircraft Modernisation Programme (AMP). This involved an upgrade to the avionics, self-protection and navigation, and weapons delivery systems. The first of these aircraft to return to the wing was 68-0050 in February 1991, just in time to deploy to Incirlik where its new systems were tested in the combat environment.

On 27 March 1987, this F-111E, 68-074, was dropping its load of fill over a range in the UK. Various ranges in the UK were regularly used by the 20th TFW. (*USAF Archives*)

Although not directly involved in the raid on Libya, the 20th TFW did provide back-up to the attacking force from the 48th TFW at RAF Lakenheath. They took off on 14 April as an airborne reserve in the event that there were problems with the F-111Fs of the 48th.

In August 1990, the 79th TFS, 20th TFW, deployed to Incirlik, Turkey, for weapons training. This was a routine deployment which coincided with the Iraqi invasion of Kuwait which began on 1 August. Operation Desert Shield commenced on 7 August. The 20th TFW reinforced its force at Incirlik with four aircraft from the 55th TFS. The F-111Es came under the overall command of the newly activated 7440 Wing (Provisional). The 20th also deployed four EF-111A aircraft to Ta'if in Saudi Arabia. Operation Desert Storm commenced in January 1991, the intention being to drive the Iraqis out of Kuwait.

From January 1991, the 20th TFW F-111Es flew combat missions over Iraq and Kuwait. Strikes were launched from both Incirlik and Ta'if. On the night of 17 January, using their TFR, the F-111s proceeded to target four radar sites in Northern Iraq. The targets were located and destroyed. The AAA and SAM missiles were often a force to be reckoned with. Crews who flew the first few nights said that the illumination from the AAA was so bright that they did not need the TFR to avoid the ground. On one particular mission, a four-ship formation hit a target and their return flight took them over Iraq's nuclear research facility at Tuwaitha near Baghdad. Here the AAA was very heavy. The tactic which the F-111E pilots developed to alleviate the danger was to fly very low through the blind spot between the guns, which could not depress too low without risking shooting at one another. Although they were formidable in the early days of the conflict, they were eventually dealt with.

Throughout the conflict until the cease fire on 28 February, the twenty-three F-111Es flew a total of 456 day and night missions from Turkey and had dropped a total of 4714 tons of ordnance. Missions were initially flown at very low level, but after the SAM sites had been suppressed, the Aardvarks dropped their ordnance from 20,000 feet, out of the reach of the AAA. Targets in Northern Iraq included petrol oil and lubricant refineries and storage facilities, biological and chemical sites, power plants, using CBU-87 combined effects munitions cluster bombs, CBU-89 'Gator' cluster bombs, containing anti-personnel and anti-tank mines, and 2,000-lb 'dumb' bombs.

The F-111Es remained in the Middle East until their return to RAF Upper Heyford on 28 February 1991. The 20th TFW was redesignated a fighter wing (FW) in 1991. The F-111Es remained in the UK until December 1993 when the wing moved to Shaw EFB in Carolina and converted to the General Dynamics F-16.

5

The 42nd Electronic Combat Squadron

The 42nd ECS had for a long time been associated with Europe, first arriving with USAFE as the 42nd TRS in March 1954 when it also had the distinction of being the first squadron in the command to have an electronic warfare role. At that time, the unit flew specially modified Douglas RB-26 Invaders in what was then a very clandestine role. Its mission was 'to provide ground air and naval forces in areas of joint air-ground operations with information concerning the location and character of electronic emissions; and instrumented weather reconnaissance'.

In mid-1956, the squadron received its first Douglas RB-66Cs to perform its mission which very often took them very close to the borders of the Warsaw Pact countries. Following the dismissal of all nuclear forces from France in July 1959, the 42nd TRS moved to the UK, having been displaced at Spangdahlem by the nuclear capable F-100s of the 49th TFW which had been in France at Étain-Rouvres. The 42nd moved in to RAF Chelveston where they remained until July 1965 when the squadron moved to the 25th TRW at Chambley in France where it remained until it was deactivated, and its aircraft, now designated EB-66B, returned to the US.

Reactivated at Takhli Royal Thai Air Base in 1968 as the 42nd TEWS in September, the squadron served with distinction in SE Asia until its deactivation in March 1974 at Korat RTAFB.

The 42nd ECS was reactivated at RAF Upper Heyford in 1983 flying the EF-111A. In June 1985, control passed to the newly activated 66th ECW based at Sembach, Germany. The 66th ECW was a component of the 65th Air Division which was responsible for all USAFE's electronic combat assets.

The EF-111A Raven

Since the departure of the Douglas EB-66 Destroyer from the European theatre of operations in 1972, the USAF and NATO had had no electronic warfare (EW) assets on the continent. In fact, since May, 1966, when the 42nd TRS left Chambley, France, with its EB-66Bs, the provision of dedicated ECM capability had been spasmodic to say the

least. In June 1969, the 39th TEWS had been activated at Spangdahlem, Germany, with Douglas EB-66E Destroyers, but the demands from Vietnam for aircraft equipment and personnel impacted heavily on the resources of the squadron; in January 1973, the unit was returned to Shaw AFB, South Carolina, in the US.

It was with some relief and a great deal of enthusiasm that on 3 February 1984 the personnel of the 20th TFW at RAF Upper Heyford, Oxfordshire, in the UK, greeted Lt-Col. Dave Wesley when he flew General Dynamics/Grumman EF-111A 66-037 into the base. The aircraft was the first to be delivered to the newly activated 42nd ECS, assigned to the 20th TFW.

The EF-111A was popular with its pilots. Capt. Robert Zaehringer came to the EF-111 after flying the Fairchild Republic A-10A with the 81st TFW based at RAF Bentwaters:

> I went from simple, slow and manoeuvrable to fast high tech. I thought the EF-111 was a great aeroplane. It went straight and fast really well. It was a really heavy aeroplane; 88,000lb fully loaded, 34,000lb of which was fuel. It took a long take off roll; but when flying low level in Europe it was like driving a Cadillac or a Rolls Royce. It was a luxury ride. There's no doubt about it.[1]

The primary mission of the EF-111A was to protect friendly aircraft which were engaging the enemy by locating and jamming the enemy's radars and providing effective countermeasures against them. The means by which this was accomplished were varied. Maj. Jim Howard was an EWO with the 42nd ECS:

Above and below: On 3 February 1984, Lt-Col. Dave Wesley flew General Dynamics/Grumman EF-111A 66-037 into the base. The aircraft was the first to be delivered to the newly activated 42nd Electronic Combat Squadron (ECS), assigned to the 20th TFW. (*USAF via Art Sevigny, 20th TFW Historian*)

> We did three basic kinds of jamming missions in NATO. In Escort Jamming missions we were in, or slightly ahead of, a fighter formation. We ingressed very low, and then popped up to line of sight with the threat radars, usually two or three thousand feet, and jammed just long enough for the bombers to deliver their ordnance on their targets. Very often we'd have F-4Gs [McDonnell Douglas F-4G Phantom] ingress the general area at the same time to help light up the radars and give them something to think about other than killing me!
>
> A Close In Jamming mission was flown in an orbit located about 12-20NM from the FEBA. These were flown around 3000 to 5000 feet, just high enough to jam the radars of the enemy front lines and still keep us just outside of the SAM envelopes. In the event of hostilities breaking out in Europe NATO's war plan was for a string of close-in jamming mission orbits parallel to the FEBA to support attacking aircraft, both incoming and outgoing.
>
> Stand-off Jamming missions were flown in fairly high orbits, by F-111 standards, at around 15000 feet, located well back from the FEBA. The theory was that we were protecting high altitude platforms like tankers, AWACS, and intel collectors. I hated these, I don't think we did much good high and far back. A problem I ran into all the time as an instructor EWO and on my follow on assignment to the HQ Air Combat Command EW staff was that people just did not understand the inverse square law, that is, that received jamming power of a target radar drops off proportional to the square of the distance from the receiver. I always thought that close counts in jamming.[2]

The roles of the pilot and EWO in the EF-111A were quite independent. It was not considered necessary for the pilots to be knowledgeable about the specifics of the EWO's role and equipment. The EWO, on the other hand, was expected to know about the aircraft and its systems. Capt. Robert S. Held was a pilot with the 42nd ECS:

> The roles were independent because on any mission that we were flying, the EWO had specific objectives that he had to accomplish. I was expected to fly the mission and get the EWO to where he was supposed to be. I was only minimally involved in what they were doing on the other side [in the right-hand seat].[3]

Both pilot and EWO were involved in the mission planning conferences. Often these would take place at RAF Lakenheath or RAF Mildenhall. They would involve all aircrew who were to be involved in the mission. At this conference, the aircrews involved would come up with a package as to the general roles of all the participants. The EWOs part in the planning process included navigation to the target area and, most importantly, the programming of the AN/ALQ-99E. Jim Howard stated:

> The AN/ALQ-99E had ten transmitters of between 1000 and 3000 watts. The ALQ-99E jammer was programmed by the EWO, either by a very long and time consuming key entry system using the cockpit keypad (located where the right control stick as on other F-111s) or by a flight planning device which could save the program to a data tape. The EWO could program the system to look for specific threats based on received radar characteristics and position from the Raven, or it could be set to pre-emptively jam targets, received or not.

> There was a program for each transmitter. One aspect of the EF-111A/ALQ-99E system that isn't well known was the Raven had steerable horn antennas for all frequencies above the VHF band. This feature is why we could fly parallel to the FEBA and still deliver high power jamming to threat radars. The ALQ-99E would steer the antennas automatically based on how the EWO programmed the system, or the EWO could manually steer them. Most of our antennas have beam widths around 30 to 45 degrees.[4]

The inclusion of the NATO star in the official unit insignia of the 42nd ECS is symbolic of its commitment to the alliance. To that end, the unit exercised all over Europe and with all the NATO countries. Regular courses and briefings about electronic warfare were held by the alliance at HMS Dryad at Portsmouth, Hampshire. Newly arrived 42nd ECS EWOs attended two-week courses at Dryad as part of their acclimatisation.

Regular deployments took place to other NATO bases for exercises. One such was to Incirlik, Turkey. Their primary mission on these deployments was to support US Navy and Turkish fighters operating over a range in the centre of the country. Regular deployments were made to other countries in the Mediterranean area in support of exercises involving countries on NATOs southern flank. This included Turkey and also involved Portugal, Spain, Italy, and Greece. Exercise Display Determination was an annual NATO exercise which took place in the Mediterranean and was designed to develop and rehearse the tactics that would be used to support and reinforce the

The General Dynamics/Grumman EF-111A Raven was developed from the General Dynamics F-111A. The large pod carried on the top of the vertical stabiliser of the aircraft housed the receivers for the AN/ALQ-99E Tactical Jamming System (TJS), seen here being wired at Grumman's Riverhead plant in New York, USA. (*USAF*)

countries of NATO in the event that they were threatened. The 42nd ECS Ravens were involved in these exercises, basing at Moron in Spain and Aviano in Italy in addition to Incirlik. Open Gate was yet another exercise which focussed on NATO's southern area. This exercise was designed to simulate air and sea power tactics required to keep the Straits of Gibraltar open during a crisis. It took place in the area of Gibraltar, the Moroccan and Spanish Coasts, and the Spanish island of Alboran. This exercise was also an occasion for photo opportunities of Ravens over the straits of Gibraltar!

It was, however, in Northern Europe that the EF-111s were mostly deployed on regular exercises. Every country in NATO at that time worked with and was supported by the 42nd ECS Ravens. Jim Howard noted:

> We played in pretty every major NATO exercise held while I was in the UK. In fact, we supported other NATO countries much more often than we supported the F-111E's at Heyford and the F-111F's at Lakenheath, because those guys really didn't want jamming support in many cases, relying instead on just being very low and very fast. I flew in support of the French Air Force and the RAF out of home station several times. We supported the Dutch, German, and Norwegian Air Forces. I recall deploying to a base in Belgium for an NATO exercise, where we stayed in a Holiday Camp near the base. I remember one mission where we had a Belgium F-16 in our formation as an escort. That was pretty cool, but really, tactically, not the best use of an F-16, since if he tried to keep up with us he'd bingo out [run out of fuel] pretty quickly.[5]

Regular missions were flown over the UK and many of these were at low level. Jim Howard noted: 'Air Traffic Control was different in the UK. I was astounded at the freedom we had to plan low level flights all over the United Kingdom from the Scapa Flow down to the tip of Lands End. We could fly almost anywhere and it made flying in the UK ever so much fun'.

Scotland was an environment which was particularly favoured by the aircrews of the 42nd. In March 1986, Jim Howard and Bob Zaehringer flew their check ride up to Scotland. But things did not quite go as planned. Jim Howard stated:

> We planned a pretty simple low level mission. We were flying up to RAF Macrahanish in Kintyre, which had a radar station we were going to jam. As we climbed up into our medium altitude jamming orbit, one of our generators went out. The EF-111 differed from the regular F-111 in that we had the 90kVA [Kilovolt Amperes] generators as opposed to the 60 kVA generators of the standard F-111 because we needed so much more power. Nonetheless when you threw those jammers on it could blow a generator, and in this case it did. We had to get one jamming orbit in to complete the check ride. If we had aborted the mission right there and then we would have to do the whole check ride again, and the preparation took a week! We flew the jamming pattern and completed our check ride. We had to return to Heyford at medium altitude because we had a lost generator.
>
> We got to be good friends with RAF radar stations, especially the ones off the west coast of Scotland as these were our favourite jamming targets. They would always ask us for a

Above and below: EF-111As of the 42nd ECS were based at Aviano air Base in Italy for the duration of Exercise Display Determination, which was an annual NATO exercise that took place in the Mediterranean and was designed to develop and rehearse the tactics that would be used to support and reinforce the southern countries of NATO in the event that they were threatened by Soviet navy activities in the region. (*USAF*)

> 'bubble check' ostensibly to check the state of their radar dome, but really to overfly them fast and low so we could add a little excitement to their day.
>
> I went up to Spadeadam range where the RAF had some pretty good equipment similar to that which the bad guys had. We got four F-111s to attack the base. One EF-111 at a time would try to defend the wave of bombers. I would judge who the best EWOs were.
>
> I flew down Loch Ness every chance I got and on one occasion I flew up to Scapa Flow to see if I could see any of the scuttled ships that were up there.[6]

The forces of the Warsaw Pact, in common with their opponents in NATO, were constantly upgrading their electronic warfare assets, including their acquisition radars and SAM engagement and fire control radars. The responsibility for acquiring the information on Warsaw Pact systems lay primarily with the RC-135s of Strategic Air Command's 55th Strategic Reconnaissance Wing. Information thus gained was handed down to the EW squadrons through the squadron intelligence officers.

When the 42nd ECS was attached to the 66th ECW at Sembach in 1985, Jim Howard was appointed wing EWO and had to divide his time between Heyford and Sembach. He recalls a particular occasion when, in addition to making a routine flight to 66th ECW headquarters, he also identified a newly activated radar in East Germany:

> The mission was to fly to Germany where the USAF had some threat radar simulators that had good signal analysers that could provide jammer waveform data. They sent this data to me as Wing EWO. I would take these plots to the Jammer maintenance shop where I'd work with the maintainers to tweak the ALQ-99 jammers if they were out of spec.
>
> I remember flying parallel to the east-west buffer zone, where I noticed an unfamiliar radar on the other side.
>
> We had not been tasked to fly this near buffer zone flight, we just did it because we had the gas and time. I wrote down the parameters: scan rate, pulse repetition frequency etc. When I got back [to Upper Heyford] I reviewed our intel data and determined that I had seen a new Soviet radar that we knew about, but as far as we knew back then had not yet been operationally deployed. I was able to tell our Intel that this radar was in fact operating just on the other side of the inter-German border.[7]

The EF-111As of the 42nd were involved in combat in two different theatres of combat while based at Upper Heyford. In Operation Eldorado Canyon in April 1986, the aircraft provided EW support to the attacking force of F-111Fs from the 48th TFW based at RAF Lakenheath. The Ravens worked in harmony with the US Navy's Grumman EA-6B Prowlers from the Sixth Fleet. Their job was to jam Libyan radar systems. Twenty-four F-111Fs and six EF-111As took off in the late afternoon of 14 April accompanied by a tanker force of McDonnell Douglas KC-10A Extenders and Boeing KC-135 Stratotankers. France denied overflight rights so a large tanker force was required. After the first refuelling, six F-111F air spares and one EF-111A returned to their bases. The air armada was due to strike Libyan targets at around 2 a.m. on 15 April. Ten minutes beforehand, the EF-111As and EA-6Bs began jamming

F-111E aircraft of the 79th, 77th, and 55th Tactical Fighter Squadrons, 20th Tactical Fighter Wing, fly in formation with a 42nd ECS EF-111A Raven aircraft over snow-covered mountains in northern Scotland in March 1987. (*USAF*)

Maj. Jim Howard stands in front of EF-111A 66-034 *Let em eat Crow* at Upper Heyford. (*Jim Howard*)

Libyan air defence radars and communications. It was not until the ground attack aircraft egressed the area that the Ravens left their jamming orbits and returned to their tankers.

During Desert Storm, between January and February 1991, the 42nd ECS flew missions from Incirlik in Turkey and Ta'if in Saudi Arabia. The aircraft at Incirlik had been on deployment since the commencement of the conflict in August 1990 and remained there until the onset of Desert Storm with six aircraft taking part in operations. The four EF-111s at Ta'if had deployed there from Heyford on 2 December 1990.

The Ravens provided jamming support for a wide range of coalition aircraft in Desert Storm. For example, on the first day of the campaign, 17 January, three aircraft supported Lockheed F-117A Nighthawks when they attacked targets in Baghdad. The same day one of the Ravens was credited with the first aerial kill of the campaign by causing a pursuing Mirage F-1 to crash into the desert. The EF-111A had been one of two supporting twenty-two F-15 Strike Eagles conducting a raid on an Iraqi airfield when it was attacked by the Mirage. Evading a missile by deploying chaff and flares, the

On 27 March 1987, a Utah Air National Guard KC-135 Stratotanker aircraft refuels a 79th Tactical Fighter Squadron F-111E aircraft. A 77th Tactical Fighter Squadron F-111E and a 42nd ECS Raven await their turn while in flight over the English Channel. (*USAF*)

Raven then descended rapidly to low level and the enemy fighter flew into the ground while trying to follow.

During the campaign, the 42nd EF-111As flew 471 combat missions, totalling 1,859 hours. One aircraft was lost when 66-0023 crashed into the desert just over the border in Saudi Arabia. The precise reason for this accident in unknown. On 25 January, the 42nd ECS was reassigned to the 20th TFW.

The Ravens stayed at Incirlik after the end of Desert Storm as part of Operation Provide Comfort to assist with the protection and give assurance to the Kurds of Northern Iraq from persecution by the force of Saddam Hussein. They returned to the UK in March 1992. On 10 July 1992, the squadron was deactivated and the Ravens were returned to 429th ECS at Cannon AFB, New Mexico. Finally, in May 1998, the aircraft were retired from the USAF inventory, replaced in the electronic combat role by the Grumman EA-6B Prowler in co-operative venture with the US Navy and the US Marine Corps.

6

The 420th Air Refuelling Squadron

The 420th Night Fighter Operational Training Group was activated on 1 June 1943 at Orlando Army Air Base in Florida. Equipped with the P-61 Black Widow the group moved, in January 1944, to Hammer Field, California, under the control of 4th Fighter Command, 4th Air Force. The unit was deactivated in March 1944.

The 420th was reactivated as an Air Refuelling Squadron at Alexandria AFB, Louisiana, in March 1954 and equipped with Boeing KB-29P tanker. It was the first tanker unit to come under the control of Tactical Air Command. The tactical air forces had begun to acquire surplus SAC KB-29s in the latter months of the Korean War when it became evident that tactical fighter and reconnaissance aircraft were being obliged to operate over greater distances. During deployments of units from the USA to Europe during the late 1940s and early 1950s, it had been necessary to stop to refuel en route several times. The deployments via the northern Fox Able route, for example, refuelled at Goose Bay, Labrador, Bluie West One in Greenland, Keflavik in Iceland, and Prestwick in Scotland before proceeding to their European bases.

In 1955, the 420th was detached to RAF Sculthorpe in the UK.

The KB-29P

Upon deployment to UK in October 1955, the 420th AREFS came under the direct command of USAFE.

Tactical Air Command's acquisition of a nuclear mission at the beginning of the 1950s increased the urgency to become IFR (in-flight refuelling) capable. The first nuclear capable tactical units in Europe were the 47th BW and the 20th FBW. Both units deployed to the UK in early 1952 under the control of the newly established 49th AD. The primary wartime mission of the 420th AREFS was to support the units of the 49th AD RB-45s and F-84Gs over the European continent prior to their penetration into Warsaw Pact countries to deliver their 'special weapons'. When the 49th AD was deactivated in July 1956, this mission was extended to embrace all USAFE tactical units; and was retained by the squadron throughout its deployment to the UK.

When the 420th AREFS arrived in the UK in October 1955, it was equipped with Boeing KB-29P tankers. In 1950, Boeing had begun the conversion of a number of surplus Boeing B-29 bombers to tanker configuration following a request from SAC which was in need of refuelling support for its large long range bombers. The KB-29 used the Boeing 'Flying Boom' system of aerial refuelling.

The KB-29P was primarily used by SAC to service its bomber aircraft and was not really suitable for refuelling the upcoming generation of high-speed jets, which would often have to reduce to almost stalling speed in order to refuel, even on those occasions when the KB-29 would be flying a shallow dive in order to gain an appropriate speed. The 420th AREFS adequately serviced the RB-45s, F-84Gs, and F-84Fs of USAFE with the KB-29P, but with the advent of the century series jets to the European theatre it became evident that this aircraft would have to be complemented, and eventually replaced by a tanker with a greater speed and the ability to refuel more than one aircraft at a time. Enter the Boeing KB-50.

Sadly just before the advent of the KB-50s into the inventory of the 420th, tragedy struck the squadron. On the morning of Saturday 2 February 1957, two KB-29P aircraft, 44-83906 and 44-69846, took off from RAF Sculthorpe to rendezvous with a flight of fighters over western France. The fighters were to be refuelled before flying down to Nouasseur AB in Morocco for bombing and gunnery training. While passing

Boeing KB-29P 44-086349 of the 420th Air Refuelling Squadron (AREFS) in the company of three Republic F-84F Thunderstreaks of the 81st Fighter Bomber Wing (FBW). (*USAF*)

KB-29Ps of the 420th AREFS at RAF Sculthorpe. The KB-29 used the flying boom system of aerial refuelling developed by Boeing. This enabled the aircraft to refuel one aircraft at a time. (*Courtesy of the Tac Tankers Association*)

This Boeing KB-29P was present at an open house at RAF Burtonwood on 19 May 1956. (*R. A. Scholefield*)

Three F-84Fs of the 78th FBS, 81st FBW, formate with a KB-29D, 44-84007, of the 420th AREFS at low level over the English countryside. (*USAF*)

over the north of France at approximately 16,000 feet, the two aircraft collided and both plummeted to the ground in a field near Morigny, just south of Saint-Lô in Normandy. The exact cause of the collision and subsequent crash was not determined. Tragically, all ten of the crewmembers aboard 44-83906 perished. On board 44-69846, five crewmembers survived while four others were killed.

The KB-50D/J

When the B-50D was retired from its atomic bombing role in SAC, many were converted to tanker configuration using the probe and drogue system of aerial refuelling. The first KB-50D tankers arrived with the 420th AREFS in January 1957 and the first KB-50Js in November of that year.

The squadron retained some KB-29Ps to service the B-45 Tornados, which were replaced by the Douglas B-66 Destroyer in the spring of 1958. In 1955, the 20th FBW had replaced its F-84Gs with the F-84F, and the 81st FBW replaced its F-86 Sabres with the F-84F, when this unit acquired a nuclear delivery mission. The F-84F also used the ‘flying boom ‘ method of in-flight refuelling.

In the European theatre of operations in the mid-1950s, there was a significant upgrading of the aircraft and capabilities of the tactical forces of USAFE. The F-84F

The KB-50 commenced operations with the 420th in 1957. KB-50J 47-0170 was displayed at the open house at RAF Alconbury on 16 May 1959. This aircraft has the three hoses unreeled. The KB-50 used the probe and drogue system of in-flight refuelling, which enabled three aircraft to be refuelled simultaneously. (*Robert Robinson collection*)

Thunderstreaks of the 20th FBW were exchanged for North American F-100D/F Super Sabres in 1957. At this time, all tactical fighter units were renamed tactical fighter wings. McDonnell F-101A/C Voodoos replaced the F-84Fs of the 81st TFW in 1958. In that year, the B-66 Destroyers arrived to replace the B-45 Tornados at RAF Sculthorpe. At the same time, USAFE assets on continental Europe also converted to the new generation of fighters: the F-100C for the 36th TFW and F-100D/Fs for the 48th, 49th, and 50th TFWs; RF-101 Voodoos for the 66th TRW; and RB-66 Destroyers for the 10th TRW. In 1961 and 1962 respectively, the 49th TFW and the 36th TFW converted from the F-100 to the Republic F-105D/F Thunderchief. All these aircraft were equipped for probe and drogue refuelling. The Voodoo and the Thunderchief were equipped with both a probe for the drogue and a receptacle for the boom.

It was the responsibility of the 420th AREFS to service all these units and their aircraft with their KB-50 tankers. It was a formidable task. All USAFE tactical fighter units deployed to 'sun bases' for fair weather weapons training during the 1950s and early 1960s, and the 420th AREFS was required to support every one of the deployments in addition to maintaining its regular routine and training missions. The 420th also had a mission to support all tactical aircraft movements from the US to Europe and *vice versa*. With the advent of air refuelling the chosen route for deployments to Europe was directly from the USA to the Azores and on to the European mainland. On this route, there were three principal air refuelling areas: north of Bermuda, the Azores, and southern France. The 420th AREFS was responsible for the Azores, southern France, and the Mediterranean area, including North Africa.

This KB-50J is refuelling three USAFE aircraft simultaneously: a North American F-100D Super Sabre, a McDonnell F-101 Voodoo, and a Douglas RB-66B at the open day at Prestwick on 28 May 1960. (*Gordon Macadie*)

KB-50D 49-0831 was at the open house at RAF Biggin Hill on 14 September 1957. The 'Dumbo' badge of the 420th AREFS is worn on the front port side of the fuselage on this aircraft. (*Courtesy of the Tac Tankers Association*)

The mission of the 420th AREFS was supplemented by the SAC KC-97 Stratotanker units temporarily attached to USAFE. The Stratotankers were equipped with the flying boom which had a probe extension that enabled the F-100s of the USAF units to refuel satisfactorily, although only one at a time.

The crews of the tankers of the 420th AREFS were highly experienced and dedicated professionals. Walt Larimer flew as a navigator with the squadron from 1957 to 1959; he recalls:

> Most of the aircraft commanders in the 420th were older men and were extremely proficient in both leadership and flying skills. Most had SAC KC-97 [Boeing KC-97 Stratotanker] backgrounds and thousands of hours in the SAC bomber air refuelling business. They knew and sincerely appreciated the importance of crew integrity and individual crewmember professionalism.[1]

Praise indeed. However, many of the pilots of the new high-performance jets had to work hard to obtain proficiency in aerial refuelling using the 'triple nipples' of the 420th's KB-50s.

Much of the squadron's flying time was spent in training sorties with the purpose of giving the pilots of the F-100s and F-101s as much practice as possible. Walt Larimer noted:

> From a KB-50 standpoint we had all kinds of refuelling incidents with inexperienced and junior fighter jocks learning to refuel, such as our refuelling hoses being completely ripped off the aircraft reel; couplings breaking at initial engagement; the drogue hitting the receiver's canopy, cracking it and depressurising the receiver's cockpit; the sudden movement of the receiver's aircraft breaking off the probe and the probe getting stuck in the refuelling hose coupling; erratic movements of the receiver in relation to the tanker, making the hose wrap completely around the receiver's wing or getting tangled in his dive breaks; and hoses dropping off tankers refuelling reel and dropping all the way to the ground, all 50 feet of heavy black hose.
>
> During one refuelling incident over England, the hose was ripped off the KB-50 by one of the Woodbridge-based F-100s and the hose fell to the ground from about 16,000 feet of altitude. The hose fell into the playground of a British school during recess and miraculously missed hitting a single British child. All of the school children in that school were invited soon thereafter for a tour of RAF Sculthorpe, crawling through all of its aircraft, and they were given a wonderful lunch at the Officers Club. On another similar mishap, the hose fell into a British forest and was never found, at least during the years I was assigned to the 420th.[2]

These 'teething troubles' were gradually overcome as the pilots of the receiving aircraft became more proficient at in-flight refuelling and it became part of their everyday routine.

The 420th AREFS regularly deployed to Wheelus, Nouasseur, and Moron in support of the tactical units detached there. The extremely good weather conditions prevailing around these bases enabled not only weapons proficiency training, but, also, training and practice in aerial refuelling.

When Morocco gained its independence from France in 1956, the US was asked to remove its military bases from the country. The request was delivered with greater urgency after the US intervention in Lebanon in 1958 and withdrawal from Nouasseur and the other Moroccan facilities began in 1959 and was completed by 1963. Fortunately, Moron in Spain became available to the USAF in 1958 when it was designated as a Reflex base for B-47 Stratojets of SAC. Units of USAFE used the base and the Bárdenas Reales gunnery range. In 1966, USAFE assumed control of the base from SAC. Wheelus remained in use by the USAF until 1970 when events in Libya and the rise of Muammar Gaddafi rendered continued use of the base untenable.

There were some exceptional missions that were flown while on detachment to North Africa. In February 1960, in the aftermath of the Agadir earthquake in Morocco, McDonnell RF-101 Voodoos of the 18th TRS based at Laon, France, were detached to Nouasseur, Morocco, to photograph the devastation. A KB-50 of the 420th AFRES refuelled the Voodoos. A little later that year, two KB-50Js of the 420th supported four RF-101s when they deployed to Wheelus to search the Sahara for the remains of the crew of the ill-fated Consolidated B-24 Liberator *Lady B Good* which had gone missing over the desert whilst returning to its base at Soluch near Benghazi, Libya, on 4 April 1943.

The wreckage of the B-24 had been found in November 1959 and a subsequent search of the wreckage revealed no human remains and no parachutes. The Voodoos were detached to Wheelus on 6 April 1960 and flew regular photo recce missions to 'map' the desert area around the wreck to aid the search for the remains of the missing airmen. The mission was completed on 20 April 1960.

During 1958, the USAF was involved in what has become known as the Lebanon Crisis, when the USAF, US Army, and US Navy units were deployed to the Western Mediterranean to support the government of Lebanon against a potential revolution. USAF aircraft were based at Incirlik in Turkey during the crisis and for a period after. During the aftermath of the crisis and into the 1960s, the 420th made regular detachments to the Turkish base to support the deployments of USAFE fighter units.

From the heat of the Middle East to the icy wastes of the Arctic, the 420th AFRES had a wide variety of missions to perform. One of these was to support a flight of two F-100F Super Sabre fighters making a nonstop flight from RAF Wethersfield in the UK to Eielson Air Base in Alaska. Codenamed Julius Caesar, the purpose of the flights was to ascertain the feasibility of transiting fighter aircraft directly over the Arctic Circle from Asia to Europe. If such a route were to prove practical, then the deployment of fighter units between the two theatres of operations would be considerably faster.

The F-100 flight was led by Air Force Reserve Brig.-Gen. Charles F. Blair. In his account of the operation in *Flying Magazine* of January 1960, he recalls the rendezvous with the KB-50Js of the 420th:

> There will be tankers from England astride the Arctic Circle to the north of Keflavik. They call themselves 'Amiable'. Soon after passing Keflavik we ease slowly down toward the

The KB-50Js of the 420th AREFS were regular participants in the USAF open houses during the late 1950s and the early 1960s. They were also seen annually at the air shows at Prestwick. Aircraft 48-0084 was present at the Scottish airfield in May 1960. (*George Macadie*)

This close-up of KB-50J 48-0084 at Prestwick in May 1960 shows the General Electric J47 turbojet, fitted to improve performance. (*Neil Aird*)

refuelling altitude, closing fast on our tanker friends. Their radar man vectors us in from astern and we soon catch sight of them. Those old airplanes may be hybrids but they look mighty good from where we sit. As the fuel gauges drop lower our affection for them increases.

While fattening up we track due north which will be our route for the next few hours. The north coast of Iceland at the Arctic circle passes underneath, its tan treeless cliffs rearing out of the waters of Denmark Strait. After filling our tanks we back off the hose and fly formation with the tankers for a few minutes. Its a couple of hundred miles from Denmark Strait to Greenland. We'll stick with our big brethren for part of the distance and then top off our tanks. The extra gallons will allow a safe fuel reserve to return across Greenland to Thule [Air Base] if the next tanker rendezvous north of Greenland should misfire.

There are scattered to broken cloud layers lying about but the visibility is good, so much so that the rugged mountains of Greenland come into view while still 100 miles distant. We go back on the hose taking a last gulp of fuel before taking leave of our amiable friends.[3]

On 8 November 1961, the 420th was assigned to the 47th BW.

In December 1962, the 420th received some very unusual and surprising tasking. In 1960, the Belgian government conceded independence to their African territories in the Congo. However, the path to self-governance was to prove traumatic and when the province of Katanga decided to secede from the newly established government, civil war broke out and the UN became involved when its armed forces were deployed to the country to end hostilities and establish a ceasefire. As part of this concerted effort on the part of the UN, the 420th AFRES was ordered to deploy one KB-50J to the region. The KB-50s and their crews would detach to the Congo each for a period of three weeks.

In December 1962, the 420th AREFS was ordered to deploy one KB-50J to the Congo to support the UN air forces detached to the country. Each KB-50 and crew would detach to the Congo for a period of three weeks. (*Sten Johnson via Leif Hellstrom*)

Dan Weber was the aircraft commander of the third aircraft to deploy:

> On the 29th December 1962, the 420th AREFS was alerted to deploy a KB-50 to Leopoldville, now Kinshasha, for the purpose of hauling 115/145 fuel to Elizabethville, now Lubumbashi, in southern Congo and JP-4 fuel to Kamina Air Base north of Elizabethville. Crews would offload the fuel on the ground into huge bladder or pillow tanks.
>
> On St Valentines Day, 1963, we launched out of Sculthorpe with our first stop at Wheelus AB in Libya. Because we carried a UN call sign we were not allowed to fly over France or Spain because the operation was not in keeping with the politics of those two countries. Therefore, we were forced to take a long way round by departing England via Lands End, across the Bay of Biscay, south over water along the Iberian peninsular, then a left turn at Gibraltar and up the Med to Wheelus.[4]

After a night stop at Wheelus the KB-50J flew to Kano in Nigeria and then to N'djili in the Congo. The route from Kano to N'djili was over the Atlantic Ocean. Immediately on arrival in the Congo, the crew began operations transporting fuel. UN air assets in the Congo were many and varied. Several countries were involved in sending their air force units to support the peacekeeping mission. For example, the Iranian, Ethiopian, and Philippine Air Forces detached units flying North American F-86 Sabres and the Swedish Air Force sent a contingent of Saab J-29 Tunnans. Dan Weber recalls:

> Our first mission to Kamina was interesting as it had been a Belgian Air Force training base and must have been a very pretty facility at one time, somewhat like our Randolph AFB. Now, however, much of the base was overgrown and was the temporary home for some Iranian F-86s all painted with UN markings on them.
>
> The Congo is about three times the size of Texas so our flights were several hours each way. The ground refuelling process had been fine tuned by the crews preceding us, so it became routine very quickly.[5]

However, the detachment was not always routine and there were some 'memorable' moments. Dan Weber experienced such a moment while landing at Elizabethville:

> There can be no worse feeling than being in a remote location thousands of miles from home and feel the aircraft lurch as a landing gear breaks through the asphalt taxiway crust. We were being directed by an unknown Caucasian person in civilian clothes and he had us close to the edge of the taxiway so the hoses could easily reach the tanks. Suddenly we lurched to the right and stopped. At any rate we had already cut our outboard engines and had not squared our props so this prevented damage to number four engine prop.[6]

Such events are traumatic, but immediately the professionalism and expertise of the KB-50 crew was brought to bear on the problem:

> The engineer and I talked this over and decided that we would offload the fuel we had brought in and then transfer wing fuel from the low side to the high side. When all that

On arrival at Kamina and Elizabethville, the crews would offload the fuel on the ground into huge bladder or pillow tanks. In Elizabethville, this was 115/145 fuel. While transferring the fuel, the outboard engines of the KB-50 would be run up to provide power and pressure. (*Dan Weber via Leif Hellstrom*)

KB-50J 49-0358 outside the terminal at Leopoldville getting ready to take on JP-4 and 115/145 fuel to deliver to Elizabethville and Kamina. The other aircraft on the ramp is a UN-chartered Aviation Traders ATL-98 Carvair, a modified Douglas DC-4. (*Dan Weber via Leif Hellstrom*)

> was complete, we dropped flaps and steadily brought up the power on the inboard engines until suddenly the aircraft lurched up out of the hole. I rolled forward a ways and then we put the engines in reverse and carefully backed up some distance, missing the hole, until we got to the concrete ramp and could turn round. That was enough excitement for one day.[7]

Following this incident, another occurred when an engine failed shortly after take-off; Dan was obliged to feather the engine and return to land back on the airfield after first dumping fuel to get the aircraft weight down. A period of forced idleness for the crew ensued while they waited for another engine to be sent out from Sculthorpe. The engine duly arrived on a MATS Douglas C-124 Globemaster. Within twenty-four hours, the new engine had been installed and tested and operations continued. No further incidences occurred, and on 12 March 1963, Dan Weber and his crew headed for home.

By the mid-1960s, the KB-50J had become old and obsolete. It was often necessary to cannibalise some aircraft to keep others in the air. In June 1962, the 47th BW was deactivated. At that time, on 1 October 1962, the 420th came under the control of the newly activated 7375th Support Group at Sculthorpe. Subsequently, on 1 September 1963, the squadron was assigned to the 3rd Air Force.

At this time, the century's series jets were being phased out of USAFE being replaced by the ubiquitous multi-role McDonnell Douglas F-4 Phantom. The Phantom was refuelled by the 'flying boom' system, not by the 'triple nipple' probe and drogue. USAFE's first F-4Cs arrived at RAF Bentwaters, Suffolk, home of the 81st Tactical

KB-50J was present at RAF Mildenhall's open house in 1961. (*Doug Gordon collection*)

Fighter Wing (TFW), on 4 October 1965. Just prior to this, in March 1964, the 420th was deactivated at RAF Sculthorpe.

With the demise of the 420th, the mission of in-flight refuelling USAFE's tactical aircraft fell initially to the detached units of SAC based at RAF Mildenhall and Rhine-Main AB in West Germany. In the UK and based at Mildenhall was the 303rd Air Refuelling Squadron, and in Germany, the 160th Air Refuelling Group. Both these units flew the Boeing KC-97.

When the Boeing KC-135 Stratotanker entered service with SAC in the late 1950s, regular deployments of the aircraft were made to the UK to support USAFE tactical aircraft. Eventually with the introduction of the aircraft into Air National Guard (ANG) and Air Force Reserve (AFR) units, these were also detached to the UK, to RAF Mildenhall in particular.

It was not until 1992 when a newly activated 100th Air Refuelling Wing was permanently assigned to the 3rd Air Force in the UK. The 100th ARW, now flying KC-135R, is based at RAF Mildenhall.

7
The 48th Tactical Fighter Wing

The Stature of Liberty Wing

The 48th Bombardment Group was activated at Hunter Field, Georgia, on 15 January 1941. Serving mainly as a training unit the 48th moved to Key Field, Mississippi, in August 1943 and was redesignated the 48th Fighter Bomber Group. Four squadrons were attached: the 492nd, 493rd, 494th, and 495th Fighter Bomber Squadrons flying the P-39 Airacobra and the P-40 Warhawk.

After moving to several bases in the US, the 48th eventually went to war in March 1944, deploying to RAF Ibsley with their Republic P-47 Thunderbolts. By 5 June, the group had flown more than 1,600 combat sorties and dropped 200 tons of bombs. Pilots flew another 1,900 sorties between 6 June and 30 June to support the D-Day landings. Following the landings, the group followed the Allied advance across Europe through France flying close support. Between 18 December and 17 January 1945, the Thunderbolts supported ground missions during the Battle of the Bulge. After advancing into Germany the group was based at Illesheim when the war ended. The 48th FBG was returned to the US and deactivated on 7 November 1945.

The 48th Fighter Bomber Wing was activated at Chaumont Air base in France on 10 July 1952, taking over the personnel and assets of the 137th Fighter Bomber Wing, a federalised ANG unit which returned to the USA. The unit was flying Republic F-84G-1s which were capable of in-flight refuelling, but, unlike the G-5s, they were not nuclear capable. The 137th and later the 48th did not have a nuclear delivery mission in USAFE with the F-84G. Three squadrons were attached to the 48th: the 492nd, 493rd, and 494th Fighter Bomber Squadrons.

In the summer of 1953, the 48th formed the first aerobatic team in USAFE. Known as the Skyblazers the team performed all over Europe in their F-84Gs. In mid-1954, the wing had converted to the North American F-86 Sabre. They flew both the dash 25 and the nuclear capable dash 35 models and practised the nuclear delivery mission with the latter. Victor Alert Detachment #1 was set up at Sembach air base in Germany

On 4 July 1954, the wing was awarded the official name of the 'Statue of Liberty Wing' in honour of the long association between the French nation and the USAFE. The 48th became the only wing in the USAF with a name as well as a number. A new unofficial insignia was designed and worn on the sides of the wing's F-86s.

In late 1956, the 48th converted to the North American F-100D Super Sabre. All aircraft were now nuclear capable and the alert commitment moved from Sembach to Hahn, Germany.

During the conversion to the F-100, the control of the Skyblazers was transferred to the 36th Fighter Day Wing (FDW) at Bitburg, Germany. In 1958, the 48th was redesignated a tactical fighter wing. In January 1960, as a result of the French dismissing all US nuclear forces from their territory, the three squadrons of the wing moved to RAF Lakenheath in Suffolk in the UK.

The F-100 Super Sabre

On 6 January 1960, F-100Ds of the 493rd TFS landed at RAF Lakenheath. They were followed shortly afterwards by the 492nd and 494th. By 15 January, the 493rd was pulling alert commitments. The Statue of Liberty Wing was settled in to the base it was to call home for the next sixty plus years.

RAF Lakenheath was formally a SAC base used for rotating bomber units from the USA. With the transfer of the 48th from France the airfield returned to the command of USAFE.

The initial few months at Lakenheath was characterised by considerable construction work being carried out on the base. Compared to Chaumont the facilities on the base left much to be desired. While SAC had upgraded numerous Second World War-era facilities and lengthened the runway, the 48th initiated a construction project to facilitate its three fighter squadrons and support elements. It was also necessary to develop base housing to accommodate the additional personnel and their families.

During the settling in period in the UK, it was very important to develop a good public relations. The wing held a special press conference to announce an open house event to be held on 28 May which would be attended by other USAFE units and the RAF.

The mission with the F-100 remained as it had at Chaumont, which to prepare for and conduct special weapons tactical air operations as directed. The wing was notified that it was to receive the Mk 43 'special weapon' in 1961. This special weapon was designed for low-altitude laydown delivery. Later, in the late 1960s the wing received the B-61 thermonuclear bomb.

The F-100s of the wing stood Victor Alert at Lakenheath and also for a period in Turkey. Capt. Marcus Anderson was with the 492nd TFS from June 1967 to December 1969 and recalls:

> We stood nuclear alert and did a lot of low-level training. We also trained with conventional ordnance and spent a lot of time on Holbeach and Wainfleet bombing ranges, which were not far from Lakenheath. When I first arrived at Lakenheath in '67 we were able to deploy to Wheelus AB in Libya for gunnery training, to include shooting the dart, something we couldn't do in the UK. We also sat alert at Çiğli, Turkey in the '67-68 time-frame, and at Aviano, Italy the whole time I was at Lakenheath. Generally those deployments were for three-four weeks at a time.[1]

Two F-100Ds of the 474 TFS prepare to leave their base at Chaumont to fly to their new home at RAF Lakenheath, where they arrived in January 1960. (*Jack Schmidt*)

F-100D 55-2822 was assigned to the 493rd TFS and wears three yellow colours of that unit at Lakenheath in 1960. The 493rd was the first squadron to land at the 'heath on 6 January 1960 and was pulling alert commitments at the base by 15 January. (*Author's collection*)

In March and April 1953, the 92nd and 78th FIS detached to Fürstenfeldbruck with a mission to identify unknown aircraft violating the US occupation zone of Germany. This detachment followed the shooting down of an F-84 by Czech MiG-15s. Here aircraft of the 78th FIS stand alert at Fursty. (*Joe Williams*)

Wearing the squadron colours in a band around the nose, F-86s of the 78th TFS line up ready to take off at Fursty, heading for home at Shepherds Grove. (*Joe Williams*)

The 78th FIS F-86s on the flight line at Shepherds Grove prior to taking off for Wheelus, Libya, for weapons training. All squadrons regularly detached to North Africa for gunnery training. F-86 pilots were expected to remain proficient in ground gunnery, air-to-air gunnery, dive bombing, and rocketry. It was essential for all USAFE units to have access to sunbases where they could hone their skills unhindered by the generally miserable North European weather. (*Joe Williams*)

A second refuelling stop *en route* to Wheelus was at Rome, Italy. The F-86s of the 81st FIW were not capable of refuelling in flight, hence the necessity to make stops, particularly in the face of a headwind. (*Joe Williams*)

This F-86A was assigned to the 91st FIS based at RAF Bentwaters. Of particular note are the drop tanks painted with the lightning flash in the blue squadron colours. (*R. Harlan via Dave Menard*)

F-86A-5-NA 49-1081, of the 78th FIS, photographed in 1954. This aircraft is seen in the colours worn by the 81st Sabres in their final years. The lessons of Korea led to a toning down of unit markings and standardisation on the yellow tail and wing bands. The squadron colour was carried on a band around the nose. (*via Dave Menard*)

Sabres from the 92nd FIS on the ramp at Shepherds Grove. They are armed with 5-inch high-velocity aerial rockets (HVAR). They are about to depart for the air to ground range at Dengie Flats. (*Alvin Post*)

F-84Fs of 'C' Flight of the 91st FBS on the ramp at RAF Bentwaters. (*Don Mikler*)

F-84F 52-6533 and Don Mikler's 1954 Chevrolet—a vintage pair at RAF Bentwaters in the autumn of 1955. (*Don Mikler*)

Above: Lt Harry Eckes is *en route* to Nouasseur. The flight to the Moroccan base was a distance of 1,210 nautical miles and took about two hours. (*Don Mikler*)

Below: The first F-84F Thunderstreaks arrived with the 81st FBW at Bentwaters and Shepherds Grove in October 1954. The 78th FBS was based at RAF Shepherds Grove alongside the 92nd FBS. Aircraft 52-6449 was the mount of Lt Joe Williams. (*Joe Williams*)

F-84F 52-6675 was the 78th FBS squadron commander's aircraft. Here keeping company with a Black Arrows' Hawker Hunter at Wattisham in 1958. (*Author's collection*)

F-84F-45-RE 52-6737 belongs to the 92nd FBS, which was based at RAF Manston from March 1955 to May 1958, at which time it joined the rest of the 81st FBW at RAF Bentwaters. (*Mike Hooks*)

F-101A 54-1468 was assigned to the 92nd TFS. The markings carried by this aircraft were the first of three of those applied to the Voodoos while they were at Bentwaters and Woodbridge. The sunburst on the tail were in the individual squadron colours. The squadron badge was carried on the vertical tail and the wing badge on the forward fuselage to the rear of the canopy. (*Author's collection*)

F-101A 54-1491 was the 81st wing commander's aircraft and carries all the squadron colours and badges on the tail. This aircraft eventually went on to serve with the Kentucky Air National Guard converted to an RF-101H. (*Robert Robinson collection*)

F-101C 56-0029 was a 91st TFS machine and wears the blue of that squadron. Externally, the F-101C was identical to the F-101A. The only difference was the internal structure strengthening, which was required to bring the aircraft up to the originally specified 7.33-G load that the 'A' models had not met, being stressed to only 6.33 G. (*Author's collection*)

This Voodoo is under guard at an open house at RAF Bentwaters in May 1964. The F-101 was fitted with four 20-mm M39 cannon in the nose, which can be clearly seen in this photo. (*Alan Johnson*)

These two F-101Cs are overflying the Suffolk coast near their twin bases at Bentwaters and Woodbridge. They are not carrying external tanks and are probably on a local familiarisation flight. (*Robert Robinson collection*)

Three Voodoos fly in formation above the cumulus. They are all F-101As: 54-1457, 54-1464, and 54-1476. (*Gregg Kittinger*)

F-101C-50-MC 56-0027 as at RAF Leuchars in 1965 together with 56-0009. (*Neil Aird*)

Badge of the 81st Tactical Fighter Wing.

When the McDonnell F-4C Phantoms first arrived at the twin bases of RAF Bentwaters and RAF Woodbridge in Suffolk in October 1965, they were painted in the US Navy scheme of dark gull grey upper surfaces and white under surfaces. F-4C 64-0866 carries the buzz number FJ-866 on the side of the fuselage. (*Author's collection*)

The Phantoms began to receive the SE Asia camouflage in 1966. F-4C-25-MC 64-0901 was assigned to the 92nd TFS at Bentwaters. On the inboard port pylon, the aircraft is carrying a travel pod, possibly adapted from a napalm canister. On 15 August 1968, this aircraft over-ran the runway on landing. (*Author's collection*)

F-4C 64-0891 was displayed at the Hanover Air Show in May 1966. (*Author's collection*)

F-4D-28-MC 65-0748 in front of the Bentwaters tower in 1969. The first F-4Ds arrived with the 81st TFW in 1968. (*Author's collection*)

F-4D-31-MC 66-7692 was assigned to the 78th TFS and has the tail code WR. (*Author's collection*)

In 1972, individual squadron tail codes disappeared and WR was adopted for all wing aircraft. F-4D 66-7553 undergoes final checks before take-off. (*Author's collection*)

F-4C-17-MC 63-7449 in flight somewhere over the UK. This aircraft was assigned to the 91st TFS at the time this photograph was taken as is witnessed by the blue fin tip. (*Jim Jameson via Simon Gladas*)

The red fin tip and red canopy rail on this F-4D-28-MC confirms that it belongs to the 78th TFS. (*Bentwaters Cold War Museum via Simon Gladas*)

Two F-4s of the 81st TFW on their way to the range. The furthermost aircraft wears the red colours of the 78th TFS on the tip of the fin. Both aircraft are equipped with a SUU-23A 20-mm gun pod on the centreline station and two SUU-21 bomb dispensers under the wings. (*via Graham Gilbert*)

Wearing its unique camouflage scheme, A-10A 75-0262 visited RAF Bentwaters in February 1978 while engaged in Joint Air Weapons Systems (JAWS) trials with US Army helicopters on mainland Europe. (*Trevor Hall*)

Arriving at Bentwaters in August 1978, 77-0192 was one of three A-10s assigned to the 81st TFW for maintenance training prior to the arrival of the squadron aircraft. (*Author's collection*)

Early A-10s were delivered to the 81st TFW in the two-tone 'ghost' grey camouflage. (*USAF*)

A left front view of an 81st TFW A-10A Thunderbolt II aircraft as an airman assists a pilot aboard on 28 June 1981. (*USAF*)

From May 1979, all A-10s were delivered in the European One camouflage scheme and at this time individual squadrons began to apply their insignia and colours. This 'Hog belongs to the 92nd TFS. (*USAF*)

Exercise Reforger (Return of Forces to Germany) was an annual NATO exercise designed to ensure that US forces could be deployed to Germany quickly in the event of war with the Warsaw Pact breaking out. The A-10s were regular participants in the exercise. This A-10 is carrying an AN/ALQ-119 'jamming' pod. It also has a modification to the muzzle of the GAU-8 in the form of the Battelle gun gas diverter. Some of the 81st A-10s carried these modifications for a time, but they were not particularly effective their use was short-lived. (*USAF*)

These two A-10s are armed with three mavericks apiece. Aircraft 80-0170 also carries an AN/ALQ-119 jamming pod. (*USAF*)

On 1 March 1987, a 91st TFS A-10A Thunderbolt II aircraft is firing its 30-mm cannon on a target at the Bardenas Reales bombing range during a training mission. Squadrons of the 81st regularly deployed to Zaragoza Air Base. This aircraft is the squadron commander's aircraft and is adorned with the 'Blue Thunder' nose art. (*USAF*)

Somewhere over the North Sea, this 78th TFS Warthog flies through a turbulent sky at sunset (*USAF*).

F-84E-1-RE belongs to the 512th FBS,406th FBW, and flies in echelon formation with two other aircraft from the same squadron. The tail band is used to denote the flight number. (*Lt-Col. F. E. Smith via Dave Menard*)

Resting on the summer grass at RAF Manston is F-84E-1-RE of the 512th FBS. The inboard weapon pylon can carry a 1,000-lb bomb. The primary mission of the 406th was to 'conduct fighter bomber operations under the operational control of the 3rd Air Force, to retard and stabilize any aggressor forces in Northern and Western Europe'. (*Lt-Col. F. E. Smith via Dave Menard*)

Photographed at Nouasseur in April 1954, F-86F-25-NA was assigned to the 514th FIS and wears the squadron's colour around the nose. (*via Duncan Curtis*)

Four F-86Fs of the 512th FIS on the ramp at Nouasseur are being prepared for a gunnery sortie. (*via Duncan Curtis*)

F-86D 52-4124 of the 513th FIS. Both the 513th and the 514th FIS converted to the F-86D in the first half of 1955. With the exception of the squadron colour (red) on the canopy, this aircraft is devoid of any other markings. (*via Duncan Curtis*)

F-96D 52-10019 of the 514th FIS. This aircraft carries the blue colours of the squadron on its canopy and in a lightning flash on the front lower fuselage. This aircraft was the 406th wing commander's aircraft, hence the multi-coloured bands on the fuselage. (*Col. D. Callaghan via D. Menard*)

This 512th FIS aircraft is in the company of an 81st FBW F-84F at an open house at Prestwick on 19 May 1956. The 512th took over the aircraft and personnel of the 87th FIS. The 406th wing badge is prominent on the fuselage side of this, the squadron commander's aircraft. (*via Duncan Curtis*)

F-86D 52-10935 belongs to the 512th FIS, which operated from Bentwaters under the control of Eastern Sector, 12 Group, RAF Fighter Command. The retractable rocket tray can clearly be seen. The F-86D had no guns, its only offensive armament were the rockets. (*George Pennick*)

F-86D-50-NA 52-10030 was the first single-seat fighter to use lead collision course interception. In the early months of its service in the UK, this method of interception caused some friction with the RAF. Happily this was resolved. (*Maj. J. White via D. Menard*)

F-86Ds of the 513th FIS are being refuelled at RAF Manston. The aircraft in the foreground bears the red fuselage stripe of the squadron commander. (*via Dave Menard*)

Above left: Badge of the 406th FIW.

Above right: Badge of the 47th BW.

Just prior to the move to the UK, the aircraft of the 84th BS are lined up at Langley. (*Tom Cress via Dave Menard*)

B-45A 47-029 was assigned to the 84th BS. (*Bill Mankevich*)

B-45A 47-061 in flight over the UK. No. 061 belonged to the 84th BS. (*Lt-Col. R. Satterfield via Dave Menard*)

The 47th shared the atomic strike with the 20th FBW, which flew the F-84G Thunderjet. Both units came under the control of the 49th Air Division. Here, a B-45A of the 86th BS formates with an F-84 of the 77th Fighter Bomber Squadron of the 20th FBW. (*Lt-Col. R. Satterfield via Dave Menard*)

Aircraft 47-055, here resplendent in the colours of the 86th BS, suffered a serious mishap in May 1957 when it crash landed at Shepherds Grove, collapsing its nose gear. It was salvaged, only to be flown to Dreux a year later to be used for fire practice. (*Author's collection*)

The B-45A carried a crew of four. In this photo of an 86th BS crew (*from left to right*) are Al Galyagoes, co-pilot; Bud Woods, bombardier/navigator; Clete Dold, pilot/aircraft commander; Bill Menkevich, gunner. The pilot and co-pilot would sit in tandem under the transparent bubble canopy. The bombardier/navigator's position was in the nose, and the gunner's position in the rear of the aircraft. (*Bill Mankevich*)

RB-45C of the 19th TRS in company with a squadron T-33. Aircraft 48-040 was one of the four 19th TRS RB-45Cs specially flown over to Sculthorpe for the April 1954 overflight by the RAF Special Duty Flight. (*Courtesy of the Schrecengost Archives—Col. Ray W. Schrecengost, Jnr, USAF*)

B-45A 47-092 belongs to the 47th Base Operations Flight and carries the white markings similar to the units C-119 Flying Boxcars. (*T. Cress via Robert Robinson*)

B-66B-DL 50-309 wears the red colours of the 84th BS and was present at RAF Wethersfields' armed forces display in May 1959. (*USAF*)

B-66B-DL 54-496 was assigned to the 85th BS. Targets for the 47th BW B-66s were mostly in North Eastern Europe and included the Baltic States, East Germany, and Poland. (*Author's collection*)

RB-45C 48-019: this was the aircraft of the 19th TRS's CO, Maj. John B. Anderson. In March 1955, Maj. Anderson led a three-ship penetration of the Warsaw Pact. The three RB-45s were piloted by Anderson, Capt. Bert Grigsby, and Capt. Robert A. Schambers. Maj. Anderson flew into Hungary and photographed targets in and around Budapest, Capt. Schambers flew over East Berlin, and Capt. Grigsby's overflight took him to Yugoslavia. (*MSgt Don Hyde via Dave Menard*)

F-84Gs of the 77th FBS in the air *en route* to Bluie West One, Greenland. The approaches to BW1 were difficult and required all the pilots' concentration. Dick Baughn recalls: 'In the parlance of today, you had to 'focus'. But in those days, we not only kept our eyes peeled—we gave it our unfettered concentration. My concentration was so rapt that I believe my 88 year old eyes could still focus well enough for me to negotiate the fjord and make a landing today—some 59 years later'. (*20th FW Historical Office via Art Sevigny*)

F-84G 51-902 served with the 77th FBS until 1955 when it joined the 79th FBS at RAF Woodbridge. (*Author's collection*)

Above left: Badge of the 19th TRS.

Above right: Badge of the 20th FBW.

F-84G-1-RE 51-967 is flying over Vesuvius, Italy, on its way to North Africa. (*Satterfield via Pennick and Menard*)

Resplendent in its yellow markings, an F-84G 51-951 of the 79th FBS sits on the hardstanding at RAF Woodbridge. (*Mike Hooks*)

This 55th FBS F-84G is landing somewhere in North Africa. In common with all USAF tactical units based in Northern Europe, the 20th FBW frequently detached its squadrons to Nouasseur, Wheelus, and Sidi Slimane for weapons training. (*Don Emigholz via Robbie Robinson*)

Conversion to the F-84F in 1955 was carried out at Nouasseur, Morocco. The 77th was the first squadron to convert to the aircraft. F-84F-45-RE 52-6696 overflies the North African desert. (*via Art Sevigny, 20th FBW Historian*)

Pictured at Wethersfield in 1956, F-84F 52-6738 wears the blue colours of the 55th FBS. (*Author's collection*)

F-100D 56-3888 was assigned to the 79th TFS. This aircraft is wearing the yellow colours of the squadron. The 79th were based at RAF Woodbridge. The squadron's Tiger badge was carried on the fuselage side superimposed on the lightning streak. The wing badge was carried on the tail. (*Author's collection*)

The blue colours adorn this Hun, which belongs to the 55th TFS. 20th TFW, which was based at RAF Bentwaters. The squadron markings changed in 1960 when the fuselage flash was removed. The tail flash remained with the wing badge carried in the same position as before. (*Author's collection*)

Triple Zilch was the wing commander's aircraft. Col. Raymond Tolliver was assigned to the 77th TFS. (*Robert Robinson collection*)

F-100D 55-3644 is *en route* to Wheelus, flying over the Alps in 1962. In 1961, the aircraft began to wear the three colours of the squadrons of the wing. This was a direct result of a maintenance reorganisation whereby aircraft were assigned to the wing and not to individual squadrons. (*Howard S. Loitwood Jnr via Art Sevigny 20th FW Historical Office*)

The 20th TFW line up at Wheelus. Aircraft from all three squadrons are represented as can be seen from the colours of the nose bands. The aircraft nearest the camera is flown by the twentieth commander and carries the three squadron colours and badges. (*Harv Segrest via Art Sevigny, 20th FW Historical Office*)

F-100D 55-3685 of the 20th TFW fires an AGM-12 Bullpup air-to-ground missile over the North African desert. (*Glenn Ramsden*)

This Aardvark photographed in 1972 was assigned to the 79th TFS. It is loaded and headed for the range, carrying twelve Mk 117, 750-lb bombs. (*Author's collection*)

This flight of four F-100s belong to the 79th TFS, although they carry no individual squadron markings. (*William L. May via Art Sevigny, 20th FW Historical Office*)

A formation of 20th TFW F-100s poses for the camera ship; in this case, the wing's T-33. (*via Art Sevigny, 20th FW Historical Office*)

In 1976, on the 200th anniversary of the signing of the Declaration of Independence, the 20th TFW in common with many other units in the USAF, painted one of their F-111Es, 68-028, in a commemorative scheme. (*via Art Sevigny, 20th TFW Association Historian*)

F-111E 68-043 is carrying an SUU-21 bomb dispenser under its starboard wing. (*Author's collection*)

Two F-111Es fly over their base at RAF Upper Heyford in January 1983. (*USAF Archives*)

An F-111E on its way to the range with a full load. The blue tip of the vertical fin marks this Aardvark as belonging to the 55th TFS. (*USAF Archives*)

A 55th Tactical Fighter Squadron F-111E aircraft lifts off from the runway at Aviano, Italy, as it departs on a mission during the USAFE exercise Display Determination '89. (*USAF Archives*)

The tiger markings on the fin tip of F-111E 68-002 mark this aircraft as belonging to the 79th TFS. (*Richard Crandall*)

Above left: Badge of the 42nd Electronic Combat Squadron.

Above right: Dumbo patch of the 42nd AREFS.

EF-111A 66-052, assigned to the 42nd ECS and named *Cherry Bomb*, was at RAF Mildenhall's air fete in 1987. (*Author's collection*)

On an approach turn over the sand bars of the River Severn, everything hangs down on this 42nd ECS EF-111A, 66-052. (*USAF*)

An F-16C Fighting Falcon aircraft of the 50th Tactical Fighter Wing leads an EF-111A Raven aircraft of the 42nd ECS, 66th ECW, and an F-111E aircraft of the 20th Tactical Fighter Wing in June 1987 over Germany. (*USAF*)

The 42nd ECS sent EF-111As to participate in Exercise Open Gate in 1989. The exercise took place in the Mediterranean in the area of Gibraltar, the Moroccan and Spanish Coasts, and the Spanish island of Alboran. The Ravens were based at Moron Air Base in Spain for the duration of the exercise. (*USAF*)

Raven 66-057 flies over the Mediterranean during the course of Exercise Open Gate. This exercise, which involved the air and naval forces of the NATO southern Europe states, was designed to simulate air and sea power tactics required to keep the Straits of Gibraltar open during a crisis. (*USAF*)

In September 1991, four EF-111As were detached to Incirlik in Turkey in Operation Provide Comfort. They were to support to eleven F-111Fs of the 48th TFW, giving support to the Iraqi Kurds in their revolt against Saddam Hussein. This Raven is about to move out of its shelter at Upper Heyford to take off for Turkey. (*USAF*)

Resplendent in the red livery of the 420th AREFS, KB-50J 49-0360 dominates the skyline at RAF Sculthorpe in 1960. (*Jack Friell via Steve Hill/EMCS*)

A detailed photo of the starboard refuelling pod and the J-47 jet engine, which was fitted to increase the speed of the KB-50 and facilitate the refuelling of the higher-performance century series of fighters which entered service with the USAFE in the mid-1950s. (*Courtesy of the Tac Tankers Association*)

KB-50J 48-0061 is at Sculthorpe in 1960. In addition to the 420th AREFS, the base also paid host to the 47th Bomb Wing, which was equipped with North American B-45 Tornados until they were replaced by the Douglas B-66 Destroyers in 1958. (*Jack Friell via Steve Hill/EMCS*)

During the 420th's deployment to the Congo in 1962, KB-50J sits on the ramp at Kamina Air Base, which was one of the bases to which the 420th had to haul fuel from Leopoldville (now Kinshasa), the other being Elizabethville. (*S-O Erikson via Leif Hellstrom*)

One of the stop overs for the KB-50s was the base at Port Etienne (now Nouadhibou) in Mauritania, West Africa. Sharing the ramp with the 420th tanker were the peace-keeping Swedish Saab J-29s wearing their UN markings. (*Dick Stenberg via Leif Hellstrom*)

KB-50D 49-381 was at RAF Wethersfield's open house in June 1957. The KB-50J was fitted with two General Electric J-47 jet engines of 5,900 lb thrust each installed under the wings in order to increase speed and altitude. (*Paul H. Minert collection via Robert Hopkins*)

Offloading JP-4 jet fuel at Kamina air base, which was the home to a unit of North American F-86F Sabres of the Philippine Air Force. (*Dan Weber via Leif Hellstrom*)

In common with other units, the 48th TFW used Wheelus base in Libya for its nuclear and conventional weapons delivery practice. F-100D 56-3226, belonging to the 494th TFS, is *en route* to this North African base. (*Phil Hawkins*)

Badge of the 48th TFW.

The primary mission of the 48th TFW was the delivery of special weapons. This F-100D is being readied for a visit to the range for practice delivery of this Mk 7 atomic bomb. (*Author's collection*)

The 48th line up at Wheelus in 1959 just prior to the move to Lakenheath. F-100Ds of all three squadrons are in evidence: the 492nd sporting blue stripes; the 493rd, yellow; and the 494th, red. (*Phil Hawkins*)

In late 1960, the markings on the F-100s began to change. The stripes were gone from the tail and the wing tips. The squadron badge was moved to the tail and placed with an alar in the squadron colour. F-100D 56-3209 was assigned to the 494th TFS. (*Author's collection*)

Three F-100Ds line up at the end of Lakenheath's runway for a formation take-off. Two of the 'Huns' carry the LT tail code in white, which identifies them as belonging to the 494th TFS. The fin tips are also painted in the squadron colour red. (*Author's collection*)

F-100D 56-3672 wears the tail code LS of the 493rd TFS. It also has the yellow fin tip of that squadron. The 48th TFW badge was carried at the top of the fin. (*Author's collection*)

Most of the early years of the F-4D with the 48th TFW were spent in practising for conventional war. For these purposes, the wing used British ranges in addition to their regular visits to Zaragoza, Spain; Aviano, Italy; and Çiğli, Turkey. Prior to its service with the 48th TFW, F-4D-28-MC 65-0742 had served the 3rd TFW at Kunsan in Korea. (*Author's collection*)

Following the phase out of the Phantom with the 48th TFW in 1977, F-4D-29-MC 65-0777 was assigned to the 388th TFW at Hill AFB, Utah. (*Author's collection*)

Before arriving at Lakenheath with the 48th TFW, F-4D-27-MC 65-0615 served with the 8th TFW, the famed 'Wolf Pack', in SE Asia, based at Ubon AB in Thailand. (*Author's collection*)

These two F-111Fs belong to the 494th Tactical Fighter Squadron. They were on detachment to Zaragoza air base in Spain for weapons training and carry Mk 82 high-drag bombs. (*USAF*)

F-111F 72-443 is carrying twelve Mk 82, 500-lb practice bombs on weapon training over the Bardenas Reales range in Spain in October 1986. (*USAF*)

Wearing the special identification number on the tail, this F-111F is taking part in the Strike Command Bombing Competition held between the USAF and the RAF at RAF Lossiemouth in June 1981. (*USAF*)

Two 495th TFS Aardvarks fly a mission out of Moron Air Base during Exercise Open Gate in April 1989. Open Gate was a NATO exercise designed to simulate air and sea power tactics required to keep the Straits of Gibraltar open during a crisis. (*USAF*)

Carrying four Mk 84 laser-guided bombs and equipped with an AN-AVQ-26 Pave Tack laser target designator, this F-111F belonging to the 493rd TFS is flying over Loch Ness on a live-firing practice mission in July 1982. (*USAF*)

On 23 January 1991, F-111F 70-2390 *Miss Liberty* taxis from its hangar as it prepares for deployment to Saudi Arabia to take part in Operation Desert Shield. (*USAF*)

Miss Liberty is armed with a Paveway laser-guided bomb on the outside pylon and a GBU-15 modular glide bomb on the inside pylon. (*USAF*)

At Taif Air Base, an Aardvark of the 48th is prepared for a mission armed with two GBU-24 laser-guided bombs (LGBs). (*USAF*)

F-111F 71-0891 of the 493rd TFS winds down after returning from a mission. (*USAF*)

Miss Liberty, the flagship of the 48th TFW, flies over the desert. Hostilities in Desert Storm ceased in February 1991 and the 48th TFW returned to RAF Lakenheath in May. (*USAF*)

F-111Fs of the 493rd and 494th Tactical Fighter Squadrons fly in formation with *Miss Liberty* and an EF-111F electronic warfare aircraft assigned to the 366th Tactical Fighter Wing. (*USAF*)

The four RB-66 squadrons of USAFE were united under the 10th TRW in December 1957. This superb photograph shows the 10th's markings applied to the 1st TRS RB-66B in the foreground, which carries the four-coloured plume on the tail and the blue band on the nacelles. The three aircraft in the background are all belonging to the 42nd TRS and have the distinctive wing tip ECM pods. The 42nd Squadron colour was red and can again be seen on the nacelles. (*R. Ganci*)

RB-66B 54-421 of the 19th TRS, 66th TRW, at an open house at RAF Wethersfield in UK in 1957. The 19th served with the 66th for a brief period before joining the 10th TRW in December 1957. (*Mike Hooks*)

An RB-66B at Alconbury in 1960. This aircraft does not have the squadron colours on the engine nacelles. (*USAF*)

Badge of the 10th TRW.

In June 1969, 64-1013 was photographed while at Moron. In the early months of camouflage a number of aircraft retained their white radomes. (*George Fennell*)

Aircraft 64-1077 was often the mount of Kirk Ransom. While on detachment to Moron in 1966, the aircraft required an engine change, and during this time, Kirk witnessed the arrival and departure of four B-58 Hustlers and their accompanying KC-135s from the 305th BW at Grissom AFB, Indiana. (*Kirk Ransom*)

These two RF-4Cs belong to the 1st TRS. When tail codes were introduced in 1970, the 1st TRS was AR and the 30th and 32nd TRS, AS and AT respectively. The squadron colours adorned the tip of the vertical stabiliser, with blue for the 1st TRS. (*via Don Karges*)

The tail code AR became standard for all Alconbury 10th TRW aircraft. Later with the introduction of low visibility markings the Vietnam camouflage scheme of the RF-4Cs of the 10th was wrapped around the whole aircraft and the codes appeared in black. Authors Collection

The pilot of this 509th TFS A-10A, 81-0964, at RAF Alconbury is doing last-minute checks before take-off for the range. In the Gulf, this A-10 was assigned to the 511th TFS and flown by Capt. Todd 'Shanghai' Sheehy when he shot down an Mi-8 helicopter on 15 February 1991. (*David Taylor*)

After the return from the Gulf, A-10A 80-172 *Jennie Mel* of the 511th TFS wears it kills proudly—including radar sites, Scud launchers, artillery, tanks, armoured personnel carriers, and trucks. (*USAF*)

Aircraft 74-01533, also in 'Ghost' camouflage, entered service with the 527th TFTAS in May 1976. It was later damaged in an accident at Spangdahlem, Germany, and after an extensive rebuild, finished its days with the US Navy. (*USAF*)

An A-10A flies over a target in Operation Desert Storm in 1991. Desert Storm A-10 units were based at King Fyad International Airport until February 1991 under the direct control of the 354th TFW (Provisional) and worked as one unit. (*USAF*)

Capt. Spence Roberts stands beside F-5E 74-1534. Capt. Roberts was one of the few 527th pilots who had to eject from an F-5E when his aircraft, 74-1550, went into a flat spin during an engagement with an F-15 over the Mediterranean while at Decimomannu. Roberts ejected successfully and the F-5 plunged into the sea. (*Spence Roberts*)

The F-5E had two Colt Browning M-39 machine guns installed in the nose. In a/c 74-01550, a contributory factor in Capt. Roberts's accident was that ammunition cans, feeder chutes, and dummy ammunition had been removed. This affected the relationship between the centre of gravity and the centre of lift, which compromised manoeuvrability. Another contributory factor could have been the asymmetry between the finned AIM-9 on the port wing-tip and the unfinned ACMI pod on the starboard. (*Alan Wisniewski*)

In 1988, the 527th Aggressors Squadron moved to RAF Bentwaters and was re-equipped with the F-16 Viper. Aircraft 85-0479 was the CO's aircraft and poses in front of the hangar adorned with the Russian bear of the 527th. (*USAF*)

Aircraft 74-1560 being prepared for flight at Deci in 1986. '60' was painted in a light grey scheme. (*Alan Wisniewski*)

F-16C 86-0231 on finals at RAF Lakenheath in March 1989 during a detachment with the F-15Es of the 48th FW. Capt. Bill Clark recalled: 'It was essentially business as usual after we switched air-planes. The mission was always to make as accurate a threat presentation as possible. While the F5 was a perfect MiG-21 sim and decent MiG-23 sim, it couldn't replicate the next generation of fighters. The 16 performance and avionics allowed us to simulate the Fulcrum and Flanker pretty well. There was actually some pretty significant pushback from the F-15 community about our new "threat presentation" along the lines of "too strong"'. (*Robert Robinson*)

Aircraft 56-216 sits on the ramp at Heyford. The natural metal finish was quickly replaced by Vietnam-style camouflage shortly after the Voodoo's arrival in the UK. (*Author's collection*)

The patch of the 527th Tactical Fighter Aggressor Squadron, activated at RAF Alconbury in April 1976.

On a rain-soaked day in 1968 at Heyford, ground crew from the 66th AMS (Avionics Maintenance Squadron) sort out an ILS problem on the 18th TRS ramp. (*Ed Bardwell*)

RF-101C 56-058 wears its new coat of tan and two shades of green at Heyford in 1967. The arrival of camouflage was the death knell for any form of individual unit markings for a while. There is nothing about this Voodoo that announces its affiliation to the 66th TRW or any of its squadrons. (*Author's collection*)

For a short while the Voodoos of the 18th and the Phantoms of the 17th worked side by side from Upper Heyford; until the 17th TRS was assigned to the 86th TFW at Zweibrücken and the 18th TRS returned to the home of USAF reconnaissance at Shaw AFB in Carolina. (*Author's collection*)

The Skyblazers retained the standard markings of the 22nd Fighter Squadron of the 36th Fighter Wing on their F-80Bs, with the exception of the team's name on the nose of the aircraft. (*Richard Kamm*)

F-84E 49-2229 shows clearly the colour scheme adopted by the team. (*Richard Kamm*)

In July 1954, the Skyblazers were equipped with the F-86F-35 aircraft. Six Sabres were assigned to the team and these were painted up in a special colour scheme and the team became a special flight within the wing. (*Author's collection*)

On 26–27 May 1956, the Skyblazers with their F-86Fs performed at Dübendorf Air Base in Switzerland for the Zurich International Air Show. (*Werner Berger via Hans Peter Tschanz*)

The Skyblazers flew the F-100C. This aircraft, 54-2002, is in an experimental colour scheme that was ultimately not adopted for the team. (*Don Emigholz via Robbie Robinson*)

Five F-100Cs of the Skyblazers on the ramp at Bitburg. (*Don Emigholz via Robbie Robinson*)

F-111D 68-145, 522nd TFS, takes off from RNAS Yeovilton during the air show on 16 May 1980. The 522nd was deployed to RAF Boscombe Down for Coronet Hammer with the 27th TFW. (*Chris England*)

Coronet Wrangler, 13 April 1982. Nellis-based F-86A 79-392 is on finals to RAF Bentwaters in the late afternoon. (*Doug Gordon*)

The District of Columbia ANG deployed to RAF Finningley, South Yorkshire, for Coronet Shield in June 1983. The 113th TFW flew F-4D Phantoms. (*USAF*)

When the Tiger Meet was held at the International Air Tattoo at RAF Fairford in 1991, the 53rd TFS sent this F-15C Eagle suitably adorned with tiger stripes. (*Steve Hill*)

This A-7D belongs to the 4451st TS, which deployed to RAF Woodbridge in October 1984 and May 1986. The 4451st was the training squadron for the F-117 Nighthawk pilots based at Tonopah, Nevada, and carried the LV Las Vegas tail code. (*USAF*)

De Havilland L-20 Beaver 52-6139 of the 20th FBW photographed at RAF Wethersfield's open house in 1957. The selected by USAF in 1951 as its principle liaison aircraft. (*Author's collection*)

Lockheed T-33A-1-LO 51-17416, assigned to the 78th FBS, 81st FBW, at RAF Shepherds Grove in 1955. This aircraft transferred to the Royal Netherlands Air Force in 1963. (*Vic Mitrishin*)

Lockheed T-33A-5-LO 57-0687 was assigned to the 81st TFW and wears the same colours as those applied to the F-101 Voodoos of the wing. (*Author's collection*)

Lockheed T-33A-1-LO of the 20th TFW at RAF Wethersfield's open house on 23 August 1958. (*Author's collection*)

During the second Berlin crisis in 1961–62, several of the deployed Operation Stair Step aircraft visited the UK and took part in armed forces days at various TAC bases. This Lockheed F-104C Starfighter was present at RAF Sculthorpe on 19 May 1962. It belongs to the 476th TFS of the 479th TFW from George AFB, which was detached to Hahn, Germany, in the latter stages of Stair Step—from 8 April to 10 August 1962. (*R. A. Scholefield*)

Also at Sculthorpe on 19 May 1962 was Republic F-84F Thunderstreak 52-6936. This aircraft was assigned to the 166th TFS of the Ohio ANG based at Columbus, Ohio. The 166th was detached to France, to Étain-Rouvres, in October 1961 along with three other ANG Thunderstreak squadrons. On 8 May 1962, these four squadrons were assimilated into the newly activated 366th TFW. The 166th became the 391st TFS. Aircraft 52-6936 retained its Ohio ANG insignia. (*Author's collection*)

Several of the Stair Step units flew the northern route to Europe making their UK landfall at Prestwick AB in Scotland. These North American F-86H Sabres of the 102nd TFW were *en route* to Phalsbourg in France in October 1961. Of the first two in line, F-86H 53-1290 was assigned to the 101st TFS and F-86H 52-2122 to the 138th TFS. The 101st was assigned to the Massachusetts ANG and the 138th to the New York ANG. (*USAF*)

F-86H 52-2068 was assigned to the 131st TFS at Phalsbourg. The Sabres of the 131st carried six 0.5-inch Colt Browning M.3 machine guns instead of the four 20-mm M-39 cannons. It was a very wet day at RAF Sculthorpe on 19 May 1962. (*Robert Robinson collection*)

F-100F 56-3907 belonged to the 494th TFS. Every squadron had some two seaters assigned for training, familiarisation, and liaison purposes. (*Author's collection*)

In 1962, the wing markings changed again. This time all three squadron colours were carried on the tail alar and the vee on the front of the fuselage. The wing badge was placed behind the alar on the tail. Initially, as on F-100D, pictured here, the wing badge was the standard shield design. Later this was changed to a round. (*Author's collection*)

Wheelus was closed to the USAF in June 1970. Just prior to the closure, in September 1969, Gen. Muammar Gaddafi led a revolution and deposed King Idris. It was this event which prompted the USAF to cease operations at the base. During the closure, Capt. Fred Abrams was involved in several trips to Libya:

> I had two other 48th TFW connections with Wheelus. First, one of the F-100s, tail number 037, with my name painted on it, was in maintenance when we were ejected. It was somewhat later that we finally repatriated it to RAF Lakenheath in a ceremony involving me and my crew chief, Sgt Benevides That got good press coverage. The second was that several us were working on forming a Lakenheath Aero Club and had a loan application into HQ USAFE. We were told that our loan to buy aircraft would not be approved and that we were being given the assets of the Wheelus Aero Club, three aircraft: a Cessna 150, Cherokee 140 and a Commanche 250. Several of us were whisked to Wheelus in a T-39 to plan the move. I ended up flying the Cessna 150 solo, only a 'whisky compass' from Wheelus to Lakenheath in 24 hours of flying time. First leg was Wheelus to Luqa AB on Malta. As an instructor (CFI) I taught in that aircraft soloing the first female student in the Lakenheath club and later married her.[2]

David Kramer was with the 492nd TFS from 1 February 1970 until 6 July 1974. He flew the Hun until September 1971 when he converted to the McDonnell Douglas F-4D Phantom and recalls the Victor Alert commitment at Lakenheath:

> Qualification for this duty involved academics ('Bomb School') and flying a low-level route in France, simulating a nuc delivery on a bridge on the Loire before returning to Lakenheath. A Stan-Eval pilot flew chase to evaluate your low-level accuracy and time on target.
>
> The Alert facility was at the eastern end of our runway and the hangars contained your aircraft, cocked and loaded with a B-61 on the centreline station. Safety restrictions were rigorous with a 'no lone zone' around the aircraft. Frequent 'Gunsmoke' exercises tested our ability to get to the aircraft before standing down.
>
> We never started the engine and there was a physical barrier to prevent any rogue start-up and taxi.[3]

In common with all NATO units, the squadrons of the 48th also engaged in exercises and exchanges with other units throughout Europe. Marcus Anderson remembers one particular exercise he was involved in:

> One exercise that stands out was when the Squadron was selected to participate in an Allied Forces Central Europe (AFCENT) Weapons Meet in Germany, which had teams from the UK, Germany, Canada and the U.S. To get our team better prepared (we hadn't participated on one of these before) we deployed our team to Sollingen AB, Germany where the Canadians were based, and learned some valuable techniques on low level flying They were very good at it. We also had a great time with them! As I recall, this was in 1968.[4]

At an open house somewhere in the UK, this F-100D has been opened up to expose some of its interior to the common gaze. (*Author's collection*)

The nickname for the 492nd TFS was 'The Mad Hatters'. Here three pilots are returning from a mission sporting their prized bowlers, one wearing a Tam o' Shanter and one a standard forage cap. (*Author's collection*)

Photographed in 1965, this F-100D, 55-2842, was assigned to the 493rd TFS. The B-2 on the fin tip indicated that it was flown at this time by the squadron's 'B' Flight. (*Author's collection*)

SE Asia camouflage began to arrive with all TAC units from 1965. The former colourful F-100s of the 48th TFW being no exception. Flying high over the UK, this F-100F seems drab compared to its predecessors. (*Author's collection*)

Towards the end of their service with the 48th TFW, the F-100s were beginning to show their age. Lining up ready for take-off is 56-2987, now carrying the '0' introduction to the serial on the tail. (*Author's collection*)

In 1971, Fred Abrams and David Kramer was selected to be two of fourteen pilots to convert to the F-4D. The pilots were selected from the three squadrons. For their conversion training, they detached to Luke AFB in Arizona from September to December 1971.

McDonnell F-4D Phantom

From 1972, the 48th TFW at RAF Lakenheath in Suffolk replaced its F-100s with the newer variant of Phantom. The first F-4D for the 48th TFW arrived on 1 February 1972. New aircraft were slow to arrive as virtually all of the F-4Ds scheduled for the 48th were coming from Southeast Asia. As the demand in that theatre for F-4Ds fluctuated, so did the supply to Lakenheath.

By the end of 1972, only the 492nd and 493rd TFS were operational. It was not until July 1974 that the 494th TFS reached the same level of readiness. Not all of the Hun pilots who converted to the F-4D viewed the move as a positive one. Capt. Fred Abrams flew with the 492nd TFS from 1969 to 1972 and relinquished his beloved F-100 for the Phantom. He was not impressed:

> We hun jocks were dismissive of the F-4 jocks calling them F-4 Pukes. When we started converting I had a bunch of patches made that looked like our traditional F-100 patch but had an F-4 outline and said F-4 puke. The higher ranking F-4 guys were not amused. I loved the F-100, all 1000+ hours in it. Honest airplane, knew about adverse yaw and you could feel the onset and avoid it, unlike the F-4 which just departed controlled flight.

F-4D-31-MC 66-7753 comes in to land at RAF Lakenheath. Two of the 48th TFW F-4Ds carried the tail code LK for a short while before the wing adopted the LN code in August 1972—the LK code passing to the C-130s of the 314th TAW at Little Rock AFB, Arkansas. The first F-4D for the 48th TFW arrived on 1 February 1972. (*Author's collection*)

Conversion to the Phantom from the F-100 was very slow and it was not until 1974 that the whole wing could be deemed operational. F-4D-27-MC 65-0644 was displayed at RAF Greenham on 7 July 1974 alongside Marineflieger Starfighter 21+31. The 48th Wing badge was carried on both sides of the fuselage to the rear of the jet intakes. (*Author's collection*)

The primary mission of the 48th TFW was nuclear strike. However, throughout the 1970s, more stress was laid upon the secondary mission of conventional strike. On the ramp at Lakenheath is F-4D-28-MC 65-0685. This Phantom came to the 48th directly from the 81st TFW at Bentwaters. The three squadron colours of the wing were carried in a flash on the fin tip. (*Author's collection*)

> One of the issues in moving from a single seat aircraft to a crew aircraft during weapon delivery was that after a 1000 hours of doing all the delivery parameter cross checks, dive angle, airspeed, release altitude while looking at the target, was that the WSO was providing verbal info helping with the delivery and by the time he could verbalise his input, the hun pilot was doing the next update. There are advantages to a two place complex fighter so this is not to belittle WSOs. It's just that it really didn't help after doing it all oneself. In air-to-air, the second set of eyes was very beneficial. Very beneficial to someone who had not developed the cross-check ability in ground attack.[5]

Capt. Richard Jarvis (Ret.) was a WSO and flew with the 492nd TFS from April 1972 to April 1974. He recalls:

> The mission of the 48th TFW was the same as that of the Wings at Bentwaters and Wethersfield i.e. to prepare for the delivery of tactical nuclear weapons if the Cold War got hot. However, the Wing did not get certified for that mission until after I left in '74. Our targets would likely have been Warsaw Pact airfields. We had begun preparing for the necessary training; but the wing was asked to send several crews on temporary duty to Southeast Asia for [Operation] Linebacker [an airborne offensive during the Vietnam War]. That, I believe delayed our beginning certification training.

Certification training for proficiency in the nuclear mission was delayed for the Phantom aircrew. This was due as much to the constant movement of aircrews between Lakenheath and SE Asia, as to the shortage of aircraft. F-4D-28-MC 65-0735 currently resides on top of a stand at Hastings Municipal Airport, Nebraska, USA. (*Author's collection*)

He added:

> Most of our flying in the years I was there was devoted to conventional weapons delivery at Holbeach [weapons range], Lincolnshire, Aviano, Italy and Zaragoza in Spain [for ranges near them]. I believe most of us enjoyed our time at Zaragosa the most. Good food, great weather and lots of fun shooting up targets with guns, rockets and bombs. We also often flew low-level navigation missions in Scotland and Wales in preparation for the nuke-delivery mission. Finally, we practised radar low-level navigation and bombing, using a town north of the Wash as our aiming point and getting scored by an RAF radar facility somewhere in the area. Although our radar was designed primarily for air-to-air intercepts, at which it performed wonderfully; it did provide us a ground-mapping mode which was usable.
>
> I recall a conventional scramble exercise shortly after I arrived at L'heath in which we were to get to the aircraft, preflight it and the ordnance (the loading of which was part of the exercise that involved our weapons crews) and be strapped into the cockpit ready for engine start. Typically, it's the GIB's job to preflight the ordnance while the pilot checks out the aircraft. Preflighting bombs (we were loaded with twelve Mk-82 500# bombs) involved checking the condition of the fuses and ensuring that safety wires were in place and the timers on the bombs were correctly set for the mode of delivery we were intending to use. The timers prevented the bombs from exploding before X seconds had passed, thus keeping us from blowing ourselves to smithereens. Our delivery mode had been briefed as 30 degree dive-bombing, with release at around 3,000' above the target. The timers on the bombs

F-4D-28-MC 65-0696 had served in Europe since 1969 when it had been assigned to the 78th TFS, 81st TFW, at RAF Woodbridge. It passed to the 493rd TFS in 1975 and wears the squadrons yellow on its fin tip. (*Author's collection*)

> had been set to 12 seconds. Having flown dozens if not hundreds of dive-bombing passes, I knew that a twelve second delay would simply plant the bombs, unexploded, in the ground. So, suspecting that this was part of the test, I began resetting all the fuses to a correct four seconds. The exercise marshals came screaming up in their van—horn blaring—jumped out and said what are you doing? I explained the physics of dive bombing (which they, of course, knew, having been combat pilots themselves). Well, I set the fuses back to 12 seconds and we didn't kill a single target that day.[6]

It was not until July 1974—after the US had made up the losses suffered by the Israeli Air Force in the previous year's Yom Kippur War—that the F-4Ds began to arrive at Lakenheath in the required numbers. By the end of September, the wing had a total of seventy-three aircraft. In July 1975, the wing was ready to resume its full NATO commitment. However, in October 1976, it was announced the 48th TFW was to convert to the General Dynamics F-111F.

The General Dynamics F-111F

The F-111F was the final version of the Aardvark produced. Upgrades included in this model were derived from the parallel development of the FB-111A and the F-111D, and included upgraded navigation and digital computer systems, AN/APQ-144 attack radar, improved landing gear and new upgraded Pratt and Whitney TF-30-P-100 engine with improved thrust. The 48th TFW received their first two F-111Fs on 1 March 1977, replacing that units F-4D Phantoms.

The 48th TFW received their first two F-111Fs on 1 March 1977, replacing that unit's F-4D Phantoms. (*USAF*)

A line-up of F-111Fs on the ramp at RAF Lakenheath. The 48th Tactical Fighter Wing would eventually receive eighty-four Aardvarks. (*USAF*)

The 48th TFW had four squadrons assigned: the 492nd TFS, 493rd TFS, 494th TFS, and 495th TFS, with the 495th having been activated on 1 April 1977. Capt. Jim Jimenez flew with the 493rd and 495th TFS in the mid-1980s:

> I remember very well my first impression of the F-111. It was like sitting in a space capsule. The cockpit was very 'switch intensive', which combined with the heavy cockpit hatch and limited visibility reminded me of the first space capsules. Plus, the two crewmen sat side-side. There was no bubble canopy, the back of the cockpit was the fuselage bulkhead. It was impossible to see past about 5 o'clock to the rear. Also, the airplane had this huge canopy rail down the centre of the cockpit. When flying I was constantly shifting in the seat to see around the rail. It was like flying with one eye stabbed out.
>
> The F-111 was very good at flying fast, low, and delivering ordnance at night or in adverse weather. But, it was big, with very high wing loading and very poor visibility. Although it was extremely fast and stable at low-level, it bled-off airspeed at an extraordinary rate when turning.
>
> The mission was all-weather strike, both conventional and nuclear. The airplane was outstanding at it. I can't think of another tactical airplane to this day that had the legs/range of the F-111. We could go farther, faster, and carry more iron than anyone else.[7]

When the Aardvarks were first deployed to the UK, their primary mission was nuclear strike, and, in accordance with the NATO policy of 'flexible response' in the event of an invasion by forces of the Warsaw Pact, their secondary mission was that of conventional strike. Both these missions were practised regularly and rigorously by the pilots and WSOs of the 48th Tactical Fighter Wing. The 'special weapon' routinely carried by the F-111F was the B-61; though the aircraft was capable of carrying both the B-53 and the B-57 bombs. Throughout the 1970s, the aircraft could carry three nukes—two on the wings and one in the weapons bay. The later development of the AN/AVQ-26 'Pave Tack' electro-optical targeting pod and its subsequent fitting to the weapons bay of the F-111F restricted the use of the weapons bay in that aircraft, so only two 'special weapons' could be carried on the wings. Lt Richard Crandall was a pilot with the 48th TFW; he recalls his nuclear role:

> The mission was to stop the Soviets. We sat nuclear alert to be always ready to counter any aggression on their part. We trained to fight them as they poured through the Fulda gap. Every crew member I served with at RAF Lakenheath thought it was a case of when we would fight WWIII, not if we would fight it. We were basically the best night time capability for USAFE.
>
> I was absolutely convinced I would have to nuke a Warsaw Pact nation, as that was about all we could hit with the F-111. We had a couple of targets in Russia where we would have had to recover with emergency fuel at one of the far northern bases in Norway. But really, we all knew the base would be gone and we would have to punch out.[8]

The F-111F could carry a large assortment of ordnance, and practice in both nuclear and conventional delivery was carried out routinely in order to maintain proficiency in

In addition to detachments to Spain, the 48th F-111Fs also detached regularly to Incirlik in Turkey for weapons training. This operation require in-flight refuelling. A McDonnell Douglas KC-10 Extender tanker refuels this Aardvark over Sicily in March 1987. (*USAF*)

a variety of delivery techniques with a variety of ordnance. Most of the ranges in the UK were used on a regular basis. Richard Crandall recalls a routine mission for a 48th TFW crew out of RAF Lakenheath:

> We would come in and find out if we had a range scheduled. If it was Tain [RAF Tain is a Ministry of Defence air weapons range on the Moray Firth near Tain in Scotland] or Rosehearty [RAF Rosehearty near Fraserburgh in Aberdeenshire], then we would plan a low level to end up North. If it was Jurby [RAF Jurby on the Isle of Man], then we might plan through Wales. We would talk to the weather guessers to get their best bet on where the weather was good to get down low and fly. We would then pull out the 1:500,000 charts and start to plan the low level, making sure we avoided all the noise sensitive and restricted areas. This was hard to do as we had to manually check the coordinates and plot them all on our maps. We would 'CHUM' the charts (Chart Updating Manual) to ensure we had the towers and any other obstructions plotted. We would take our planning plotters, turning diameters, pick turn points and practice targets, plan an attack, put the distance marks and timing marks on it, plan the fuel burn and create a map for our use in the cockpit. This would take a long time to do. There were some preplanned routes we could use but we would often make our own. We would then go in and brief up the mission, plan what we needed, brief what we must, fly what we are able. We were legally allowed to brief up three different ranges. On each range we would plan our deliveries and get the appropriate ballistics planned, wind corrections, etc. This took a lot of time. Then we would step out to the jet. They would drive us to the appropriate shelter though there were jets we could walk to. It just depended on where the jet was. We would then do our pre-flight, get in and start up. It took a while for the INS to spin up. That was critical because if the INS dumped it was harder to fly the low levels. We would call for taxi and do the Standard departure. We would get cleared by the British ATC though sometimes we would fly to France or the Netherlands or Germany to fly a low level though not as often as just staying in England. The missions averaged 2.4 hours or so. We would come back and do an Instrument Penetration/radar pattern. If it was a clear day we would beat up the pattern with overheads, land, taxi in and debrief. It was nice that the F model had the video as could review the radar and Pave Tack info during the debrief and settle the bets for bombs of course.[9]

The armament carried by the F-111F included Mk 82 500-lb bombs, Mk 84 2,000-lb bombs, CBU-24 Cluster Bombs, and the French Designed Matra BLU-107 Durandal runway penetration bomb. For practice and training purposes, the F-111s used the BDU-33 practice bomb for all slick bombs and the Mk 106 for the high-drag-type bombs. The ballistics were not perfect for the Mk 82/84 slicks with the BDU-33 but were close enough for the delivery to be very similar in release altitude and range. The Mk 106 was not exact for the high-drag bombs, initially the Mk 82 snake eyes but in the '80s, they switched to the Mk 82/84s. They had the ballutes that would inflate like a balloon behind the bomb. The SUU-21 practice bomb dispenser normally carried two MK 106s and four BDU-33s, and had doors which enclosed the bombs as to avoid accidental release in populated areas.

The F-111F initially used the weapons bay which could carry a variety of stores. Pave Tack enabled the laser-guided bombs (LGB), GBU-10, GBU-12, GBU-15, GBU-24, and GBU-28 to be carried and delivered.

At Lossiemouth, during the Strike Command Bombing Competition, aircrew approach their aircraft to fly a mission on 15 June 1981. (USAF)

This F-111F is carrying French-designed Matra BLU-107 Durandal runway penetration bombs. In the conventional role, the 48th TFW F-111F targets included Soviet and Warsaw Pact airfields. (*USAF*)

Although much of the training for both the nuclear and conventional missions was carried out in the UK, the 48th TFW deployed regularly to Europe, North Africa, and the Middle East, on exchange visits and for weapons training. Jim Jimenez recalls two of the regular training venues visited by the 48th TFW:

> We had two semi-annual weapons deployments a year for concentrated weapons training. One was to Incirlik, Turkey. The other was to Zaragoza, Spain. We couldn't drop live ordnance in Spain, but we dropped plenty of inert heavy-weight bombs on Bardenas Reales Range. Our redeployment sortie from Zaragoza in the fall of 1985 was pretty memorable. In those days there was still a U.S. Air Force F-16 wing at Torrejón. They asked us if we could support them during one of their exercises. We said we were redeploying back to the UK, but could hit them on the way. They were stunned. The F-16s would have needed a tanker to fly to the UK and we were going to fly low-level and attack their airfield before heading out. We rocked em. Two noticeable things about the F-111F were flame and noise. The afterburner was visible during the day, and to this day, the F-111F in afterburner remains the loudest airplane I've ever heard. The folks around Torrejón still talk about that simulated attack. We exited feet wet over the Atlantic going the speed of stink. The Torrejón F-16s didn't have the gas to chase us. After a bit we got tired, pitched-up, brought the wings forward, and flew north to Lakenheath.[10]

The Aardvarks took part in a variety exercises, including the southern region Display Determination annual NATO exercise.

If the F-111 had one problem, it was the difficulty experienced by the ground crews in maintaining the aircraft to the standard required for the mission. As with F-111Es of the 20th TFW, there was a serious shortage of spares and MC rates were high. This had a significantly adverse effect on mission capability and effectiveness. Richard Crandall recalls:

> The F-111 was 9% of Tactical Air Command's aircraft yet commanded 25% of the budget for maintenance. It had fantastic capabilities but it always broke. The F model was the best, most reliable, but I still remember spending hours and hours sitting in the cockpit as the cannibalized parts off of other jets to try to get mine flying. We really did have a hard time getting our formation requirements done as it was hard to get a formation up together.[11]

When Gen. Gaddafi of Libya had tested the US patience to breaking point with his constant acts of terrorism against them, Operation El Dorado Canyon was planned to deliver an unequivocal message. The operation was for USAF aircraft to fly from the UK and bomb targets in and around the Libyan capital of Tripoli. The US Navy's Sixth Fleet in the Mediterranean was to support the operation in addition to carrying out their own raids on targets around the city of Benghazi.

It was decided that the attacking force for Eldorado Canyon would be conducted by the F-111Fs of the 48th TFW based at RAF Lakenheath in Suffolk. They would be supported by EF-111A Ravens from the 42nd Electronic Combat Squadron from RAF Upper Heyford. The role of the Ravens was to work in harmony with the Navy's Grumman EA-6B Prowlers in jamming Libyan radar systems. Twenty-four F-111Fs and

Maintenance make the final adjustments to this Pave Tack laser target designator during a press briefing day at Lakenheath in October 1981, prior to its entering service in early 1982. On the F-111F, the AN-AVQ-26 was carried in the internal bomb bay and could be retracted when not in use. (*USAF*)

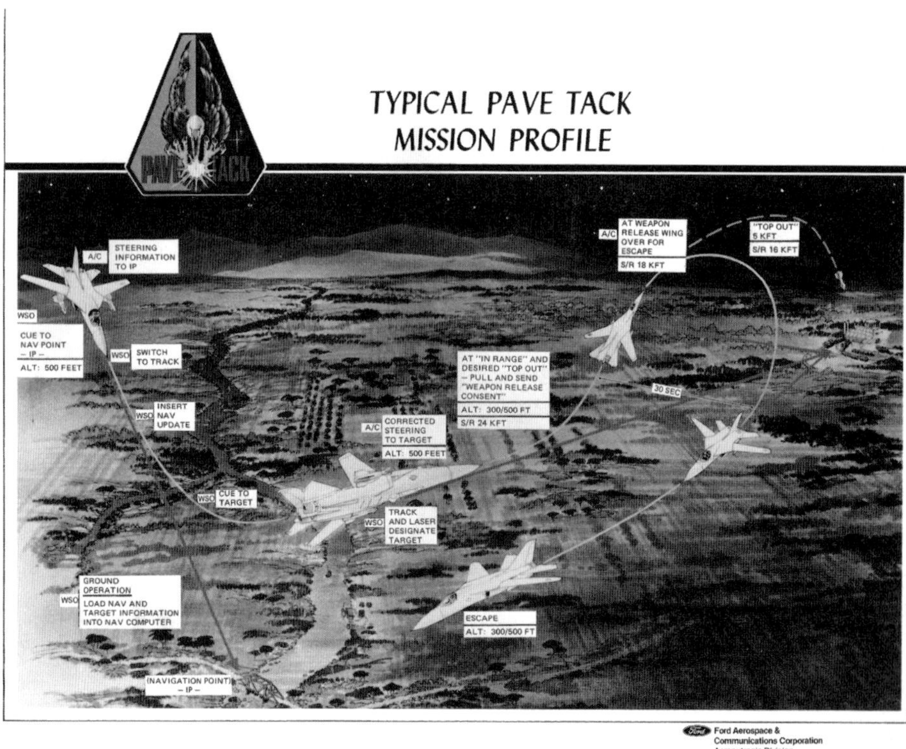

A 'Typical Pave Tack Mission Profile' publicity document published by the Ford Aerospace and Communications Division. (*Ford Aerospace*)

This F-111F is waiting to take on fuel from a Wisconsin ANG KC-135 somewhere over the Mediterranean. (*USAF*)

On 14 April 1986, an F-111F takes off at Lakenheath to fly the retaliatory strike against Libya, codenamed Operation Eldorado Canyon. (*USAF*)

A ground crew prepares an F-111F aircraft prior to take-off for Eldorado Canyon. An arming supervisor gives hand signals to the pilot of the aircraft as the crewman under the wing pulls arming pins out of the GBU-10 modular glide bombs. (*USAF*)

six EF-111As took off in the late afternoon of Monday 14 April 1986 and headed south in radio silence, accompanied by a tanker force of McDonnell Douglas KC-10s and Boeing KC-135s. After the first refuelling six F-111F spares and one EF-111A returned to base. The remainder proceeded south, each with their 'mother' tanker.

The armada was due to strike their Libyan targets at approximately 2 a.m. on 15 April. Ten minutes before this time, the EF-111As and the EA-6Bs began their jamming of the Libyan air defence radars and communications. Jim Jimenez was one of the pilots with the strike force. He takes up the story:

> The sky was overcast, and the moon had set about four hours earlier. We had flown the entire route 'comm out'. Our last weather brief, before takeoff, had forecast a 20mph tailwind from Lampedusa to the target, but instead we were fighting a 23-mph headwind. If the winds were this off, maybe our forecast altimeter setting was just as wrong.
>
> Without afterburner, the airplane's max speed was 655 mph. Approaching the starting point for the bomb run, we were 10 seconds slow, so I selected afterburner to accelerate to 690 mph for two minutes. The airplane jumped at the chance to go faster, and I had to fight off vertigo to keep it level. When we hit the start point, I turned left toward the target, hacked my stopwatch, and again selected afterburner. Our target run was planned for 690 mph at 200 feet. We didn't dare descend, but we had to nail the timing or we'd risk hitting someone else's airplane or bombs.

> The target run was a sensory overload. The terrain-following radars gave off an incessant, blaring 'fly up' alarm. Even though we did not have them engaged, we didn't dare turn them off, since the radar scope was picking up a faint return from the waves. On top of that noise, the radar warning receiver was sounding a constant 'New-Guy Audio'. The audio was to warn us of a new priority radar threat. The Libyans were turning their search radars off and on and using their beamed tracking radars to search for us. Each search radar cycle or sweep of the target trackers triggered our radar warning. The end effect was like a broken record. I would have punched off the audio but was afraid I'd accidentally punch off something important, like the intercom or radio.
>
> As we approached Tripoli, the sky was filled with tracers and surface-to-air missiles, but the real threat was of plunging into the water. With our unreliable altimeter setting and no radar altimeter, we didn't know how high we really were, and at 700 mph, it wouldn't have taken much of a distraction for us to smack the waves.
>
> We arrived at our pull-up point, with 18 seconds to go to the target. Our tactic was to 'toss' the bombs, do a wing-over, and then remain at altitude to laser-guide the bombs. Just prior to pull-up, I de-selected the afterburner and reset the wing sweep to 54 degrees. At the pull-up point, I initiated a 4-G pull, concentrated on centring the steering, pressed the bomb release button (the 'pickle'), and let the armament system compute when to drop the bombs. I relied on my training and acted on reflex. Chaff, pull, pickle, chaff. 'Bombs gone.' Chaff/flare, wing-over. '18 seconds to impact.' Chaff/flare. '10 seconds.' Chaff/flare. '5 seconds.' Chaff/flare. 'Impact.' Chaff/flare.
>
> Just after our bombs hit, I saw a large, napalm-like explosion across the harbour. It had to have been Karma 52, the F-111 that was lost on the raid. Neither of us could afford to dwell on our feelings. There was still too much flying to do. With the bombs gone, I swept the wings back and got out of Dodge as fast as possible without using the afterburner, since it had proven to be an anti-aircraft-artillery magnet.[12]

Following the attacks on the various targets, the F-111Fs egressed the area. It was not until they had departed that the EF-111s left their jamming orbits and headed for their tankers. They had been the first in and the last out of the area.

Opinions vary regarding the success or otherwise of the raid on Libya. Undoubtedly, the Libyans were unprepared for the attack and the F-111s initially met with little resistance in terms of anti-aircraft fire and fighter interception. Indeed, no Libyan jets were scrambled. However, only three of the eighteen targets were hit, and although a number of Libyan military aircraft were destroyed on the ground, one of the principle targets, Gaddafi himself, was not touched. His support for terrorist operations continued unabated.

Although initial opposition was minimal and the raid only lasted approximately twelve minutes, one F-111F was downed by anti-aircraft fire or a missile probably as a result of the attacking aircraft attacking in trail, thereby giving the defenders times to respond to the last in line. Captains Fernando Ribas-Dominicci and Paul F. Lorence of the 495th TFS, flying F-111F 70-2389, crashed into the Gulf of Sidra.

The refusal of the French and Spanish authorities to allow the attacking aircraft to overfly their territory certainly complicated mission planning. The flight to the target area took the aircraft fourteen hours to cover 5,500 nautical miles, and would certainly have contributed to aircrew fatigue and could, arguably, have contributed to the overall operation of the mission. Although aircrew error was responsible for some of the targets not being hit, the extremely restrictive ROE, which stated that no bombs were to be released unless the aircrew were absolutely certain of hitting the target, also had a detrimental effect on the operation. On the positive side, the lessons learnt from working with the Pave Tack systems were to prove invaluable some four years later when the 48th went to war in the Gulf.

On 2 August 1990, the Iraqis invaded Kuwait. So commenced Operation Desert Shield. Desert Shield was followed by Desert Storm, which commenced on 17 January 1991. Between August 1990 and May 1991, the entire 48th TFW deployed to the Middle East to take part in the operations against Iraq.

Eighteen F-111Fs departed Lakenheath for their base at Ta'if in Saudi Arabia on 5 August 1990. By December 1990, sixty-six aircraft were based at Ta'if. Missions flown by the Aardvarks were many and varied. Targets included artillery, SAM sites, bunkers, hangars, runways, hardened aircraft shelters (HAS), bridges, Scuds, and tanks and armour. In total, the wing flew 2,500 sorties of which 2,200 were deemed successful. This constituted a formidable 88-per cent mission success rate.

By far the most successful of these missions were those flown at night against tanks and other armour. A total of 920 targets in this category were put out of action. 'Tank plinking' as it became known was a new mission for the 48th TFW. To adequately prepare for the mission the 48th F-111s took part in two exercises in the theatre during Desert Shield: Night Camel and Night Cannon. Both these exercises involved medium-altitude missions against friendly armour using simulated cluster bombs. One of the lessons learnt from these exercises was that the missions would be more certain of success if LGBs were used. The aircrews soon became so proficient at the role of 'tank plinking' that this soon became their primary mission, with as many as sixty sorties per night flown against tanks. The standard weapons load for the anti-tank missions was four GBU-12 500-lb LGBs.

Many of the missions flown over Iraq were met with considerable anti-aircraft opposition. On the first night of the war, 17 January 1991, Lt-Col. Dennis R. Ertler was engaged on an attack on a HAS near Ali Al Salem airfield. Heavy defensive fire had caused some of the Aardvarks to turn back, but Lt-Col. Ertler and his WSO, Capt. Keith Zuegel, continued on to the target with the remaining aircraft. In an account of the mission in the 48th TFW *Jet48* publication, he recalled:

> We were getting AAA, radar warnings and SAM [Surface to Air Missile] activity, so I set the jet on automatic terrain following radar [TFR] when I saw the first launch of a SAM on the side of the aircraft. The TFR seemed to be flying us directly into the path of the climbing AAA. I was forced to fly the jet manually at low level because of that.[13]

The F-111F was carrying two GBU-24 2,000-lb LGBs. The bombs were released and Capt. Zuegel marked the target. At this crucial time in the mission, Ertler received a second SAM warning: 'I released some chaff and the SAM blew up right behind us. Our bombs were still on target and they hit dead centre'. For this mission, Lt-Col. Ertler was

Armed with two laser-guided bombs, F-111F 72-1443 taxis out at Ta'if to fly a mission. F-111Fs flew 2,500 combat sorties in the Gulf War, achieving an 88-per cent bombing success rate. (*USAF*)

Capt. Bradley Seipel (WSO) and Capt. Michael Russell (pilot) strap themselves into the cockpit of a 48th Tactical Fighter Wing F-111F aircraft in preparation for a mission during Operation Desert Storm. On 26 January 1991, Seipel and Russell of the 493rd TFS flew the successful mission against two oil-pumping stations in Kuwait, which were pumping thousands of gallons of crude oil into the Gulf. To prevent an ecological disaster, the flow had to be stopped. Seipel and Russell were one of four crews that undertook the mission to place two 2,000-lb GBU-15 LGBs directly on to the pumping stations and destroy them. Brad Seipel noted: 'The mission went exactly as planned. Two jets flew towards the target at Mach 1, released their bombs and escaped the heavy anti-aircraft artillery and surface to air missiles. The other two jets, located miles from the target, guided the bombs directly onto the pumping stations'. (*USAF*)

awarded the Air Force Silver Star. There were four other such awards for gallantry to 48th FW aircrew during the Gulf War.

Two Aardvark aircrew, pilot Lt-Col. James F. Slaton and WSO Capt. John F. Daughtry, were awarded the Silver Star for their part in the attack on the Al Tuwaitha nuclear Research facility on the outskirts of Baghdad on 4 February 1991. The target was protected by nineteen SAM systems and some 200 AAA emplacements. Eighteen F-111Fs were involved in the strike accompanied by four McDonnell Douglas F-4G 'Wild Weasel' Phantoms for SAM suppression, four McDonnell Douglas F-15C Eagles for fighter cover, and two General Dynamics EF-111A Ravens for ECM. The F-111Fs were carrying GBU-24 bombs.

The anti-aircraft environment over the target was so intense that only three aircraft managed to reach their targets, led by Lt-Col. Slaton's aircraft. He takes up the story in the *Jet48* journal of 24 April 1991:

> The clouds were too thick for our equipment, so we had to fly lower to get a look at our targets. The only problem was, this put us in the heart of their defences. Bear (Captain Daughtry's call sign) guided the bombs directly on target and we got out of there. By that time the whole sky was lit up. At least that's how it looked to me.[14]

He was a great believer in the use of the GBU-24 for this type of mission: 'It has steep impact angles and a long cruise range, so we could release the bomb several miles from the target. During peace we train to get into precise parameters, but, during the war, you're getting shot at and dodging SAMs and AAA. These hi-tech weapons make the difference'.

The first successful delivery of the GBU-28 4,700-lb LGB was by an F-111F of the 48th TFW. On 27 February 1991, Lt-Col. Dave White (pilot) and Capt. Tom Himes (WSO) destroyed the Iraqi Command and Control centre north of Baghdad which was buried 100 feet underground. The GBU-28 had the distinction of being developed and delivered to the wing within seventeen days of the request for a more powerful bomb for attacking the harder targets.

The 48th TFW returned to RAF Lakenheath from the Gulf on 13 May 1991, hostilities effectively having ceased on 23 February. Not only had the aircrew and the Aardvark acquitted themselves with distinction during the conflict, but they had done so with the unfailing commitment of the maintenance personnel who kept a mission capable rate in excess of 85 per cent throughout the conflict and had never failed to provide a crew ready jet during Desert Storm.

On 1 October 1991, the 48th Tactical Fighter Wing was redesignated the 48th Fighter Wing and the 495th TFS was deactivated. In February 1992, the wing began conversion to the McDonnell Douglas F-15E Strike Eagle. The last F-111Fs left Lakenheath in December 1992 when the 493rd FS was deactivated.

In January 1994, the 493 TFS was reactivated and received the F-15C Eagle, being tasked with an air superiority and air defence mission in support of USAFE and NATO.

F-111F 73-0715 takes off from Ta'if. During operations in the Gulf, the 48th TFW lost no aircraft in combat. (*USAF*)

8

The 10th TRW, TFW

The 10th Photographic Group was activated at Key Field, Mississippi, in December 1943. It took over the personnel of the 73rd Observation Group. In the first months of 1944, the group deployed to the UK and joined the 9th Air Force, being based at RAF Chalgrove in Oxfordshire. The 10th comprised six operational squadrons flying a variety of aircraft in the photographic and observation roles. The squadrons were the 15th TRS and the 30th, 31st, 33rd, 34th, and 425th Photographic Reconnaissance Squadrons. The principle aircraft flown were the Lockheed F-5 Lightning and the North American F-6 Mustang.

Operating from Chalgrove in May 1944, the 10th Photographic Group played a major part in the preparations for the D-Day landings, photographing key tactical targets. The 30th PRS moved to RAF Middle Wallop in May and was replaced at Chalgrove by the 423rd Night Fighter Squadron. This unit flew the Douglas F-3A Havoc and the 10th acquired a night photo reconnaissance role. The 42nd was redesignated the 155th Photographic Reconnaissance Squadron.

After playing a major role in the Normandy invasions in June 1944, the 10th PRG moved to France at the end of June. The units was attached to the United States 3rd Army, and between August 1944 and the end of the war, it flew reconnaissance missions in support of the Allies' advance, taking part in the Battle of the Bulge and the crossing of the Rhine, eventually being based at Fürth in Germany at the war's end.

After the war, the 10th remained on the continent assigned to USAFE. In 1947, it was transferred on paper back to the US, to Langley AFB, Virginia. In September 1947, at Larson Field, Georgia, it was equipped with the F-6 Mustang and redesignated the 10th TRG. Two squadrons were attached, the 1st and the 15th TRS. In June 1948, the group was redesignated the 10th Tactical Reconnaissance Wing at Pope Field, North Carolina (now Pope Air Force base). The wing was deactivated in April 1949. In July 1952, the 10th TRW was reactivated and assigned to USAFE, based at Toul-Rosières Air Base in France, taking over the personnel and equipment of the Air National Guard's federalised 117th TRG. In May 1953, the 10th moved to Spangdahlem in Germany. In 1959, as a part of 'Red Richard' reshuffles, the 10th (its four squadrons now equipped with the Douglas RB-66 Destroyer) was obliged to move to the UK.

The Douglas RB-66 Destroyer

The story of the Destroyers of the 10th Tactical Reconnaissance Wing (TRW) in the UK begins in Germany, at Spangdahlem and Sembach air bases.

The 66th TRW, which was based at Sembach, and the 10th TRW, at Spangdahlem, both had night photo squadrons attached. With the 10th at Spangdahlem were the 1st TRS and the 42nd TRS, and at Sembach with the 66th TRW were the 30th TRS and the 19th TRS; the 19th TRS was already based in the UK, at RAF Sculthorpe. The 19th TRS had, until January 1957, been attached to the 47th Bombardment Wing, flying the North American RB-45C Tornado. The 1st and 30th TRS flew the Martin RB-57A Canberra, and the 42nd TRS, which had an ELINT role, flew the Douglas RB-26 Invader. In 1957, the four squadrons began conversion to the Douglas RB-66 Destroyer.

Conversion to the RB-66 progressed throughout the year, with all four squadrons fully equipped by the end of 1957. In December of that year, HQ USAFE issued General Order 88, which assigned the 19th and 30th TRS from the 66th TRW to the 10th TRW, and the two 10th TRW day reconnaissance squadrons, flying the RF-84F Thunderflash, were assigned to the 66th TRW.

Thus the 10th TRW became an all RB-66 wing; the 1st, 30th, and 19th TRS flew the RB-66B; and the 42nd, the RB-66C and the WB-66D, the latter being ostensibly for weather reconnaissance.

The missions flown by the squadrons were mostly routine with two notable exceptions. Routine for the 42nd TRS involved regular electronic surveillance missions along the borders of the Warsaw Pact countries. One such mission caused some headaches for USAFE command. In the early part of the year, an RB-66C had inadvertently violated the East German Air Defence Zone (ADIZ). Fortunately for all concerned, the aircraft was not intercepted by air defence fighters and returned to its proper course. Subsequent investigation of the incident revealed that the navigational radar was inoperative and other aids were unreliable. This prompted 10th HQ to issue a directive forbidding any of its squadrons to fly east of the Rhine River if the navigation radar was in any way suspect. Regular Space Cadet missions were defined for the 42nds WB-66Ds at this time also requiring them to fly close to hostile borders in the ADIZ for the purposes of obtaining weather information for the use of USAFE tactical units.

Another of the missions of the weather reconnaissance WB-66Bs of the 42nd TRS was the Wild Goose mission, which was to provide weather reconnaissance for all USAFE aircraft detaching to North Africa.

In 1959, the 1st TRS undertook trials for Operation Taxicab, which was designed to develop a pathfinder role. Taxicab was initially conceived as an experiment to ascertain whether or not the RB-66 could be used to lead in F-100 fighter bombers to a target in bad weather or at night, i.e. when IFR were required. For the purposes of the evaluation exercise RB-66s of the 1st TRS and F-100Ds of the 49th TFW deployed to Nouasseur. When the details had been worked out and practised the 1st TRS aircraft returned to Europe to manoeuvre with the F-100Cs of the 36th Tactical Fighter Wing. At a

The 19th TRS at RAF Sculthorpe also began receiving the RB-66 in early 1957, replacing its RB-45C Tornadoes. The 19th was transferred to the 66th TRW in January 1957, and for a short while wore the colours of that wing. A blue band around the engine nacelles with white stars superimposed. (*Courtesy of the Ray Schrecengost archives*)

This RB-66 of the 30th TRS still carries the markings of the 66th TRW while at an open house somewhere in Europe. (*via Robbie Robinson*)

RB-66B 54-435 of the 19th TRS still wearing its 66th TRW markings. (*R. Ganci*)

Author Jackie Collins, sister of Joan, visited the 19th TRS at RAF Sculthorpe in 1957 and had an RB-66B named after her. (*USAF*)

specified distance from the target, the fighter bombers broke away and, at a signal from the navigator of the destroyer, performed their target run. After a successful bombing run had been accomplished, the RB-66 would fly over the target and photograph the damage. The 'Pathfinder' concept was tried and successful and was to become part of USAFE's operations systems from July 1959, when two WB-66Ds of the 42nd TRS formed the alert force at Bitburg with four F-100Cs.

The move of the 10th TRW to the UK went smoothly enough but was to have a considerable effect on the missions of the squadrons. Taxicab, barely started, was cancelled. The component parts of the alert force were based too far apart to make it viable. The 19th TRS, having just moved from Sculthorpe to Spangdahlem, was obliged to move yet again, to RAF Bruntingthorpe. The 1st and 30th TRS went to Alconbury and the 42nd to RAF Chelveston.

It became necessary for the 42nd TRS to plan new ECM routes. The increased distance to the borders of the Soviet zone of Germany and Czechoslovakia, coupled with the ATC procedures of the UK, considerably restricted 'watch time' over target. Just prior to the redeployment of the aircraft to the UK, they had been fitted with refuelling probes. From 15 October 1959, daily KB-50 refuelling exercises were introduced for the RB-66s in an attempt to overcome this problem, and as a result, watch time was increased to two hours twenty minutes. However, poor weather took its toll of some missions and it was estimated that ECM missions were cut by as much as 50 per cent after the move to the UK.

On 22 December 1959, the 42nd undertook a covert operation against two Soviet radar complexes in East Germany located near the towns of Zerbet and Morseburg. The two radars, codenamed Barlock and Stonecake were unknown quantities and the object of the exercise was to ascertain whether they were synchronised one with the other, as well as to intercept and record Soviet Air Defence transmissions. In this mission, the 42nd was aided by F-102s of the 86th Fighter Interceptor Wing. These aircraft made supersonic incursions into East German airspace to encourage the Soviets to turn their radars on so that they could be checked out by the 42nd ECM crews. The mission was successful.

These 'probe' missions were often carried out by the 10th TRW. However, on occasions when the RB-66B was used as the probe aircraft, it was imperative that actual penetration did not take place. The destroyer did not have the performance to escape any interceptors sent up after it! 'Doc' Partridge was the commander of the 19th TRS from 1958 to 1962:

> We were tasked on rare occasions to fly fake penetrations of the Russian border. Normally those missions were given to fighter units but as I said we would get one every now and then. The 42nd TRS would be on station with their C models so that when the border lit up they could analyse their signals. I flew one of the border missions. We were under ground control, on a heading straight at the Russian border. My navigator informed me that if we didn't start a turn immediately that we would probably have a border violation on our hands. I started the turn immediately and ground called and said my turn would not put us close enough to the border to have any affect. I told them that this was not a fighter and

In 1959, the squadrons of the 10th TRW moved to their new bases in the UK. The wing headquarters was at RAF Alconbury where the 1st and 30th TRS were to be based. The arrival of the first RB-66s was enthusiastically welcomed at Alconbury: 'I remember the day they first arrived. I knew we were getting new planes but never knew what or when. Then, on a clear day from out of nowhere several B-66s were circling fairly low overhead and banking 90° as they rolled in before landing. It gave us a good view of how neat they looked'. (*Tom Burns via Bob Green*)

Col. James D. Kemp arrives at Alconbury. Kemp was the commander of the 10th TRW. (*via Bob Green*)

Lt-Col. Edward Ellis carries the shield of the 10th TRW to its new home at Alconbury. (*via Bob Green*)

The 42nd TRS was based at RAF Chelveston. The RB-66Cs of the 42nd were equipped with a multitude of sensors for their electronic warfare role. Particularly noticeable are the wing tip antenna pods, which housed the AN/APD-4 instantaneous airborne direction finder, used to detect and catalogue radar emissions in the frequency range of 1,000 to 33,000 megacycles per second. (*USAF*)

Landing at Alconbury is RB-66B 54-512. It is in the process of deploying its drag chute. (*10th TRW Historical Office*)

Aircrew from the 1st TRS, 10th TRW, and aircrew from 543 Squadron, RAF, stand in front of their respective aircraft at Alconbury. There was a good deal of co-operation between the two units, not only because many aspects of their role were similar, but also because Wyton and Alconbury were so close there was a joint air traffic control system, with each station being allotted a block time for arrivals and departures. (*Gerry Reponen*)

> that we would have had a border violation if we hadn't started our turn when we did. As it was we did get close enough to light up some radars.[1]

The 42nd weather recce missions continued much as they had done before the move to the UK. The Wild Goose mission based three WB-66Ds at Nouasseur to support all movements from Europe to the North African bases.

Another of the 42nd's weather tasks was the Tac Strike mission. These were weather reconnaissance flights into the refuelling areas used by fighter aircraft moving between the US and Europe. In the main, these were routine missions, but on two occasions the crews of the WB-66Ds were involved in the rescues of downed aircrew. In the first incident, an F-100 crashed into the Mediterranean off Wheelus. The destroyer crew pinpointed the area and circled the site of the crash until naval forces arrived. The second event involved the collision between an F-100D and a two seat F-100F over the Bordeaux area. The former managed to limp to Chateauroux, but the F-100F crashed and the WB-66 followed the parachutes down and radioed their position, maintaining station until the unfortunate airmen were picked up.

The notorious UK weather had an adverse effect on the operations of the 10th Tactical Reconnaissance Squadron. Rex Davis was a navigator with the 30th TRS and related:

> The weather in the UK was always a factor. Pea soup fog could come on in an instant. We would try to contact the French radar but usually they couldn't find us so we would leave their frequency and do whatever we needed to do. Quite often when the weather was bad all over the UK, we could find decent weather in Dijon area. The weather in Germany was often bad and because of the border with the East more complicated. Each crew would decide where they wanted to go to fill training requirements. I favoured Scotland, Northern Ireland and the Brest peninsula, France. All our night missions were over a water target in the Wash near Kings Lynn or off to the west side of the Isle of Man. We had a range north of Holland that we would use if the weather was bad in the UK.[2]

One necessary consequence of the move to the UK was the pressing need to take full advantage of the opportunities the sun bases of North Africa offered. In 1960, Moron, Spain, also became available as a regular detachment for the 10th TRW squadrons. Gerry Reponen was with the 30th TRS:

> At RAF Alconbury the weather was not very conducive for flying so we were sent to Moron AB at least once a month beginning in October. We would fly our night mission over the Salvage Islands range dropping the M123A1 photoflash cartridges with the four second delay fuse or the M120 photoflash bombs. During 1960 our night missions at Moron were changed to fly over the Mar Menor Bomb Range.[3]

In North Africa, the RB-66s used Nouasseur in Morocco. This detachment did not sit well with some of the aircrew: 'Morocco sucked! The French had left Casablanca and taken the good chefs and restaurants with them. It was an hour drive down town and not much to do when you got there. Such a contrast with Seville'.

One of the advantages of Moron over Nouasseur was the availability of suitable photographic targets. Moron normally had good weather and photo targets were more diverse. Nouasseur had the better weather, but photographing small villages in a wasteland was not challenging. As many as twelve RB-66s were sent to Moron for a week at a time. For each aircrew, an average of fifteen hours' training and operational flying took place.

One of the most significant events for USAFE tactical reconnaissance began in January 1960 when the Green Dragon mission was assigned to the 10th TRW. To implement Green Dragon, the 10th TRW was assigned twelve specially modified B-66Bs. The B-66B was the bomber variant of the destroyer and some of these aircraft had been stationed at RAF Sculthorpe with the 47th Bombardment Wing. The modification consisted of the installation of a special pallet in the bomb bay of the aircraft in which were installed a suite of electronic countermeasures equipment including the AN/ALE-1 chaff dispenser, AN/APS-54 radar warning set, and an array of jamming equipment. The tail gun barbette was removed from the aircraft and a special ECM tail cone fitted. In fact, all RB-66s of the 10th TRW underwent this modification to the tail of the RB-66 over a period of months. The K-5 bomb navigation system was also installed. The job of modifying the aircraft was a considerable one and fell to the Roma Air Material Area (ROAMA) who completed the job in just four weeks. Following on from the modification the Brown

Cradle, B-66Bs were tested by the 801st Air Division of Air Defence Command in the USA where further modifications were made following recommendations following the trials. These included the addition of stub antennae.

After modification, the Brown Cradle B-66Bs were assigned to the 42nd TRS, which phased out its WB-66Ds during the first half of 1960.

Although assigned to the 42nd TRS, the Brown Cradle aircraft were crewed by personnel from all the squadrons of the 10th on a rotational basis. However, before being permitted to fly the aircraft on a regular basis, the pilots were obliged to check out. The ECM suite as installed had considerably altered the centre of gravity of the aircraft and both take-off and landing speeds were markedly different for both aircraft.

Echo Alert went into operation on 1 May 1960 at RAF Alconbury. The purpose of the alert was to support USAFE F-100D fighter bombers in the event of war breaking out, by providing electronic countermeasures designed to confuse the enemy sensors as they flew to their targets. Two aircraft were on alert at all times. Gerry Reponen noted: 'In April the Alert facilities had been completed and we kept two B-66B aircraft on alert at all times. With two aircraft over the continent of Europe, we would be able to block all radar with the ECM jamming equipment we carried'.

In order to increase time on station, the 10th TRW considered FOLs for its Echo Alert B-66s. Commencing in October 1960, Toul-Rosières AB in France received and refuelled the Brown Cradle aircraft on a regular basis.

The testing of the efficiency of the jammers on board the B-66Bs was carried out on the Hot Check mission. Prior to going on Echo Alert the aircraft would turn on all its jammers and pre-set to known Soviet frequencies. After take-off, the aircraft would fly out over the Atlantic in company with an RB-66C. Once well away from land the B-66B would turn on its jammers one by one and these would be verified by the crew of the RB-66C for frequency range and output. Once all had been found to be satisfactory, the Brown Cradle aircraft could proceed to Toul-Rosières and alert duty. This was costly in terms of flying hours and also required an RB-66C to be on Hot Check duty daily. In 1962, the 42nd TRS detached permanently to Toul-Rosières.

Meanwhile, back in the UK, at Chelveston, the 42nd TRS played host to personnel from the 9th TRS based at Shaw AFB. Deployments of these crews and aircraft continued throughout the year, for sixty-day periods, the object being for the Shaw-based crews to be integrated with the 42nd TRS and fly ECM missions over Europe.

In February, the 42nd was ordered to detach and maintain on station two WB-66Ds at Wheelus, Libya. They were to launch one sortie a day in order to ascertain high-altitude wind direction for a minimum period of three weeks. The operation, code named Golf Ball, was ordered as a direct result of the French nuclear tests in the Algeria. It was necessary for the USAF to have data relating to the high-altitude air currents in order for the B-57 and WB-50 aircraft to efficiently collect fallout samples from the tests. Thirty-one missions were flown over uncharted areas of desert.

A programme of fitting the RB-66s of the 1st, 19th, and 30th TRS with ECM tail cones got under way in 1961. These replaced the tail barbettes and guns. It enabled all aircraft of the wing to undertake ECM missions, although these were limited in comparison to those carried out by the 42nd TRS.

These RB-66s of the 1st TRS wait in the inclement weather at night. Some aircraft were kept on standby, fuelled up and ready to go. (*Frank Doyle*)

Exercise Cold Turkey in 1961 involved the 42nd Brown Cradle B-66Bs. These aircraft did not often on turn their jamming devices except over the UK and the open ocean. Cold Turkey marked the first time since the Second World War that the USAF had conducted active ECM over the continent of Europe. At this time, Brad Mosher flew with the 30th TRS out of Alconbury:

> We had very specific targets located inside East Germany. They were RR marshalling yards, RR bridges, major highways, tunnels, troop movement, any SAM sites we happened upon, and airfields not already identified. After many years it dawned on me that we only learned one target, they must not have planned on many successful missions. All of our practice missions were similar to the actual target site, these we flew in France and Germany. I have no idea as to declassification of targets, or equipment that was installed on the RB-66Bs. I do know that if we turned all the ECM gear on at one time while at cruise altitude we could blank out most of Western Europe.[4]

Rex Davis also flew ECM missions when the 30th TRS detached to Toul-Rosières in France.

> In 1961, we went to Toul-Rosières, France, to pull Electronic Warfare alert. Toul-Rosières was painful due living in a WWII hanger, restricted to the alert area, the weather and never being allowed off base. We could only leave the alert area two of the seven days. Our

> mission was to jam all the Ruskie and East German radars. We tested the equipment coming from Norway into the UK. We put the entire radar and communications system down from the Shetlands to Jersey. Flight controllers at Heathrow were not amused. We only had the equipment on for 15 seconds.[5]

In the summer of 1961, the 10th TRW was tasked to provide ECCM training for the NATO air defence units, both ground based and airborne, using the ECM tail cone-equipped RB-66Bs. Willi Bruenner was the EW (electronic warfare) officer responsible for the programme:

> This was the start of the Dancing Doll program ,which eventually included the Dutch, Belgians ,Danes, French, UK, Italians, Greeks, Turks, our sixth Fleet, and the German Navy. To get final approval, I had to also brief the BFS (the German FAA) in Frankfurt, because we were going to use jammers and chaff in a very crowded air traffic environment. We usually flew three missions per week, using one or two RB-66s. Both the RB-66 aircrews and the NATO air defenders enjoyed these sorties, because they provided more realism than the canned training provided by the ground radar computers. The RB-66s were the only in-theatre capability NATO had for this type of training at the time, except for a few RAF Coastal Command WWII 4 engine bombers. Major problem arose when the navs did not calculate the chaff drop winds aloft correctly and chaff drifted over neutral Switzerland in bad weather obstructing Zurich radar which did not have any ECCM features. For me, the major by product was that the Soviets, who could observe these exercises, were constantly reminded of the West's technical superiority in electronics. The exercises lasted till the RB-66s had to be deployed to SEA in 1965.[6]

In July 1961, an RB-66C of the 42nd TRS crashed at Chelveston. Of the seven crewmembers on board, only three survived. Both engines had flamed out over the runway. The EWO compartment had ejected downwards as it was designed to do. The aircraft was too low and the three were killed instantly. The gunner was also killed. Doc Partridge was president of the accident investigation board:

> The accident happened on an intentional go-around after a GCA approach. That was a normal procedure after completing a mission. The RB-66C had a modified Bomb bay area for the Electronic Warfare Officers or jammers as we called them. They had downward ejection seats. When the ejection procedure is initiated the first thing that happens is the hatch under the seat is blown off and that triggers the ejection of the seat itself. The aircraft was at approximately 400 feet when both engines flamed out. The pilot gave the order to eject. The navigator went first followed by the engineer. The pilot assumed that everyone in the back had ejected but by that time he was too low to eject. He put the airplane down in a field off the end of the runway without too much damage. Too his surprise he found one of the EWO's exiting the ECM compartment. His hatch had blown off but the seat malfunctioned and didn't go. He believed he was the only one in the aircraft and was going to die when it hit the ground. The three EWO's that ejected hit the runway before their parachutes deployed. The engineer had hung onto his seat and rode it into the runway and was killed. The navigator made it safely.[7]

In March 1962, the 10th TRW took control of Toul-Rosières in France and moved the 19th and the 42nd TRS there. Both RAF Chelveston and Bruntingthorpe were closed down for military operations.

The 10th TRW regularly took part in the annual recce competition Royal Flush on a regular basis as part of the 4th ATAF. In 1960, the competition took place at Bremgarten in Germany and the 30th TRS fielded all the crews for the competition representing the 10th TRW. Rex Davis was associated with Royal Flush for three years from 1960 to 1963:

> The 30th had provided all three crews in 1960. Prior to 1960, there had been a crew from 1st, 30th and 19th from Buntingthorpe near Leicester. The wing went back to a crew from each squadron in 1961. The crew from the 30th had been selected from crews who were very experienced. The opportunity to fly 'Flush' was very competitive. It definitely made crews pay attention to missed targets and various screw ups that crew members often make.
>
> I couldn't have been more surprised to find out the RF-101s out of Loan AFB, France, were grounded and unable to fly day time competition in Flush and that the 10th Wing would provide crews and aircraft for both day and night competition for 1961 and would be going to a base near Brussels for the competition. I was even more surprised to find that I was on the day crew to represent the 30th. The pilot, Bill Sears, was a legend in his own time and sniffed out the opportunity before most people in the sqd. The Radar/Nav (Nickerson) had the most experience in the squadron having spent a tour in SAC. I probably qualified because Bill Sears had gone on weekend cross countries all over Europe the previous year. We were assigned our own aircraft and maintenance crew as were the other two squadrons. There were only two flying slots in the competition so we went head to head with other two crews. Sears, Nickerson and I won that competition. Our first flight was on Mar 9th 1961. We had 36 practice flights prior to going to Beauvechain, Belgium for Royal Flush V1. The goal on each flight was to practice on targets over military areas in France and Germany. We would photograph the entire complex so we would be familiar with the terrain etc. The important part of these missions was to establish an IP (initial point) that would show up on radar and hopefully visually. The targets for us were almost always in Germany and France. The other competitors flew all over from Norway to Italy. In 1961, our day targets were primarily on bombing ranges, military bases and airfields. They were quite easy to find and photograph. The PIs had their hands full trying to get all the data. The night targets in 1962 and 1963 were always on an army base, bombing range or military air field. The reason being is that photo flash cartridges were dangerous if they were duds and could set fires if only partially expended. We would drop at least seven on each target. They'd really light up the countryside. The pilot would try not let the light affect his night vision when they went off. I don't recall many of the targets except for one at Nordholm range in Germany. We had a perfect IP in the city some five miles SE. In addition to being a good radar site, there was a neon sign in the middle of town that said 'Joe's Tavern'. I could see the sign about two miles out. We would line up so when we went over the sign we were on heading for the target. We would start a stop watch. If I could see the target (tanks in this case) the cameras were turn on by my command. If not, we use the pre-determined time and dropped using the stop watch. We used a ferris wheel in the city of Caen, France, to line up on their airfield.

> An interesting thing happened two years in a row at Caen. In 1961, the PIs saw an air-to-air missile in the launch position. Wrong ... it was a truck with a ladder like thing sticking up in the air. In 1962, Caen was again the target and in the same place was actually a missile. Our PIs missed it both years. RAF did not.[8]

One of the great advantages of Royal Flush was that it provided an opportunity for NATO crews to share their expertise and to engage in constructive dialogue about their respective missions. Of course, it was at the same time an opportunity to 'get one over on the other chap' and a good deal of creative scoring undoubtedly went on.

In March 1962, the 10th TRW gained control of Toul-Rosières and the 19th and 42nd TRS left the UK and moved to the French base. There they remained until they transferred briefly to the 25th Tactical Reconnaissance group at Chambley. The 1st and 30th TRS remained at RAF Alconbury and the RB-66s were replaced by the RF-4C Phantom in 1965.

The McDonnell RF-4C Phantom

On 13 May 1965, two McDonnell RF-4C Phantom II photo jets landed at RAF Alconbury in Huntingdonshire. It was the beginning of an association with the base that was to last twenty-two years. The 10th Tactical Reconnaissance Wing at Alconbury had

'Royal Flush' was a regular annual NATO Recce competition. The 10th TRW Destroyers, and their RB-57s before them, had taken part in the night time part of the exercise. Of the greatest importance was the speed in which the film was downloaded and delivered to the photo interpreters. In this photo, taken at the time of Royal Flush V111, Lionel Barfield is seen running to deliver the developed film, while the other runner carries the undeveloped film. (*Mike Barfield*)

two squadrons assigned in 1965: the 1st and the 30th. The first two Phantoms 64-1019 and 64-1025, resplendent in their grey and white livery, were flown in by Col. DeWitt Spain and Maj. Gary Wright to a base and media welcome. They were assigned to the 1st TRS.

The 10th TRW was the second unit in the USAF to be equipped with the RF-4C, the first being the 16th TRS which was based at Shaw AFB and from there began a tour of duty in SE Asia in October 1965.

The first pilots and GIBs of the 1st and 30th TRS came from a variety of backgrounds. Some were from RF-101s, some from RB-66 units, and some straight from pilot training. Dean Maurer was among the latter:

> Upon graduation from pilot training I headed to Shaw AFB for training in the RF-4C. There were several of us newly graduated pilots and we were all excited about flying the Phantom II. I don't remember if it was the first or second day of class that we were 'paired up' with our front seaters. We were originally given the title of Pilot Systems Operator, although GIB was more commonly used in reference to our back seat position. I had orders to Mountain Home, ID, but these were changed to RAF Alconbury about mid-way through our training.[9]

As time passed, several Vietnam veterans of the 16th TRS joined the 10th, and some of those pilots too were obliged initially to take the rear seat. Jim Wilson arrived at Alconbury fresh from a Vietnam tour: 'The nine GIBs in my group were a sought after commodity because of our back seat radar experience in Vietnam. We all had over 200 night missions each. And of course we were all pilots and chomping at the bit to get upgraded to the front seat, which happened in fairly short order'.

In 1967, the 32nd TRS joined the wing at Alconbury. The 32nd TRS had been a part of USAFE for a long time, and immediately before attachment to the 10th TRW, it had been based at Toul-Rosières in France as part of the 26th TRW. During this time, it had converted to the RF-4C.

As more and more aircraft arrived so the squadrons' operational readiness developed and the regular training, deployments, and exercises became routine. There were some initial problems with the Phantoms, however. Because of the demands of the war in SE Asia, many of the initial RF-4s at Alconbury did not have all the equipment. Some cameras were awaited as were radar scopes. Jim Wilson noted:

> Since aircraft production was ahead of radar scope production, I believe the initial airplanes that went to Alconbury did not have the radar scope. I don't believe this was much of a problem in Europe because there was a still a major daytime mission ... night being lower priority. So although I didn't arrive at Alconbury until Sept 1966 after my Vietnam tour, I believe the shortfall prior to IOC at Alconbury was the rear seat radar scope. As I recall most of the radar scope backfill had been completed at Alconbury by about December of 1966.[10]

Larry Garrison was the commander of the 32nd TRS from 1969 to 1970. He stated: 'The photo systems were quite a ways behind the airplane and the RF-4 at Alconbury

Aircraft 64-1020 was the RF-4C flown into RAF Alconbury by Col. Dewitt Spain on 13 May 1965. One of the things noticed by the aviation press present on the day was the profusion of stencilling on the aircraft, very evident on this photo. (*Randy Romancheck*)

Aircraft 64-1019 was flown by Maj. Gary Wright. The transatlantic crossing required the use of two underwing tanks and the fuselage tank. (*USAF via Bill LaRoche*)

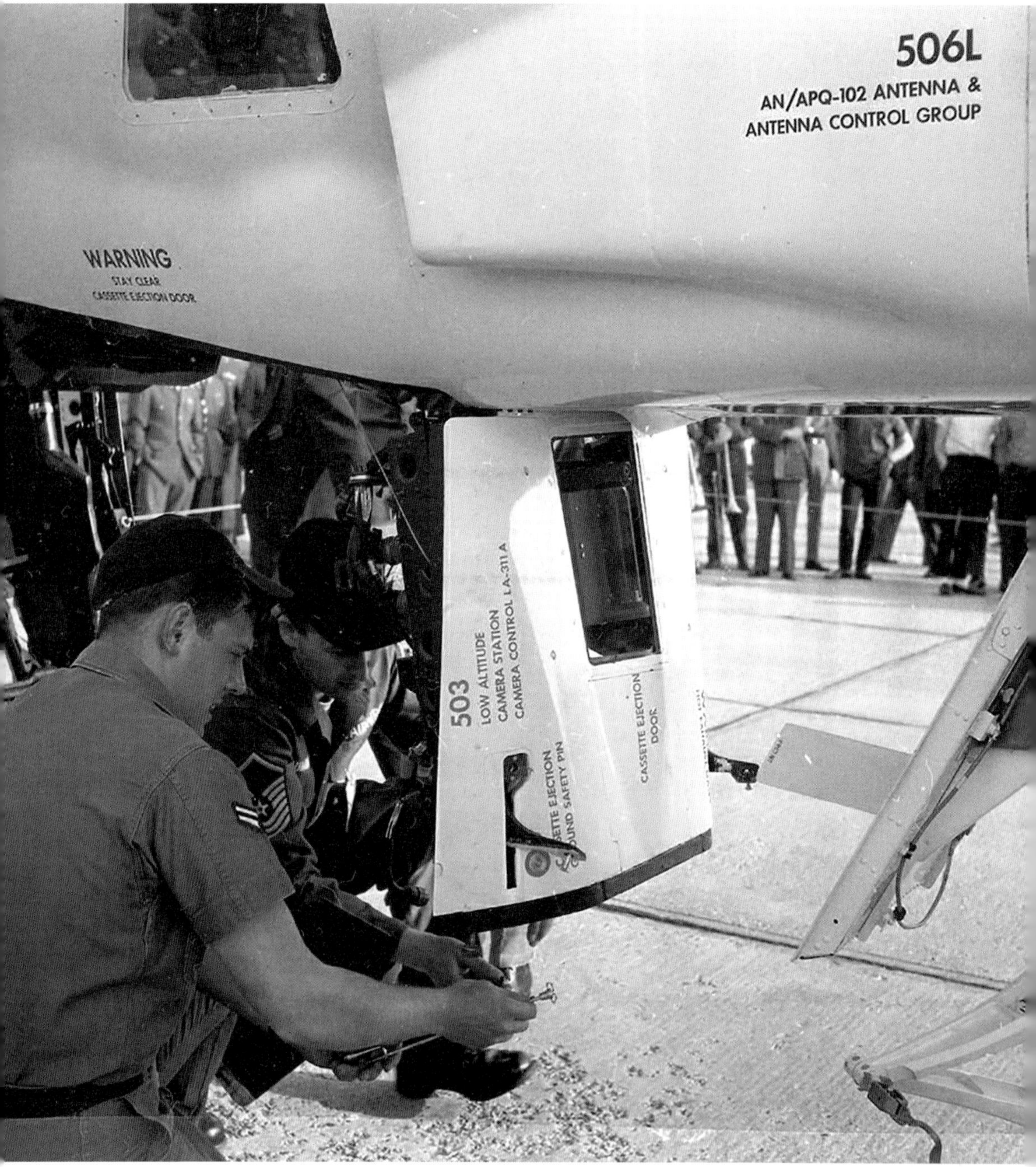

The curiosity of the 'camera troops' is evident as they examined the open camera doors in the nose of 64-1019 on arrival at Alconbury. (*USAF via Bill LaRoche*)

The first squadron to equip with the RF-4 at Alconbury was the 1st TRS. Taken in November 1966, all the pilots in this photo were veterans of the war in SE Asia, including the squadron commander, Lt-Col. John E. Buchanan, at the centre. (*USAF*)

RF-4C 64-1026 is proudly displayed at the Paris Air Show in 1967. The 10th TRW sent an RF-4C to Le Bourget in 1967 and 1969. (*USAF via Bill LaRoche*)

was unable to take many photo for the period 65 to about 67. They essentially had a great flying club for a while'.[11]

During the mid-1960s, the USAFE was losing its bases in North Africa. Nouasseur and Sidi Slimane in Morocco were closed in 1963. This left Wheelus in Libya, the future of which, towards the end of the 1960s, was very uncertain. It was essential for USAFE to have good 'sun bases' where pilots could enjoy good climatic conditions in order to hone their skills and exercise. To this end, they utilised bases at Moron in Spain, Aviano and Sigonella in Italy, and Larissa in Greece. The principle TDY base for the 10th TRW and its squadrons was at Moron and the squadrons detached there for thirty-day periods on a regular basis. One such detachment took Kirk Ransom and others there with a special assignment:

> I do not recall the name of the operation but there was a year long operation out of Moron to monitor the movement of the Soviet fleet in the Mediterranean Sea. These were 30 day deployments to Moron by each recce squadron in USAFE, including the RF-101s and the RF-4Cs from *Zweibrücken. On some missions we would fly two ship from Moron, refuel north of Algeria, proceed all the way to the eastern end of the Mediterranean and refuel again on the return trip. These were about 5+ hour missions. Other missions were single ship in the western or central part of the Mediterranean.* Very early in this operation, I had an aircraft with the new RHAW gear. That made it really easy to find the Soviet fleet. On the first mission where we found the fleet, we dropped down to photograph them as we were supposed to. On this first occasion there were fourteen ships in two columns and we flew at about 200 feet, 360 kts, down between them with the cameras running. It was spooky as every gun and missile tracked us the whole way.[12]

When Fred Mills detached to Moron, he also was dispatched on a special mission on behalf of the US Navy Mediterranean fleet:

> We were on fair weather training at Moron and were tasked to fly out into the Med to take pictures of the Enterprise shadow. We made a low approach to the Enterprise and then they vectored us to the shadow. It looked like a fishing boat but there were too many dipole and parabolic dish antennas for fishing.[13]

Of course, the weather in Northern Europe was not always restrictive and it was necessary for the squadrons to exercise regularly. After all, it was over countries of Western and Eastern Europe that the RF-4Cs would be plying their trade in the event of hostilities commencing with the Warsaw Pact.

Missions flown did not always involve reconnaissance. The wing was regularly tasked with missions testing the air defences of other NATO member countries. One such took ten RF-4Cs to Aalborg in Denmark on a mission to fly back to the UK simulating a hostile force in order to test the UK's air defences. Denmark was a regular destination for RF-4Cs from Alconbury. The base at Karup was the venue for exchange visits with the Royal Danish Air Force and a regular destination for cross-country flights as were bases in the Federal Republic of Germany. Air Defence missions were also flown from German bases. Kirk Ransom noted:

Moron was a regular 'sun base' detachment for many USAFE units, including the squadrons of the 10th TRW. From here many different missions were flown, including exercises with the US Mediterranean fleet and the shadowing and photographing of the Soviet Mediterranean fleet. (*Kirk Ransom*)

Ramp Rat was the somewhat uncomplimentary name given to 64-1077 shortly after the application of 'Vietnam' camouflage. Mark Temple was the crew chief. 'The *Ramp Rat* was put onto the aircraft for Royal Flush that year. It only stayed on the aircraft for the duration of Royal Flush and was painted over soon after the exercise was complete as this sort of thing was not authorized!' (*via Dave Menard*)

> Another mission was in support of air defence exercises. These would usually involve a single mission flying to southern Germany and then fly high altitude back to the Netherlands while being intercepted. On one very large exercise, the wing was tasked to send about 15 aircraft, a couple an hour, on this same route but at 1.1 Mach at 41,000 feet. The charts in the dash-1 did not give a good reading on what the fuel requirements were, so I was tasked to fly the mission before the exercise and record actual fuel use during the high speed portion to build a fuel profile for crews to use.[14]

The German plains provided the terrain for much of the low flying undertaken by the squadrons of the 10th. The RF-4Cs did use the Scottish low-flying areas but not regularly. One of the problems was that while over Scotland the pilots had to file their position every ten minutes in case they went missing.

Creek Hatrack was a regular mission to test the photo processing capability of the photo laboratories at USAFE fighter bases. It was vital that these facilities were always at a high state of readiness. In the event of a war, the recce Phantoms may have to divert to other bases at short notice to offload their film. Creek Hatrack required the RF-4s the fly a recce mission and divert to a fighter base such as Hahn or Bitburg. They would only tell the tower that they were on Hatrack mission just before touchdown. They would be met by the photo lab people and the canisters would be offloaded and taken to the labs for immediate processing.

Another regular mission flown by the RF-4s out of Alconbury was in support of the SALT Treaty. These missions were flown regularly throughout the day over a period of a week; the purpose was to determine if, in fact, optical photography could accurately verify compliance on the ground with SALT requirements. These missions were considered so important that each one had a spare airplane ready to go in case of a problem.

The RF-4Cs had many equipment upgrades during the years they were based at Alconbury. The original 'fit' of forward oblique KS-87, low pan KA-56, KS-72 framing and AN/AAD-5 Infrared cameras, and SLAR, and the FLR sensors was supplemented by additional cameras such as the KA-91 High altitude Panoramic camera. One of the significant upgrades was the AN/ARN101 DMAS (Digital Modular Avionics System). This upgrade replaced the existing navigation computer with an all new capability to load an entire flight plan containing many waypoints. This system was fully integrated with the FLR and the AN/ALQ-125 TEREC. TEREC was a recce system providing precision direction finding, passive ranging, and emitter threat identification. The 1st TRS had two TEREC equipped RF-4s. The DMAS was also compatible with the AN/AVQ-26 Pave Tac. Jack Griffin was a GIB with the 1st TRS from 1983 to 1985:

> I believe we had about six or eight Pave Tac pods in the squadron. It was really the cat's me'ow !!!! I loved it and seized every chance I could to jump on the schedule when one was available. The pod had a control stick, in the rear cockpit. It was a real mind-bender at first. Pulling back on the aircraft control stick of course makes the nose of the aicraft pitch up. Pulling back on the Pave Tac control stick caused the seeker head to tilt down. Sooner or later, we couldn't resist trying to fly the aircraft with our left hand and track a target

> using Pave Tac with our right hand. Everything could be recorded, so this was a great night sensor, especially since it was steerable and allowed you to "stand off" from the target. Pave Tac also had a laser designator so an RF-4 could lead the way and designate the target with the laser, and bomb-droppers could follow and unload on the designated target. We did not train for this, but the capability was there.[15]

The 10th TRW was usually represented by the 32nd TRS in the Royal Flush competitions. Often crews were rotated from either of the two other squadrons so that they could take part. Success in the competition was mixed for the 10th. They were a part of the USAF team which comprised crews from both the 38th TRS from Ramstein and later Zweibrücken, and, in the years 1966 through to 1970, the 18th TRS from Upper Heyford fielded the RF-101 Voodoo.

Royal Flush X11 in 1967 did not bring any accolades to the 10th TRW, which prompted the pilots of the 18th TRS to fly their Voodoos over Alconbury while giving a characteristic impolite RF-101 salute with their refuelling probes.

The following year, Kirk Ransom and Tom Dorset flew in Royal Flush X111 and recounts part of his contribution to the 10th TRW effort:

> We flew out of Alconbury. Three days, and I think only two targets on each sortie and three sorties each day. There were very fixed TOTs and crews were not allowed within 20 miles of the target before the TOT. All targets required visual sighting reports via HF.
>
> The PPIF was moved into the phase hangar. We would taxi up to the hangar and when the camera crew was ready, shut down the engines which started the 30 minutes time when the final photo interpretation report had to be in the judges hand. As soon as the engines were shut down the camera crew rushed to the airplane and removed the film canisters and tossed them in a chain to the PPIF. We would go into the PPIF and assist the PIs [Photo Interpreters] in locating the target on the film, then rush back to the squadron to get the next mission.
>
> Usually the mission had already been planned and drawn so we would just pick up the map and go. We would rush back to the airplane, which had been serviced and start it up for the next mission. On one occasion after a target in Scotland (which was a long mission), the next targets were all railroad bridges in Belgium. Because time was critical, we were just given the map with the targets marked on it. All the targets were on a railroad line so I flew IFR, I follow railroad! As we passed the first target I did a roll and continued following the railroad. But Tom had forgotten to turn off the low pan. When we were in the PPIF watching the film come out of the Versamat and over the light table, I pointed out the first target and the PI took the cut of film to take to his light table. The film was taped together and continued to be rolled back on the spool, the DO who was watching the film saw the roll and said, 'What was that?' And I answered without a pause, 'Clearing turn, Sir.'
>
> On another mission our TOT for a target deep in southern Germany was long after the first target. So as we entered Germany, I switched to the ANG KC-97L frequency and called 'Taxi Tanker, are you up?' They answered they had just taken off from Rhein-Main. I caught them at 13,000 feet climbing out and plugged in.[16]

Royal Flush in 1970 was held at Deelen in the Netherlands. RF-4C 64-1063 is here having its film downloaded. George Fennell and crew managed it in fifty-one seconds: 'It was 6 cameras including the IR. We had a forward 72, left oblique 72. KA -56 lowpan, and twin 3in 72's in the HighAlt station'. This aircraft has been zapped by just about every other participant in the competition. (*George Fennell*)

In May 1971, Royal Flush was held at Ramstein. The camera troops wait for the RF-4C to stop moving before commencing the download, which began fifteen minutes after the engines had shut down. The PPIF (Photo Processing and Interpretation Facility) was situated just off the taxiway. (*George Fennell*)

The Royal Flush competitions were not without controversy and, on occasions, there was a degree of mistrust as to the antics of the opposing teams. Mike Kostelnik recalls the 1974 competition:

> I trained for the 1974 Competition which was held in Belgium and was crewed with John McCoy. That year, in the interest of fairness, a competition team for each Wing was determined by blind draw, and John and I did not get the chance to go! That year, a 10th TRW crew won the outstanding crew award at the competition. That crew was Steve Monagan and Benny Copeland. I had done a lot of homework on in-flight identification guides, and Steve and Benny used my guides during the competition. The targets for the competition were provided in Europe along the navigation routes by various countries, and on one day of the competition, the French were supposed to provide a target group of five Allouette helicopters as one of the competition targets. Unfortunately, due to some unforeseen circumstance, the five helicopters failed to show at the proper location and time. Every team in the competition, including Steve and Benny, reported a no sighting at the target point. The French team in the competition on the other hand reported Five Allouette Helicopters.[17]

Not all the Royal Flush competitions were straightforward. George Fennell was with the camera crew at Deelen in the Netherlands in 1970:

> We went to Deelen, Netherlands expecting to win the whole thing. Unfortunately we flew one less sortie than any of the other teams. On the 3rd day of the competition we were only a couple points out of the lead with the Canadian 436 Squadron. That morning we pre-flighted a/c 64-1023 as normal before a sortie. We all watched it take off from our camera van but noticed after a minute or so that it was returning to base. Capt Hull did a low flyby and we noticed the nose gear had not retracted. He recycled the gear as he came over but the nose would not retract. So the decision was made to do a touch and go to see if that would jar the nose gear and make it retract. We all watched as it did the touch and go but unfortunately he picked up some FOD in his left engine.
>
> He went full afterburner to get back in the air because he did not have enough runway to stop. Everything looked fine until he tried to blow his wing tanks. He was losing altitude so he blew the tanks but his nose was too high and the tanks didn't release as normal. The explosive charge blew holes in the tanks and they exploded as they dropped off the plane. I had my camera but didn't think to take a picture until a minute later. We all were expecting the crew to eject but Capt Hull managed to keep the plane flying and managed to get it back to base on one engine. The tanks went down in the forest and they said it burned about 10 acres of Dutch Pines. They taxied just a short ways from the active runway and we met them along with the fire/rescue trucks. Capt Caffarelli was out of the back seat almost before they stopped. He climbed down the ladder, laid face down and kissed the ground. Capt Hull took his time and climbed out as if it was a normal flight. About 10 days before RF-XV started they were struck by lightning during

> RF practice in a/c 641011 and had to bail out in a thunderstorm. Both pilots had small bruises all over their neck and hands from from the hail in the storm. The loss of this sortie cost us any chance of winning the competition.[18]

In addition to the Royal Flush competitions, the 10th TRW also took part in Best Focus and Big Click.

Throughout the 1960s and 1970s, the detachments to warmer climes around the Mediterranean continued. In 1970, Gordon Ranum was tasked for a special mission over Gaddafi's Libya:

> In the month before U.S. Forces were removed from Libya the 10th TRW was tasked to send two aircraft to Wheelus AFB to photograph six of the airfields in the country, except the one at Tripoli, which already had MIGs I believe. This was to update the intelligence data before the pull-out. George Wehling from the 32nd was in charge. I flew the second aircraft from the 30th. We flew about 3 sorties out of Wheelus covering all the airfields with two aircraft to ensure camera coverage. On one of the sorties we were briefed that on our return, the active runway would be a specific runway regardless of the wind direction. The approach path to this runway would bring us over the harbor and the docks when Soviet ships were unloading equipment. We made a two-ship landing approach with all the cameras running.[19]

RF-4C 69-0370 stands outside 32nd Maintenance Hangar in March 1971. The aircraft is in desert camouflage as it had been one of two lent to the Israelis while they were waiting for the arrival of their RF-4Es. It was quickly repainted in standard Vietnam camouflage. (*Art Krenzel*)

Larry Garrison, a veteran of the secret RF-86 flights over China, commanded the 32nd TRS in 1972 and recalled an unusual trip to Italy and yet another mission over Libya:

> One of the only rare things that happened was sending a pilot to Aviano to pick up and RF-4C that had been used by the Israelis on photo missions until their purchased aircraft arrived. It stood out with desert camouflage. I did take six aircraft to Athens for a couple weeks to do Infra Red work in the Med for the Navy trying to spot Soviet Naval Units with the Libyans threatening to shoot down the next aircraft entering the Gulf of Sidris, which, of course, they did not do. The Aircraft recovered at the Naval Base in Italy and came on home after downloading the film.[20]

In 1976, the 30th and 32nd TRS were deactivated and the 1st TRS became the sole recce squadron in the 10th TRW. But, of course, the squadron's RF-4Cs were not alone on the base. They were joined by the F-5s of the 527th Tactical Fighter Training Aggressor Squadron (TFTAS), and later, in 1982, by the Lockheed TR-1s of SACs 95th Reconnaissance Squadron.

Surprisingly, the 1st TRS did not regularly receive dissimilar air combat training from the resident F-5s. Jack Griffin was a RF-4C WSO with the squadron:

> Our ACM Training was limited to one to one DCM, which we usually did in house with our own airplanes which were clean RF-4's without external fuel tanks; flown by our own specially certified Instructor Pilots. I do recall one training flight where we briefed and flew a one to one with an F-5 from the aggressor squadron. During the bad weather months the 527th conducted most of their training at a detachment in the Med, where other squadrons would join them.[21]

Most missions fragged for the 1st TRS were 'hi lo hi'—i.e. an approach to target at medium to high altitude, then a drop to low level for the target run, followed by a return to altitude and a run for home. Missions were also at this time predominantly night missions. Both of the two recce units in USAFE—the 1st TRS and the 38th TRS, based at Zweibrücken—complemented each other. The 38th RF-4 missions were invariably at medium altitude, utilising the TEREC equipment. They had a number of aircraft so equipped.

In 1986, the 1st TRS took part in the first Reconnaissance Air Meet competition at Bergstrom AFB in the US. RAM 86 was the first competition of its kind to be held. It was open to all Air Force and Air National Guard units, the US Navy and Marine Corps, and any of the allied nations that chose to take part. The 1st TRS represented USAFE. There were altogether six RF-4C units represented and the navy fielded a TARPS equipped F-14 and the marines an RF-8 Crusader. The allies were represented by two RF-111Cs of the Royal Australian Air Force. The 1st TRS came seventh overall in the competition; the winners were the RF-4Cs of the 123rd TRG of the Nevada ANG. RAM 86 allowed the units to fly missions in formation. Gone were the days of 'Alone, Unarmed and Unafraid'. Aggressors were also introduced into the competition. Flying missions in formation allowed for a wingman to be watching the skies while the lead aircraft took the photos.

RF-4C is seen here in the company of two F-5Es of the 527th TFTAS. When the F-5Es arrived at Alconbury, the 1st TRS was the only RF-4 squadron operating from the base. The 30th and 32nd TRS were deactivated in 1976 when the F-5s arrived. (*USAF*)

In 1986, the 1st TRS competed in the Reconnaissance Air Meet 86 held at Bergstrom AFB in the USA. RF-4Cs were very much in evidence in this competition. Ken Thorne was the crew chief on RF-4C 68-0583, and recalled: 'I did spend many hours preparing the aircraft for the competition. The entire aircraft was repainted, we replaced all the decals throughout the wheel wells and refinished the cockpit with new black paint and instruments. The biggest job was polishing the blast panels and tail-hook to a mirror like shine'. The 1st TRS came seventh overall in the competition. (*USAF*)

RAM 86 was to be the swansong for the 1st TRS and the RF-4C at Alconbury. In June 1987, the 1st TRS deactivated and the Phantoms returned to the US. The 10th TRW became a Tactical Fighter Wing in August, flying the A-10 Thunderbolt 11.

The 10th Tactical Fighter Wing

The A-10A Thunderbolt II

In order to fulfil its new mission, two squadrons of Republic A-10A Warthogs were moved into RAF Alconbury. They were the 509th and the 511th TFS. Their move to Alconbury in 1988 followed the deactivation of the 1st TRW, the last remaining tactical recce squadron at the base which had taken place in June 1987, and was followed by the movement of the 527th TFTAS from Alconbury to Bentwaters, which took place in June 1988.

Both the 509th and the 511th TFS retained the mission that they had with the 81st Tactical Fighter Wing—that of close air support—regularly detaching to the Ahlhorn and Nörvenich FOLs in Germany.

In December 1990, the 511th TFS detached to Saudi Arabia to take part in Operation Desert Storm. In addition to the 511th, there were six other A-10A tactical fighter squadrons units detached to the gulf and one OA-10 FAC units; these were the 353rd and 355th TFS from Myrtle Beach, the 74th and 76th TFS from England AFB, the 706th TFS based at New Orleans NAS, and the 23rd TFS from Davis Monthan AFB flying OA-10s. They units were based at King Fyad International Airport from until February 1991 under the direct control of the 354th TFW (Provisional). The squadrons detached to the gulf worked as one unit.

The pilots of the 354th TFW were charged with two other missions in addition to the close air support role, which their training had emphasised. One of the new roles was that of air interdiction (AI), which involved working behind enemy lines attacking selected priority targets that, though not posing an immediate threat, constituted a future potential threat to the allied coalition forces, for example Iraqi artillery. In addition to these tasks the A-10s were tasked with the destruction of Iraqi GCI sites. These sites were of vital importance to the Iraqi in controlling their air force assets opposing the coalition armies.

On the first day of the conflict, 17 January 1991, two A-10s of the 511th were the first to take-off from Fyad. They were piloted by Lt-Col. Mike O'Connor and Maj. John Condon. During that day, the A-10s attacked a total of twenty-six GCI sites and destroyed ninety-six radars. The pilots on AI were on search and locate missions to locate and destroy artillery sites. At the end of the day, all aircraft returned to Fyad. There was some battle damage. Capt. Rod Glass brought his A-10A, 81-0694, home with a bullet hole through the top of his wing.

When Saddam Hussein shifted his strategy on to firing Scud missiles into Israel, the A-10s acquired another mission—that of Scud hunting. A FOL was set up for the A-10 units at Al-Jawf in north-west Saudi Arabia. Ten A-10s were detached to the FOL, changing every five days. The pilots flew sometimes for as much as twelve hours a day.

A-10A of the 509th TFS assigned to the 10th TFW based at RAF Alconbury. The 509th and 511th TFS were transferred to the newly redesignated 10th TFW in 1988 from the 81st TFW at RAF Bentwaters. (*Author's collection*)

During Desert Storm, all 511th TFS Warthogs were given nose art painted by Sgt James Trago and A1C David McCartney. *JUST-A THUMP IN* was applied to 81-0987. (*USAF*)

Eleven days into the conflict, the A-10s had attacked tanks, artillery units, GCI sites, and Scud missile emplacements. On 27 February, they received a new mission. They were targeted against the formidable Tawakalna Republican Guard unit with their tanks and artillery. The plan was to put eight aircraft from each squadron in to attack with a ten-minute time over target. They would fly a total of six missions in each day amounting to a total of one hour over target with maverick missiles, guns, and bombs. On the first assault on day one, the 511th TFS followed the 76th TFS and the 353rd TFS. At the end of the three days, the offensive capability of the Tawakalna division had been considerably reduced.

It was at this point that the Iraqi army again changed tactics and began to make sorties into Saudi Arabia on several fronts. This drew some A-10s away from the assault on the Tawakalna. They provided support to the ground troops under attack by the Iraqis which were forced to withdraw, but not before they had shot down two USAF aircraft, an AC-130 and an OA-10A, both hit by AAA.

The 144 A-10As in Desert Storm flew 30 per cent of the air force's total sorties. They accounted for more than half of the confirmed Iraqi equipment losses and fired 90 per cent of the precision-guided Maverick missiles launched during Desert Storm in the great variety of missions that they flew. They also accounted for two air-to-air kills, one of these by a 511th TFS pilot.

On his twenty-seventh combat sortie, Capt. Todd 'Shanghai' Sheehy, flying A-10A 81-0964, had the rare distinction of achieving an air-to-air kill in his Warthog. On 15 February 1991, he was flying on a mission to locate and destroy a Sukhoi SU-22 Fitter

Jennie Mel artwork on A-10A 80-172. (*USAF*)

which the Iraqi Air Force had secreted in revetments alongside a road adjacent to an airfield. Having successfully killed the SU-22, Sheehy and his wingman were returning home when they were vectored by an AWACS that had identified a slow low-flying target the vicinity of the heavily defended city of Kerbala. He spotted a large helicopter, which he identified as hostile. It was an Iraqi Mi-8 Hip, a large transport and attack helicopter. His A-10 was armed with Sidewinder air-to-air missiles, but he decided to go for a gun shot. He secured the target in the gunsight of his GAU-8A 30-mm Avenger Cannon and fired two short bursts. The second burst hit the Mi-8, but did not kill it. It turned in the direction of the city and the protection of its AAA, which by now was beginning to make its presence known in the sky around Sheehy and his wingman, Jay Keller. Sheehy decided to pursue and take one last shot. At low altitude, he rolled in again and fired one more short burst before turning quickly away and gaining altitude. Looking back, he saw the burning wreckage of the helicopter.

The 511 TFS returned to RAF Alconbury in June 1991 and was deactivated at RAF Alconbury in December 1992 together with its sister squadron, the 509th TFS.

9

The 527th Tactical Fighter Training Aggressor Squadron

Originally designated the 312th Bombardment Squadron (Dive) and activated at Will Rogers Field, Oklahoma, the unit was assigned to the 86th Bombardment Group, flying a variety of aircraft including the Douglas A-24 Banshee, the Vultee A-31 Vengeance, and the North American A-36 Apache. The 312th was deployed to the Mediterranean theatre of operations in August 1942 and initially based at La Senia in Algeria. During the following months until 1 July 1943, the squadron operated in Algeria, Morocco, and Tunisia before moving to Sicily. The 312th was renamed the 527th Fighter-Bomber Squadron on 23 August 1943 at Gela in Sicily and moved to Barcelona, Sicily, three days later. Between August 1943 and October 1944, the 527th participated in several campaigns in Italy, including Naples-Foggia, Anzio, and Rome-Arno. On 30 May 1944, the squadron was redesignated the 527th Fighter Squadron at Ciampino, Italy, assigned to the 86th Fighter Group. Between October 1944 and the end of the war, the 527th FS followed the Allied armies up through France and into Germany, eventually basing at Schweinfurt in Bavaria. The squadron returned to the US in February 1946 to Bolling Field, where it was deactivated on 31 March 1946. A few months later, on 20 August 1946, the squadron was reactivated at Nordholz in Germany and, once again, assigned to the 86th FG. At the beginning of December, the 527th moved to Lechfield, Germany, and in March 1947 to Bad Kissingen. Both bases were in Bavaria. After a brief sojourn in the US at Langley AFB from June to December 1947, the squadron moved back to Germany, arriving at Neubiberg on 30 December, assigned to newly-activated 86th Fighter Wing, flying the Republic F-47D Thunderbolt. Three squadrons were assigned to the 86th: the 525th FS, the 526th FS, and the 527th FS. The 86th was redesignated a fighter bomber wing in January 1950 and the 527th entered the jet age when it acquired its Republic F-84E Thunderjets during that year.

The 86th FBW moved to Landstuhl AB on August 1952 and the three squadrons converted to the North American F-86F Sabre. In October 1954, the 527th was redesignated a fighter day squadron. It was deactivated on 8 February 1956.

On 1 April 1976, the 527th Tactical Fighter Training Aggressor Squadron was activated at RAF Alconbury in the UK.

The Northrop F-5E Tiger II

The 527th Tactical Fighter Training Aggressor Squadron was activated at RAF Alconbury on 1 April 1976 with a primary mission 'to improve the air-to-air capability of USAF Europe by realistic simulation of the enemy threat'. On 21 May, the first of eight Northrop F-5E Tiger II aircraft arrived at the base aboard Lockheed C-5A Galaxy transports from McLennan AFB, California. Twelve further F-5Es were delivered in June. The aircraft were packed in specially designed pallets with the wings and other parts detached. The first flight out of Alconbury took place on 1 June 1976.

For the remaining six months of 1976, the 527th developed and perfected its training schedule and concepts and became fully operational on 1 January 1977.

Because the 527th was a part of USAFE, most of the pilots were selected from USAFE units, at first primarily, though not exclusively, from the F-4 Phantom wings. Some pilots were drafted in from the other USAF Aggressor squadrons. Only pilots with considerable experience were considered for the training and had to be recommended by their squadron commander. Good air-to-air experience was considered desirable, but not essential, as was the ability to work with others as a team. In addition, those chosen would have demonstrated good leadership and teaching skills.

The first port of call for those selected for 527th was with USAF Intelligence in Washington, DC, learning about Soviet training, tactics, and culture. From here, they went to Nellis AFB for their aggressor training.

Shortly after arrival in the UK, this publicity photo was taken by the USAFE. The colour schemes of the F-5Es were designed to replicate those used by the operators of the MiG-21. They were given specific names. In this photo two 'Snake' aircraft formate with a 'Patches'. (*USAF*)

Alconbury had for a long time been the home of the 10th Tactical Reconnaissance Wing, and it was to this unit that the 527th TFTAS was attached. Here an RF-4C Phantom of the 1st Tactical Reconnaissance Squadron is accompanied by two F-5Es in 'Snake' camouflage. (*USAF*)

F-5E 74-01535 is in 'Ghost' camouflage. This aircraft was eventually sold to the Tunisian Air Force. (*Author's collection*)

Capt. Jon 'Goldy' Goldenbaum joined the 527th TFTAS in 1979. Originally with the 20th TFW at RAF Upper Heyford flying F-111s, he was a not a typical choice for aggressor training. His experience had been in 'air to mud' with time on Skyraiders in SE Asia as well as a spell with Training Command flying T-38s:

> Nellis aggressor training was a difficult no-nonsense program. It was built on the building block approach, first simple air fighting tactics: 1 *versus* 1, then 1 *v* 2, then 2 *v* 2, then 2 *v* many, etc. The emphasis was not so much on your individual successes in air combat, rather on your ability to accurately remember and debrief an entire air-to-air engagement.
>
> As we progressed the emphasis was on teaching. It was not enough to fly well. One had to make valid points to adversaries that helped them improve in DACT. If you could not reconstruct complex fights with pertinent learning points, you were out. We carried crude little cassette tape recorders wired into the map cases of the aircraft to record our running narratives of each battle. After the flight it was our job to reconstruct the fight solely by listening to the tape. We soon learned exactly what to say to be able to reconstruct a complex, high G, swirling fight. The syllabus was flexible, you could not move from one block to the other without demonstrating proficiency. The instructors were relentless, no slack given for slow learners. At the end of the program we flew and led large formations of 'red air' in Red Flag exercises at Nellis, the culmination of our training.[1]

During his time with the 527th, Jon Goldenbaum was promoted to major. The commanding officer of the 527th at the time of its activation at Alconbury was Lt-Col. Bruce MacLennan; it was his responsibility to get the squadron up and running to perform its mission, which was a significant task. USAFE was, with the other air forces of NATO, in the front line in countering any eastern bloc incursions into Europe. They would not only have to stop the ground offensive but successfully take control of the air. This where the dissimilar air combat training provided by the aggressors could make the difference. Lt-Col. MacLennan noted:

> Most air forces, including our own, have a lot of missions to perform and they don't particularly concentrate on just flying air-to-air or dropping one type of bomb. Our F-4 pilots are highly qualified in their aircraft and their mission, but most of them haven't had the opportunity to see a dissimilar aircraft in air-to-air combat. When they complete their F-4 training they've got their bachelor's degree in tactical fighters, but after they complete the aggressor training program, they've got their masters.[2]

The principle fighter of the Soviet bloc was the MiG-21 in many variants. The F-5E was chosen as the aggressor aircraft because it could most successfully simulate the MiG-21 in air-to-air combat. It was small, nimble and agile. The MiG-21 was the fighter which USAF and NATO pilots would most likely have to face in a wartime scenario. Before the arrival of the 'Alconbury Aggressors', most of the USAF and NATO fighter aircraft had only flown simulated combat against similar aircraft: F-4 against F-4, Lightning against Lightning, and so on. Flying against a highly experienced pilot in an F-5 was a whole new experience.

The pilot's helmet, complete with red star, adorns the cockpit of F-5E 74-01548, which was on static display at RAF Wattisham's open day in August 1981. '48' has the 'Silver' colour scheme. This aircraft later crashed in Germany while operating out of Jever. (*Author's collection*)

A 527th Squadron photo taken in 1981. (*Jeff Brown*)

Not only did the 527th fly a dissimilar aircraft, but they also adopted other Soviet practices which further enhanced their role and the learning experience of their 'pupils'. 'Goldy' Goldenbaum stated:

> During the Cold War, western intelligence had spent a great deal of time and effort studying Soviet and Warsaw Pact tactics. This was done by radar and voice intercepts from intelligence ground and airborne sources. The Soviet system was very different from ours. They employed a close relationship of fighters, GCI radars and air defense weapons. Fighter aircraft did not roam independently, they were closely directed by GCI, and had to be cleared to fire by a ground commander. We made every effort to replicate this system; in fact, we had a dozen aggressor GCI controllers attached to our squadron. On most occasions we travelled with our GCI folks. They would control us from local ground radar stations in the initial part of our simulated battles exactly like the soviets did. We knew and simulated soviet tactics, our intent was to give those NATO forces we trained radar pictures and tactics right out of the Soviet play book. Once we merged however, we fought our hearts out, high G manoeuvring, and close- in dog fighting. We tried to use the weapons parameters of Soviet missiles, mostly Atoll heat seekers and guns.[3]

The 527th also trained unarmed RF-4Cs in evasion tactics. There was, of course, no way that the recce Phantom pilots could be trained to turn the tables on the F-5 and shoot it down, but they could be taught how to evade the enemy and avoid being shot down themselves. Also based at Alconbury, the RF-4Cs of the 1st Tactical Reconnaissance Squadron, 10th Tactical Reconnaissance Wing, played a significant role in helping the 527th TFTAS develop its mission and tactics. Maj. Don Pickard, an RF-4C veteran of SE Asia, was one of the pilots of the 1st TRS to get involved with the aggressors. He was an RF-4 instructor and check pilot for the 10th TRW. Following a request from a UK aviation journal to participate in a simulation of F-5 *versus* RF-4C, Don found himself scheduled, in February 1977, to fly a mission against Capt. Karl Whittenberg and his F-5E:

> We had just bedded down the 527th. They gave me a short air-to-air refresher in F-4Ds at RAF Lakenheath and tasked me to start up the Alconbury dissimilar counter-air RF-4 program and check out instructors for a similar effort at the recce wing at Zweibrücken. We had barely begun the program when we got a request for this flight from 3rd AF. The 527th was excited about doing it, but there was a great deal of trepidation at the wing level. I was given strict instructions not to go offensive and not use any of our classified RHAW (Radar Homing and Warning) gear or flares and chaff.[4]

Don was unhappy with the restrictions imposed on him by the director of operations, but the work that he and others did in these early days of the 527th helped to refine the mission and tactics of the squadron. Don later returned to Alconbury in 1984 to command the 10th TRW.

When flying out of Alconbury, the 527th used three closed training areas—one which was centred on the Wash; one which was off RAF Bentwaters in Suffolk; and one which was out in the North Sea. In both the North Sea and the Bentwaters areas, the engagements were allowed to be at supersonic speed. The Wash, however, was subsonic. The training for the pilots began in the classroom with some ten hour of lectures and discussion which covered the doctrine, tactics, philosophy, and training of the enemy. After this, the aggressors and their students took to the air. Lt-Col. MacLennan stated:

> The first few missions pit one F-4 against one F-5. We start by giving the F-4 the offensive position against us and let him try to maintain it. We fly our airplane as hard as we can to try to destroy their tracking solution, or we try to manoeuvre back to their 6 o' clock position where we can get a shot at them. These missions are followed by two F-4s *versus* one F-5. Now we get them to use flight tactics, working together to maintain mutual support to sequentially attack the bandit, us, forcing him into manoeuvres that would allow them to get a shot or separate and go home together.[5]

The program then developed this theme with varying numbers of F-4s and F-5s manoeuvring together, in groups or singly. Of paramount importance was the debriefing after each flight, which could take up to as much as two hours.

With the mission of the squadron clearly defined, the 527th began to extend their areas of operations, so as to reach as many units of NATO as they could. To this end, the unit established a detachment at Decimomannu in Sardinia. Decimomannu boasted an ACM range off the western shore of the island, which enabled a far more accurate analysis of the missions flown. The range was essentially a series of buoy mounted receivers. Maj. Goldenbaum noted:

> These buoys received transmissions from transmitters mounted on aircraft, interestingly in the hollowed bodies of air-to-air missiles. These signals were sent back to a central receiving station on Deci where a huge computer converted them to images of aircraft on a huge playback screen. These images showed every aircraft carrying an ACMI missile pod.
>
> The images could be selected to show the relative position and speed of each aircraft as if one were looking straight down on the range with a 'God's eye' view, as we used to say. When a pilot pressed his fire buttons on board the aircraft, a simulated missile would fly, and if the computer decided the range and angle were sufficient, a kill was recorded on the target aircraft in the shape of a virtual coffin that surrounded the dead aircraft. This display was all recorded in real time with an overlay of the radio transmissions from both sides of the fight. This was obviously a huge boon to training. Large air-to-air fights could be replayed and analysed after landing, a far cry from chalk boards and tape recorders.[6]

The 527th kept several F-5s at Decimomannu all year round, and the detachment played host to a variety of USAFE and other NATO units and their aircraft. The F-15 Eagle had arrived at Bitburg and Soesterberg by this time, and they were regular visitors to the Sardinian base. Italian Fiat G-91s and F-104s and German F-4s and MiG-29s were 'entertained' as were units of RAF Germany.

In addition to flying from Decimomannu and Alconbury, the F-5s of the squadron also visited other NATO airfields to train pilots. Small detachments visited RAF bases

F-5E 74-1545 taxiing at Decimomannu in Sardinia. This aircraft is carrying an ACMI pod on its starboard wing tip. The Italian base boasted an air combat manoeuvring range off the western shore of the island. (*Alan Wisniewski*)

'Snake' camouflaged F-5E 74-1553 takes on fuel at Deci prior to a mission, using the base's innovative Meyerinck pantograph hydraulic refuelling system. (*Alan Wisniewski*)

in the UK such as Binbrook and Leuchars. Others went regularly to Germany, and countries as far afield as Spain, France, Turkey, Norway, and Switzerland were on the schedule. Capt. 'Jiffy' Jeff Brown enjoyed his visit to RAF Binbrook:

> RAF Binbrook was a classic. They flew the Lightning and flew it very well. A typical mission with them was two of them against one of us. The F-5E did not have a lot of gas, but the Lightning was much worse. We would take off with them, have two engagements, go with them to their tanker, two more engagements and then back to the base at 450 kts.
>
> The RAF Lightning's were a lot of fun to fly against; more so than the F-4 which was G-limited most of the time due to airframe restrictions.[7]

Although there was, in general, a mutual respect engendered between the aggressors and their students, things sometimes did not go quite according to plan. Goldy Goldenbaum recalls a visit by Royal Navy Sea Harriers just prior to the Falklands campaign:

> Most of the Sea Harrier pilots had very little air-to-air experience, and they were eager to learn. We got on very well with all of them, most were as colourful as we were, I particularly remember Sharkey Ward. They were quite sure that their vaunted 'viffing' manoeuvre would baffle us. I vividly recall flying a canned engagement behind a Sea Harrier with gun camera on during a staged gun tracking exercise. We were to put the pipper on the Sea Harrier in stabilized high G flight, then have the Harrier do his 'viff' manoeuvre to see if we could keep the pipper on. No problem, the Harrier barely seemed to have any relative movement at all when viffing as I recall.[8]

Jeff Brown picks up the story:

> A couple months later, someone in the squadron got hold of the Royal Navy magazine and we all read the article on how they had come to Alconbury and had beaten the crap out of the Aggressors in their Sea Harriers. The author of the article, John Starkey, the Sea Harrier's operations officer, was seen a couple months later and when asked about the article, he just mentioned 'Hope you chaps didn't mind, we're trying to get more Sea Harriers.'[9]

Yet another aspect of the mission of the 527th was undertaken by 'Smokey' Sundell in the spring of 1982, when he and two other pilots deployed to Switzerland for some interaction with the Swiss Air Force. The difference with this deployment and others like it was that they did not take their F-5s with them but travelled by civilian airliner as civilians. Switzerland was a neutral country and, as such, the participation of the US military in their training programmes needed to be very low key.

> We were there to fly with the Swiss Air Force instructor pilots as they prepared for the summer training cycle with their reservists. The Swiss Air Force is comprised of a small cadre of full time professional pilots with the majority being part-time reservist. They had F-5E's, F-5F's, and the Mirage V as I recall. We flew in the front seat of their two seat F's with an instructor in the back-seat. Their jets were absolutely pristine with low hours and better radars than we had in our F-5E's at Alconbury.

Enjoying the Swiss sunshine are 527th pilots Capt. Charles 'Smokey' Sundell and Capt. Paul 'PT' Taylor together with two unidentified Swiss pilots. The 527th sometimes detached pilots without their aircraft to assist other air forces with their DACT. (*Capt. Charles Sundell*)

> The flights were all 2 vs 2 F-5's against Mirage's as I recall. We even did formation take-offs on the wing of the Mirage! We also got back seat rides in their 2-seat Mirage V, nothing like seeing the peak of the Matterhorn and Eiger from 100′ out the top of your canopy! We would debrief the engagements in normal aggressor fashion, reconstructed from tape recordings using coloured chalk. The whole concept of operation for the Swiss was to validate their tactics, train new Instructors and a brush-up for the old heads. Two hops a day with a nice lunch in between and party at night. That was a typical day.
>
> There were other similar deployments by the 527th. I deployed to Jordan for two weeks with a couple other pilots to fly their F-5's. I also went to Norway alone for a week of air-to-air training for their F-5 Instructor Pilot training class, flew in the back seat of F-5B's on that deployment.[10]

In 1983, the 527th was redesignated the 527th Aggressor Squadron.

Meanwhile, back at Alconbury, in December 1982, Exercise Red Star was instituted. Lt-Col. Jim Wisdom was with the 527th at this time:

> During the two weeks in December that we had all our aircraft and personnel at the home station; the Commander at the time, Lt Col. 'Bullet' Bob Mendell, proposed that we invite one of the four F-15 units to come into town to participate in the exercise that was

Aircraft 74-1532 rests at Decimomannu. Aircraft at Deci flew with a sidewinder missile on the port wing tip and an ACMI pod on the starboard. (*Alan Wisniewski*)

given the name 'Red Star'. The fact that we had all our aircraft and personnel on station gave the Eagle units the opportunity to fly in an exercise against a large force air threat not conducted in Europe at the time. The largest force on force numbers we could ever come up with at Decimo was a four *vs* six. During 'Red Star', we started out with a four *vs.* four and gradually progressed the complexity each day by increasing the numerical ratio's throughout the week until we finished with a four *vs.* twelve or an eight *vs.* twelve, depending upon the size of the F-15 deployment.

All missions flown by the 527th emphasized very precisely flown Soviet tactics, documented Soviet weapons employment philosophy, and the use of centralized GCI close control techniques. This was the one time of the year that the F-15 units could fly against numbers of this size and allowed them to focus on their multi-entity radar sort plans, shot priorities against a large Air-to-Air Force, and how to minimize their exposure when out numbered and maintain a good kill ratio. All missions were thoroughly debriefed, normally by the Red Force Flight Lead, and at the end of the exercise, an after action report was completed by both sides to look for ways to improve the performance of the F-15's and the support the 527th provided during the exercise. This exercise was conducted every year and eventually evolved to where we started to make it a bi-annual event, the same time in December and a week in the month of July sometime around 1986.[11]

Jim Wisdom left the 527th in 1984, but was to return in 1987.

The F-16C Fighting Falcon

The advent of the F-15 and F-16 in USAFE coupled with the development of the next generation of Soviet fighters coming into service heralded more changes for the 527th Aggressor Squadron. In May 1988, it was decided to relocate the squadron to RAF Bentwaters and to re-equip it with the F-16C Fighting Falcon. Such a change in aircraft had been on the cards for some time. The F-5E was a good match for the MiG-21 but not for the MiG-29 and the SU-27 Flanker. The F-16, on the other hand, equipped as it was with the General Electric 110 Engine, APG 68 Pulse Doppler, Track-While-Scan-Radar, Radar Warning System, and a wide field of view HUD, was a quantum leap over the F-5E in performance, manoeuvrability, and avionics. The F-16C also had a video and audio recording system. Gone were the portable audio cassette recorders.

The final mission in the F-5E was flown out of Alconbury on 22 June 1988. Just prior to this, on 14 June, two F-16s had arrived at Bentwaters and the squadron joined the 81st Tactical Fighter Wing.

Gaining proficiency in the new aircraft was, of course, a priority for the pilots in the latter months of 1988 and into 1989. Lt-Col. Jim Wisdom returned at this time as operations officer for the 527th:

> The F-16's we received were BAI (Backup Aircraft Inventory); F-16 wings contributed aircraft from all over USAFE. The model was the Block 30 'C', equipped with the General Electric 110 Engine, APG 68 Pulse Doppler, Track-While-Scan-Radar, Radar Warning System, and a wide field of view Heads Up Display (HUD). This was a quantum leap over the F-5E in performance, manoeuvrability, avionics, and on station time.
>
> The challenge at hand was to ensure we provided the various threat levels and employed the aircraft as an accurate threat replicator, not flying it as a full up F-16C. We set up a training program that each pilot had to complete to validate our threat replication. We called it 'Have Grip'. A matrix was developed that addressed each aircraft's acceleration performance, manoeuvrability to include minimum airspeeds and 'G' limits; avionics constraints to reflect what we best thought the Soviets would be working with; very specific weapons employment criteria for each air-to-air weapon by aircraft, and associated formations and tactics for each aircraft type. The validation process took about six months to complete and by early 1989, we began our six ship deployments back to the Quadra National base in the Mediterranean, Decimomannu Sardinia.[12]

On 22 April 1989, Jim Wisdom became the CO of the 527th Aggressors.

In addition to the F-15 Eagles of Bitburg, Soesterberg, and Keflavik, the 527th continued to support and train other USAFE and NATO units. The RAF visited RAF Bentwaters for a week on one occasion with a squadron of Tornado F-3s. This visit prompted the following observation from Wisdom:

> The aircrews that flew those aircraft were very talented and capable, but the F-3 aircraft was underpowered and so underwhelming in all areas of performance (acceleration, manoeuvrability, radar and avionics) that it proved to be very challenging for those crews when flying against our aircraft. We occasionally flew with the RAF F-4J crews out of

F-16C 479 taxis at Bentwaters. (*Robert Robinson*)

The tail of F-16C 479 was decorated with a black bear for a short while. (*Robert Robinson*)

Wattisham; it appeared the F-4J was a more capable aircraft than the Tornado F-3 ADV variant at that time.[13]

A truly dissimilar air combat exercise took place when the F-16s were tasked to fly with the A-10 Warthogs of the 81st TFW. Both the F-16C and the A-10 had considerable endurance and on-station time, so with every sortie, a number of engagements could be flown. Those engagements were not as one sided as might be imagined. The turning ability of the Warthog coupled with its highly efficient radar warning system, which enabled it to acquire the aggressor before it deployed its weapons, gave the aircraft a commendable survival rate against the F-16.

In September 1989, the 527th received notification that it was to deactivate in 1990, in common with all USAF Aggressor squadrons worldwide.

It fell to Jim Wisdom to oversee the deactivation. Up to this point, the squadron had only received twelve F-16s. It was never to reach its planned complement of twenty. The unit was at the top of its form. Following a unit effectiveness inspection in August 1989, the 527th received an 'Excellent' rating. There can be no doubting the quality of the training that was being provided to the units of USAFE and NATO. In the final analysis, the reason for the drawdown was simply a cost saving exercise. The fact that the Soviet Union and the Warsaw Pact was beginning to disintegrate was a contributory factor, and would be cited as one of the principle reasons for the demise of the aggressor squadrons. However, subsequent events on the world stage have proved that there many potential and real enemies to be engaged and they mostly fly dissimilar aircraft. A final

Aircraft 86-0229 on the tarmac at RAF Bentwaters in May 1989. The F-16 pilots were truly getting into their stride in mid-1989 and received an 'Excellent' rating in a unit effectiveness inspection in August, just before the announcement that all USAF Aggressor units were to be deactivated. (*Author's collection*)

word from 'Jiffy' Jeff Brown who went from the 527th to the 36th TFW at Bitburg and flew against the aggressors:

> The reason for our success in the first Gulf War can be directly attributed to the training received from the 527th. They were a first class adversary and they were also a good group of guys. Not quite the group of Alconbury guys from the early 80's as that group can never be duplicated. Flying missions during the Gulf War was a walk in the park compared to flying with the 527th.[14]

On 29 November 1989, two F-16s departed for Spangdahlem. By the middle of 1990, all twelve aircraft had departed Bentwaters, and in September of that year, the squadron was deactivated.

10

The 66th Tactical Reconnaissance Wing

The 66th TRW was activated at Shaw AFB, South Carolina, in January 1953, and was equipped with the Douglas RB-26 Invader and the Lockheed RF-80 Shooting Star. In July, the wing deployed to Europe, coming under the control of USAFE at Sembach in Germany. The 66th comprised three squadrons: the 30th TRS Night Photo and 302nd and 303rd TRS Photo Jets. The 30th flew the RB-26 and the 302nd and 303rd the RF-80A.

Conversion to the Martin RB-57A for the night photo squadron began in 1955, and the photo jet squadrons received the Republic RF-84F Thunderflash. On 1 January 1957, another squadron joined the 66th TRW. Flying the North American RB-45C Tornado, the 19th TRS was resident at RAF Sculthorpe in the UK, where it was attached to the 47th Bombardment Wing. The squadron did not move to Sembach, remaining based at Sculthorpe.

On 6 December 1957, HQ USAFE issued General Order 88, which assigned the 32nd and 38th TRS, both resident at Phalsbourg, to the 66th TRW. The 19th and 30th TRS were assigned to the 10th TRW, the 30th moved to Spangdahlem while the 19th remained, for the time being, at Sculthorpe. The 66th now became an all RF-84 wing and the 10th an all RB-66 wing.

In March 1958, the McDonnell RF-101C Voodoo MTD was set up at Phalsbourg for the training of the 32nd and 38th TRS personnel in anticipation of the conversion to the new jet. When, in July, the 66th HQ moved to Laon, the 32nd 38th remained at Phalsbourg. The 32nd TRS was the first to convert to the Voodoo and had completed this conversion by the end of the year. The 17th and 18th TRS arrived at Laon in May 1959 from Shaw AFB and had replaced the 302nd and 303rd TRS, which were deactivated. The 17th and 18th were already equipped with the Voodoo.

In March 1966, Gen. Charles de Gaulle pulled France out of NATO and ordered all foreign forces to leave French soil. It was a decision that was to have considerable implications for the 66th TRW at Laon, which now comprised two squadrons: the 17th and 18th TRS. In July 1965, the 32nd and 38th TRS had come under the control of the newly activated 26th TRW based at Toul-Rosières and both squadrons converted to the RF-4C Phantom. The Voodoos of the 17th and 18th TRS were scheduled to move from Laon to RAF Upper Heyford where they arrived in September 1966.

The McDonnell RF-101 Voodoo

The move of the 17th and 18th TRS to Upper Heyford did not go quite according to plan. Just days before the move was scheduled, a problem was discovered with the Voodoos main undercarriage. George Howard flew with the 17th TRS and stated:

> A few days before the aircraft were to move, a crew chief discovered a cracked uplock actuator bracket during a pre-taxi check that resulted in checking all aircraft. I do not recall the number with the same problem but several/most were affected. Those aircraft were grounded as should the gear be retracted and the bracket failed you could not then extend the gear … not good!! In order to stay on the move timeline, it was decided to fly those aircraft with gear down and locks installed to prevent any unintended retraction. As such, we were altitude limited to about 18,000 feet thus putting us in the UK VHF only control area and the Voodoo had only UHF. It was worked out to enable us to fly at 18K. It was a real humiliation to get kicked out of France and leave with the gear down like running away with your tail between your legs. As I recall there was no press release or coverage of the move either at Laon or UH. We were just to leave and show up without anyone knowing about it.[1]

The 18th TRS had no such problems. John Lashuay was the squadron commander and stated:

> I was told of a severe problem with a landing gear strut linkage being cracked due to stress. This could only be seen by magna-fluxing. We were already in the process of moving from France to England and another headache was not needed. Nothing malicious was intended, but we immediately acquired all the replacement parts from Base Supply to fix those 18th aircraft that were affected. When the time came to move, the 17th was forced to fly directly to England with the landing gear hanging.[2]

However, the 17th, though hampered by the undercarriage problem, were not to be outdone on their arrival in the UK. George Howard noted:

> There were 5 aircraft in the 17th Sq that had good up-lock actuation brackets and could fly unrestricted. I think these were the last 5 to leave Laon but not sure. I flew one of these, Jim Waugh one, I do not recall the other 3 pilots. We were given quite direct orders that we were to take off individually, though in succession, from Laon, fly separate training missions in Germany and arrive, recover and land individually at UH. There was to be no formation or individual fly overs … just land. Collectively the five of us had a better idea in that if we were to leave France unnoticed; we should at least have some sort of an arrival ceremony. So in a covert briefing we agreed to join up in the vicinity of UH and put on a four ship fly by, which we did. While the 'troops' on the ground thought it was great, those in command took a much different view. It took a while for them to get over it![3]

Prior to their displacement to RAF Upper Heyford in September 1966, the Voodoos of the 66th TRW were based at Laon in France. At this time, all Voodoos were in natural metal and squadron markings were carried. Just before the move to Upper Heyford, many of the Voodoos were painted in Vietnam camouflage. RF-101C 56-180 overflies Laon in this photo. (*USAF via George Howard*)

Five Voodoos of the 17th TRS did not share the ignominy of having to make the trip to the UK with wheels down. Photographed here on approach to Heyford and photographed by the No. 5 aircraft, the four RF-101cs are in diamond formation for their unauthorised flypast. (*USAF*)

Pilots of the 17th TRS pose with RF-101C 56-123. *From left to right, standing*: unknown, Phil Harvell, Jim Wylie, Roger Brockoff, Don Morgan, Don Hunt, Jim Waugh, Bob Jobe, Tom Hennigan, unknown, and Howard Myli. *From left to right, kneeling*: Ray Tiffault, Pierce Hodnette Commander, unknown, Bob Gage, Warren Pierce, Tom McNierney Ops Officer, Carlos Higgins, and Dan Courtney. (*USAF via George Howard*)

The base at RAF Upper Heyford was not immediately ready for the 66th. John Summers recalls the effort required to improve facilities for the air and ground crew:

> The 17th TRS moved into buildings on the base side of the runway. They looked like left over from WWII, but usable. The 18th TRS got the building across the runway. You pulled up on the taxiway and waited for a green light from tower to cross and go to work. All the windows were broken, and pigeon poop was ankle deep on the floors. The pilots did most of the cleaning up and painting to get it halfway decent.[4]

The 17th TRS Operations buildings had been previously used for alert quarters and operations by B-47 crews who stood alert in the UK during the Cold War. That operation was called Reflex.

The Voodoo was a popular airplane with its pilots. It did, of course, have its idiosyncrasies, but, as a recce platform, it was efficient. Missions from Upper Heyford were very different from those out of Laon. Indeed, the pilots had to fly further in order to exercise efficiently. Controls for missions over Europe came under the jurisdiction of Heathrow and, subsequently, southern radar. Most practice missions not flown over the UK were flown over Germany and the Low Countries. In Europe, the Voodoos flew

Another squadron photo taken shortly after arrival in the UK. All 17th TRS personnel are included. (*USAF via George Howard*)

virtually all their missions at low level, which was the norm. In the event of hostilities breaking out with the Warsaw Pact, the object of the 101's mission would be to fly low and fast to the target, get the photos, and return by the same method. Don Karges flew the Voodoo in Europe before taking the plane to SE Asia; he noted:

> All training in Europe was based on high speed, low level tactics. The reasons were simple. We had only a day capability with no ECM or radar warning devices. We did not believe we could survive a heavy SAM environment above 1000′ and the prevailing weather in Europe would force us to photograph targets at low altitude. A typical mission was two hours and ten minutes and consisted of a high-low-high profile. We would climb to 30,000′ and cruise in a straight line for about 40 minutes, let down below the clouds and fly our planned low level mission at 420kts, 500′ for about 30–40 minutes, usually with two-three pinpoint targets like com sites, bridges etc. and one route reconnaissance of a highway or railroad. These practice missions had both photo and visual requirements since the wartime missions required us to give visual reports on the way home, in case we were shot down and to give the intel folks some advance information. After the low level portion we climbed back to altitude, around 35,000′, made our visual report back to squadron intel, and returned home. Missions near the border were very strictly controlled demanding positive radar contact at all times. They were in support of army exercises.[5]

The low-level missions did produce some unique results on occasion, as Nick Pishvanov testifies:

> For our low altitude photo missions to designated targets within the bounds of England we followed prescribed low altitude routes. One day near the south coast of England I noticed an SOS outlined in the soil. I turned back and made a photo run. The photo lab processed it and gave copies and the exact coordinates to the appropriate British authorities. The local constabulary made inquiries and discovered that a farmer was getting tired of the noise from low altitude overflights. He had been complaining about this for some time but to no avail. As a result I believe the routing was changed to avoid this area and allow the sheep to graze in peace.[6]

The mission of the 17th and 18th TRS remained primarily a daylight one, and occasionally took the pilots and aircraft further afield. Bob Gould noted:

> I went on a Med search as part of a flight of three 101s. We flew from Heyford, around France to Naples, Italy. There we spent the afternoon and night. We made a salty morning take-off to the eastern Med attempting to be invisible to make a surprise visit to a Navy Carrier task force. I made it to about a mile out on approach to the carrier before I was joined by a Navy fighter. I don't remember the type. We returned to Naples, refuelled and went home the same day. The most exciting part of the trip was the ride in a Navy bus from the base into Naples.[7]

Usually missions with the US Mediterranean Fleet were flown from Moron, Spain. The Spanish base was used extensively by the 66th TRW as a 'sun base'. It was also the base at which new pilots were transitioned to the Voodoo. Bob Gould had been one such. He had flown the RF-101 at Shaw and was current on the RF-4C when he was sent to Upper Heyford. Because he had not flown the Voodoo for some twelve months, he was obliged to fly ten transition lessons:

> Now if anyone thought you could get decent transition weather in England in February, they were in dreamland. When the English recce squadrons wanted decent winter flying weather, they went to Moron AB at Seville, Spain. That was pretty good duty. So off to Spain I went to learn how to fly the Voodoo. My IP was Roger Brockhoff. I didn't know Roger well at the time, but I soon learned that he was one hot- rock pilot. We were flying 18th TRS aircraft and we were cautioned to take good care of them. Training requires a solo take-off with a chase plane following and that was the way it happened initially. As soon as we were airborne, I called for afterburners but Roger said 'Negative—get on my wing.' Then we climbed out to about 10,000 feet and did a loop. That was the first time I had ever done a loop in formation in an RF-101. During the next 10 days, I did several more. Needless to say, transition was never more fun.[8]

Moron was a welcome detachment for the aircrews who spent time there. The city of Seville was a popular diversion from the routines of flying. There are differing attitudes to the

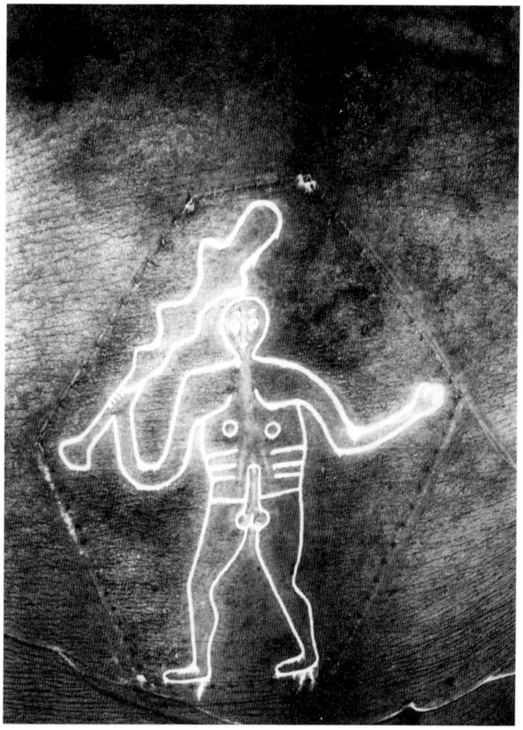

Left: RF-101C *Happy Snap*: The Giant of Cerne Abbas. This photo was thought by some to be a fake. Nick Pishvanov recalled: 'My first photo did not have the Voodoo Shadow and the photo lab technicians were convinced it was a fake. So I went on another mission with my wing man, John Boyer, and set us up to leave a shadow'. (*Nick Pishvanov*)

Below: Save Our Sheep. A disgruntled farmer left this message for the low-flying aircraft. Nick Pishvanov photographed the message and the matter was taken up by the local police and the farmer's concerns duly noted and acted upon. (*Nick Pishvanov*)

famous oranges. Ed Satterfield of the 18th TRS, however, obviously enjoyed the fruit and used his RF-101 to import some into the UK: 'I can not guess how many tons of oranges I sent back to Upper Heyford. With the cameras removed in the nose and split vert's there was a lot of room for oranges. The ramp men at Upper Heyford were not advised of the load and when they opened the bays oranges poured out all over the ramp'.

It was a matter of routine for recce pilots to carry goods, often of the liquid variety, in the camera compartments of their aircraft when on cross-country trips.

Even at this time in the mid- to late 1960s, weekend cross-country trips were allowed. John Summers recalls one he made:

> John Pell and I took one which went to Ramstein on Friday night, and Copenhagen on Saturday morning for the 600th anniversary of Copenhagen. Beer flowed freely, and free, in the streets with all the parades. Sunday am from Copenhagen to Madrid for the bullfights. That is about the max range for the 101, about 3:15 or so. Back to Heyford on Monday am.[9]

Such outings were not quite as trivial as they sound. It was necessary for all pilots to complete a fixed number of hours in the aircraft, and when the weather was good, what better opportunity was there to get the hours in and visit Europe.

In 1966, before departing for RAF Upper Heyford, the 18th TRS had performed well in the Royal Flush competition. Captains Nick Pishvanov, the 66th Russian Exchange pilot as he was sometimes known, and Leonard 'Doc' Cramer scored the highest points ever achieved by a USAFE team and the squadron came sixth out of a field of thirteen squadrons.

At Heyford in May 1967, the 18th TRS won the competition. Twelve pilots were involved, and over the three-day exercise, they flew more than 200 targets. Each pilot flew three missions a day, with three assigned targets per mission. The total of seventy-two sorties was flown without one target being aborted for any reason. The top USAF pilot in the competition was Ed Satterfield of the 18th TRS. However, he did have an anxious moment in the competition. Nick Pishvanov related:

> Ed was leading on points and had picked up on some very good, difficult targets. He was looking like a winner and sweating his last mission. It turned out good. Weather was excellent and he hit his targets dead-on. He taxied in right on the time, within seconds of his assigned chock-time. This was very important to keep the photo lab from getting overloaded by getting a group of undisciplined and untimely arrivals. It is probably something that had penalised our competitors. We had the approach time from the English Channel and touchdown plus and taxi time nailed to the second. Nevertheless the boys in the photo lab cooked up a great, but cruel, practical joke. They rushed up to the aircraft and had the camera doors open as the engines wound down; had the film canisters out of the nose and were rushing them to the photo truck. Ed was smiling like a possum eating something strange. He knew he had nailed all targets and had PERFECT photos. His in-flight report was dead-on, also. At that point, one of the camera crew clumsily dropped a canister and 50 ft of film came streaming out across the ramp. Poor man almost had a combination coronary and neuro-circulatory collapse. You could hear Ed howl clear back to the O club on the other side of the field. Unbeknownst to him, the real film was already being

On one of his TDYs to Moron AB, Bob Gould pilots RF-101C 56-101 over the city of Seville. (*Bob Gould*)

The TDYs to Moron often gave the Voodoos time to play with the local Spanish Air Force F-86s. Nick Pishvanov flies Voodoo 56-101 in company with two Sabres of the Ejército del Aire. (*Nick Pishvanov*)

The 18th TRS tribute to the RF-4s of Alconbury after their success in Royal Flush XII. 'During the flyby we activated our vulgar looking refuelling probes and gave Alconbury the famous "horse dong" salute'. (*Nick Pishvanov*)

The success of the 18th TRS in Royal Flush XII was earned through sheer hard work and determination to get it right. Here film is downloaded in record time and rushed to the processing tables. (*USAF*)

> processed. Poor Ed! He just couldn't understand why we were so mean to him. What a day that was![10]

Inevitably, there were accidents in the Voodoo squadrons while they were at Heyford. One of these was fatal. Maj. Robert 'Buster' Sipes was taking off from the base when the engine of his Voodoo failed. Because of his proximity to the local primary school, Sipes elected to stay with his aeroplane and guide it away from the building. The Voodoo crashed in nearby Follies Field and Sipes was killed. His selfless action prompted the villagers of Steeple Aston to erect a memorial to him in the village church. In the US, the airport in Jackson, Tennessee, is named after him.

In addition to the regular routine missions over Western Europe, the squadrons of the 66th TRW were also involved in exchanges with other services. The 17th TRS undertook regular exchanges with Aufklärungs Geschwader 51 "Immelmann" (Reconnaissance Wing 51 "Immelmann"). AG.51 flew the RF-104G Starfighter from Ingolstadt Manching. In September 1968, in addition to routine exercises, the two squadrons indulged in some impromptu photo shoots. One of these occasions incurred the wrath of the USAFE command. Bob Gould recalls:

> The 17th TRS was on exchange with the Luftwaffe AkG51 squadron at Ingolstadt Air base in Bavaria near Munich. A French Squadron was on exchange with another Luftwaffe Squadron at the same base. The inevitable result was a formation flight of the three nations' aircraft. Although the pilots were well briefed and covered all safety aspects, permission for the flight was not obtained from higher USAF authority and the result was some verbal reprimands for certain USAF pilots.[11]

Apparently, the German commanders of the base were not very happy about this flight either. How the French reacted is unknown. George Howard also recalled another incident related to the detachments to Ingolstadt:

> When we returned from Ingolstadt we made off with some treasures from their O club to include some unit flags and their treasured small cannon referred to as 'Tillie' I think. That hit a sore spot and shortly after we returned to UH their wing CO. arrived in his 104 not at all happy and wanted his cannon back, which we promptly gave him and he departed without any further fanfare. Squadron exchanges were always good times and fostered long time friendships that continue to today.[12]

In 1968, the inevitable tide of progress caught up with the 66th TRW and its remaining two Voodoo squadrons. It was announced that the 17th TRS was to convert to the RF-4C Phantom in 1969. The 18th TRS would continue with the RF-101C for a while longer. The first two Phantoms arrived for the 17th TRS on 27 March 1969.

For the 17th, conversion entailed a great deal of time and work. Bob Gould noted:

> Probably my busiest time at Heyford was the transition from 101s to RF-4s. I had become squadron commander and as soon as we learned we'd be converting, I was sent to an F-4 unit to get current. I had previously flown the RF-4 at Shaw for a short time before going to Upper Heyford. I needed to get recurrent before a year had passed from previous flight.
>
> There was a large exchange of pilots to and from the 17th Sqd. Pilots with less than a year remaining on their overseas tour were to be transferred out when we lost our 101s. The others were sent to Shaw to check out in the RF-4. Some of our new pilots and Navs had experience in the RF-4 and they became instructors. Some of the pilots had flown the F-101B in ADC but they knew nothing about reconnaissance. The Navs without F-4 time attended F-4 ground school but had no flight experience in the F-4. So we had an extensive and intensive training event. Headquarters was always pushing us to get combat ready. The days were long, 12 to 16 hours.[13]

The RF-101s continued in the daylight role and the RF-4Cs were capable of operating in all weathers day and night.

In the event, within a matter of months after conversion to the RF-4C the 17th TRS was assigned to the 86th TFW at Zweibrücken in Germany. The 20th TFW was to move from RAF Wethersfield to Upper Heyford and convert to the F-111E fighter bomber. The 18th TRS flew its Voodoos back to Shaw AFB in Carolina and there converted to the RF-4C. The 66th TRW was deactivated, to be reincarnated later as the 66th ECW

Carlos Higgins and Bob Gould at Ingolstadt in September 1968. One of their Voodoos has been 'zapped' with the owl of AG.51. (*Carlos Higgins*)

The exchange to Ingolstadt in September 1968 included some international formation flying. A Starfighter from AG.51, two Voodoos from the 17th TRS, and three French Mirage IIIRs of an unknown squadron. The USAFE command was not impressed as no permission had been given for the flight. (*Bob Gould*)

The F-104 Starfighter from AG-71 and a 66th TRW RF-101C formate over the German countryside during the exchange at Ingolstadt. (*Bob Gould*)

RF-101C 56-210 photographed at RAF Bentwaters's open house in 1967. Resplendent in its natural metal and grey finish this aircraft is devoid of any unit markings. (*via Mick Sudds*)

Photographed at RAF Bentwaters's open house in 1968, this RF-101C keeps company with a Royal Navy Hunter T.8 of 764 Squadron. (*Alan Johnson*)

11

The Skyblazers

It was a common practice, in the 1950s and 1960s, for the majority of military airbases throughout Western Europe to hold regular open houses or armed forces days, thereby giving the public the opportunity to see the aircraft at close quarters and meet the people responsible for supporting those aircraft and the mission of the resident unit. These open days were also attended by many visiting aircraft from other NATO air forces, glad of the opportunity to show off their machines.

One of the essential elements of any open-day air show was the flying display, and, then, as now, the highlight of any flying display was the team aerobatic display. Virtually all countries formed teams that performed regularly all over Europe. One of the first of such aerobatic teams to be formed in USAFE was from the 36th FBW at Fursty. The idea of forming a team with the F-80s came quite by chance when three pilots of the 22nd FS were returning from Malta where they had been on an exercise. They decided to engage in some impromptu aerobatic stunts and enjoyed it so much, that on the day after their return to Fürstenfeldbruck, they took their Shooting Stars up once again to hone their skills. They decided to seek approval to form an aerobatic team and this was duly granted. They added another pilot to their number and thus were the Skyblazers born. The Skyblazers were to perform regular air shows throughout Europe and North Africa for the next twelve years.

The Skyblazers flew their first public air show at RAF Gütersloh in the British zone of occupied Germany in October 1949. Although the teams time with the F-80 was to be limited, their display thrilled crowds in many countries. Richard Kamm was the crew chief of F-80B 45-8663, piloted by Bill Pattillo; he noted:

> The first air show that I can remember was a military show at RAF West Raynham and the second was at Orly Field in Paris. The Bomb Burst as originally practised by the Skyblazers was different than presently used. They did not use a four way pass after the burst. Vince Gordon gave an individual aerobatic show that required set up time. After the burst the three remaining aircraft would do a two-way pass. Two aircraft would fly very

> low (probably under 5 feet) down the runway in one direction and the third aircraft would key the slot flying between the two aircraft in the opposite direction. Though it looked spectacular this was a relatively safe manoeuvre. The two aircraft coming one way put their inboard wing-tip on the edge of the runway while the single aircraft flew the centre-line. The lack of altitude restrictions meant the pilots could fly extremely low and this was the case on that 1950 day in Paris. You would think that it would be more spectacular if the aircraft passed each other in the centre of the air show area, but this is not necessarily true. The two runway edge aircraft were just a second early and the crowd's eyes were naturally following them down the runway when the centre-line aircraft suddenly appeared from the opposite direction. If you think several hundred thousand people gasping at the same time cannot drown out a jet aircraft, you are wrong. In the 1951 air show season the team went to the more conventional four-way pass but I personally enjoyed watching the two way pass more.[1]

In January 1950, the 36th was redesignated a fighter bomber wing and was to convert to the Republic F-84E Thunderjet. The F-84E had a fearsome reputation. The in-commission rate of the aircraft was appalling. In April 1950, for example, out of the entire air force inventory of F-84s, only 50 per cent were in commission. Main cause was the chronic shortage of spare parts, particularly for the J35-A-17 engine. Engine failure of one sort or another was the primary cause of accidents in the F-84. Richard Kamm noted:

> Though the Air Force would not officially admit it was having problems with the F-84Es, they first refused to let the Skyblazers fly as an aerobatic team. I have been told that after much haggling, the decision was finally made by General Vandenberg, the Air Force's Commanding General, allowing the team to fly. The first air show of the season was again at West Raynham and the second was on 1 July 1951 at Le Bourget in Paris.[2]

Richard's memories of the Le Bourget air show illustrates clearly just how much things have changed since those days in the interests of health and safety.

> The Le Bourget air show probably had the most spectacular ending to the bomb burst ever seen. By this time the team was using the more conventional four way bomb bust practised by most of today's aerobatic teams. The bomb burst was the last manoeuvre before reforming to land. Our parking area was near the end of the runway and as I was watching my pilot diving down for the four way pass, I saw a woman walking in the grass at the end of the runway. The aircraft was actually lower than her head and Bill lifted a wing and swept over her. The aircraft was so close that upon passing over, her skirt went up and at the same time she raised her arms and fainted. Bill who does not remember the event (he probably thought it was a post of some sort) lowered the wing and continued down the runway. Upon pulling up to reform he found himself on a collision course with a staggered formation of 48 French built Vampires (the papers reported there were 50 of them, but they were in groups of four). There was nothing Bill could do because any turning would just increase the chance of collision. Someone in the formation or in air show control must have yelled the French

Pilot Bill Pattillo and crew chief Richard Kamm pose with their F-80B 45-8663. (*Richard Kamm*)

In early 1950, the 36th FW became the 36th Fighter Bomber Wing and converted to the F-84E Thunderjet. The Skyblazers used four aircraft from the 22nd FBS, which retained their squadron colours. (*USAF*)

> equivalent of 'Break' because just as he approached the formation the formation broke up. They broke up in singles; consequently the sky was full of Vampires going in all directions. The crowd on the ground applauded wildly as they thought it was a planned manoeuvre. Upon landing, while I was unstrapping Bill from the ejection seat, he looked up at me and said "I swear I went between the twin booms of a Vampire.[3]

On 21 May 1952, Capt. John P. O'Brien, one of the team's solo pilots. crashed at RAF Manston after an engine explosion occurred during a low-altitude pass. Capt. O'Brien was killed. This crash was one of the reasons for the Skyblazers being stood down at Fürstenfeldbruck in August 1952. Also, the 36th FBW was scheduled to move to Bitburg in October of that year. Responsibility for the Skyblazers passed to the 86th FBW, which had moved from Neubiberg to Landstuhl.

Coincidently, at this time, the Pattillo brothers were transferred to Air Training Command at Luke AFB. Here they were the founder members of an aerobatic team called the Stardusters. The name of this team was changed to Thunderbirds, and remains so to this day.

The Skyblazers' sojourn with the 86th FBW was short-lived. They performed their first public display on 9 January 1953 and their last at Spangdahlem on 10 July 1953.

Just prior to this, in June 1953, the 48th FBW, based at Chaumont and flying F-84Gs, was told to start practising. Capt. William N. Dillard was appointed the team captain and training got under way at once, with the prospect of flying the first displays in July.

When the Skyblazers moved to the 86th FBW, they continued to fly the F-84E. Seen here flying over Landstuhl AB, their F-84s initially carried no distinguishing markings. Later, the name 'SKYBLAZERS' was placed on the outside of the wing tip tank in red. (*via Dave Menard*)

In fact, apart from flying a limited display at the Chaumont 'Bastille day' celebrations on 14 July, the displays did not commence until September when a series of 'Battle of Britain' displays took place in the UK. It was at the Biggin Hill display that Lt Jack Bennett had an engine flame out while climbing into a loop. Disaster was avoided when he managed to restart his engine and rejoined the team for the following manoeuvre.

In October 1953, the team was disbanded as the entire wing upgraded to the F-86F Sabre. It was not until July 1954 that the Skyblazers were reformed with the F-86F-35 aircraft. Six Sabres were assigned to the team and these were painted up in a special colour scheme and the team became a special flight within the wing. Capt. Dillard remained as captain. The team performed their first air show on 9 July 1954 at Wiesbaden in Germany. The F-86s regularly came to the UK, performing their first show at RAF Wymeswold on 30 May 1955.

The 48th FBW Skyblazers, like their predecessors, displayed all over Europe. Because of the uncooperative nature of the north European weather, practice sessions were held at Wheelus in Libya and also in the south of France, the F-86s being based at Marseilles. In the spring of 1956, they were joined at Marseilles by an RF-80 photo jet from Sembach and pilot Russ Tansey, who took publicity photos for the team.

The 1956 season kicked off at Toulouse and Bordeaux and the highlights were the 'Bomb Burst' and the 'Thread the Needle'. During these manoeuvres, the Skyblazers used smoke for the first time. The Skyblazers were to be the first aerobatic team to use red, white, and blue smoke, but this did not take place until later when the team flew the F-100C.

One of the most significant shows for the team in May 1956 was the Zurich International air show at Dübendorf Airport near Zurich, Switzerland. Here the team was flying alongside a variety of other aircraft from all over Europe including other aerobatic teams: the RAF's 111 Squadron with their black Hawker Hunters, Swedish J-29s, and the Patrouille de France with Mystere 1Vs. Also present at Zurich were several Soviet aircraft.

In October 1956, the Skyblazers returned to the control of the 36th TFW, now based at Bitburg in Germany, and began conversion to the F-100C Super Sabre. The 36th had F-100C Super Sabre in its inventory at that time. The F-100Cs of the team had specially modified leading edge slats for low-speed manoeuvrability.

Don Emigholz was one of the founder members of the team and recalls those early days—things did not always go smoothly:

> When we were first getting the team started, we went through some intensive training, flying out of Sidi Slimane Air Base in Morocco. We flew twice a day for a number of weeks until Bill Creech, thought we were ready for our first show. After returning to Germany, one of his first tasks was to obtain some aerial photos of the team that were to go in to the Press Kits that would be handed out to reporters prior to any air show. These kits were made up of pilot profiles, the manoeuvres we flew and the photographs.
>
> The only two seat airplane we had at Bitburg, for these photos was the T-33. Of course, the manoeuvring airspeeds of this jet were a lot slower than the F-100 so the plan was for the four ship diamond to approach the T-33 from astern with the T-33 at max speed. Our

The Skyblazers reformed at Chaumont with the 48th Fighter Bomber Wing. Their F-84Gs received a special colour scheme. The tail surfaces were blue, the vertical carrying a white lightning flash. The outer surfaces of the tip tank were white with a blue lightning flash. The fuselage lightning flash was red edged in white and extended from the nose to the rear of the cockpit. (*48th TFW Historical Office*)

The Sabres in their original markings fly over the French countryside posing for the camera aircraft for a series of publicity photos. (*USAF*)

This portrait of the Skyblazers were taken when the team was engaged in some fine weather training based at Marseilles. They were accompanied by an RF-80A photo jet flown by Lt Russ Tansey of the 302nd Tactical Reconnaissance Squadron. (*USAF*)

The Skyblazers line up at Chaumont. The 48th FBW began conversion to the F-100D in 1956, and in October of that year, the team returned to the 36th TFW at Bitburg. (*48th TFW Historical Office*)

In tight formation, four Skyblazer F-100Cs in the colour scheme adopted for the team. (*USAF*)

leader tried to time it so that the photo could be taken when both the T-33 and our F-100 jets were going straight up. That part worked out fine, but we were so slow going through the vertical, that by the time we got to the top of the loop our airspeed was about 100 knots, as I recall. The F-100 does not fly very well at that airspeed and the next thing I knew I saw fire come out the nose of my leader's jet and then 'BANG', both of my feet were knocked off the rudder pedals from the compressor stall of the engine. I actually saw the fire ball in front of my jet too.

Needless to say, we did not have any more photo missions with the T-33. But, there was a RF-84 outfit over at Spangdahlem Air Base and that guy flew on our wing like he'd been doing it all his life and the photos from that shoot were the ones that we used in our Press Kits.[4]

The Skyblazers flew many prestigious air shows from the beginning. At one of these, the Paris International Air Show in 1957, Don Emigholz experienced a flame out during a barrel roll. Fortunately, he recovered and made a power off landing in front of over 100,000 spectators. The solo pilot, Gordon Ells, was flying just outside the show area and was called in by the leader, Bill Creech, to take Don's place on the right wing. The show proceeded as scheduled. The F-100Cs first performed in the UK in June 1957. Between June 1957 and the end of 1960, they returned to the UK regularly. *Flight* magazine reported on their show at Biggin Hill in September 1957, giving this rather biased report:

But the battle of the giants was that between the aerobatic teams of No. 111 Sqn. with their black Hunter 6s and the F-100Cs of the U.S.A.F. Skyblazers. This time there was no doubt that No. 111 Sqn. have achieved the lead. Even after giving two other shows (at Duxford and Horsham St. Faith) that afternoon, their loop and roll with nine aircraft, their constant formation changing and their smoke carried the day. The Skyblazers, too, now have very fine smoke and still do their individual rolling Fleur-de-Lys manoeuvre; but their extreme precision and after-burning spectacle do not match the Hunters' virtuosity. The leader came back for an individual show afterwards and frightened many children with a very low pass in a steep turn, blasting the enclosures with his afterburner.[5]

Gordon Scharnhorst joined the Skyblazers in December 1957, replacing Jim Portison and 'locked on to Bill Creeches left wing tip lights for many hours'.

'Horse' Scharnhorst recalls an occasion on 7 August 1959 when he experienced a mechanical failure when returning to the home base after a practice:

We headed back to Bitburg AB in spread formation and started a let down to landing approximately thirty miles from Bitburg when my elevator control became inoperative. All flight control hydraulic systems and trim controls worked correctly on the ailerons and rudder. To make a long story short I ejected at 5000 feet. I landed in a pine forest on the Luxembourg side of the German border. When the canopy of my chute hit the top of the trees I collapsed and fell to the ground. There was a bed of pine needles on the ground about twelve inches deep which acted like a mattress. I had a slight ankle sprain. I didn't lose a thing. I had to offer the helicopter pilots who picked me up my pencil so he could fill in the forms![6]

Skyblazers F-100Cs in echelon formation. Note the tail of 54-1980, which usually flies in the slot position, has had its fin blackened by the exhaust of the lead aircraft. (*Robert Robinson collection*)

The very next day, 8 August, 'Horse' was up with the rest of the team and taking off at 7:30 a.m. for the south of France for a series of air shows. He flew with the Skyblazers during the 1958 and 1959 seasons and was recalled to fly one show at Wheelus, Libya, at the beginning of the 1960 season when his replacement became ill and was grounded for a few days.

It was at a display at Kleine Brogel on 16 June 1960 that the Skyblazers trailed red white and blue smoke for the first time.

The Skyblazers eventually disbanded in January 1961. They were very briefly transferred to the 50th TFW at Hahn in December 1960, but the wing did not want the mission due to a variety of factors, not least the appalling weather prevalent at the base and the maintenance problems associated with and inventory of F-100Ds, F-100Cs, and F-100Fs. The F-100Cs of the Skyblazers were sent to various destinations. Most went to Wheelus as target tugs. One and possibly more ended up with the Iowa National Guard. One aircraft, 54-2009, eventually went to SE Asia where it was flown on a combat mission by Bill Creech who, years before, had flown it with the Skyblazers as team leader.

Skyblazers over the UK

Base	Date	Aircraft
West Raynham	June 1950	F-80B
West Raynham	June 1951	F84E
Manston	21 May 1952	F-84E
Biggin Hill	September 1953	F-84G
Wymeswold	30 May 1955	F-86F
Speke Liverpool and Hucknall	21 May 1956	F-86F
Hucknall	29 May 1956	F-86F
Coventry	15 September 1956	F-86F
Biggin Hill and West Malling	21 July 1956	F-86F
Wethersfield	15 June 1957	F-100C
West Raynham	June 1957	F-100C
Biggin Hill	September 1957	F-100C
Alconbury and Sculthorpe	17 May 1958	F-100C
Biggin Hill and Horsham St Faith	20 September 1958	F-100C
Alconbury and Bentwaters	16 May 1959	F-100C
Biggin Hill and Wattisham	19 September 1959	F-100C
Lakenheath and Wethersfield	28 May 1960	F-100C
Filton	9 July 1960	F-100C
Biggin Hill	17 September 1960	F-100C
Biggin Hill and Coltishall	16 September, 1961	F-100C
Mildenhall, Sculthorpe and Wethersfield	17 June 1961	F-100C

12

Tactical Air Command Temporary Deployments to the UK in the Cold War

Paving the Way

Commencing in the post-war years, the USAF has temporarily deployed its units and their aircraft from the US to Europe. More often than not, this was to participate in exercises or, as in the case of Operation Stair Step, to reinforce USAFE and the NATO forces in times of tension between NATO and the Warsaw Pact.

Deployment in the early days was a fairly arduous process. Many of the early flights from the US to Europe were flown in stages, taking time to refuel and rest along the route. The first pioneering transatlantic crossing by jet fighter aircraft was made in July and August 1948 by the 56th Fighter Group, which was based at Selfridge Field in Michigan. This occurred at the time of the Berlin blockade by the Soviets. It was a show of force to assure the Soviet Union that it was possible for the US to reinforce Europe with aircraft if necessary. The flight was conceived by the commander of the 56th FG, Col. David C. Schilling, who led the flight from Selfridge to RAF Odiham stopping at Bangor, Maine; Goose Bay, Labrador; Bluie West One at the southernmost tip of Greenland; Meeks Field, Iceland; and Stornoway in the Hebrides. He christened the crossing 'Fox Able' being the phonetic code for Fighter Atlantic. From Odiham, the 56th Flight moved on to Fürstenfeldbruck in Germany where they remained for ten months.

The Fox Able route to the UK and the rest of Europe was followed by nearly all subsequent deployments to Europe, including those units which were to be permanently based in the theatre. Before the 20th FBW became resident in the UK with their nuclear capable F-84Gs, they deployed to Manston in July 1950 for a five-month deployment with their F-84Ds. The F-84Ds had flown the Fox Able route with 'hot guns', fearing possible interference with the flight by the Soviets.

Frequent stops *en route*, however, slowed the Atlantic down, and in 1950, Col. Schilling and Col. William Ritchie made the first flight from the UK to the USA sustained by aerial refuelling. The flight of F-84Es took off from RAF Manston, Kent, to Limestone, Maine. The first refuelling was by an Avro Lancaster near Prestwick, the

In July 1948, Col. David Schilling, commander of the 56th Fighter Group, led a flight of Lockheed F-80As from Selfridge Field in Michigan to RAF Odiham in the UK. The Atlantic crossing was the first of jet fighter aircraft and was christened Fox Able One by Schilling—Fox Able being phonetic code for Fighter Atlantic. The CO's aircraft was 44-85464. (*Author's collection*)

RAF personnel at RAF Odiham have a good look over a 53rd FS F-80A. The 56th Flight flew on the Furstenfeldbruck in Germany where they remained for ten months before returning to the US on Fox Able Two as a show of force to assure the Soviet Union that it was possible for the US to reinforce Europe with aircraft if necessary. (*Author's collection*)

second by an Avro Lincoln over Iceland, and the third by a Boeing KB-29 off the coast of Labrador. The system used was probe and drogue developed by Flight Refuelling Ltd, and the Lancaster and Lincoln were both operated by that company. The flight lasted ten hours and eight minutes.

By the mid-1950s, in-flight refuelling had been perfected to the extent that the majority of units deploying to and from the UK and Europe could do so without a number of stops. There were two principle routes to Europe, both pioneered in Operation Longstride in August 1953. The first route, flown by David Schilling leading eight F-84Gs, became known as the southern route and flew to Europe and the north African bases with aerial refuellings west of Kindley Field, Bermuda; the second between Kindley and the Azores; and the last one in the vicinity of Lajes in the Azores. This was the route that would be regularly used by fighters deploying to Southern Europe, North Africa, and the Middle East. The second route was flown by twenty F-84Gs led by Col. Thayer S. Olds out of Turner AFB. They flew to RAF Lakenheath with three refuellings: once over Boston, Massachusetts; the second time near Labrador; and the third time close to Iceland. This was the route that would generally, but not exclusively, be used by fighters deploying to the UK and Northern Europe. Many times, the first port of call in the UK would be Prestwick in Scotland.

In 1956, Operation Shark Bait pioneered the first non-stop flight of jet fighters across the Atlantic, using the Great Circle Route. This can be defined as being the shortest route between two points on a sphere—the earth being a sphere. The flight of three F-84F Thunderstreaks, led by Col. Charles F. Blair, took off from McGuire AFB, New Jersey, on 19 April, heading for RAF Wethersfield, the home of the 20th TFW, in Essex, England. The purpose of the flight was to find the shortest route from mainland USA to Europe, but there were other targets. Col. Blair recorded in his autobiography *Red Ball in the Sky*:

> Shark Bait is scheduled to be the first non-stop flight of jet fighters across the Atlantic on the direct, great circle route, and the first one with only one in-flight refuelling. Although it is mainly a deployment exercise to demonstrate the most rapid transfer of fighter aircraft to Europe, it's also a test of my air-planes newly designed guidance equipment. Therefore part of my task is to find the Wethersfield Royal Air Force station near the east coast of England without using radio.[1]

Blair's F-84F *Excalibur IV* was fitted with a 'Star Tracker', which measures the angularity between the sun and stars, and Doppler radar, which bounces signals off the earth to verify ground speed and drift. The radio direction finder on Blair's aircraft had been deactivated.

After a crossing of 3,145 miles (5,061.4 km), *Excalibur IV* touched down at Wethersfield after six hours and fifty minutes in the air. It had only been refuelled once, by a Boeing KC-97.

With the exception of the movement of new aircraft to the established units in the UK and the co-operative exchanges and exercises with other units of USAFE, there was little regular movement of units and their aircraft on temporary deployment to UK

Standing beside F-84F Excalibur IV are Col. Charles F. Blair, centre; Capt. Cezar Martinez, left; and Maj. Robert C. Tomlinson. In 1956, Operation Shark Bait pioneered the first non-stop flight of jet fighters across the Atlantic, using the Great Circle Route from Maguire AFB to RAF Wethersfield in the UK. Blair's Excalibur IV was specially equipped with a 'Star Tracker'. The nonstop flight was refuelled in flight once and the flight took six hours and fifty minutes. (*Author's collection*)

Before the 20th FBW became resident in the UK with their nuclear capable F-84Gs, they deployed to Manston in July 1950 for a five-month deployment with their F-84Ds. The F-84Ds had flown the Fox Able route with 'hot guns', fearing possible interference with the flight by the Soviets. (*Author's collection*)

bases during the 1950s. The most significant movement of US forces across the Atlantic occurred in 1958 when the Lebanon crisis brought a CASF (Composite Air Strike Force) to the Middle East. Although several aircraft made landfall at bases in France before moving on to Turkey, there was no movement through the UK. The RF-101s, F-100s, B-57s, and RB-66s made the trip across the ocean via the Southern Atlantic route. The CASF concept was developed by TAC in 1955 in order to have a task force ready to deploy to any part of the world to deal with 'bush fires'. The CASF was designed to augment combat-ready units already assigned to USAFE, PACAF, and Alaskan Air Command.

Total Force

One of the significant developments as the 1960s dawned was the allocation of various Air National Guard units to the major USAF Commands: SAC, TAC, MATS, and ADC. At this time, TAC 'gained' a significant number of ANG fighter, tactical bomber, and reconnaissance units, which could be called upon if the need arose as witnessed by the Berlin crisis and the subsequent deployment of ANG units to Europe in 1962 under Operation Stair Step. The policy was also to have significant implications for TAC operations commencing in the 1970s.

The involvement of the USAF in SE Asia throughout the remainder of the 1960s and the early 1970s proved to be an immense strain on TAC resources. So much so that whether or not the command could deliver its mission satisfactorily was at risk. Basically it was a question of financial resources. The state could not afford to continue funding the forces at the rate demanded by the war and all that that implied in terms of the provision of material resources, training, and new equipment. A period of austerity beckoned. The question was how to move forward while managing with less money. The fact that the National Guard and other Reserve Forces had not been used to any significant degree in the SE Asia war was a frustration to many in the Department of Defence. President Richard Nixon's Secretary of Defence Melvin Laird first articulated the total force concept in a memorandum to the secretaries of the military departments on 21 August 1970:

> Within the Department of Defence ... economies will require reductions in over-all strengths and capabilities of the active forces, and increased reliance on the combat and the combat support units of the Guard and Reserves. Emphasis will be given to the concurrent consideration of the Total Forces, Active and Reserve, to determine the most advantageous mix to support national strategy and meet the threat. A total force concept will be applied in all aspects of planning, programming, manning, equipping, and employing Guard and Reserve Forces.[2]

If the country ever went to war again, the total force concept would mean, in the case of the air force and TAC, that the ANG and the AFRES would be required to play an active role. This would also imply that the ANG and AFRES equipment and training would have to be improved, and the consequence of this was that more, not less funds would be required to achieve this. The regular air force would need to bear the brunt of austerity, at least in the short term. The advantage which the air force had over the land and sea forces was that the experiences of the Stair Step and the development of the CASF units meant that concept of total force was not entirely new and was welcomed from the outset. They were soon ahead of the game.

Air Reserve Components (ARC) would be required to train and exercise together. The most significant threat of war was in Europe. The assumed superiority of the Warsaw Pact conventional forces meant that the battles would be fought over European territory and skies. In 1968, budget cuts had caused the withdrawal of land and air forces from Europe. For USAFE, this meant the loss of an entire wing, the 49th TFW which was withdrawn back Holloman AFB in 1968, with a commitment that it would be ready to deploy back should the need arise. Under Exercise Crested Gap, the 49th returned annually to Europe to participate in Reforger (REturn of FORces to GERmany) exercises, which also included the elements of the US Army withdrawn from Europe.

Under the auspices of the total force, a concept of dual basing was developed by TAC. Regular units of the air force and units from the ANG and AFRES would regularly deploy to European bases to exercise and train with NATO forces as if in wartime. The first of these regular deployments which included the UK was coded Creek Bee and started in 1972. It involved 67th TRW and the 363rd TRW deploying to Europe alternately for two weeks at a time. Creek Bee brought the 45th TRS of the 67th TRW to RAF Alconbury, home of the 10th TRW, in June 1973. In 1977, the name of these tactical reconnaissance deployments was changed to Salty Bee.

Coronet

Coronet deployments to Europe commenced in 1975. These were truly total force movements involving TAC and the ARC units, and they were intended to reflect as accurately as possible a wartime deployment. In the UK, the regular USAF bases were used and designated as MOBs (mobile operating bases). These were RAF stations Mildenhall, Lakenheath, Bentwaters, Woodbridge Alconbury, and Upper Heyford. Two further ex-USAF bases were also used and designated as SOBs (standby operating bases). These were RAF Wethersfield and RAF Sculthorpe. In addition to the MOBs and SOBs, other bases were made available to the USAF from 1978. Allocated as co-located operating bases, these were the RAF airfields at Coltishall, Wittering, Waddington, Finningley, and Leeming, and the Aeroplane and Armament Experimental Establishment (AAEE) at Boscombe Down.

Commensurate with the commencement of the Coronet deployments was the appointment of Gen. Wilbur Creech as commander of TAC in 1978. Creech took a close interest in Coronet deployments and had very firm views about how they should be conducted. He believed in bringing realism to the deployments and the training and exercises associated with them. He required each unit to become familiar with its wartime co-located base. In 1979, he instigated Checkered Flag, which embraced

Commencing on 9 June 1978, Coronet Oriole brought the F-105Ds of the 301st TFW, AFRES, to RAF Sculthorpe in Norfolk, where they remained for a just over a month departing on 11 July. (*USAF*)

the co-located base programme including the Coronet. If you are going to deploy to a wartime base, Creech argued, then it was imperative that you did so with the utmost realism, ensuring that the moment you touched down you were immediately on a war footing. This had considerable implications for maintenance as well. If you were going on a war footing, it was also imperative that you had access to spares and a maintenance regime that supported your war readiness. Creech introduced many reforms that enabled this to happen. One of the cornerstones of his philosophy was the need for decentralisation. He introduced the Combat Orientated Maintenance Organisation (COMO), which assigned maintenance units to each squadron in TAC. Not only did this make for a more efficient maintenance regime, but it also helped to engender a pride in the job and the unit and forged a bond between who flew the missions and those who enabled them to do so. He believed in the dedicated crew chief programme, which assigned a crew chief to a particular aircraft. He allowed the crew chief's name to be painted on the aircraft just like the pilots.

In May 1980, when the 522nd TFS took their General Dynamic F-111Ds to Boscombe Down for a two-week deployment called Coronet Hammer, it was more than just another deployment. They took with them a full complement of personnel, parts and other equipment, something that they could not always access at their home at Cannon AFB, New Mexico. Creech specially directed this deployment to demonstrate what could be achieved if the squadrons were properly equipped and motivated. Maintenance had the equipment and spares to ensure that the aircraft had a high in-commission rate, which, in turn, enabled the pilots could complete all scheduled missions. It was a triumph. The pilots flew their full range of missions and the squadron achieved an 86.4-per cent mission rate compared to only 34 per cent back at Cannon, an improvement of almost 150 per cent. A total 505 sorties had been scheduled and 554 were actually flown. The War Readiness Spares Kit (WRSK), which they had taken with them, was fully sourced and met 95 per cent of their requirements, the remaining 5 per cent able to be sourced locally from other bases and supply depots.

The missions flown by the F-111Ds in Coronet Hammer fell under four categories. The interdiction mission was the primary mission of the Aardvark and this accounted for the majority of missions flown from Boscombe Down. Realistic mission profiles were flown against a variety of targets in the UK and mainland Europe against simulated enemy defence systems. Missions against airfields on mainland Europe known as offensive counter air (OCA) missions formed the second category. The third category was battlefield air interdiction (BAI) and close air support (CAS). This was not a task for which the 522nd regularly trained. It was, however, a requirement of NATO. These were missions which were performed under the direction of a forward air controller (FAC) from the ground. The BAI mission was essentially a deep penetration mission usually flown beyond the forward edge of the battlefield area (FEBA) and over enemy territory. It targeted forces not immediately engaged with the friendly forces. Gen. Creech was a firm advocate of BIA and the co-operation of the army, which that involved. The final category of missions flown was tactical air support of maritime operations (TASMO). This required flying sorties against Royal Navy vessels as part of Exercise Dawn Patrol, which was an annual exercise which took place in the Mediterranean and, in 1980, involved the naval forces of the USA, UK, Italy France, the Netherlands, and Turkey.

Coronet deployments were many and varied. During the period from 1975 through to 1991, there were twenty-two deployments by TAC squadrons, thirty by ANG squadrons, and one by an AFRES squadron.

By far the most frequent visitor was the Vought A-7D Corsair II, which deployed on twenty-seven occasions with the ANG and twice with TAC's 4451st Training Squadron of the 4450th Tactical Group. The 4451st Tactical Squadron was the training squadron at Nellis AFB, Nevada, for the F-117 Nighthawk. The cockpit layout and the flying characteristics of the A-7D were similar to those of the F-117. The 4451st deployed to RAF Woodbridge in 1984 and 1986. These deployments were surrounded by a great deal of security. One spotter recalls the occasion when his attempts at photographing the A-7s was thwarted when a security vehicle was consistently imposed between his camera and subject. The underwing stores carried by the A-7s were also covered right up the moment just prior to take off.

There were occasions when Coronet exercises coincided with other exercises in the UK. For example, Coronet Castle in April 1983 coincided with the NATO Exercise Mallet Blow 83, when the A-7Ds of the Ohio ANG were deployed to RAF Sculthorpe. The Mallet Blow exercises were held twice every year commencing in 1980. They were for 'mud movers' and were focused on the Scottish ranges. TAC participants were generally, but not exclusively, those that were based in the UK such as the A-10s of the 81st TFW and the F-111s of the 20th and 48th TFWs.

F-111D 68-122, seen here at Greenham Common's air show on 31 May 1980, was assigned to the 522nd TFS of the 27th TFW and deployed to the UK in May and June 1980 to RAF Boscombe Down for Coronet Hammer. (*Chris England*)

In June 1984, the F-16s of the 428th TFS, 474th TFW, from Nellis AFB arrived at RAF Bentwaters for Coronet Raider. (*USAF*)

An F-16B of the 429th TFS, 474th TFW, taxis to its hardstanding at RAF Bentwaters on 13 April 1982. In both 1982 and 1984, the 474th TFW deployed to RAF Bentwaters. In 1982, it was for Coronet Wrangler. (*Doug Gordon*)

In June 1984, the F-16s of the 474th TFW were accompanied by the F-16As of the 57th Fighter Weapons Wing ADS, the Thunderbirds, under the auspices of Coronet Thunder. (*Doug Gordon*)

F-4C Phantoms of the 110th TFS, 131st TFG, of the Missouri ANG took part in Coronet Cactus at RAF Leeming in June and July 1982. This aircraft had to take the arrestor cable on landing after a sortie. (*USAF*)

Coronet Mail bought the A-7Ds of the 150 TFG, New Mexico ANG to RAF Wittering in July 1983. (*USAF*)

The A-7Ds of the Air National Guard were regular visitors to the UK throughout the 1980s. In February 1983, this A-7D is being pre-fighted prior to a sortie in Coronet Castle at RAF Sculthorpe. (*USAF*)

Deployments of TAC aircraft to the UK often coincided with air shows. This Ohio ANG A-7D at RAF Marham in 1983 was a participant in Coronet Castle based at RAF Sculthorpe. (*Doug Gordon*)

The 81st TFW at the twin bases of RAF Bentwaters and Woodbridge regularly welcomed deployments of A-10A 'Warthogs'. This aircraft belonged to the 75th TFS of the 23rd TFW and was at RAF Woodbridge for Coronet Cross in June 1983. (*USAF*)

Coronet Venom brought the A-10As of the 356th TFS, 354th TFW, to RAF Bentwaters in August 1989. (*USAF*)

Other Deployments

In addition to Coronet, other deployments of TAC aircraft visited the UK from time to time.

The NATO Tiger Meets, which were a regular feature of NATO's aircrew training, took place in the UK for the first time in 1961 at RAF Woodbridge. Any squadron with a tiger as its emblem was allowed to join the tiger club. The Tiger Meets were the brainchildren of two squadron commanders: John Howe of the RAFs 74th Squadron and Ed Rackham CO of the 79th TFS. The two squadrons got together for the first time at Woodbridge in 1961. The year 1962 saw eight NATO 'Tiger' squadrons participating. Since its inception, the squadrons have met every year at bases throughout Europe with the exception of 1995 and more recently 2020.

The first event was hosted by the 79th TFS, which was part of the 20th TFW and flew the F-100D Super Sabre. The only other regular TAC participant at the UK Tiger Meets was the 53rd TFS of the 36th TFW based at Bitburg in Germany. This unit initially flew the F-4D Phantom, later converting to the F-15 Eagle. The 79th TFS converted to the F-111E when the 20th TFW moved to RAF Upper Heyford in 1970. In 1993, the 20th FW moved stateside to Shaw AFB and flew the F-16C/D. The 79th FS returned to the UK for the 1997 Tiger Meet, when the 494th FS of the 48th FW made its first appearance at the meet with the F-15E Eagle. The purpose of the meets was to foster professional co-operation and understanding between the NATO allies and to share tactics and ideas. The exercises usually lasted a week.

Tiger Meets were a regular part of NATOs exercise schedule through the years since the first one at RAF Woodbridge in 1961. The 53rd TFS of the 36th TFW deployed from Bitburg in Germany for the meet every year while based in Europe. RAF Woodbridge hosted the NATO Tiger Meet in 1969. On that occasion, the 53rd brought the F-4D Phantom.

Exercise Excalibur was hosted by the 48th TFW and held annually at RAF Lakenheath, commencing with Excalibur I in 1985. It was a gunnery, strafing, and bombing competition. Originally designed as a USAFE exercise, it evolved to welcome participants from numerous NATO air forces. For the purposes of the exercise, units deployed aircraft to Lakenheath. The ranges used for the competition were Holbeach and Wainfleet, and Nordhorn on the Netherlands' German border. The pilots flew air-to-ground missions, refuelling on their way to the target. They were assigned a certain time to hit the target and could be intercepted *en route*. Pilots were graded on their ability to accurately deliver their bombs on a specific target from a high and low altitude, dive bombing, and low-altitude gunnery. Awards were given for the top-scoring pilot in each event and for the top-scoring flight and wing. Regular USAFE TAC units deployed to Lakenheath from their European bases were the F-15s of the 32nd TFS from Soesterberg, the Netherlands; the F-15s of the 36th TFW from Bitburg, Germany; the F-16s of the 52nd TFW from Spangdahlem, Germany; the F-16s and A-10s of the 50th TFW from Hahn, Germany; the F-16s of the 86th TFW from Ramstein, Germany; and the F-16s of the 401st TFW from Torrejón, Spain. The last of the Excalibur competitions, Excalibur IX, was held at Lakenheath in 1993.

Tactical Fighter Meets were another regular NATO exercise and welcomed TAC units, not only from Europe, but, occasionally, from the USA as well. One such was the meet held at RAF Waddington from 4–8 August 1986. In addition to USAFE's 525th TFS of the 36th TFW and the 612th TFS of the 401st TFW, the base also welcomed F-15Cs from the 1st TFW from Langley AFB and the F-16As of the 428th, 429th,and 430th TFS of the 474th TFW out of Nellis.

Participation in the RAF Tactical Bombing competitions was also open to TAC units, both based in the UK and elsewhere. The 23rd TFW deployed from England AFB to take part with A-7Ds in both 1977 and 1978 and, in both years, won the team trophy. In 1981, TAC was represented by the 388th TFW from Hill AFB flying F-16As.

The participation at UK airshows of TAC aircraft based with USAF are, of course, numerous and need not detain us here.

With the end of the Cold War, the number of USAF tactical units in Europe and the UK was considerably diminished and so were the deployments from TAC units in the USA. During Desert Storm and subsequent Middle East and Baltic interventions, many TAC and ANG units were deployed through UK bases to the areas of conflict.

This F-16A of the 388th TFW is taxiing out at RAF Lossiemouth to take-off for the range in the RAF Tactical Bombing Competition in 1981. (*USAFE*)

F-16As of the 388th Tactical Fighter Wing from Hill AFB, Utah, attended the RAF Tactical Bombing Competition at RAF Lossiemouth in May and June 1981. The aircraft are being loaded with two AIM-9 sidewinder and six laser-guided bombs. (*USAFE*)

TAC Temporary Deployments to the UK 1962 to 1991

DATE	EXERCISE	BASE
1962		
August	NATO Tiger Meet	RAF Woodbridge
1966		
July	NATO Tiger Meet	RAF Leuchars
1969		
August	NATO Tiger Meet	RAF Woodbridge
1971		
	NATO Tiger Meet	RAF Upper Heyford
1973		
June	Creek Bee II	RAF Alconbury
1975		
Nov/Dec	F-111 familiarisation	RAF Upper Heyford
1976		
March	Coronet Rally	RAF Alconbury
March	F-111 familiarisation	RAF Upper Heyford
April/May	Coronet Prize	RAF Lakenheath
Oct/Nov	Coronet Fife	RAF Lakenheath
1977		
June	NATO Tiger Meet	RAF Greenham Common
Sept/Oct	RAF Tac Bombing Competition	RAF Lossiemouth
1978		
June	Coronet Oriole	RAF Sculthorpe
June/July	RAF Tac Bombing Competition	RAF Lossiemouth
July	Coronet Heron	RAF Coltishall
July	Coronet Teal	RAF Wittering
July	Coronet Teal	RAF Wittering
July	Coronet Teal	RAF Wittering
1979		
July/August	Salty Bee 79	RAF Alconbury
Aug/Sept	Coronet Stallion	RAF Waddington
Aug/Sept	Coronet Stallion	RAF Waddington
1980		
May/June	Coronet Hammer	Boscombe Down
Sept/Oct	Coronet Gyro	RAF Alconbury
1981		
May/June	RAF Tac Bombing Competition	RAF Lossiemouth
May/June	Coronet Canvas	RAF Wittering

T	AIRCRAFT	COMMAND
TFW/53 TFS	F-105D	TAC
TFW	F-84F	TAC
TFW/53 TFS	F-4D	TAC
TFW/53 TFS	F-4D	TAC
TFW/53 TFS	F-4D	TAC
TRS/67 TRW	RF-4C	TAC
th TFW	F-111F	TAC
TRS/363 TRW	RF-4C	TAC
TFS	F-111A	TAC
TFS/122 TFW	F-100D/F	Indiana ANG
TFS/113 TFW	F-105D/F	District of Columbia ANG
TFS/192 TFW		Virginia ANG
TFW/53 TFS	F-15A	TAC
TFS/23 TFW	A-7D	TAC
TFS/507 TFG	F-105D/F	AFRES
TFW	A-7D	TAC
TRS/363 TRW	RF-4C	TAC
TFS	A-7D	Ohio ANG
TFS/112 TRG	A-7D	Ohio ANG
TFS/169 TFG	A-7D	Ohio ANG
TRS/363 TRW	RF-4C	TAC
TFW	A-7D	Iowa ANG
TFS/114 TFW	A-7D	South Dakota ANG
TFS/27 TFW	F-111D	TAC
TRS/186TRW	RF-4C	Kentucky ANG
TFW	F-16A	TAC
TFS/138 TFG	A-7D	Oklahoma ANG

1982		
April/May	Coronet Wrangler	RAF Bentwaters
May/June	Salty Bee 82	RAF Alconbury
June	Coronet Brave	RAF Finningley
June/July	Coronet Cactus	RAF Leeming
1983		
April	Coronet Castle	RAF Sculthorpe
May/June	Coronet Cross	RAF Woodbridge
June/July	Coronet Joust	RAF Coltishall
July	Coronet Mail	RAF Wittering
September	Coronet Archer	Boscombe Down
1984		
April	Coronet Patriot	RAF Wethersfield
June	Coronet Thunder	RAF Bentwaters
June/July	Coronet Raider	RAF Bentwaters
Oct/Nov	Coronet Spark	RAF Woodbridge
1985		
April	Coronet Barracuda	RAF Wittering
May June	Coronet Buffalo	RAF Waddington
	Coronet Crusader	RAF Bentwaters
July/August	Coronet Comet	RAF Woodbridge
1986		
April	Coronet Chinook	RAF Bentwaters
May	Unknown	RAF Woodbridge
June July	Coronet Miami	RAF Sculthorpe
July August	Tactical Fighter Meet	RAF Waddington
	Salty Bee 86	RAF Alconbury
Aug/Sept	Coronet Comanche	Boscombe Down
	Coronet Papago	Boscombe Down
September	Coronet Mobile	RAF Coltishall

TFS/474 TFW	F-16A/B	TAC
TRS/363 TRW	RF-4C	TAC
TFG	F-4D	Illinois ANG
TFS/131TFG	F-4C	Missouri ANG
TFS/121 TFG	A-7D	Ohio ANG
TFS/178 TFG		
TFS/180 TFG		
TFS/23 TFW	A-10A	TAC
TRW	RF-4C	Alabama ANG
TFG	A-7D	New Mexico ANG
TFS/112 TFG		Pennsylvania ANG
TFS/27 TFW	F-111D	TAC
TFS/103 TFG	A-10A	Connecticut ANG
FWW	F-16A	TAC
TFS/474TFW	F-16A	TAC
1 TS/4450 TG	A-7D	TAC
TFS/138 TFG	A-7D/K	Oklahoma ANG
TFS/132TFW	A-7D/K	Iowa ANG
TFG		
TFS/114TFG		South Dakota ANG
TFS/474 TFW	F-16A	TAC
TFS/354 TFW	A-10A	TAC
TFS/23 TFW	A-10A	TAC
1 TS/4450 TG	A-7D	TAC
TFS/121 TFG	A-7D	Ohio ANG
TFS/178 TFG		
TFS/180 TFG		
TFW	F-16A	TAC
FW	F-15C	TAC
TFW/525 TFS	F-15C	TAC
TFW/612 TFS	F-16A	TAC
TFW/428,429TFS	F-16A	TAC
TRS/363 TRW	RF-4C	TAC
TFS/27 TFW	F-111D	TAC
ECS/366 TFW	EF-111A	TAC
TRS/117 TRW	RF-4C	Alabama ANG

1987 July/August	Coronet Gemini	RAF Wittering
1988 June	Coronet King	RAF Wittering
1989 April May June June June/July Aug/Sept	 Coronet Hoop Coronet Pine Coronet Diamond Coronet Python Coronet Venom	 RAF Alconbury RAF Sculthorpe Boscombe Down RAF Bentwaters RAF Bentwaters
1990 July August September	 Coronet Lariat Coronet Gun NATO Tiger Meet	 RAF Sculthorpe RAF Sculthorpe RAF Upper Heyford
1991 June July	 Coronet East 97 NATO Tiger Meet	 RAF Waddington RAF Fairford

TFG TFS/112 TFG	A-7D/K A-7D/k	New Mexico ANG Pennsylvania ANG
TFS/138 TFG	A-7D	Oklahoma ANG
TRS/117 TRW TFS/178 TFG TFS/180TFG TFS/27 TFW TFS/354 TFW TFS/354TFW	RF-4C A-7D A-7D/K F-111D A-10A A-10A	Alabama ANG Ohio ANG Ohio ANG TAC TAC TAC
TFS/128TFW TFS/23 TFW TFW/53 TFS	A-10A A-10A F-15C	Wisconsin ANG TAC TAC
TFS/138TFG TFW/53 TFS	A-7D F-15C	Oklahoma ANG TAC

Epilogue

On 1 June 1992, the USAF was reorganised. Tactical Air Command, Strategic Air Command, and Military Airlift Command were deactivated and replaced by Air Combat Command.

Following the end of the Cold War, the 3rd AF oversaw the inactivation of units and bases in the UK. In 2006, following the deactivation of the 17th AF, the 3rd AF assumed control of all USAFE European units and bases and moved its headquarters from RAF Mildenhall to Ramstein, Germany. In 2006, the 3rd AF was briefly deactivated between November 2005 and December 2006 when the 16th AF took moved to Ramstein and took control of all USAFE's assets. Following deactivation of the 16th AF in December 2006, the 3rd AF was reactivated at Ramstein with responsibility for European operations. In 2012, following the deactivation of the 17th AF, the 3rd AF took over responsibility for the USAF in Africa, retaining its responsibilities for Europe.

In 2022, there is only one active USAFE tactical unit in the UK, and that is the 48th FW based at RAF Lakenheath. The 48th has four squadrons assigned: the 492nd, 493rd, 494th, and 495th Fighter Squadrons. The 492nd and 494th FS fly the McDonnell Douglas F-15E Eagle, and the 493rd, the F-15C/D Eagle, and the 495 , the Lockheed Martin F-35A Lightning II. The 48th FW is assigned to the 3rd Air Force.

Several of the other units previously on permanent detachment to the UK are still active, albeit with different roles. The 10th TFW was reactivated as the 10th Air Base Wing in November 1994 providing support to the USAF Academy in Colorado. The 20th FW continues to be based at Shaw AFB in South Carolina, its three squadrons flying the F-16. The 47th Bomb Wing was reactivated as the 47th Flying Training Wing at Laughlin AFB, Texas, on 1 September 1974, conducting pilot training flying the Northrop T-38 Talon, the Raytheon T-1A Jayhawk, and the Beechcraft T-6 Texan II. In July 1993, the 81st was redesignated as the 81st Training Wing at Keesler AFB, Mississippi. The 81st TW is a non-flying unit conducting specialised technical training. The 42nd ECS was reactivated in 1994 as the 42nd Airborne Command and Control

Squadron at Davis-Monthan AFB Arizona flying the Lockheed EC-130E. It was subsequently deactivated in 2002 and reactivated as the 42nd ECS at Davis Monthan in March 2006, attached to the 55th Electronic Combat Group and flying the EC-130H. The 527th AS was reactivated as the 527th Space Aggressor Squadron at Shriever AFB, Colorado, on 29 September 2020. It assigned to the 57th Adversary tactics Group based at Nellis AFB. It is a non-flying unit conducting training in countering Space threats. The 420th AREFS was reincarnated as the 420th Test Squadron in October 1992 at Edwards AFB and was involved in the testing of the Northrop-Grumman B-2 Spirit. It was redesignated the 420th Flight Test Flight Squadron in March 1994 and deactivated again in 1997. Reactivated in 2001 at Phoenix-Mesa Gateway Airport, Arizona, the squadron was responsible for the testing of the cockpit modifications for the T-38 Talon. It was deactivated on completion of this work in October 2007 and reactivated again in October 2019 to conduct the testing of the Northrop-Grumman B-21 Raider.

Only two of the previous UK-based units are presently inactive. The 66th ECW was reactivated in 1994 as the 66th Air Base Wing at Hanscome AFB in Massachusetts, inactivating again in September, 2010. The 406th FIW was resurrected as the 406th Air Expeditionary Wing on 30 March 2011 at Moron AB, Spain. It was inactivated shortly after.

Of all the bases used by the TAC units, only RAF Alconbury and RAF Woodbridge are currently operating as military facilities. Alconbury is still active, on a stand-by basis, managed by the 423rd Force Support Squadron but is reportedly up for sale by the Ministry of Defence. RAF Woodbridge is operated by the British Army and is home to two Royal Engineer regiments. It is divided into two separate areas, Rock Barracks and Woodbridge Airfield. In 2017, the airfield was used for rough field landing trials for the Airbus A400M.

However, in spite of their closure and inactivity as military airfields, much work is being done to preserve the history of many of the airfields. The Bentwaters Cold War Museum is one such example of this. It is situated on the former base and in addition to a growing aircraft collection its collection includes some of the former facilities used by the 81st TFW when in residence. RAF Sculthorpe is home to the RAF Sculthorpe Heritage Centre, with many exhibits reflecting the history of the base when it was home to the 47th BW. Manston, which closed in 1999 hosts the Manston History Museum and the Spitfire and Hurricane Memorial Museum.

Appendix I

The Tactical Aircraft Assigned to the Tactical Units based in the UK

The first three decades of the Cold War from 1950 to 1970 were characterised by the relatively short service careers of the, predominately, jet fighter aircraft that served with the wings and squadrons of the USAF in the UK. Technology advances in design and systems, coupled with a seemingly endless supply of funds, meant that no sooner had one aircraft joined a wing than its successor was hot on its heels. An example of this is the 20th TFW, which, during the 1950s, changed its aircraft three times beginning the decade with the Republic F-84G Thunderjet, then converting to the F-84F Thunderstreak, and passing into the 1960s with the North American F-100 Super Sabre.

During the Second World War, the Lockheed P-80 Shooting Star, Gloster Meteor, and Messerschmitt 262 saw service in the final stages of the conflict. The technology that created these aircraft led to the design of other straight wing subsonic jets purpose built for a variety of roles, principally air defence, ground attack, and reconnaissance. In the USA, this included the F-84 Thunderjet and the F/RF-80. Only the F-84 Thunderjet, with the 20th FBS and the 406th, was based in the UK. Commencing in November 1951, the F-84E arrived with the 406th FIW at Manston, and in June 1952, the F-84G at RAF Wethersfield with the 20th FBW.

Following the Second World War and the appropriation of much of the German research into jet engines and swept-wing technology, more advanced fighters began to enter service in the late 1940s and early 1950s. These aircraft are exemplified by the North American F-86 Sabre and its opposition in Korea, the Mikoyan MiG-15. These jets were transonic, i.e. capable of supersonic flight in a dive, but not in level flight. They were also developed by the manufacturers to fulfil a variety of different roles. Republic's F-84F Thunderstreak was a fighter bomber and, in the guise of the RF-84F Thunderflash, an accomplished reconnaissance platform. Just as aircraft design evolved, so did the weapons they were designed to carry and deliver. The F-86D, an air defence fighter, carried a pack of 'Mighty Mouse' rockets in its mission to kill the attacking bomber. It was not fitted with a gun. The advent of the 'special weapon' into TAC's armoury required computer systems for successful delivery. The F-84F, the F-86F-35, and the F-86H were equipped for the nuclear role. The Thunderstreak, F-86A/E/F Sabre, and the F-86D were based in the UK.

The second generation of fighter aircraft were supersonic. The century series aircraft belong to this category, of which two served in the UK with USAFE: the F-100D/F and the F-101A/C Voodoo. These aircraft entered service with USAFE in the UK in 1958 (the reconnaissance RF-101C Voodoo did not arrive in the UK until September 1966). These aircraft had a longer service life than their first generation predecessors. The F-100D/F served with the 20th TFW for a total of twelve years from 1958 to 1971. It was an era that saw considerable developments in self-protection systems, radar, and missile technology.

The Super Sabres and the Voodoos were followed into service in the mid-1960s by the McDonnell F-4C/D Phantom, and, later, in the 1970s, in the case of the 20th and 48th TFWs, by the General Dynamics F-111E/F Aardvark. The role of these aircraft was determined in no small degree by the doctrine of flexible response, which NATO adopted in 1967. Although these aircraft maintained the nuclear delivery role of the Super Sabres and Voodoos, their primary mission gradually turned to conventional attack and, to a lesser extent, air defence. The development of new systems including look-down/shoot-down radars, RHAW, TFR, laser-guided bombs, advanced air-to-ground missiles such as the AGM-65 Maverick, and evolving offensive and protective ECM systems defined the development of fighter aircraft at this time, and the experiences of the war in Vietnam ensured that those older aircraft that were still in service, such as the F-100 and the F-105, also benefited from these developments.

The Northrop F-5A Freedom Fighter and F-5E Tiger evolved at this time and served with many overseas air forces as well as the USAF. The need for an aircraft to replace to fill the gap left by the ECM dedicated EB-66C led to the development of the EF-111A Aardvark, which equipped a reactivated 42nd ECS at RAF Upper Heyford in 1984.

Of all the lessons learnt from the war in SE Asia, the need for air superiority aircraft and armaments was what led to the development in the USA of the next generation of fighter aircraft. These included the McDonnell Douglas F-15 Eagle, the Grumman F-14 Tomcat, the McDonnell Douglas F-18 Hornet, and the General Dynamics F-16 Fighting Falcon. Both the F-16 and the F-18 sprang directly from a competition for a lightweight fighter. Both designs developed into multi-role aircraft. The only one of these fighters that concerns us in this narrative is the F-16, which flew with the 527th TFTAS at RAF Bentwaters from June 1988 to November 1989.

The evolution of the dedicated tactical reconnaissance aircraft paralleled fighter development. The RF-101C Voodoo served in USAFE from 1958. It did not arrive in the UK until 1966 when the 17th and 18th TRS of the 66th TRW moved from Laon, France, to RAF Upper Heyford. The RF-4C served with the 10th TRW at RAF Alconbury in the UK from 1965 to 1987. The evolution of digital sensors to supplement the standard cameras used by the early RF-84Fs and the RF-101Cs during the Cold War greatly enhanced the later Voodoo and Phantom capability. These included Hycon KS-72 cameras with automatic controls, which were part of Modification 1181 for the RF-101C. This modification was completed in 1967 and improved the Voodoos low-altitude and high-altitude performance. The Hycon KS-72 was originally designed for the RF-4C.

As the recce Phantom developed, various sensors were developed that greatly enhanced performance. These included a Texas Instruments AN/APQ-99 two-lobe mono-pulse J-band radar, an AN/ALR-46A radar warning receiver, a Litton AN/ALQ-125 TEREC sensor with data link equipment for transmission in near real-time, a Goodyear AN/APQ-102 side-looking mapping radar, and the AN/APQ-102A side-looking radar.

When the RF-4C left the UK in 1987, it was the end of USAFE's tactical recce presence in the country.

The reconnaissance variants of the B-45 Tornado and B-66 Destroyer bombers were, like their fighter counterparts, developed alongside the bombers. The service of the RB-45s was limited and is best remembered as the aircraft that took UK aircrew over the Soviet Union in two spy flights in the 1950s codenamed Ju Jitsu. In fact, these were missions conducted in association with SAC, and do not fall into the remit of this book. The flight of the RB-45s of the 19th TRS has been included in the narrative.

The spy flights were apart from the routine missions of the 19th TRS, which was to support the nuclear mission of the 47th BW. The RB-66s that succeeded the RB-45s in service with the 19th TRS and subsequently the 10th TRW had a varied tactical mission including photographic reconnaissance, weather reconnaissance, and electronic reconnaissance gathering mission.

Republic F-84 Thunderjet

The GOR for a jet fighter to replace the Republic P-47 Thunderbolt was published on 11 September 1944. It called for a mid-wing day fighter capable of a top speed of 600 mph, a combat radius of 850 miles, and armament of eight .50-calibre machines or six .60-calibre machine guns. The power-plant was to be the General Electric J-35 turbojet.

In the event the original specifications proved to be too ambitious and the final version of the P-84A had a reduced armament of six .50-calibre machine guns and a combat radius of 705 miles. The subsequent reduction in weight served the aircraft well as the low thrust of the engine was causing difficulties in development. The first flight of the first prototype XP-84 took place on 28 February 1946, and the second in August of the same year. In 1946, the AAF awarded two contracts for 141 and 271 aircraft.

Development problems throughout 1946 and into 1947 caused a slippage of the production of the P-84 and threatened the continuation of the programme. However, in February 1947, the AAF received their first aircraft in the form of fifteen YP-84s. These aircraft were fitted with an uprated J35-A-15 engines. In December 1947, the first production P-84Bs entered service with the 14th Fighter Group at Dow Field in Maine. The initial period in service with the 14th FG was fraught with problems. There was a marked scarcity of spares and flying was restricted by structural problems. Wrinkling of the skin limited the maximum speed permitted.

With the foundation of the USAF, all aircraft prefixes were changed, and the P-84 became the F-84. In total, 226 F-84Bs were accepted by the air force. Those aircraft not accepted were modified and subsequently received other designations. A further in-service mandatory modification programme was approved in 1949.

The F-84C followed the 'B' model into production. The only marked difference between the 'B' and the 'C' model was the change to the J35-A-13 engine and a new electrical system. Regrettably, the service lives of both the 'B' and the 'C' models of the Thunderjet was not a happy one. The accident rates in the squadrons were high, many of these due to pilot error. A USAF awareness programme was instigated which laid heavy emphasis on the training of new jet pilots and, with the cooperation of the manufacturers, on the flight characteristics and limitations of the aircraft.

The F-84D followed the F-84B/C in to production and, because of previous problems, was subjected to stringent testing by the air force. The tests were to ascertain whether or not the 'D' model was, in essence, a better aircraft than its predecessors, and indeed, how its performance as a fighter compared with the Lockheed F-80. The F-84D had received structural improvements and some other engineering changes. Testing concluded that the developmental changes made in the F-84D did in fact give it a better performance than the F-84B/C and that, overall, it performed better than the F-80 in range, acceleration, versatility, load-carrying ability, high-altitude climb, and level flight speed. The procurement of the F-84D was assured, but some modifications needed to be made. The F-84D served with Strategic Air Command's 27th Fighter Escort Group in Korea.

The F-84E featured a new higher thrust engine, the J35-A-17, a strengthened wing, a longer fuselage, a radar gunsight, and a fuel system which enabled the combat radius to be increased to over 1,000 miles. The fuel would be carried in two external tanks under the wings. The F-84E entered service in 1949 and a year later went to Korea replacing the F-84Ds in the 27th Fighter Escort Wing. In total, 843 aircraft were produced, 100 of these for foreign air forces under the MDAP.

The F-84G Thunderjet introduced several new features to the design. The aircraft incorporated in-flight refuelling equipment, which enabled it to be refuelled by the Boeing 'Flying boom' system. The F-84G was the first fighter with this capability. It was fitted with the J35-A-29 engine, an autopilot, a new A-4 gunsight, and an instrument landing system. The F-84G was the most successful of the Thunderjets. A total of 789 were produced for the USAF and 2,236 for the MDAP, and it served with distinction in Korea. One of the most significant developments for the F-84G was the ability to carry and deliver the atomic bomb. As such, it was assigned to the 20th Fighter Bomber Wing of the 49th Air Division and, in 1952, deployed to the UK with a mission of nuclear attack.

Republic F-84F Thunderstreak

The F-84F was developed as a low-cost response to an air force revision of the GOR of September 1944 that had led to the development of the original F-84. Republic claimed that its new aircraft would be a development of the F-84E and that as a consequence 55 per cent of current tooling could be used in production and subsequent air force maintenance. On the basis of this, the air force allocated one F-84E for the company to build a prototype. This was in December 1949. The aircraft would introduce many new features, including swept wings and tail with a 40-degree sweep at 25 per cent of the chord; the wings were fitted with leading edge slats. The engine would be a J35-A-25 turbojet, the F-84F could be refuelled in-flight using the same 'flying boom' system as used by the F-84G. It would be capable of carrying a nuclear weapon and a heavier load of external stores.

The prototype YF-84F was delivered to the air force at Edwards Air Force Base in May 1950. Tests were conducted in two phases, the first of these flown by a Republic test pilot and phase two by air force pilots. The J35-A-25 engine was considered to be completely inadequate for the F-84F and a decision was made to use the Wright J65-W-3 turbojet with 7,220-lb static thrust instead. The Wright engine was a licence-built version of the British Armstrong Siddeley Sapphire. However, the first F-84Fs were to be fitted with the lower-powered J65-W-1 engines, which led to problems with performance.

It was not until 14 February 1951 that a new prototype was flown. On 9 April 1951, the air force contacted to buy 274 F-84Fs. This was later revised to a total of 719 aircraft. In the event, innumerable problems with the power plant and the airframe effectively delayed the programme. Wright could not deliver the engine on time and when they did they ran into innumerable problems. Problems also persisted with the airframe. There was far less compatibility with the F-84E than was previously envisaged. Construction of the airframe component fell foul of the shortage at that time of aluminium alloy.

On 3 December 1952, the air force finally accepted the first two F-84Fs. However, further production delays and deficiencies with the aircraft's systems set back the programme and the Thunderstreak did not enter operational service until January 1954 when the first aircraft went to SAC's 508th Strategic Fighter Wing at Dow AFB Maine. They were not welcomed. They were underpowered and maintenance was an issue. In May 1954, the 405th FBW at Langley AFB was the first TAC unit to receive the aircraft.

Further deficiencies in service caused several aircraft to be grounded. In September 1954, the air force placed the order on hold while operational tests were carried out concerning the Thunderstreak's fitness for the role for which it was needed. These tests, called Project Run In, were completed by November and declared the aircraft fit for purpose and that it was a considerably better aircraft than its predecessors, the F-84E and F-84G.

However, after a further grounding in early 1955, the F-84F went on to give a satisfactory account of itself for the remainder of its service life. Altogether, 2,348 F-84Fs were produced, 1,496 for the USAF and the remainder for MDAP. The USAF began to retire its Thunderstreaks in 1954. Both TAC and SAC transferred their aircraft to the ANG. By January 1964, all F-84Fs had left the air force inventory, to be replaced, in most cases, by the North American F-100 Super Sabre, one of the exceptions being the 81st FBW at RAF Bentwaters and Woodbridge, which converted to the McDonnell F-101A/C Voodoo.

The F-84F continued in the ANG until 1972. In 1961, the Berlin Crisis brought four ANG squadrons of the F-84F to Europe to reinforce USAFE When these squadrons returned to the US, they left their Thunderstreaks to the newly activated 366th Tactical Fighter Wing. The aircraft served with the European air forces of Denmark, West Germany, Italy, Belgium, the Netherlands, Greece, and Norway, in addition to the Republic of China and Turkey.

> Its overall performance was very good, had a tremendous rate of turn. It was an honest airplane. It had to outlive a prior bad name. It was heavy, but I don't consider that an idiosyncrasy. Prior to flying the F84F I flew the F86-A/F. Comparisons regarding the aircraft

are not valid. Both had different missions and could not be compared objectively. You are basically talking apples and oranges.

Col. Robert R. Fredette Snr USAF RET, 78th FBS, 81st TFW[1]

They took our beautiful F-86 away from us and equipped us with the F-84F fighter bomber. The F-84's were shipped to Lisbon, Portugal to a Republic Aviation crew that installed the wings and was then test hopped by a Republic test pilot. I flew down there and set up an 81st operation to 'buy' the air-planes after the test hop. I took off for England with the first F-84 airplane. I was requested to do a flyby at Sculthorpe so all the Generals could see this 'great' nuclear carrier. I did and they asked what I thought of the new fighter. I said, 'It's no F-86'.

Lt-Col. Arlie Blood, 78th FBS commander, 81st FBW[2]

North American F-86A/E/F Sabre

In May 1945, the Army Air Force published a GOR, which called for a day fighter of medium range that could work as an escort fighter and dive bomber. There was an emphasis on speed: a minimum speed of 600 mph was stipulated.

North American had been in the process of developing the XFJ-1 Fury for the navy—a straight-wing jet fighter. In November 1945, they proposed to the AAF that the design of the Fury be modified with a swept wing. They had already proved that this would lead to a significant increase in speed. On 20 June 1946, an order for three prototypes was placed. Before the prototypes had flown, a production order was placed for thirty-three P-86s.

The first flight of the prototype took place on 1 October 1947. This aircraft was powered by a General Electric J35-C-3 turbojet engine. This was replaced shortly after by a more powerful J47-GE-3. The first production aircraft first flew on 20 May 1948, and in the following month, the designation was changed to F-86A. In February 1949, the F-86A entered service with the 94th Fighter Squadron of the 1st Fighter Group at March Field, California.

Production F-86As were initially fitted with the J47-GE-3 engine, but during the course of the production run, this was supplanted by upgraded models culminating with the J47-GE-13. Armament was six Colt 0.50-inch Browning M-3 machine guns.

In November 1950, the first F-86As were urgently deployed to Korea with the 4th Fighter Interceptor Wing (FIW). The success of the F-86A in Korea is legendary; within weeks, the units had established air superiority over the MiG-15. This was due more to the skill of the pilots than the inherent superiority of the aircraft, which, in reality, probably had only a marginal performance advantage over the MiG. There were some problems with the F-86A which were identified in combat against the MiGs. The M-3 machine guns were not very efficient and accounted for a high number of 'probables', which should have been kills. The aircraft was also over weight and carried excess weight from some systems that could have been modified or dispensed with, including self-sealing fuel tanks that were useless against the 23-mm and 27-mm cannons of the MiG-15. The electronic gunsight was also unreliable.

The next model of the Sabre, the F-86E, sought to address some of these problems and upgrade other design and systems features. The M-3 guns were, however, retained, but an A-1CM gunsight was fitted. This was coupled with an AN/APC-30 radar fitted in the upper lip over the nose intake. The F-86E featured a new tail with power-controlled tailplane and elevators. The first F-86Es joined the fight in Korea in mid-1951. The aircraft was successful in Korea and, in early 1952, claimed eighty-three MiGs killed for the loss of six Sabres.

Operational suitability tests were carried out on the F-86E in early 1952 and completed in July that year. The biggest challenge was how to increase the performance of the aircraft to meet the challenges that the MiG-15 represented. To replace the engine with the more powerful J47-GE-27 would have been the most logical solution; unfortunately, these engines were in short supply. One solution which did give the F-86E an increase in speed was to remove the slats on the wings leading edges and extending the wings sweep-back by increasing the length of the inboard edges by 6 inches and the outboard by 3 inches. Unfortunately, the kits for this modification did not reach the squadrons in any great numbers.

The F-86F evolved as a fighter bomber rather than as an escort or air defence fighter. The J47-GE-27 engine became standard for the aircraft as did the modified slat-less wing fitted retrospectively to the F-86E. The 'F' model would incorporate four underwing pylons for bombs and other external stores. It was also configured for the carriage of HVAR, and in the F-86F-35, for the carriage and delivery of a nuclear store, larger 'drop' tanks could be carried, which increased combat radius. A new gunsight, the A-4, replaced the A-1. The F-86F-35 was fitted with the LABS computer for nuclear delivery. A later modification involved the refitting of slats in conjunction with extensions to the leading edge and the wing tip. This dramatically improved aspects of performance, manoeuvrability at high altitude, and reduced landing and take-off speeds. In common with its predecessors, the F-86E acquitted itself well in Korea, not only in air-to-air combat, but also as a reliable and competent air-to-ground fighter bomber.

In Europe, the F-86F's primary role with USAFE was the delivery of nuclear bombs. In the UK, the F-86F-25s that equipped the 81st and 406th TFWs were for conventional attack and air defence.

> I loved the F-86A. I have never flown a more fun airplane than the A model for all around flying. At one time our squadron, the 78th Fighter Interceptor replaced their A models with the F-86E and F. But they decided we should not have two different models in the same Squadron, so they took away the hard wing F and replaced them with the slatted E's. We were the best airplane in Europe at the time and could out fly anything in England the whole time we were there.
>
> Lt Joseph Williams, 78th FIS, 81st FIW[3]

North American F-86D Sabre

The F-86D Sabre bore little resemblance to its Sabre stablemates. In fact, the only thing it had in common with the F-86A, 'E', and 'F' was the wing. The 'Dog' as it became known was developed alongside the other F-86s and began development in 1949. It was a novel concept at the time. An all-weather day and night interceptor with only one crewmember. The navigator was replaced by a fully automated fire-control system. The aircraft was not fitted with guns. Its offensive weapon was to be air-to-air rockets. The air intake was retained under a much enlarged upper lip, which housed the scanner of the AN/APG-37 radar. The engine was initially the J47-GE-17, but later models used the higher thrust J47-GE-33. Enlarged tail surfaces compensated for the increase in fuselage area.

The fire-control system, designated E-3, was designed by the Hughes corporation. The E-3 was tested on the prototype YF-86D in October 1950. Shortcomings were identified and there was a delay before production of the first E-3s. Meanwhile, development of the E-4 replacement for the E-3 was proceeding and the first of these were delivered to North American in December 1951.

The armament of the F-86D was the Mighty Mouse 2.75-inch Mk 4 FFAR. The rockets were fired in salvos from a tray or pod carried by the interceptor. In the case of the F-86D, twenty-four rockets were carried in a retractable tray positioned under the forward fuselage. The folding fins would unfold when the rocket left its firing tube. The rockets systems were specifically designed to attack enemy bombers and were fitted with a 6-lb (2.7-kg) HE warhead.

Although one rocket was sufficient to destroy a bomber, the systems were notoriously inaccurate and with a rapidly expanding spread from a salvo being adversely affected by gravity, wind, and other factors, because of the slow speed and spin rate of the rocket, it was a distinct possibility that not one rocket would find its target. The Mighty Mouse eventually evolved into an effective air-to-ground weapon and the air force turned to guided missiles for air-to-air.

In March 1951, the air force had 341 F-86Ds on order. By May, this figure had risen to 979 aircraft. Sadly, the fire-control E-4 system was not performing as promised and overall deliveries to the air force were considerably delayed. It was not until April 1953 that the fully equipped F-86Ds reached the squadrons and Air Defence Command (ADC) could be confident in fulfilling its mission. However, there were recurring problems, most notably with the engines. In December, all the F-86Ds were grounded after a series of fires had destroyed thirteen aircraft. The fault was traced to a faulty fuel system, which was corrected.

Project Pull-Out in 1953–4 sought to address the systems and maintenance problems and rectify them. The F-86D, even with its deficiencies was still a better aircraft than the F-89 and F-94 which it was due to replace and the air force needed it, not only in Air Defence Command, but also in USAFE and PACAF. Pull-Out involved 300 modifications on 1,128 aircraft, which were withdrawn from service in batches to ensure that their missions were not compromised. Unfortunately, in spite of the best efforts of the modification programme, the E-4 fire-control system still proved unreliable and throughout the service life of the aircraft it never allowed the aircraft to reach its full potential.

The F-86Ds was assigned to the 406th and 86th FIWs in USAFE. The 406th was based at RAF Manston in the UK and the 86th at various bases throughout West Germany. When the 406th was deactivated, its F-86D squadrons joined the 86th FIW in Germany.

> I was crew chief on F-86D 51-10033 for four years. The F-86D was different; electronic fuel controls, rocket pod, radar and single point refuelling. The electronic fuel control gave us most trouble I think. The English weather wasn't good for fuel control. We only had two pilots to fly our F-86Ds at the beginning, so we did a lot of ground run-ups to check new pilots. We got a lot of the bugs ironed out and by April 1954, we had got all the F-86Ds and transferred out all the F-86Fs. Then it was down to getting all our F-86Ds inspected and combat ready. We had to pull inspections on all our F-86Ds on arrival and everyone was busy for a while.
>
> We would stand runway alerts quite often at Manston on the south end of the runway. We had a ramp for two F-86Ds with pilots in the cockpit and crew chiefs on the ground with a power unit on just in case. We only had a few minutes to get the aircraft off if the alert call went off.
>
> S/Sgt Norman Harris[4]

North American F-100D Super Sabre

One of the most recognisable and iconic fighters of the Cold War was the North American F-100 Super Sabre. With the USAF and the air forces of several other countries, the 'Hun' had a service life in excess of three decades.

The F-100 Super Sabre was developed by North American Aviation initially as a private undertaking. Their proposal for a supersonic day fighter was originally designated the Sabre 45 because of the aircraft's 45 degrees of wing sweep-back. North American submitted their design for consideration in January 1951, but there was, at that time, no GOR published by the USAF. The company had to wait until October 1951 before getting a response from the Air Force Council when, following the publication of a GOR in August, which called for an air superiority aircraft, they were given the go ahead to proceed with development. The schedule was tight. The requirement was for the aircraft to be operational by 1955. In November 1951, the Sabre 45 was designated F-100.

On 3 January 1952, the air force issued a contract for two F-100A prototypes. Following hot on the heels of this came a second letter contract for twenty-three F-100As. The mock-up inspection on 21 March 1952 met with general approval, and in August of that year, the air force issued a requirement for 250 additional F-100As.

On 25 May 1953, the first prototype YF-100, 52-5754, took to the air, flown by test pilot George S. Welch, a veteran of Pearl Harbor. On this flight, Welch took the aircraft past Mach 1. However, some major deficiencies were identified during the flight testing of the first prototype. These related primarily to stability and control issues. However, the air force needed the F-100 and maximum effort was made to get the F-100A into squadron service. Black boxes were installed in the yaw and pitch axis of the aircraft to eliminate stability and control problems at certain speeds. Two further modifications were the installation of 'wet' wings on future production aircraft and to give the F-100 both a conventional and nuclear bombing capability. This last modification was to have massive implications for the role of subsequent models of the F-100 in service. Modifications to the fin and rudder of early production Super Sabres were made to mitigate control and stability problems.

The first F-100As entered service with the 479th FDW of the USAF on 27 September 1954. All F-100As were grounded following a series of accidents in November 1954. The first casualty was George Welch who was killed while flying the ninth production aircraft, 52-5764, on 12 October 1954. On 8 November 1954, RAF officer Air Commodore Geoffrey Stephenson was killed at Eglin AFB when his F-100A went out of control. There were further accidents. The grounding lasted for two months, and during this time, the causes of the problems were investigated and solutions sought. Three modifications were recommended: to increase the height of the vertical tail, extend the wing-tips, and modify the aileron and stabiliser control systems. Until these fixes were made to all F-100As, restrictions were placed on flying, although the grounding was lifted in February 1955.

Meanwhile, the F-100C was being developed by North American. The new features in this aircraft were 'wet' wings, additional hard points on the wing to carry additional stores in accordance with the aircraft's secondary fighter bomber mission, and, in later versions, the installation of the higher thrust J57-P-21 engine. The first F-100C entered service with the 450th FDW on 14 July 1955. As with the F-100A, there were yaw and pitch problems with the F-100C. Modifications were introduced, which largely solved these problems. They included the installation of a hydraulically activated and electrically controlled yaw damper, and the addition of a pitch damper in the horizontal stabiliser system.

In May 1954, TAC request for a more sophisticated fighter bomber led to the development of the definitive Super Sabre, the F-100D. This aircraft was to be a fighter bomber first and an interceptor second and the new features for the F-100D reflected this change in mission included increased wing and tail area, autopilot, provision for 'buddy' air-to-air refuelling, two 450-gallon air refuellable external tanks, and inboard landing flaps. The F-100D entered service with the air force in April 1956. To enhance the aircraft's air superiority role, provision was made for the carriage of AIM-9B sidewinder missiles. In 1958, some F-100Ds were modified to carry GAM-83 Bullpup air-to-surface missiles. Between 1962 and 1965, all F-100Ds underwent extensive modification under the High Wire programme.

The F-100F was developed in tandem with F-100D as a two-seat trainer. The two seater first entered service with TAC in January 1958, and by December of that year, it had reached the majority of the overseas F-100D squadrons.

The F-100Cs were the first variants of the Super Sabre to be deployed to USAFE. These aircraft were assigned to the 36th Fighter Day Wing and the 32nd FDS based at Camp New Amsterdam in the Netherlands.

The advent of the F-100D to the inventory of Tactical Air Command in 1956 greatly enhanced the number of Super Sabres in service with USAFE. Surprisingly, the 36th TFW retained its F-100Cs, eventually relinquishing them in 1961 when the unit converted to the Republic F-105 Thunderchief. The F-100D equipped a total of four wings in USAFE: the 20th TFW, the 48th TFW, the 388th FBW (later, in 1957, to be redesignated the 49th TFW), and the 50th TFW.

> Was the F-100 a good aircraft to fly? Absolutely, but you had to pay attention to adverse yaw at high angles of attack. The aircraft would depart controlled flight if you 'horsed'

> it around and used aileron instead of rudder at low speed/high angles of attack. I never departed one, but had some friends that did. The Hun was the first fighter I flew, so I had nothing to compare it with. I really enjoyed flying the Hun and accumulated 1,000 hours in it. I later flew the F-4 and F-15, which were also great airplanes. I wouldn't have traded those experiences for anything.
>
> Maj. Marcus Anderson 492nd TFS, 48th TFW[5]

McDonnell F-101A/C Voodoo

The F-101 Voodoo was developed from the XF-88 strategic penetration fighter, which first flew on 20 October 1948 and which was cancelled by the air force in August 1950, just months after the second prototype's first flight. Reasons for the cancellation were many: the increased finance put into the large bombers such as the B-36; the production debut of the F-84, which could satisfy immediate demands for a penetration fighter; and not least the quite poor performance of the XF-88 in meeting the requirements placed upon it.

However, SAC in January 1951 outlined the minimum characteristics it required of an escort fighter to accompany its long-range B-36s, and a new reconnaissance variant. GOR 101 was published in February 1951, and although there were many contenders for the contract, McDonnell's newly configured F-88 won the day—although production was not to go ahead until October 1951.

Originally intended as an interim fighter, it soon became clear that the Voodoo could be developed to satisfy the air force's requirements for a long-range fighter. Fiscal year 1952 funds previously allocated to the F-84 and F-86F were released to get the F-88 into production without delay. Because of the quite significant difference in configuration between the original XF-88 and the new aircraft, the air force council directed a new designation of F-101 on 30 November 1951.

The time from designation to first flight of the F-101 was almost three years. On 29 September 1954, the aircraft was flown at Edwards Air Force Base with encouraging results. Mach 1.07 was achieved in a dive and the programmed test profile was completed satisfactorily. Before the end of the year, three further F-101s were accepted by the air force.

From then on, the programme proceeded fitfully and was fraught with problems. By mid-1956, the twenty-nine F-101s accepted by the air force were experiencing structural, propulsion, aerodynamic, and armament problems. A production halt was ordered by the air force in May 1956, and although short-lived, it was indicative of the concern felt at that time. One of the biggest drawbacks for the Voodoo was the inability to match GOR 101's requirement for an aircraft capable of surviving forces of 7.33 G. Initial F-101s were only capable of loads of 6.33 G. The air force reluctantly accepted the downgrading of capability in the initial aircraft, but stipulated that the 7.33-G requirement must be adhered to in the subsequent model Voodoo, which it designated F-101C. This aircraft would be internally strengthened to meet GOR 101 requirements.

One of the most significant of the Voodoo's dangerous idiosyncrasies was the tendency to 'pitch up'. The 'T' tail configuration of the airframe was responsible for this phenomenon. At high angles of attack and high-G manoeuvring the wing blocked or disrupted the airflow causing the stabilisers to become ineffective, thus causing the nose to pitch up at a high degree, creating dramatic loss of air speed and subsequent stall and spin. Solving the pitch-up problem had to be a top priority before the Voodoo could enter squadron service. Eventually, an inhibitor system was developed by McDonnell, which provided the pilot with an audible warning as pitch up was approached, thus enabling evasive action to be taken. Although the device satisfied the air force, it did not eliminate pitch up occurring in emergency or unexpected circumstances.

The first of the F-101As were assigned to the 27th Fighter Bomber Wing at Bergstrom AFB, which was a SAC unit. However, in July 1957, the whole unit and their aircraft were transferred to TAC. In 1958, all of the F-101As were transferred to the 81st TFW at RAF Bentwaters in the UK.

In September 1957, the first F-101Cs were delivered to the 523rd FBS of the 27th FBW. These too were transferred to the 81st TFW in 1958. The 81st TFW was the only unit in the USAF to fly the single-seat F-101A/C.

> Superb performance and capability for mission. It had more performance than previous aircraft. Great speed, great range, ideal for its mission. It was better than anything I had flown before for its mission. As a side note, we subsequently ferried our F-101s across the ocean and converted to the F-4 in 1964.

Col. Robert R. Fredette, Snr, USAF RET, 78th FBS, 81st TFW[6]

McDonnell F-101C, 81st TFW, RAF Bentwaters, 1961. (*Alan Scholefield*)

McDonnell RF-101C Voodoo

Development of the reconnaissance RF-101A proceeded alongside the fighter version and experienced the same problems, including G loading and pitch up. The RF-101C would be developed according to the same structural principles as the F-101C and would retain the RF-101A's 'special weapons' delivery capability.

The RF-101A reconnaissance version of the Voodoo was soon succeeded in production by the RF-101C. The air force had also decided in December 1956 to limit production of the F-101A/C and convert to reconnaissance configuration the last ninety-six aircraft under contract. The first flight of the RF-101C took place on 12 July 1957, and the aircraft entered service with the 432nd TRW in September 1957.

In late 1964, a substantial upgrade was initiated in the RF-101Cs' reconnaissance equipment. Because it was planned to continue the aircraft in operational service before being phased into the Air National Guard, it was essential that something was done to upgrade a suite that was very dated and had outlived its usefulness. Modification 1181 was designed to give the Voodoo an improved high-speed, low-altitude capability, a night capability, in flight processing, cassette ejection, and an increase in sensor reliability due to automatic exposure control. The centrepiece of the modification was the Hycon KS-72A framing camera being developed for the McDonnell RF-4C Phantom. Initially, there were problems; the 66th TRW in 1964 reported many failures of the system and spares deficiencies. These problems were ironed out, however, and in the final analysis, the upgrade did all that was intended for it, and, indeed, enabled the RF-101C to serve with distinction in SE Asia.

> Barnard, 17th Ops Officer, brought the first RF-101A into Shaw on May 6th 1957. Shortly afterwards he took a flight of four out to Clovis, New Mexico for the dedication of Cannon AFB. During the briefing conducted by the F-100 Fighter Group commander, he indicated how the aircraft would line up depending up on the wind. He asked Barney how much of a tail wind the 101s could take and was informed anything up to 40 KTS. That produced the desired effect from the fighter jocks in whose dust we had trailed for so long. The remark wasn't too far off the mark except for time limitations. I think we were limited to as few as two or three flights when carrying two 450 external tanks, between tire changes.
>
> Capt. Bob Sweet 17th TRS, 66th TRW[7]

> In 1957, the 17th began to transition into the RF101A. In fact, the entire squadron accomplished the check outs in just two a/c, # 41503 and 41504. The Voodoo had growing pains much like any new bird. Hydraulics were the primary problems. We learned to respect the infamous pitch-up characteristics and worked around them. The pitch-up trait was brought to reality during the operational testing at Eglin AFB, Fla. Lonnie Moore, I think, was killed when he pitched up on take off. Since he was a Korean War ace, the feelings among the higher ups were that if a test pilot could do it what were the garden variety jocks going to do? What we garden variety pilots did was to read the flight handbook and fly the a/c like the book said!
>
> Scotty Schoolfield, 17th TRS, 1957[8]

McDonnell RF-101C, 17th TRS, 66th TRW, RAF Upper Heyford, 1967. (*Author's collection*)

McDonnell F-4C/D Phantom II

The first Phantom II variant for the USAF was the McDonnell Douglas F-110A, subsequently redesignated the F-4C. It was derived from the US Navy's F-4B, but with specific modifications, defined in November 1961 in Standard Operating Requirements (SOR) 200. The document outlined the entire USAF tactical mission: close air support, interdiction, and counter air.

The F-4C had to be capable of air-to-air refuelling and was equipped with a boom receptacle. It also needed to carry the AIM-7D and 'E' Sparrow, AIM-9B and 'D' Sidewinders, and AIM-4D Falcon air-to-air missiles as well as the AGM-12 Bullpup air-to-ground missile, napalm, plus conventional and nuclear bombs, in the latter case, the B43 and B57 thermonuclear bombs. The F-4C-15-MC was powered by two General Electric J79-GE-15 engines.

The first production F-4C flew on 27 May 1963 and was accepted by the USAF on the same day. It entered service with the 4453rd Combat Crew Training Wing in November 1963, and its first operational unit, the 12th TFW, in January 1964. In early 1965, the first F-4Cs went to SE Asia. The first aerial victories by the F-4s took place on 10 July 1965 when two Phantoms of the 45th TFS, 15th TFW, shot down two MiG-17 fighters over North Vietnam with their AIM-9 Sidewinder missiles. By March 1966, there were seven F-4C squadrons in South Vietnam and three in Thailand. Attrition rates were high. During the first two years of the aircraft's time in SE Asia, fifty-four F-4Cs were lost. One of the major problems was the lack of a gun. The reliance on missiles was not as effective as a gun would have been. The fix for this was the provision of a 20-mm M61A1 Vulcan six barrel rotating cannon carried in the SUU-16A pod on a centre-line weapon station. Unfortunately, this had an adverse side effect, which was to degrade overall aircraft performance. Several F-4Cs were fitted with a radar homing and warning (RHAW) system.

The F-4D first flew in December 1965 and was a considerable improvement on its predecessor. From the start, the F-4D could carry the AIM-4D Falcon air-to-air missiles. An AN/APQ-109A bombing computer was installed and the range of ordnance carried increased to include the AGM-12 Bullpup and the AGM-65 Maverick. Interestingly, in 1968, the capability of carrying the AIM-9 Sidewinder was given to the F-4D at the same time as it was restored to the F-4C. In SE Asia, the Falcon had proved wanting in close air-to-air combat, though effective in shooting down slower less manoeuvrable aircraft. The F-4D could carry the General Electric M61 20-mm cannon in an SUU-23 pod on the centre fuselage station. The version of the cannon used in the 'D' variant had more range than that used on the earlier Phantom. The F-4D had a better bombing capability than the 'C' model due to an improved computer. Like the 'C' model, the F-4D could carry the M61A1 Vulcan cannon but in a SUU-23 pod. The RHAW system with its APS-107 radar installed in the F-4D was more accurate than the APR-25/26 system of the F-4C.

The desire to rush the F-4D into service did not allow for a considered development. The aircraft had inherited many of the deficiencies of the F-4C. In November 1969, there was a significant development for the F-4D. Philips Ford (later Ford Aerospace) had designed a laser designator, which could be fitted in a pod to be carried on the wing of the Phantom.

The AN/AVQ-10 Pave Knife consisted of a steerable pod and TV camera installed in the pod, which would be operated by the WSO from the rear seat of the F-4. The only six pods were destined for the USAF in SE Asia where they were fitted on six modified F-4Ds. An additional six aircraft were modified to receive pods but these were not forthcoming

The withdrawal of the F-4D units from Vietnam took place in the early 1970s. This was good news for USAFE's 48th TFW at RAF Lakenheath, which, because of the high demand for the Phantoms in SE Asia, had spent several years waiting to convert all three of its squadrons to the aircraft.

> The F-4 was an excellent, multi-role fighter aircraft. Those roles included aircraft intercepts, air-to-air combat, very-low-altitude navigation, and air-to-ground weapons delivery, including nuclear weapons.
>
> Most aircraft, but perhaps not fourth and fifth generation fighters like the F-35 and Su-25, will stall, even at high speeds, if you roll into a steep-banked turn and apply a lot of back pressure for a hard turn. That generates a lot of G-forces and a high angle of attack. As you approach the high-speed stall, the F-4 would start to vibrate ('shudder'). The plane was telling you to ease off. If you didn't, or even pulled harder, the F-4 might snap-roll over and back in the opposite direction. At that point, you were out of control, and immediate

corrective action was required. I never went that far, but, in 1972 at Luke AFB, a student F-4 pilot in the front seat tried to do that to me 200 feet above the ground in the landing pattern. I seized the controls and went maximum afterburner. We lived. He failed that ride.

Lt-Col. James McGorry, 92nd TFS, 81st TFW[9]

The F-4 'smoked' like a coal powered locomotive and could fly at twice the speed of sound. Using air-to-air refuelling, the F-4s range and airborne duration was limited only by aircrew restrictions. It wasn't the most 'agile' of the fighters but flown at optimum parameters by a skilled pilot, it could and did hold its own in aerial combat situations. We nicknamed the F-4 *Double Ugly* but in flight it was a beautiful machine. It reminded me a lot of a pelican: ungainly on the ground but poetry in motion when airborne!

Lt-Col. John Hugie 92nd TFS, 81st TFW[10]

Nearly everybody in the late '60s–early '70s trained in C-models that had been returned to the States following combat duty in the war. Most of us were trained at Davis-Monthan AFB in Tucson, Arizona. There was no significant difference between the C and D except the addition of some equipment for nuke delivery (which I never practised). The principal difference with the E was the addition of a 20 mm six barrelled gun in the nose. To

McDonnell F-4D, 81st TFW, RAF Bentwaters, 1970. (*Author's collection*)

counterbalance the added weight in the nose, a seventh fuselage fuel tank was added under the vertical stabilizer. Later versions of the E had leading-edge slats on the wings for improved manoeuvrability, but that was after my time. I did fly in Es during my second tour in SEA, during Operations Linebacker I and II. With a little more power and a little more weight, I believe it had pretty much the same flight characteristics as the D. The real value of the F-4 as a combat aircraft was its versatility, provided by its size and its seat for a WSO. In SEA, our D models were constantly being retrofitted with new weapons delivery equipment, advanced LORAN receivers and computers, laser designators, Electro-Optically Guided bomb delivery using a TV monitor in the back seat) Of course, none of these were used in USAFE while I was there, which is the principal reason I volunteered to return to Ubon on temporary duty for Linebacker in late '72. I flew another 50 combat missions before returning to the 'heath in Jan. '73.

Capt. Richard Jarvis, WSO, 492nd TFS, 48th TFW[11]

McDonnell Douglas RF-4C Phantom II

The McDonnell Douglas RF-4C Phantom was developed in response to SOR 196 which called for an all-weather reconnaissance version of the F-4C fighter bomber. SOR 196 was published on 29 May 1962, and in addition to the reconnaissance requirement, it also requested a nuclear delivery role. The mock-up inspection took place on 29 October 1962 and demanded 150 configuration changes. Most of these were designed to ease maintenance of the aircraft's systems and components such as better access to cameras, infrared sensors, and side-looking radar sensors. The air force also endorsed a less sophisticated forward-looking radar system.

The first flight of the RF-4C, actually a reconfigured Navy F-4B (62-12200), took place on 8 August 1963. Subsequently, McDonnell test pilots undertook extensive testing of the aircraft's reconnaissance systems prior to the delivery of the first production model to the air force, which took place in September 1964 at Shaw AFB to the 33rd TRTS. All initial production aircraft were delivered to this unit. In 1965, they were transferred to the first operational RF-4C squadron, the 16th TRS, with the first aircraft arriving on 30 April 1965.

Initially, the 16th TRS experienced problems with safety aspects of the new aircraft. The RF-4C suffered significant flight and directional control problems while taking off from wet runways.

The war in SE Asia demanded that the 16th TRS become combat ready in the RF-4C in a very short period of time. On 31 July, the first forward-looking radars, APQ-99, were delivered to the squadron. On 27 October 1965, the first element of the squadron deployed to Tan Son Nhut with nine aircraft and two spares. The second element deployed on 28 December.

During its initial service in SE Asia, certain shortcomings were identified. Shortages of funds dogged any modifications that needed to be made. In order to mitigate the problems with sensor resolution, it was decided to streamline the whole nose section covering the camera bays. It was a mammoth task and was estimated to take some four years. Replacement of the RHAW APR/25/26 radar with the much improved ALR-46 began in 1973 but this was constrained by shortage of funds and was also scheduled over several years. Some RF-4Cs received a new side-looking radar (SLR). An interim installation until a newly developed system would come available in 1976.

Also in 1965, the RF-4C began deployment to USAFE with the 10th TRW and the 32nd and 38th TRS of the 26th TRW. The PACAF squadron, the 15th TRS then assigned to the 18th TFW received their first Phantoms in 1967 and saw action in SEA.

The regular air force service career of the RF-4C spanned almost thirty years, and during that time, the aircraft underwent many system changes and developments. As well as SE Asia, the aircraft saw action in The Gulf war.

> Overall the plane was excellent. It was extremely fast, capable of attaining very high altitudes, and it was very stable in addition to being very fast in a low altitude environment. It had excellent acceleration, along with more than enough power for its mission.
>
> Another aspect of the RF-4C that everyone appreciated was having two powerful and highly reliable J-79 engines with afterburners. We could sustain a lot of battle damage, lose an engine and still outrun an enemy and make it back home.
>
> IR and photo sensor arrays on the RF-4C were superior. They worked very well at high, medium and low altitudes. Photo-flash at night was OK at low altitudes in a low-threat areas, but hardly desirable otherwise. In high-threat areas the IR was first choice; especially, for night missions.
>
> Charles K. Munroe 38th TRS, 26 TRW[12]

McDonnell RF-4C, 32nd TRS, 10th TRW, RAF Alconbury, 1967. (*Denis Dawes*)

> The RF-4C had dual controls in the rear seat; whereas the navy's RF-4B did not. The USAF decided initially to place young pilots just out of flying school in the rear cockpit to act as Weapons Systems Officers (WSOs). It was felt that the Phantom was too complicated for young pilots to handle. This, in my opinion, was not the case. I always believed that it was so simple and easy to fly that it could have been used as a basic training aircraft, although the cost to equip and operate would have been excessively high.
>
> Scotty Schoolfield 16th TRS TSN, 1966[13]

General Dynamics F-111E/F Aardvark

The General Dynamics F-111 Aardvark had the hardest and probably the most acrimonious gestation of any modern jet fighter to enter service with the USAF. Its development was plagued by ill-informed negative media attention and wallet-watching politicians. Almost everything about the aircraft was innovative from its variable sweep wings to its Mach +1 ultra-low-altitude terrain-following capability. It is no wonder that there were delays in its development when new innovations in technology were being introduced regularly. But, in spite of this, the F-111 emerged as one of the most successful fighters the USAF had ever flown, displaying its prowess in SE Asia and later in Operation Eldorado Canyon and in the Gulf, where there was no other aircraft, from all the other nations involved, capable of performing the missions at which the F-111 excelled.

The first production F-111A flew for the first time on 12 February 1967, three years after the first flight of the first RDT&E F-111A. In October 1967, the aircraft entered operational service with the 474th Tactical Fighter Wing at Cannon AFB, New Mexico. On 17 March 1968, six F-111As were deployed to SE Asia, arriving at Takhli Royal Thai Air Base. Unfortunately, after three losses, the aircraft returned to the US in November 1967. There followed a lengthy period of modifications and upgrades that lasted for over three years and served to further encourage the aircraft's detractors. However, in spite of the unwelcome media and political attention, the 474th TFW was eventually declared combat ready in July 1971. In September 1972, the F-111A returned to Takhli and immediately undertook bombing missions over North Vietnam and Laos. One F-111A could deliver the same bombload as five F-4 Phantoms in weather that would have grounded all other aircraft. In spite of some problems, which included spares shortages, the TFR, and attack radars, the return of the Aardvark to the war in SE Asia was deemed a success. They performed their missions without ECM, escort aircraft, EC-121s to vector them, or tankers.

The F-111E was the third variant of the Aardvark to go into production for the USAF. In spite of the nomenclature, the FB-111A and the F-111D succeeded the F-111E into production. The F-111E bore a close resemblance to the F-111A, sharing most of that aircraft's features. One significant difference was the Triple Plow 11 air inlets, which were a development of the Triple Plow 1 inlets fitted to the F-111A. The modification to the intake improved engine operation at high speed and high altitude. The 2TF-30-P-3 engine was as fitted to the F-111A. The first flight of the production F-111E took place on 20 August 1969, which was, coincidently, the same day as the delivery of the last

F-111A to the USAF. The F-111E entered service with the 27th Tactical Fighter Wing on 30 September 1969. A year later, on 11 September 1970, the first F-111Es landed at RAF Upper Heyford in the UK, joining the 20th TFW. The F-111Es of the 20th TFW acquitted themselves well in Europe, but were plagued by spare shortages and maintenance problems for several years.

The F-111F was the successor of SAC's FB-111A and the F-111D, both of which had received significant modifications over the F-111E. These upgrades to these aircraft's systems and configuration were incorporated into the F-111F, and, in some cases, considerably improved, including the Avionics package, which combined both F-111D and FB-111A navigation and digital computer systems, including the APQ-144 attack radar. The engine was the 2TF-30-P-100 delivering 25,100 lb of static thrust and increased take-off thrust by 40 per cent, although problems with the new engines did mean that the first F-111Fs were fitted with the earlier P-9 engine. Later, the P-100 was fitted to all in-service F-111Fs but continued to prove troublesome throughout the operational life of the aircraft. The F-111F entered service with the 347th TFW at Mountain Home AFB in 1972. The 366th TFW replaced the 347th at Mountain Home in October 1972, taking over the F-111Fs. Operation Ready Switch in August 1977 replaced the 366th's Aardvarks with the F-111As of the 474th TFW, which received F-4Ds from the 48th TFW at RAF Lakenheath in the UK. The 48th TFW received the F-111Fs from the 366th TFW. By the end of 1977, there were two wings of Aardvarks in the UK. With their all-weather, day and night role, the F-111s complemented the Phantom force in USAFE and would prove to be a very valuable asset in the theatre.

> I flew the F-111 and then the F-15E. I flew it in air-to-air against the F-5—it beat us every time. Poor visibility was its greatest drawback. It also had a high energy bleed off when you would manoeuvre, higher than the F-4, though we had similar thrust to weight with the F model. It's biggest disadvantage was lack of air-to-air ordnance or even HARM. It would have been excellent in the anti-SAM role as the A-6 proved. The USAF however likes to have mission specific aircraft. Only the F-16 is a true multi-mission aircraft—they do it all though with limited payload and range. The RAF was better. They even put an AIM-9 on some of their heavy aircraft during the Falklands war. The strength of the F-111 was its air-to-ground radar, best of its time, and its Terrain Following Radar. Another strength was fuel efficiency/speed. We were very fast with a full load of bombs and could carry it a really long way. Great in the weather. No problem to do our mission night or in weather.
>
> Lt Richard Crandall, 48th TFW[14]

Northrop F-5E Tiger II

The Northrop F-5 series of lightweight fighter aircraft were developed to satisfy a demand to provide allied nations with an affordable, relatively unsophisticated, and versatile weapons system. The prototype flew for the first time on 30 July 1959. The USAF funded the development of two further prototypes, and in April 1962, the aircraft was selected for the MAP and was designated the F-5.

General Dynamics F-111F, 48th TFW, RAF Lakenheath, 1989. (*USAF*)

The aircraft was tested in combat conditions in SE Asia under Project Skoshi Tiger in mid-1964 by TAC's 4503rd TFW and based at Da Nang. The aircraft flew air-to-air, air-to-ground, and reconnaissance missions. So successful was the project that TAC initiated a training programme for F-5 replacement pilots.

First customers for the F-5A were the South Vietnamese Air Force who received the Skoshi Tiger aircraft. They were followed by the Philippines, Chinese Nationalist, and Turkey. By the middle of 1972, fifteen nations had been equipped with the aircraft, which included some reconnaissance RF-5As supplied to Norway, Libya, and Morocco.

The basic armament suite of the F-5A was two 20-mm M-39 cannon in the nose and two AIM-9 Sidewinder air-to-air missiles on the wing tips. Two hard-points on each wing were available for a variety of stores. Two-seat F-5Bs were also supplied under MAP and FMS. The two-seat T-38 was also developed alongside the F-5A.

The F-5E was initially developed as a private venture by Northrop. New features included an uprated J-85-GE-21 engine with afterburner that replaced the dash 13 engine of the F-5A and F-5B. The 'E' model was also to carry 10 per cent more fuel and would include manoeuvring flaps, landing edge wing root extensions, and an integrated fire control system. Dubbed the Advanced International Fighter the F-5E was to retain its simplicity and ease of operation and maintenance. Its improved performance would also enable it to compete on an equal footing with those aircraft that it would be most likely to encounter in a hostile environment, such as the MiG-19 and the MiG-21.

Between February and November 1970, the air force, in response to a demand from Congress, invited aerospace corporations to tender proposals for the International Fighter Aircraft. Four companies tendered proposals. McDonnell proposed a stripped F-4E; Northrop, the F-5A advanced version; Lockheed an F-104 variant; and Ling-Tempo-Vought, a development of the F-8 Crusader. Northrop's proposal was chosen and the F-5 Tiger 11 was born.

The first production F-5E flew on 11 August 1972, and the aircraft entered operational service with the 425th TFTS in April 1974. The development Aggressor programme in the USAF and the USN demanded an aircraft which could successfully imitate the MiG-21 in aerial combat. The USN and the US Marine Corps, in the Top Gun programme, used A-4 Skyhawks to represent the MiG-17 and the T-38 to represent the MiG-19 and MiG-21. The advent of the F-5E into the inventory provided all services with another option, the F-5E which was quickly adopted in this role. The USAF activated several aggressor squadrons in the 1970s equipped with the F-5E. One of these was the 527th TFTAS based at RAF Alconbury in the UK.

> The F-5E was a very small aircraft, almost exactly the same size as the MiG-21s and MiG-23s of the era. Western aircraft had become large and unwieldy, like the F-4 which was designed for multiple missions. In Vietnam, American forces had been hurt badly by small, nimble aircraft that were hard to see and could generally out manoeuvre our larger aircraft. For this purpose, the F-5E was a great simulator, we had every advantage in the initial stages of a fight, and we could usually see our adversaries miles before they could see us, even if they had us on radar. This allowed us to almost always enter the fight with an advantage; we began manoeuvring offensively long before they did. This was a great learning point for our NATO forces and made the F5E a great training aid. The F5E could always out manoeuvre the majority of the aircraft we faced: F-4s, Lightning's, Mirages, F-104s, A-10s, Buccaneers, etc. The F-15 and F-16 were more powerful and in the right hands could out dogfight an F5E, but our small size and proficiency in air-to-air we more than held our own. On average, we probably flew twice as many hours and sorties monthly than the average NATO pilot. And since our only mission was air-to-air, we got pretty good at it.
>
> Maj. John 'Goldy' Goldenblaum, 527th TFTAS[15]

General Dynamics F-16C Fighting Falcon

The General Dynamics F-16 first appeared in the UK in 1977 at the annual air show at RAF Mildenhall in Suffolk when YF-16 72-1568 made a visit on its way to the Paris Air Show. In spite of having been in regular USAF service since 1980, the F-16 was not based in the UK until 1988 when F-16Cs became based at RAF Bentwaters with the 527th TFTAS.

In 1971, the LWF programme got funding approval. Proposals were invited from aerospace companies in the US to submit a design. The culmination of the programme would be that two designs would be selected for competitive evaluation. In the event, the General Dynamics Model 401 and Northrop's P-600 were selected—the prototypes to be named YF-16 and YF-17 respectively.

Northrop F-5E, 527th TFTAS, RAF Alconbury, 1983. (*USAF*)

In April 1974, the secretary of defence announced that the proposal would become the ACF or advanced combat fighter. The proposed mission for the new fighter would not be confined to air defence but would encompass air-to-ground as well as air-to-air—in effect, a multi-role fighter.

In January 1975, the YF-16 was selected and an initial order was placed by the USAF for 650 aircraft. It had been hoped that the US Navy would come on board with this design, but alas, it was not to be. On 13 December 1973, the first YF-16 prototype, 72-1567, rolled out. Air-to-air armament was to be two AIM-9 Sidewinder missiles and the integral 20-mm M61A1 Vulcan cannon. The aircraft could carry two 2,000-lb bombs, four Maverick missiles, or eight 500-lb bombs. An ALQ-131 ECM pod was also to be a standard store. A new radar was in development. The engine was the Pratt and Whitney F100-PW-100. The first production F-16A flew on 8 December 1976.

Meanwhile, some NATO allies and other air forces were concerned with replacing their Lockheed F-104 Starfighters and were looking for a replacement. The F-16 was ideally placed to exploit this market and no time was lost by the US in presenting its new multi-role fighter.

Development and upgrades through several models of the F-16 not only improved its efficiency, but also its saleability overseas. Principle developments commenced with the F-16A Block 15 aircraft. These included an upgraded AN/APG-66(V)2 pulse Doppler planar radar, two additional hard-points under the engine inlet and strengthened wing hard-points. The horizontal stabilisers were enlarged to compensate for the increased weight of the additional hard-points.

The F-16C Block 30 introduced an improved AN/APG-68 long-range radar and a new engine in the form of the General Electric F-110-GE-100. Later Block 30 models were fitted with enlarged engine air intakes. Armament improvements enabled the AGM-45 Shrike and AGM-88 HARM air-to-ground missiles, and the AIM-20 Advanced medium-range air-to-air missile to be carried. The 527 TFTAS at RAF Bentwaters flew two F-16C Block 30A and ten Block 30C models.

> We were very confident that we could effectively replicate the MiG-21, MiG-23, MiG-29 and Sukhoi-27. The only problem was that we had a total of 12 aircraft as opposed to the 18 aircraft we had with the F-5E and the utilization rates were also lower for the F-16, due to its increased complexity and sophistication, than they were for the F-5E. Additionally, another significant improvement was the Video and Audio recording system that the F-16C had. No longer did we have a little audio-cassette recorder to carry around or the Gun Camera Film cartridge every time we went to the aircraft. We did have to take a VHS tape to the aircraft and as part of our preflight; we had to ensure we installed the tape before engine start. The VHS tape was good for 30 minutes of recording time and recorded both Audio in the cockpit and the Visual view through the Heads Up Display for simulated weapons employment validation. This enhanced our debriefing ability and established more credibility for the shots that were taken. Inclusion of the ability to captive carry the AIM-9M all aspect infra-red training missile gave us the ability to accurately replicate all the various Soviet infra-red missiles by complying with the specific employment parameters for each type. The F-5E we flew was configured the majority of the time with the captive carry AIM-9E infrared training missile. It did not have all aspect capability and could only validate the shots keeping the missile seeker head in the caged mode during simulated launch. With the AIM-9M we could and did un-cage the captive carry missile seeker head, and coupled with the HUD able to display a more dynamic missile performance envelope, being video recorded, we could more accurately validate the simulated shot.
>
> Lt-Col. Jim Wisdom, 527th TFTAS[16]

General Dynamics EF-111A Raven

As the Vietnam War drew to a close in the early 1970s, it became increasing evident that the USAF would need a new updated electronic warfare aircraft. The last of the EB-66s was retired at Shaw AFB in mid-1974, when the 39th TEWS was inactivated. Replacements for the destroyer had been considered for some time. The only other dedicated EW platform that was available at the time was the Grumman EA-6B Prowler, which the USAF was set against acquiring for a variety of reasons, most notable being the different operational requirements of the air force that the Prowler would not meet in terms of range, loiter time on station, endurance, and speed among other things. Lack of available funding excluded the possibility of developing an entirely new EW aircraft. It was decided to modify an existing airframe. The General Dynamics F-111A was chosen for the modification and two prototypes were to be developed by Grumman, with work commencing in 1974. Various delays affected the progress of the work and

General Dynamics F-16C, 527th Aggressor Squadron, RAF Bentwaters, 1988. (*USAF*)

it was not until November 1981 that the first production aircraft was delivered to the 388th TFW at Mountain Home AFB, Idaho.

The EF-111A retained the F-111's navigation, RHAW, and terrain-following radar (TFR) systems. The primary EW system employed by the EF-111A was the AN/ALQ-99E tactical jamming system. The receivers were housed in a pod carried on the top of the vertical stabiliser of the aircraft. The electronic components were installed in the weapons bay and the transmitters in a canoe-shaped fairing on the underside of the aircraft. The AN/ALQ-99E worked in conjunction with the AN/ALQ-137 threat-warning system and the AN/ALR-62 digital radar-warning system. The EF-111A had a crew of two: the pilot and the EWO. The cockpit was arranged so that all EW systems instrumentation and controls were on the EWO's position on the right and all the flight and navigation instrumentation and controls were on the left (the pilot's side). The aircraft carried no offensive armament; it relied on its speed and countermeasures systems to keep it out of trouble.

> While still 'training' in the low-level environment, the Raven pretty much turned into a magic carpet ride of scenic wonderment for at least a handful of minutes each flight. I know that Rob [Capt. Robert S. Held], Jim [Maj. Jim Morgan], and I, in particular would create some fantastic low-fly routes to enjoy as we went about our missions. I recall doing a pylon turn around Mont Saint-Michel so low and close you could practically see the visitors' eyes

bugged out of their heads! Ah, those were the days. If you were lucky, a flight of Mirages, Phantoms, or Jaguars would swoop down and 'bounce' you leading to a challenging set of defensive manoeuvres.

Capt. Robert 'Z-Bob' Zaehringer, Pilot, 42nd ECS[17]

After a short 'high' altitude phase, I would always drop down to an extraordinarily low altitude route that would be outstanding in terms of the view and the thrill. I routinely flew over white cliffs of Dover, Loch Ness, between the towering mountain peaks near Grenoble France, and over the Shetland Islands; all extremely close to the ground and at very high subsonic speeds. Because of our range and the swing wing, the Raven could cruise for many hours at high level or do fast low level training with much of western Europe being in our wheelhouse.

Capt. Robert S. Held, Pilot, 42nd ECS[18]

Boeing KB-29/50 Superfortress

The Boeing KB-29 was basically a B-29 bomber modified as a tanker aircraft to refuel other aircraft in flight. The first of the Superfortress was the KB-29M. The system of aerial refuelling developed for this tanker was what became known as the looped-hose method invented by FRL in the UK. The tanker was named the KB-29M and the receiving aircraft, the B-29MR. SAC was anxious to get the refuelling programme under way and ordered the modification of eighty B-29s into tankers and receivers. From 26

General Dynamics EF-111A, 42nd ECS, 66th ECW, RAF Upper Heyford, 1985. (*USAF*)

February to 3 March 1949, a B-50 nicknamed *Luck Lady* circumnavigated the world using the looped-hose method of in-flight refuelling.

Meanwhile, both in the UK and the USA, two alternative methods of aerial refuelling were being developed. In the US, Boeing developed the 'flying boom' system, which became the preferred method of in-flight refuelling for SAC. The rigid boom was mounted at the extreme rear of the aircraft. It was fitted with two small wings that enabled the boom operator to 'fly' it into the refuelling receptacle on the receiving aircraft, which the pilot had manoeuvred below and the rear of the tanker. Commensurate with this, in the UK, FRL was developing the 'probe and drogue' system. This system entailed the tanker aircraft to trail three hose, on the end of which was a cone-shaped drogue. The receiving aircraft would be fitted with a probe which would be inserted in the drogue and take on the requisite amount of fuel. The advantage of the latter method was that three aircraft could be refuelled simultaneously.

Following the successful development of Boeing's flying boom system, SAC's KB-29 were modified and were named KB-29P. KB-29s served with six TAC air refuelling squadrons during the 1954 to 1958. These were progressively replaced by Boeing KB-50 tankers.

The KB-50 was fitted with the probe and drogue refuelling system. Designated KB-50D, the first of these aircraft carried three hoses on reels. One of these reels replaced the tail turret while the other two were in pods situated outboard of the 500-gallon underwing tanks. In spite of a much-improved performance over the KB-29P, the KB-50D was still not fast enough to adequately service the high-performance aircraft it was designed to refuel. In 1957, a modification saw the installation of two General Electric J-47 jet engines of 5,900-lb thrust each installed under the wings, replacing the underwing tanks. This modification improved not only speed for refuelling but altitude performance. The modification was carried out by the Hayes Aircraft Corporation and the aircraft was designated the KB-50J. The KB-50J served until the mid-1960s when all TAC air refuelling squadrons were deactivated.

> All of the KB-50Js each had four powerful reciprocating engines as well two J-47 engines, one of either side of the reciprocating engines on each wing for a total of six engines. This gave the KB-50s a lot of power and significant performance improvement. We could refuel three aircraft from one KB-50 aircraft, as before the J-47 jet engines were installed, but we could do it at higher altitudes and at faster airspeeds making it much easier and safer for the jet fighters and light jet bombers to refuel. The KB-50 refuelling aircraft does not use the single flyable, controllable, refuelling probe. It uses three refuelling drogues, one on each wing and one at the tail of the aircraft, that release refuelling hoses. When I joined the 420th AREFS, I was assigned to a KB-50 crew and a few months later with the same flight crew to the KB-50Js. Simultaneously, all of the USAF F-84s previously used by fighter squadrons located in the UK and at bases in Europe were replaced by F-100s. Thus all USAF flying organizations in the UK and in Europe experienced very significant equipment upgrades. What this meant was that during USAFE alerts, we were no longer refuelling fighter bombers over the English Channel, we refuelled F-100s, B-66s and RB-66s from refuelling orbits over Western Europe, thus enabling USAF bombers to fly to deeper targets

in the Soviet bloc or perhaps all the way into Russia if their war plans called for that extension of range.

Col. Walker A. Larimer, Master Navigator-Bombardier, 420th AREFS[19]

North American B/RB-45 Tornado

Towards the end of the Second World War, in April 1944, the US Army Air Force issued a requirement for a jet bomber with a speed of 500 mph, a radius of 1,000 miles, and a bombload of 8,000 lb. In response to this requirement, North American proposed the XB-45; Convair, the XB-46; and Martin, the XB-48. In the event, three prototypes of the XB-45 were ordered in December 1944. The first flight took place on 17 March 1947 at Muroc (later Edwards AFB).

The B-45A bomber entered service with the 47th Bombardment Group at Biggs AFB, Texas, in November 1948 and almost immediately received orders to move to Barksdale AFB, Louisiana. Pilot training took place at Muroc. Unfortunately, the supply of B-45s to the 47th at Barksdale did not keep pace with the return of pilots eager to fly their new jet bomber. The first aircraft arrived on 23 March 1949. By July, the wing had received twenty-five Tornados

The entry into service of the B-45A was marred by several accidents, of which two were fatal. There were repeated groundings for a variety of reasons. In October 1949, the 47th fell subject to budget cuts and was deactivated. The B-45s were transferred to the 363rd TRG at Langley AFB together with the 84th and 85th BS. The 363rd was ill equipped to deal with their new asset, and the Tornados languished without a clearly defined mission and role.

The acquisition of a nuclear role by TAC at last gave the aircraft a *raison d'être*. In August 1950, Operation Back Breaker introduced a series of upgrades and modifications to support the nuclear delivery role. Modifications included the fitting of an AN/APQ-24 bombing and navigational radar, a Norden M9C bomb sight, an AN/APT-5 jammer, and an AN/APN-3 SHORAN coupled with an AN/CPN-2 transmitter. On 29 December 1951, the 47th BW received notice that it was to deploy overseas as part of the 49th Air Division. The B-45A Tornado had a mission and it was a vital one of pioneering TAC's newly acquired nuclear mission.

The RB-45C reconnaissance version of the aircraft was the final production model. The B-45C on which it was based was cancelled by the air force after only ten aircraft had been built. The reconnaissance Tornado differed from the bomber version in many respects. The transparent nose of the aircraft was completely covered and a forward oblique camera installed. Two 214-gallon drop tanks were carried underneath the nacelles. These carried water for the water injection system employed to increase the take-off thrust of the J-47 engines. Wing tip tanks, each carrying 1,200 gallons of fuel, considerably increased the range of the aircraft. The RB-45C was also capable of air-to-air refuelling. A total of twelve cameras were carried. In addition to the forward oblique in the nose, there were four in the vertical position in the rear compartment, four split verticals, and a trimetrogon mounted on a pallet centrally. The bomb bay was retained and contained extra fuel tanks and twenty-five M-122 photo flash bombs.

The first RB-45C flew in April 1950 and the first delivery to the air force took place on 26 August to the 91st Strategic Reconnaissance Wing at Barksdale AFB, Louisiana. All of the RB-45Cs were destined for SAC and the 91st. By the end of 1950, twenty-seven aircraft had been assigned. This figure rose to the full complement of thirty-three in early 1951.

The early service career of the RB-45C was fraught with difficulty, due in no small part to the rush to get it into production and into service. Of the thirty-three aircraft assigned to the 91st SRW, eleven had been written-off by the end of 1952. One of these had been shot down by MiGs in Korea. The others had perished as a result of flying accidents. This was almost a wartime attrition rate, not a peacetime one.

In spite of this, the Tornado went on to serve for several more years in the air force. The 91st had detachments in the Far East, at Yokota, and in Europe at RAF Sculthorpe. It was from Sculthorpe that several overflights were undertaken in the aircraft by RAF crews in RB-45s painted in RAF colours.

In 1953, as the RB-47 entered the SAC inventory, the RB-45Cs were transferred to TAC. Aircraft in Yokota were assigned to the 6021st Reconnaissance Squadron. Those at Sculthorpe were assigned to the 47th Bombardment Wing, which, at that time, flew the B-45A in the nuclear attack role. In May 1954, the 19th TRS was assigned to the 47th BW and took over control of the RB-45Cs. In 1957, the 19th TRS became assigned to the 66th TRW.

Douglas B/RB-66B Destroyer

The Douglas B/RB-66 evolved out of a response to a requirement published by the air force in 1951 for a reconnaissance/light tactical bomber experimental (RBL-X). A long-term replacement for the B/RB-26 was needed. The RB-57 would be fulfilling the role in the interim. The expectation was that the new aircraft would be in service by 1954. To meet this requirement, Douglas submitted a revised version of their A3D Skywarrior. Other designs submitted were modified versions of the Boeing B-47 Stratojet, the Martin 'Super Canberra', the Martin XB-51, and the North American B-45 Tornado. A British design, the Vickers Valiant, was also tendered.

In November 1951, the USAF expressed its preference for a version of the Navy's Douglas A-3 Skywarrior. The reconnaissance version of the new aircraft would take precedence in the production schedules. The GOR for the future RB-66 was published in January 1952 and for the bomber B-66 in April of the same year.

An order for five pre-production RB-66As was placed in February 1952. In many ways externally similar to the Skywarrior, the RB-66 was a substantially different aircraft. In addition to shedding some of the uniquely naval equipment such as arrestor hooks and strengthened undercarriage, some 400 alterations were made to the basic design. These included the use of anti-icing technology to enable an all-weather and night capability, and modifications that recognised the low-level, high-speed mission such as upward exiting ejection seats and strengthening of the airframe. To accommodate alterations in the cockpit layout, this had become wider and longer. The nose had been widened to accommodate the 45-inch radar dish, which had been required in order to give the aircraft a greater radar range. The wing had been redesigned and altered in appearance from the Navy aircraft. In spite of considerable difficulties, not least in the selection of the power plant for the RB-66, the favoured engine for the B-66 was the Pratt and Whitney J-57. Unfortunately, this engine was in high demand by SAC and for civil projects and the pressure was on Douglas to accept another power plant, namely the Allison J71, which it reluctantly did. In retrospect, this proved to have been a bad decision. Many of the Destroyer's in-service problems would concern the engine. Following this flight, subsequent test flights revealed more problems with the aircraft, many related to control and stability. In 1955, so serious were the problems and the slippage in the schedules that it was feared that the project would have to be cancelled. In the event Douglas instigated an intensive engineering and systems programme and by the middle of the year the RB-66A was much improved. However, no RB-66As made it to the squadrons.

The first RB-66B flew in October 1955, and the first aircraft entered service with the 9th TRS, 363rd TRW, at Shaw in January 1956, replacing that unit's RB-26 Invaders. Over the succeeding two years, the RB-66B reached USAFE and PACAF squadrons as well as three more at Shaw replacing the RB-26s and the RB-57As. Although the problems were mostly ironed out by the time the aircraft reached the squadrons, the early service life of the RB-66 was often fraught with difficulties. In 1966, some RB-66B aircraft were redesignated EB-66E in recognition of their change of equipment and role in the SE Asia war.

The RB-66C was designed from the outset as an electronic version of the aircraft. It differed from the RB-66B in that, the bomb bay, which in the RB-66B accommodated the cameras, became a pressurised compartment with space for four ECM operators and their equipment. The RB-66C was redesignated EB-66C in 1966.

The WB-66D was designed as a weather reconnaissance aircraft. It was the last variant of the aircraft to fly, initially doing so in May 1957. Similar to the RB-66C, the bomb bay compartment was occupied by two weather observers and their equipment.

The B-66B first flew in January 1955 and began to join TAC squadrons in March 1956, one year behind schedule. Initially, the total force of B-66Bs served with the 17th BW at Hulbert Field in Florida. These aircraft were transferred to the 47th BW at RAF Sculthorpe in the UK commencing in September 1957.

In May 1959, thirteen B-66Bs were modified as 'Brown Cradle' aircraft for use by USAFE. These aircraft were redesignated EB-66Bs in 1966 and were deployed to SE Asia.

> I have no adverse comments about the RB-66's flying characteristics. It was a little underpowered and on a hot day with a full load it did take quite a bit of runway for lift off. Both Sculthorpe and Bruntingthope had plenty of runway so it was never a real problem. I did miss not having a co-pilot on long flights. The auto pilot was good but a co-pilot is nice to have around in case of an emergency.
>
> Col Lewis (Doc) Partridge USAF Ret., 19 TRS, 10th TRW[20]

The A-10 Thunderbolt II

The A-10 was designed for one specific purpose: to find and destroy Warsaw Pact armour and vehicles in the event of an invasion of Western Europe by the Soviet Union and its allies. The aircraft was armed with a formidable primary weapon: the 30-mm GAU-8 Avenger Gatling gun. The Avenger can fire up to 4,200 armour-piercing rounds per minute. The A-10 can also carry up to six AGM-65 Maverick anti-tank missiles. Mavericks were only able to be fired from stations three and nine. The LAU-88/A triple rail launcher on each of those stations could carry up to three missiles each. Other stations were not wired for Mavericks. The aircraft also has the capacity to carry a variety of other under wing stores on, originally, eleven weapons carriage stations. Three stations were later removed. The aircraft was highly manoeuvrable at low speed and at low altitude and was designed to withstand a considerable amount of hostile fire, the pilot's 'office' being protected by an armoured titanium 'bathtub'. The A-10 was not an attractive aircraft, except to its pilots and maintenance crews, and earned the nickname early on of 'Warthog', often abbreviated to just 'Hog'.

The A-10 story starts in 1966 when, in December, a RAD was issued for a close support aircraft. This was to be known as the A-X project. The GOR for the aircraft required that it be highly manoeuvrable at low speed, survivable in the battle area, extreme firepower, and long loiter times in and around the battlefield. The operational qualities of the Douglas Sky raider were often cited as a model for the A-X. In 1970, more specific requirements were published. One of these requirements was that the aircraft be fitted with the 30-mm rotary cannon, had a take-off distance of 1,200 metres (4,000 feet), could carry a load of 7,300 kg (16,000 lb), had a maximum speed of 740 km/h (460 mph), and a 460-km (285-mile) combat radius. This was not to be a multi-role aircraft, but one specifically designed for close air support. The GAU-8 cannon was to be built by General Electric.

The proposals of two companies eventually reached the prototype stage, the Northrop YA-9 and the Fairchild Republic YA-10. In the fly-off between the prototypes, the YA-10 was selected by the USAF. The first production A-10 flew in October 1975, and deliveries to TAC commenced in March 1976.

Europe was where the threat from Soviet and Warsaw Pact invasion was considered to be most likely, and deliveries to the 81st TFW in the UK commenced in January 1979. The 81st was very much at the forefront of the resistance to any incursion by WP forces into Germany, but it was not in Europe that the 'Warthog' was to be 'blooded', but in the Middle East in the battle against the forces of Saddam Hussein in Iraq. Later, the aircraft would fight in the Balkans and in Afghanistan. Several attempts have been made to retire the aircraft, but the USAF has nothing with which to replace it and it has received several upgrades to enable it to face further challenges well into the twenty-first century.

> The A-10 is a wonderful weapons delivery platform. Somewhere 'back in those days', we read 'expected attrition rates' for the A-10 in a European 'high-threat' scenario. Those numbers were certainly not comforting! However, as a young Captain and especially later as an A-10 squadron commander, I would not dwell on those attrition numbers, as we trained

the way we planned to fight and we trained hard. I was most confident that A-10 would get me to/from the target area without fail.

The A-10, in my opinion, was the perfect weapon system for the wartime mission against the Warsaw Pact order of battle and the anticipated threat. I was most confident that A-10 would get me to and from the target area without fail. Its advantages were manoeuvrability; visibility; stability; durability; survivability; 'stand-off' capability and short take-off and landing ability. The A-10 was highly manoeuvrable and had excellent 360 degree visibility. Adversary aircraft had a difficult time coming in from our rear aspect without A-10 pilots being able to detect them. Once detected, the A-10s turning ability allowed great defence against an air-to-air threat. Plus, any adversary had to 'honour' the GAU8 30mm in the A-10. Manoeuvrability and visibility also were huge advantages when working Close Air Support (CAS).

Lt-Col. Bill Rial, 78th TFS commander, 81st TFW[21]

Republic A-10A, 78th TFS, 81st TFW, RAF Woodbridge, 1983. (*USAF*)

Appendix II

Wing and Squadron Support Aircraft

Throughout the USAF, all units were assigned support aircraft, commonly known as 'hacks'. These aircraft were assigned to a wing base flight, which, in turn, sometimes assigned individual aircraft to a squadron. Within TAC units in the UK, a variety of aircraft were assigned for different purposes. Each wing would have at least one Lockheed T-33A two-seat trainer. This aircraft would be used for pilot proficiency training and testing, area familiarisation flights, and for general liaison flights to other bases.

For general light utility and liaison purposes, each wing also had one or more de Havilland L-20A Beavers. The L-20 was a versatile aircraft of rugged construction and capable of operating from a variety of surfaces. It would be used as a light equipment and passenger transport.

For heavier equipment and multi-passenger transport, each wing usually possessed one Douglas C-47 Skytrain. When the wing went on a deployment, the base flight C-47 would usually carry personnel and equipment to support the operations. Some wings were also assigned Fairchild C-119C/F Flying Boxcars for such transportation duties. The 47th BW at RAF Sculthorpe was one such. The 47th Air Base group had nine C-119C/Fs assigned to its Flight A. This unit had a very special role: to transport nuclear bombs to the two nuclear strike fighter units which were based in the UK, the 20th FBW at RAF Wethersfield and the 81st FBW at RAF Bentwaters and Woodbridge. It was not safe to transport these cargoes on the roads.

Some units, for example, the 20th TFW, 48th TFW, and 81st TFWs, were also assigned North American T-39A Sabreliner twin-jet transports. The aircraft was used in an executive passenger role and could carry up to seven passengers.

Douglas C-47 Skytrain 44-76600 of the 48th TFW. The wing badge was positioned just aft of the cockpit. (*Author's collection*)

Lockheed T-33A-1-LO 54-1535 of the 19th TRS based with the 47th BW at RAF Sculthorpe in 1955. This aircraft passed to the German Air Force in 1957. (*Author's collection*)

North American T-39A 62-4462 of the 20th TFW photographed while at the open house at RAF Wethersfield on 8 August 1964. (*Author's collection*)

De Havilland L-20A Beaver 52-6138 at the open house at RAF Bentwaters in May 1960 wears the badge of the 81st TFW on the tail. (*Robin A. Walker*)

De Havilland L-20A Beaver 52-6139 assigned to the 55th FBS, 20th FBW. (*Author's collection*)

Lockheed T-33A-1-LO 51-8754 of the 10th TRW, RAF Alconbury, 28 May 1960. (*Robert Robinson collection*)

Fairchild C-119F Flying Boxcar 51-8247 attached to the 47th BW at RAF Sculthorpe. (*Robert Robinson collection*)

Douglas C-47A 43-48083 was assigned to the 47th BW at RAF Sculthorpe. The tail flash is in yellow and the flashes emanating from the rear of the squadron badge are in the three squadron colours of red, yellow, and blue. (*Robert Robinson collection*)

Appendix III

The Policy of 'Massive Retaliation'

The decision to employ nuclear weapons as a first response to a Soviet invasion of Europe was endorsed by the NATO in a strategy document, DC 6/1, published in August 1949. The fact that NATO was incapable of countering an invasion by conventional means prompted the unambiguous statement that the organisation 'should carry out strategic bombing promptly by all means possible with all types of weapons, without exception. This is primarily a U.S. responsibility assisted as practicable by other nations'.

In October 1953, the NSC published paper NSC 162/2, which addressed the Soviet threat and clearly stated:

> The capability of the USSR to attack the United States with atomic weapons has been continuously growing and will be materially enhanced by hydrogen weapons. The USSR has sufficient bombs and aircraft, using one way missions, to inflict serious damage on the United States, especially by a surprise attack.... The risk of Soviet aggression will be minimised by maintaining a strong security posture, with emphasis on adequate offensive retaliatory strength and defensive strength. This must be based on massive atomic capability, including necessary bases...[1]

When President Dwight Eisenhower endorsed this document, the policy of massive retaliation was born. The principles were adopted by NATO, who accepted not the possibility that nuclear weapons would be used as a first response, but the certainty that they would.

Appendix IV
Red Richard

In July 1959, Gen. Charles de Gaulle, the president of France, ordered all foreign nuclear forces from French soil. This necessitated a major reshuffle of USAFE units on the continent and had consequences for the 3rd Air Force in the UK. This realignment of assets in France and Germany was called Project Red Richard.

USAFE nuclear units resident in France at that time were the 48th TFW at Chaumont-Semoutiers, the 49th TFW at Étain-Rouvres, and the 50th TFW at Toul-Rosière. The 48th TFW was scheduled to move to RAF Lakenheath, the control of which was relinquished by SAC and transferred to the 3rd Air Force. The 49thTFW moved with their F-100Ds from Étain-Rouvres to Spangdahlem, displacing the 10th TRW, which moved to three bases in the UK: Alconbury, Chelveston, and Bruntingthorpe. The 50th TFW moved to Hahn in Germany. The 66th TRW remained at Laon, now being the only USAF recce unit on mainland Europe. The reconnaissance RF-101s of the 66th TRW were nuclear capable even though they did not have a nuclear strike mission. In fact, in 1961, in response to the Berlin Crisis, the 38th TRS detached from Laon to Ramstein, Germany, to stand Victor Alert in their Voodoos.

Appendix V

The Hungarian Uprising 1956

During the Second World War, the Hungarians supported the Nazi regime and fought on the side of the Axis powers. Following the defeat of the Nazis in 1945 by the Allies and the Soviet Union, the country tried to constitute a democratic state. Initially this succeeded, but Soviet influence and power encouraged and supported the establishment of a one-party communist state based on the Soviet model. A gradual process of intimidation and other repressive measures against the democratically elected parties resulted in one-party elections being held in 1949, culminating in the foundation of the People's Republic of Hungary.

Under the leadership of Mátyás Rákosi, the people of Hungary were severely oppressed. Hundreds disappeared and were killed or sent to concentration camps in the Soviet Union. For two years, from 1950 to 1952, the Security Police, the ÁVH, were given a free reign and brutally enforced the will of the Communist government and its Soviet overlords.

Although the 'elections' of 1952 produced a more moderate prime minister in the shape of Imre Nagy, the influence of Rákosi, who was still general secretary of the Communist Party, was such that, in 1955, Nagy was removed from office. In February 1956, as the policies of Josef Stalin were being denigrated in the Soviet Union by Nikita Khrushchev, Rakosi was replaced by Ernő Gerő. Gerő, though not a Stalinist was, nonetheless, not a reformer. Meanwhile unrest was growing.

The 23 October march in Budapest was not greeted sympathetically by the government and subsequently led to more people taking to the streets. The ÁVH police and soldiers opened fire on the crowds and the ill-fated revolution had begun. The day after the march, the Soviet Union entered Hungary on the invitation of Gerő and, assisted by the Hungarian army and the ÁVH, attempted to put down the revolution. Gerő was forced to resign and Nagy was reinstated as prime minister in the expectation he would persuade the people to return to their homes. He succeeded in persuading the Soviets to withdraw, and he began to draw up proposals for a new limited multi-party government. Such liberal plans were too much for the Soviets and they determined to put an end to the revolution. On the morning of 4 November 1956, Warsaw Pact forces invaded Hungary under Operation Whirlwind. With considerable violence, they succeeded in crushing all opposition and took Nagy back to Russia where he was systematically tortured and hanged after a show trial.

The dangers for world peace of the actions of the Soviet Union and its allies cannot be underestimated. Their actions prompted western forces to be placed on high alert in case the manoeuvres of the WP armies threatened nearby NATO states. In the UK, all TAC nuclear forces were placed on alert for the duration of the emergency.

Appendix VI
The Cuban Missile Crisis

Following the Cuban revolution in 1959 and the ascent of Fidel Castro, the newly born socialist country aligned itself with the Soviet Union politically, economically, and militarily. This occurred at the height of the Cold War. Understandably, the rapprochement between Moscow and Havana caused the Americans some concern. Russian pilots arrived in Cuba to train pilots for the new air force and, in 1961, the first Mikoyan MiG-15s arrived on the island. More Russian pilots arrived throughout 1961 and, in addition to training Cuban pilots in the air defence role, they also flew interception missions against the RF-101 Voodoos and RF-8 Crusaders, which frequently conducted reconnaissance overflights over Cuba. Meanwhile, more Cuban pilots went to China and Czechoslovakia for training. Russian Ilyushin Il-28 bombers were also sent to the island.

The development of the fledging air force did not alarm the Americans unduly. Their air superiority over the Caribbean was secure, and they conducted their overflights without a great deal of inconvenience or loss. However, on 14 October 1962, a Lockheed U-2 aircraft conducting a high-altitude overflight of Cuba returned with photographs of an SS-4 medium-range ballistic missile being assembled. This missile, NATO reporting name 'Sandal', had a range of approximately 1,600 km and was capable of delivering a 1-megaton warhead. For the US, this was very alarming. With these missiles, the Soviets could threaten the southern and eastern states of the union. Up to this point, the US had enjoyed a monopoly of placing their missiles close to the borders of the Soviet Union without the facing a similar threat themselves. The Soviets saw the placement of missiles on Cuba as a way of balancing the situation.

On receiving the news of the presence of the missiles on Cuba, President Kennedy and his advisors considered their response—their options were limited: they could invade Cuba and destroy the sites or they could launch an aerial bombing attack which would destroy the missiles. The eventual strategy decided by Kennedy was to order a naval 'quarantine' of Cuba and Soviet ships transporting any offensive weapons were to be turned back. Kennedy was unequivocal in his announcement to the American people:

'It shall be the policy of this nation to regard any nuclear missile launched from Cuba against any nation in the Western Hemisphere as an attack by the Soviet Union on the United States, requiring a full retaliatory response upon the Soviet Union'.

US Forces went to Defcon 3—the air force on fifteen minutes' readiness. During 24–25 October, the quarantine strategy appeared to be working in spite of Soviet Premier Khrushchev declaring it an act of aggression. However, US tactical reconnaissance flights revealed that the missiles already on the island were nearing completion. Invasion by US Forces seemed the only realistic means of destroying them. Tensions grew further and Strategic Air Command went to Defcon 2.

On 26 October, Khrushchev sent a letter to Kennedy stating that, if the United States would undertake not to invade Cuba, the Soviets would remove the missiles. On 27 October, a further letter arrived stating that any deal must include the withdrawal of American Jupiter medium-range missiles from Turkey. Kennedy responded publicly to the first letter and gave his assent. He sent his brother, Robert, to the Soviet ambassador in Washington to state that the Jupiters would be removed from Turkey, but that could not be stated publicly. The Soviets accepted this and the crisis was over. The SS-4 missiles were removed from Cuba along with the Il-28 bombers. In 1963, the US removed all its Jupiters from Turkey.

During the Cuban Missile Crisis, the tactical nuclear units based in the UK were on high alert status, ready to launch an attack on their targets in the Warsaw Pact countries and the Soviet Union.

Appendix VII

Able Archer

It was NATO exercise Autumn Forge 83 that contributed in no small measure to the thawing of relations between NATO and the Soviet Union and eventually led to the end of the Cold War. The early 1980s had been characterised by an increase in tension between the US and the Soviet Union. President Ronald Reagan's public sabre rattling and seeming belligerent attitude prompted Soviet leader Yuri Andropov to declare in June 1983 to the US envoy in Moscow, Averell Harriman, that the administration's provocative demeanour was in danger of causing a confrontation which could lead to nuclear war by 'miscalculation'.

Autumn Forge was comprised of a number of smaller exercises: Reforger 83, Cold Fire, Crested Cap, Display Determination, Oksoboel, and Able Archer 83. As was to be expected, the exercise was watched very closely by the Soviet Union and its WP allies. The Able Archer simulation, which took place from 7–11 November, included a nuclear dimension. Blue forces (NATO) B-52 and KC-135 operations were directed in accordance with an operational plan which included hostile actions against the Orange Force (Soviet and Warsaw Pact forces). The objective being to test the concept of 'flexible response' and the transition from the use of conventional to nuclear weapons.

Orange had been increasing its chemical weapons onslaught on Blue, which prompted Blue to request from SACEUR (Supreme Allied Command Europe) permission to use nuclear weapons. This occurred on 9 November, two days before the exercise finished.

On the final day of the exercise, eight KC-135 Stratotankers were launched from their bases in the UK, and Blue Force simulated further nuclear strikes with B-52s on the same day. Meanwhile, behind the Iron Curtain, all this activity was being monitored by a variety of means and the possibility that a real nuclear attack was imminent prompted the air forces of the Warsaw Pact to be placed on high alert. For the first time since the Cuban Missile Crisis, the world had stood on the brink of Armageddon. When it became apparent that the NATO allies intended no such hostile action for real, the crisis was over, but in the aftermath, both sides of the Cold War mutually decided that they must never allow such a situation to develop again and east and west entered into a new era of *détente*. One of the outcomes of the exercise questioned the participation of the UK-based B-52s. Undoubtedly, the tension between NATO and the WP was as a result of the careless use of the word 'strike' in reference to the B-52 missions. Bearing in mind that the Soviets would have been actively engaged in electronic (ELINT) and communication (COMINT) intelligence gathering during all phases of the exercise, such language could have been misunderstood and would have elicited an appropriate response. B-52 deployments to the UK continued right up to the present day, but were confined to a conventional role.

Appendix VIII

1966 France Leaves NATO

In March 1966, Gen. Charles de Gaulle pulled France out of NATO and ordered all foreign forces to leave French soil. For some considerable time, the French had become disenchanted with the alliance. There were several reasons for this. Paramount was the American dominance over all matters nuclear. The French would like to have seen a nuclear strategy that was decided by Europe, and one that recognised the USA solely as an equal partner. Also, the doctrine of flexible response which the USA attempted to impose on its European allies in the early 1960s was not widely welcomed. Although a nuclear Armageddon would clearly render the entire planet uninhabitable, the doctrine of massive retaliation had been seen to be working and was by many seen to be preferable to a strategy that envisaged, at least initially, a conventional war that would have caused countless casualties, particularly in Germany, which was on the frontline. The war would have been confined to Europe and so would the damage. The US mainland would remain untouched.

Tensions in the alliance were also exacerbated by the fact that the NATO countries steadfastly declined to cooperate with the USA and get involved in its South East Asia conflict. De Gaulle envisaged France as part of a Europe independent of the influence of the US. In 1959, he had demonstrated his rejection of the US policy of maintaining its control over nuclear weapons in France by ordering the withdrawal of all such weapons from French soil. In the early 1960s, and independently of the US, he made several attempts at *détente* with the Soviet Union, visiting Khrushchev in Moscow in 1964. In the meantime, France was developing its own nuclear capability, exploding its first device in the Sahara in February 1960.

Eventually, in February 1966, France withdrew from NATO's Military Command Structure, while still remaining in the organisation. He also ordered all foreign military personnel and equipment to be removed from France within a year, a decision that brought the 17th and 18th TRS from Laon-Couvron Air Base to RAF Upper Heyford in September 1966.

Appendix IX

The 1961 Berlin Crisis and Operation Stairstep

Since the end of the Second World, the city of Berlin had been administered by four powers: the Soviet Union, the US, the UK, and France. The Allied sectors were collectively known as West Berlin and the Soviet sector as East Berlin. West Berlin was governed by an elected mayor and an elected senate, but the ultimate power resided in the hands of the occupying forces and the commander-in-chief.

Movement between East and West Berlin was initially relatively free, but the massive migration to the west of citizens of the GDR soon led to more and more restrictions being put in place. These restrictions eventually led to the construction of a barbed-wire fence overlooked by watch towers that separated the two states. Berlin, however, remained open, and the haemorrhaging of some of the east's population continued through this route. In November 1958, in Moscow, Soviet Premier Nikita Khrushchev declared that he wished to see an end to all military occupation of Berlin. He followed up with an ultimatum which demanded that, within six months, the Allies either left Berlin or the Soviets would sign a treaty with the GDR, one of the clauses would be that the GDR would be given control of all of Berlin.

The threat was clear and the firm response from the Western Allies equally so. Khrushchev withdrew his ultimatum, and in 1959, a four-power conference was held to address the Berlin question. It ended with no agreement being reached. The flood of refugees to the west through Berlin did not lessen and became critical. The drain on the human resources of the GDR was profound, particularly in terms of professionals, teachers, lawyers, doctors, engineers, and others. Early in 1961, Khrushchev revived his demands that the Western Allies leave Berlin and that he would sign a peace treaty with the GDR. In August, construction of the Berlin Wall began effectively cutting off the city. President Kennedy who had engaged Khrushchev in discussions on several occasions drew the line. The integrity of West Berlin would be maintained at all costs.

In September, he authorised an augmentation of USAFE with units deployed from the US. Several Air National Guard were federalised and ordered to deploy to Europe. These comprised: four Republic F-84F Thunderstreak squadrons, four North American

F-86H Sabre squadrons, one RF-84F Thunderflash squadron, and three Lockheed F-104A Starfighter squadrons. These units were supported by units from the Military Air Transport Service.

All the ANG fighter and reconnaissance RF-84Fs were destined for bases in France and Spain, and the Atlantic crossings were flown by the northern route via Labrador, Greenland (Bluie West One), Iceland, and Scotland (Prestwick), before continuing to their French bases. The alternative route traversed the southern Atlantic via the Azores. Deployments commenced in October and were complete by the end of November. By mid-1962, the crisis had receded and the units returned to ANG control and the US. The F-84F squadron personnel returned home without their aircraft, which were allocated to the newly activated 366th Tactical Fighter Wing, four squadrons of which were based at Chaumont-Semoutier, Chambley, and Étain-Rouvres.

In addition to causing the deployment of tactical units to Europe, the effect of the Berlin Crisis in 1961 was felt by the tactical units based in the UK, all of which were maintained on a high state of alert until the threat was dissipated. The deployments were also a boon for the UK aviation enthusiasts who got the opportunity to see many of the deployed aircraft, at USAF open days, and when many of them passed through Prestwick.

The armed forces day at Sculthorpe in May 1962 also played to F-84F 52-6963 of the 366th TFW. This Thunderstreak was also originally assigned to the 166th TFS of the Ohio ANG. (*R. A. Scholefield*)

Both RAF Wethersfield and RAF Sculthorpe had an armed forces day on 19 May 1962. Present at RAF Wethersfield was F-86H 52-2009 of the 131st TFS based at Phalsbourg in France. The 101st was a Massachusetts ANG squadron. (*USAF*)

Appendix X
The Suez Crisis 1956

On 6 July 1956, in Alexandria, Egypt, Egyptian President Col. Gamal Abdul Nasser announced the nationalisation of the Suez Canal. The Suez Canal was at that time owned and administered by the governments of the UK and France. For many years prior to this event, the tensions between Egypt and the colonial powers had been growing. This was for a variety of reasons.

Nasser wanted the British and their military bases out of Egypt; he wished to present himself as the leader of the Arab world against what he viewed as colonial oppression. The French in Algeria and the British in Egypt symbolised oppressive colonialism. Nasser supported the FLA rebels in Algeria against the French. Furthermore, the arming of the Israelis by France and the UK, and their refusal to sell arms to Egypt, further exacerbated the situation. The US in the meantime was managing the Cold War with the Soviet Union. The US desperately wanted to keep the Soviets out of the Middle East, but they too refused to sell arms to Egypt, principally because of their friendship with Israel which had been in a state of conflict with Egypt since 1954. Nasser had no option but to turn to the Soviets for his arms. He approached Khrushchev, who was only too glad to be of assistance, and he brokered an arms deal between Czechoslovakia and Egypt. This, of course, infuriated Britain, France, Israel, and the US. However, USA President Eisenhower believed that it was possible to have a rapprochement with Egypt, and in early 1956, he tried to organise a peace deal with Israel. He also offered to pay for the construction of the Aswan Dam if Nasser would co-operate. Neither was the American president particularly sympathetic to the colonial motives of the French and British.

Immediately following the Alexandria speech by Nasser, Egyptian forces seized the canal and the crisis had begun. The UK, France, and Israel met secretly at the town of Sevres to plan their response. They did not involve the US. Israel was to attack Egypt across Sinai. The French and British would then intervene and present an ultimatum that demanded that the two warring sides withdraw away from the canal. Should this be refused, then the French and British would invade Egypt after destroying the Egyptian Air Force. All ran according to this plan. The Israelis launched Operation Kadesh across the Sinai on 29 October 1956. The ultimatum was ignored, which gave the French and British the green light to launch Operation Musketeer, the invasion of Egypt, on 31 October. The Egyptians responded by sinking ships in the canal and effectively blocking it.

The Soviet Union was apoplectic in response to what they saw as an invasion of their Middle Eastern ally. Khrushchev stated that they would go to war if necessary to defend Egypt. Premier Bulganin threatened the cities of Britain and France with rocket attacks. The fact that the crisis in Egypt coincided with the Hungarian uprising created grave concerns should either situation escalate into a wider conflict. The US did not support the invasion of Egypt for two principal reasons: in the light of their strong criticism of the Soviet treatment of Hungary, they could hardly have supported an invasion of a sovereign state by colonial powers, and they were also extremely anxious to reach an understanding with Egypt, a country that they saw as pivotal to security in the Middle East.

Under intense pressure from the US, both directly and through the UN, the British and French forces accepted a UN ceasefire on 6 November 1956. They withdrew their forces and a UN peacekeeping force was sent to guard the canal, which was reopened in March 1957.

Appendix XI

The Doctrine of Flexible Response

In 1967, NATO adopted a policy of flexible response (FR). This strategy replaced the Eisenhower doctrine of massive retaliation. Effectively, the defence of NATO in the event of a Soviet-led invasion using conventional weapons would be met, not by immediate large-scale nuclear response, but by a staged three-fold reaction: conventional counterattack, battlefield tactical nuclear weapons, and, finally, if all else fails, strategic nuclear attack.

The implications for the air forces of NATO in the adoption of the FR strategy were quite profound. For USAFE, it implied a greater stress on developing better and more efficient conventional weapons and intensive training in their use. It took some time before these developments became apparent. It was not until the late 1970s and 1980s that new weapons systems and aircraft would come into service. Meanwhile, the USAFE tactical nuclear strike units developed and practised for conventional war in addition to retaining their nuclear capability. Many of the new aircraft that joined USAFE units in the final decade off the Cold War sat Victor Alert just as their predecessors did. The pilots and WSOs of the F-111s at Upper Heyford and Lakenheath still rushed to their aircraft at the sound of the klaxon, but they did it in the knowledge that the conventional response to the Warsaw Pact aggression had failed. The F-111 could carry multiple B-61 warheads. When the 81st TFW replaced its F-4Ds starting in 1979 with the Fairchild A-10 Thunderbolt II, NATO was provided with a potent weapon to counter the threat of Soviet tanks raging through the Fulda Gap in Germany; while at the same time, at Hahn, AB General Dynamics F-16s were on Victor Alert with B-61 bombs. Victor Alert in USAFE effectively finished at the end of the 1980s.

The USAF still retains B-61 bombs in Europe and the weapon has been upgraded to be carried by the Lockheed Martin F-35 Lightning II. It remains to be seen whether or not Victor Alert will ever be reinstated. Current tensions between the alliance and the Russian Federation and the fact of the overwhelming superiority in TNWs by the Russians certainly raise uncertainties for the future.

Appendix XII
Tables

Wings, Squadrons, and Tail Codes

Tail codes or 'distinctive unit aircraft markings' were first introduced on camouflaged aircraft operating with PACAF in SE Asia, and subsequently applied to all USAF aircraft, being adopted by USAFE in 1970. The code consisted of two letters. The first letter designated the wing and the second the individual squadron. The letter selected for the wing was usually the initial letter of the base name. However, in the case of aircraft occupying two bases (as in the case of the 81st TFW at Bentwaters and Woodbridge), one base letter was used (in this case 'W' for Woodbridge). The 'B' initial letter was applied to 36th TFW aircraft based at Bitburg, Germany. The second squadron letter was 'R', 'S', 'T', 'U', or 'V' depending on the number of squadrons in the wing.

In April 1972, following the transference of maintenance from squadron to wing level, the individual squadron tail codes gave way to a single tail code designated the whole wing. This system remains in operation to the present day.

WING	SQUADRON	AIRCRAFT	TAIL CODE 1970 to 1972	TAIL CODE 1972 onwards
10th TRW	1st TRS	McDonnell RF-4C	AR	
	30th TRS	McDonnell RF-4C	AS	AR
	32nd TRS	McDonnell RF-4C	AT	
10th TFW	509th TFS	Republic A-10A		
	511th TFS	Republic A-10A		AR
20th TFW	55th TFS	GD F-111E	US (not used) JS from 4/1971	
	77thTFS	GD F-111E	UT 10/70-1/71 JT from 1/1971	UH
	79th TFS	GD F-111E	UR 10/70-1/71 JR from 1/1971	
	42nd ECS	GD EF-111A		UH
48th TFW	492nd TFS	NA F-100D/F	LR	
	493rd TFS	NA F-100D/F	LS	
	494th TFS	NA F-100D/F	LT	
48th TFW	492nd TFS	McDonnell F-4D		
	493rd TFS	McDonnell F-4D	LK Only 27 F-4Ds carried this code between October 1970 and	LN
	494th TFS	McDonnell F-4D	July 1972	
48th TFW	492nd TFS	GD F-111F		
	493rd TFS	GD F-111F		LN
	494th TFS	GD F-111F		
	495th TFS	GD F-111F		
81st TFW	78 TFS	McDonnell F-4C/D	WR	
	91 TFS	McDonnell F-4C/D	WS	WR
	92 TFS	McDonnell F-4C/D	WT	
81st TFW	78 TFS	Republic A-10A		
	91 TFS			
	92 TFS			
	509 TFS			WR
	510 TFS			
	511 TFS			
	527 TFTAS	F-16C		

USAF Air-Launched Tactical Nuclear Weapons 1950 to 1990

Within the context of USAFE and the TAC units in the UK, a tactical nuclear weapon can be defined as a short-range weapon with a range of approximately 600 km. The 'special weapons' carried by the fighter bombers of the 3rd Air Force evolved over the course of the years of the Cold War, from the Mk 7 to the Mk 61 carried.

WEAPON	AIRCRAFT	YIELD
Mark 7 atomic bomb 'Thor'	Republic F-84G Thunderjet Republic F-84F Thunderstreak NA B-45A Tornado NA F-100D Super Sabre McDonnell F-101A/C Voodoo	6 Yields: 8 – 61 kilotons
Mark 28 (B28) thermonuclear bomb (Mk 28RE/Mk-28 RE)	Douglas B-66 Destroyer NA F-100D/F Super Sabre McDonnell F-101A/C Voodoo McDonnell F-4C/D Phantom GD F-111E/F Aardvark	FUFO 5 Yields Y1: 1.1 Mt Y2: 35 Kt Y3: 70 Kt Y5: 1.45 Mt
Mark 43 thermonuclear bomb	NA F-100D/F Super Sabre McDonnell F-101A/C Voodoo GD F-111E/F Aardvark McDonnell F-4C/D Phantom II	5 Yields: 70kt to 1mt
Mark 57 Thermonuclear bomb	NA F-100D/F Super Sabre GD F111E/F Aardvark McDonnell F-4C/D Phantom	Yield; 5 - 20 Kt
Mark 61 Thermonuclear bomb	NA F-100D/F Super Sabre GD F111E/F Aardvark McDonnell F-4C/D Phantom	FUFO 4 Yields: 0.3 to 340 kt

LABS—low-altitude bombing system
LDD—low-altitude drogue delivery
FUFO—full fusing options (dial a yield)

ERY	NOTES
all	Airburst and contact In service with USAF 1952 to 1967
all B28EX, B28IN 3-28EX, B28IN B28RE, B28RI Laydown B28EX, B28IN	Airburst and contact. In service with USAF 1958 to 1991 Redesignated B58 in 1968. Four models for use by tactical aircraft: B28EX External, B28RE, External retarded B28IN, Internal B28RI, Internal Retarded
all vn	Airburst and Contact In service with USAF 1961 to 1991 Two models; Mod 1 and Mod 2
all vn	Airburst and contact In service 1963 to 1993
all vn	Airburst and contact

Appendix XIII

Maps

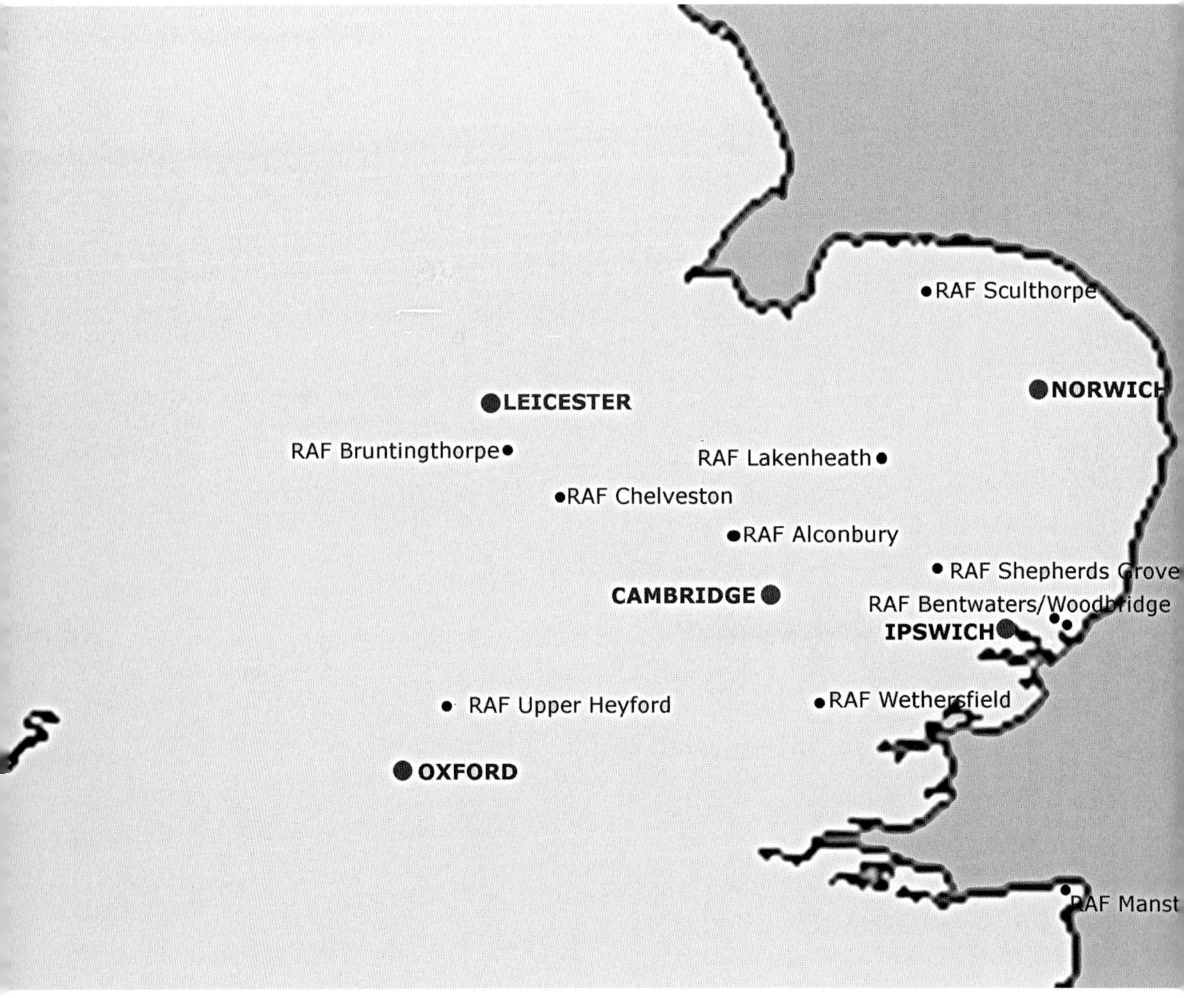

Map of USAFE tactical unit bases in the UK.

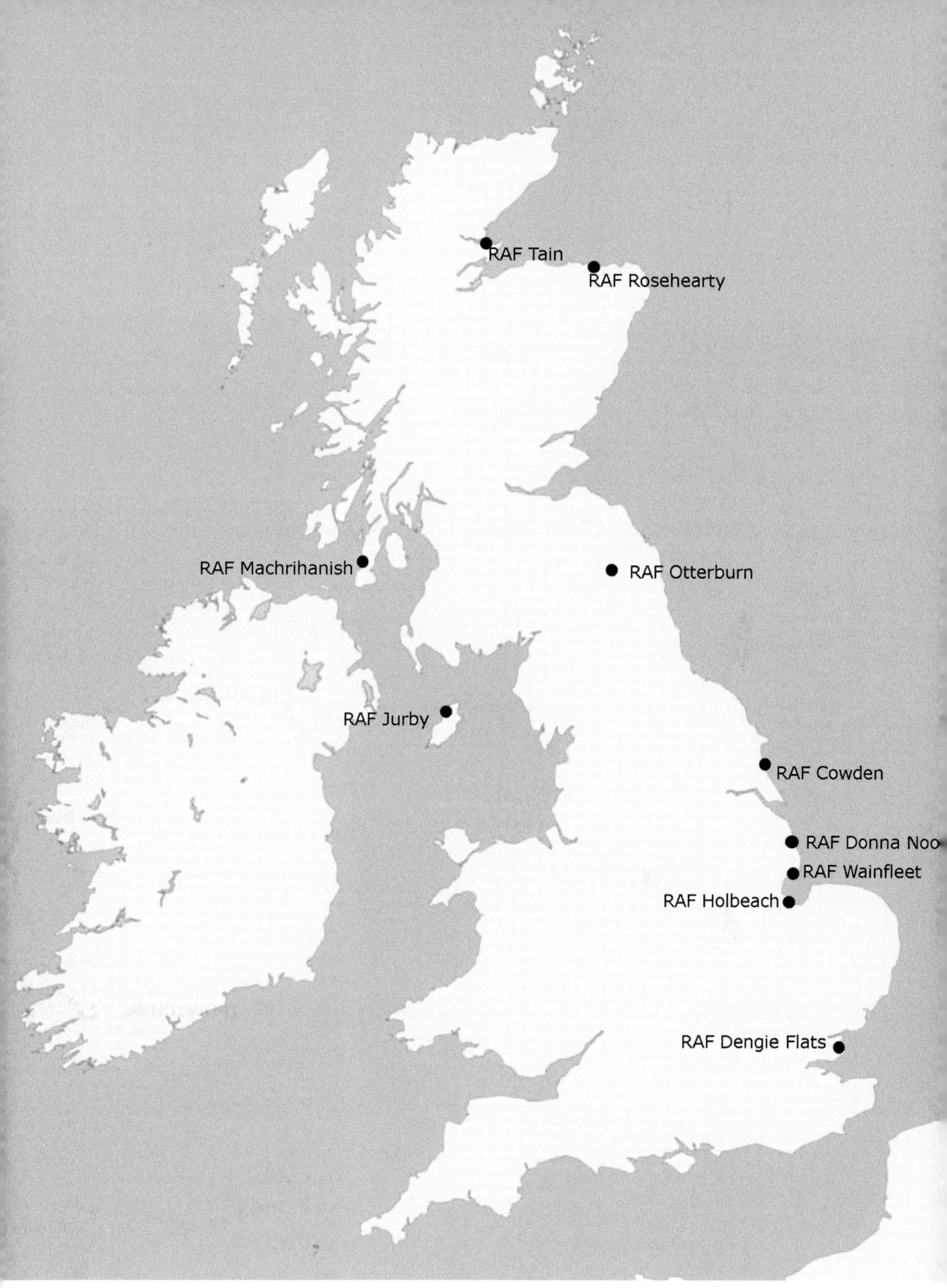

Map of RAF gunnery and bombing ranges in the UK used by UK-based USAFE tactical units.

Map of European and North African gunnery and bombing ranges used by USAFE tactical units.

Endnotes

Chapter 1

1 In an email to the author, 11 August 2010.
2 In an email to the author, 26 July 2010.
3 In an email to the author, 6 June 2010.
4 In an email to the author, 26 July 2010.
5 Ibid.
6 In an email to the author, 8 August 2010.
7 In an email to the author, 6 June 2010.
8 In an email to the author, 3 September 2010.
9 Blood Arlie J. Only Angels have Wings (Golding 1997), p. 136.
10 In an email to the author, 12 June 2010.
11 Ibid.
12 In an email to the author, 19 July 2010.
13 In an email to the author, 28 August 2011.
14 In an email to the author, 23 August 2011.
15 In an email to the author, 18 November 2011.
16 In an email to the author, 16 January 2012.
17 Ibid.
18 In an email to the author, 23 August 2011.
19 In an email to the author, June 1999.
20 Ibid.
21 In an email to the author, 2 February 2020.
22 In an email to the author, 10 April 2019.
23 Ibid.
24 In an email to the author, 21 May 2019.
25 In an email to the author, 10 April 2019.
26 In an email to the author, 27 March 2019.
27 In an email to the author, 2 August 2019.
28 In an email to the author, 21 May 2019.
29 Ibid.
30 In an email to the author, 2 August 2019.
31 In an email to the author, 7 April 2019.
32 In an email to the author, 10 April 2019.
33 In an email to the author, 7 April 2019.
34 In an email to the author, 10 April 2019.

35 In an email to the author, 27 May 2014.
36 In an email to the author, 20 May 2014.
37 In an email to the author, 27 May, 2014.
38 In an email to the author, 20 May 2014.
39 In an email to the author, 27 May 2014.
40 Ibid.
41 In an email to the author, 25 May 2014.
42 In an email to the author, 11 June 2014.
43 In an email to the author, 21 February 2013.
44 In an email to the author, 29 January 2017.
45 In an email to the author, 27 May 2014.

Chapter 2

1 In an email to the author via Duncan Curtis, 17 November 2000.
2 Ibid.
3 Ibid.
4 In an email to the author, 18 November 2000.
5 In an email to the author, 9 November 2000.
6 In an email to the author, 17 November 2000.
7 In an email to the author, 14 November 2000.

Chapter 3

1 In an email to the author, 25 May 2011.
2 In an email to the author, 20 July 2011.
3 Taken with permission from the video Cold War Remembered; produced by Glenn Ludlow and published in Vancouver, Canada by GCL Productions Ltd.
4 In an email to the author, 25 May 2011.
5 Taken with permission from the video Cold War Remembered; produced by Glenn Ludlow and published in Vancouver, Canada by GCL Productions Ltd.
6 Ibid.
7 In an email to the author, 22 May 2011.
8 In an email to the author, 25 May 2011.
9 Ibid.
10 In an email to the author, 22 May 2011.
11 Ibid.

Chapter 4

1 In an email to the author, 17 October 2012.
2 Richard M. Baughn BGen USAF, Retd., '20th fighter wing first in nucs & bare bones over-the-shoulder bombing'. Air University.
3 Ibid.
4 In an email to the author, 1 January 2011.
5 In an email to the author, 20 January 2011.
6 Ibid.
7 In an email to the author, 15 January 2011.
8 In an email to the author, 25 January 2011.
9 The Wingman journal of the 20th TFW.

10 In an email to the author, 14 January 2011.
11 In an email to the author, 15 January 2011.
12 In an email to the author, 1 January 2011.
13 In an email to the author, 28 November 2017.
14 Ibid.
15 Ibid.

Chapter 5

1 Audio conference call, 1 February 2017.
2 In an email to the author, 1 January 2017.
3 Audio conference call, 1 February 2017.
4 In emails to the author, 6 and 7 February 2017.
5 In an email to the author, 1 January 2017.
6 Audio files by email to the author, 7 October 2013.
7 In an email to the author, 1 January 2017.

Chapter 6

1 In emails to the author, 3 and 4 May 2019.
2 Ibid.
3 Gen. Charles F. Blair, Flying Magazine, January 1960.
4 Dan Weber, 'The 420th AREFS Great Adventure in the Belgian Congo', published in TAC Tanker Tales, Volume 2, Issue 1, September 2001. Reproduced with kind permission of John Bessette, Historian of the Tac Tankers Association.
5 Ibid.
6 Ibid.
7 Ibid.

Chapter 7

1 In an email to the author, 8 January 2020.
2 In an email to the author, 14 April 2020.
3 In an email to the author, 17 February 2020.
4 In an email to the author, 8 January 2020.
5 In an email to the author, 14 April 2020.
6 In an email to the author, 7 January 2017.
7 In an email to the author, 21 February 2018.
8 In an email to the author, 25 October 2017.
9 Ibid.
10 In an email to the author, 21 February 2018.
11 In an email to the author, 26 October 2017.
12 In an email to the author, 21 February 2017.
13 Jet48 journal of the 48th TFW, 24 April 1991.
14 Ibid.

Chapter 8

1 In an email to the author, 19 January 2012.
2 In an email to the author, 6 September 2011.

3 In an email to the author, 22 March 2002.
4 In an email to the author, January 2002.
5 In an email to the author, 6 September 2011.
6 In an email to the author, 4 January 2002.
7 In an email to the author, 19 January 2012.
8 In an email to the author, 6 September 2011.
9 In an email to the author, 7 October 2011.
10 In an email to the author, 5 October 2009.
11 In an email to the author, 25 September 2009.
12 In an email to the author, 5 October 2009.
13 In an email to the author, 5 October 2009.
14 In an email to the author, 5 October 2009.
15 In an email to the author, 7 October 2009.
16 In an email to the author, 5 October 2009.
17 In an email to the author, October 2009.
18 In an email to the author, 5 October 2009.
19 In an email to the author, 2 October 2009.
20 In an email to the author, 27 September 2009.
21 In an email to the author, 7 October 2009.

Chapter 9

1 In an email to the author, 24 December 2012.
2 Quoted from The Bandits by Tsgt Herman J. Kokojan and SMSgt Harold Newcomb; a 10th TRW publicity paper introducing 527th TFTAS to the Alconbury community.
3 In an email to the author, 24 December 2012.
4 In an email to the author, 24 January 2013.
5 Quoted from The Bandits by Tsgt Herman J. Kokojan and SMSgt Harold Newcomb; a 10th TRW publicity paper introducing 527th TFTAS to the Alconbury community.
6 In an email to the author, 24 December 2012.
7 In an email to the author, 16 January 2013.
8 In an email to the author, 24 December 2012.
9 In an email to the author, 16 January 2013.
10 In an email to the author, 1 February 2013.
11 In an email to the author, 21 February 2013.
12 Ibid.
13 Ibid.
14 In an email to the author, 8 February 2013.

Chapter 10

1 In an email to the author, 7 June 2010.
2 Email to Carlos Higgins, Recce Reader, Spring 2002.
3 In an email to the author, 7 June 2010.
4 In an email to the author, 9 May 2010.
5 In an email to the author, 22 August 1999.
6 In an email to the author, 24 October 1999.
7 In an email to the author, 16 December 2010.
8 Ibid.
9 In an email to the author, 9 May 2010.
10 In an email to the author, 19 September 1999.
11 In an email to the author, 16 December 2010.

12 In an email to the author, 7 June 2010.
13 In an email to the author, 16 December 2010.

Chapter 11

1 Memoirs of Richard Kamm are reproduced with the kind permission of the 'Aircraft Engine Historical Society' website.
2 Ibid.
3 Ibid.
4 In an email to the author, 13 March 2012.
5 Flight magazine September 1957.
6 In a letter to the author, 29 March 2012.

Chapter 12

1 Col. Charles F. Blair, Red Balls in the Sky, Random House 1969.
2 Memorandum Secretary of Defense Melvin Laird to military department secretaries, 21 August 1970.

Appendix I

1 In an email to the author, 23 August 2011.
2 In an email to the author, 28 August 2011.
3 In an email to the author, 18 November 2011.
4 In an email to the author, 20 January 2011.
5 In an email to the author, 8 January 2020.
6 In an email to the author, 23 August 2011.
7 Letters to the author, November 2004.
8 In an email to the author, 17 November 1999.
9 In an email to the author, 21 May 2019.
10 In an email to the author, 10 April 2019.
11 In an email to the author, 7 January 2015.
12 In an email to the author, 3 October 2003.
13 In an email to the author, 24 October 2002.
14 In an email to the author, 25 October 2017.
15 In an email to the author, 24 December 2012.
16 In an email to the author, 21 February 2013.
17 Audio conference, 1 February 2016.
18 Ibid.
19 In an email to the author, 3 May 2019.
20 In an email to the author, 12 November 2011.
21 In an email to the author, 29 January 2017.

Appendix III

1 Policy Paper 162/2 of the United States National Security Council, 30 October, 1953.

Bibliography and Other Sources

The content of this book is based primarily on official histories obtained in microfilm from the USAF Historical Research Agency (AFHRA) at Maxwell AFB, Alabama, and primary evidence in the form of conversations, letters, and email exchanges with individuals who were directly involved in the events. Secondary evidence referenced relevant books, journals, and websites.

Books

Anderegg, C. R., *Sierra Hotel, Flying Air Force Fighters in the decade after Vietnam* (Office of Air Force History, CreateSpace Independent Publishing Platform, 2015)

Anderton, D., *North American F-100 Super Sabre* (Osprey, 1987)

Blair, C. F., *Red Ball in the Sky* (Random House, New York, 1969)

Blood, A. J., *Only Angels have Wings* (Golding, 1997)

Bowers, P., and Menard, D., *Buzz Numbers* (Speciality, 2006)

Boyne, W. J., *Beyond the Wild Blue* (Thomas Dunne Books)

Cosner, W. E. *We called You Hauled: The history of the Fairchild C-119 Flying Boxcar*

Curtis, D., *Rise and Defend. The USAF at Manston 1950–1958* (Flight recorder Publications, 2006)

Dancy, P., *Cold War Containment, Americans in Britain* (Lulu, 2013)

Davies, P., *F-111 and EF-111 units in Combat* (Osprey, 2014)

Davies, P., *USAF McDonnell Douglas F-4 Phantom II* (Osprey, 2013)

Davies, P., *General Dynamics F-111 Aardvark* (Osprey, 2014)

Downer, L., *Major General USAF Retd. 'Victor Alert'* (CreateSpace Independent Publishing Platform, 2016)

Ellis, P., *Aircraft of the USAF* (Janes, 1980)

Frederickson, J., *The B-45 Tornado* (McFarlnd & Co., 2009)

Gordon, D., *Tactical Reconnaissance in the Cold War* (Pen and Sword, 2005)

Grimes, USAF Retd., Col. B., *The History of Big Safari* (Archway, 2014)

Gunn, P. B., *Sculthorpe, Secrecy and Stealth* (The History Press, 2014)

Gunston, B., *Modern Combat Aircraft. F-16 Fighting Falcon* (Ian Allan, 1983)

Haynes, G., *Bentwaters and Woodbridge* (Woodfield, 2007)

Jones, N., *Able Archer 83* (The New Press, New York, 2016)

Knaak, M., *Encyclopaedia of USAF Aircraft and Missiles. Volume One: Post World War Two Fighters 1945–1973* (Office of Air Force History, 1978)

Knaak, M., *Encyclopaedia of USAF Aircraft and Missiles. Volume Two: Post World War Two Bombers 1945–1973* (Office of Air Force History 1978)
Martin, P., *Tail Codes* (Schiffer, 1994)
Maurer, M., *Combat Squadrons of WW2* (Office of Air Force History, 1982)
McAuliffe, J., *US Air Force in France, 1950–1967* (Milspec Press, 2005)
McPeak, Gen. M. A., *Hangar Flying* (Lost Wingman Press, 2012)
Menard, D., *Before Centuries. USAFE Fighters 1948–1959* (Airlife, 1999)
Ravenstein, C., *Air Force Combat Wings* (Office of Air Force History, 1984)
Robinson, R., *Volume One USAF Europe in Colour 1948–1965* (Squadron Signal, 1982)
Robinson, R,. *Volume Two USAF Europe in Colour 1947–1963* (Squadron Signal, 1990)
Robinson, R., and Menard, D., *F-100 Super Sabre in Colour* (Squadron Signal, 1992)
Robinson, R., *North American Aircraft, NATO F-86D/K Sabre Dog* (Edition Mini Monde 76, 2018)
Robinson, R., *F-84F/RF-84F Thunderstreak-Thunderflash* (Merlin Massara, 2015)
Samuel, W., *Glory Days* (Schiffer, 2008)
Scutts, J., *Modern Combat Aircraft, Northrop F-5/F-20* (Ian Allan, 1986)
Smallwood, W. L., *Warthog, Flying the A-10 in the Gulf War* (Potomac, 1993)
Slife, J. C., *Creech Blue* (Air University Press)
Smith, R. K., *75 Years of In-flight Refuelling* (Office of Air Force History, 1998)
United States Air Force, '*Winged Shield, Winged Sword, A history of the US Air Force, Volume II 1950–1997*' (Office of Air Force History, CreateSpace Independent Publishing Platform, 2015)
Warnock, T., (ed.), *Short of War-US Contingency Operations* (Office of Air Force History, 2000)
Walpole, N., *Voodoo Warriors* (Pen and Sword, 2007)

Websites

forgottenjets.warbirdsresourcegroup.org—Jet Aircraft serial database
nara.getarchive.net—US National archive Public Domain
nsarchive2.gwu.edu/—National Security Archive
nuclearweaponarchive.org—List of US Nuclear weapons
supersabresociety.com—F-100 Super Sabre Society
www.af.mil/News/Photos—US Air Force Archives
www.afhra.af.mil—Air Force Historical Research Agency
www.designation-systems.net—Designations of US Nuclear weapons
www.dhc-2.com/—Prestwick Portraits Aircraft
www.enginehistory.org/—Aircraft Engine Historical Society
www.sharpshooter-maj.com—Coronets, Crested Gaps and Salty Bees
www.tactankers.com—Tac Tankers Association

Videos

'Cold War Remembered, The US Air Force in the United Kingdom 1952–1957, A tribute to the 47th Bomb Wing.' Produced by Glenn Ludlow, GCL Productions. Produced by Video Publishing Group, Vancouver, Canada.

Official Histories

Air Force Historical Research Agency Microfilm. Official Histories of the 10 TRW; 20 FBW/TFW; 47 BW; 48 TFW; 66 TRW; 81 FIW/FBW/TFW; 406 FBW/FIW.

Journals

10th TRW Public Relations Kokojan, Herman and Newcombe, Harold, 'The Bandits' 527 TFTAS.
20th TFW 'Wingman' July 1964, 'NATO Weapons Meet, Chaumont'.
20th TFW 'Wingman', August 1964, 'Open House Wethersfield'.
48 Fighter Wing Office of History, 'The History, Heritage and Heraldry of the 48 FW'.
Aeroplane, 25 January 1957, MacDougall, Neil 'USAF in Africa'.
Aeroplane, 8 February 1957, MacDougall, Neil 'USAF in Morocco'.
Aeroplane, September 1984, Crouchman, Alan, 'Skyblazers'.
Aircraft Illustrated, January 1971, March, Peter M., 'The USAF at Upper Heyford'.
AirFan 37, Loubette, Fabrice, 'Operation Stairstep'.
Air Force Magazine, January 2008, 'The Years of Wheelus'.
Airfix Magazine, April 1979, Richards, Steve, 'USAFE Squadron Codes'.
Aviation News, June 2020, Wright, Dr Kevin 'Reinforcing the UK' Key Publishing
Aviation Review, August 1959, '420th AFRES in-flight refuelling with the KB-50J'.
Aviation World, March–April 1979, Archer, Bob, 'The USAF in the UK'.
Aviation World, December–January, 1989–90, 'Arthur Pearcy, The Origins of USAFE'.
Flight, 7 September 1951, News item Arrival of Sabres at RAF Shepherd's Grove.
Flight, 25 July 1952, 'The 49th Air Division in Britain'.
Flight, 23 July 1954, Wynn, Humphrey, 'Exercise Dividend'.
Flight, 22 April 1955, Lambert, CM., 'At the Controls of the B-45'.
Flight, 1 July 1955, 'Exercise Carte Blanche'.
Flight, September 1957, Biggin Hill Airshow report.
Flight, 22 May 1959, 'Open Day with a NATO Flavour' Wethersfield Open House.
Flight, 20 April 1961, 'Shores of Tripoli,' (Wheelus).
Flight, 12 March 1971, Gilson, Charles, 'Tiger on your Tail,' (527th TFTAS).
Flying Magazine, January 1960, Blair, Charles, 'Operation Julius Caesar'.
Heyford Observer (66 TRW), 26 May and 16 June 1967 'Royal Flush' articles.
Jets, Spring 1999, Hooks Mike, 'Armed Force's Days'.
Recce Reader Journal of the Tac Recce Association, Spring 2002.
Scale Aircraft Modelling, August 1995, 'Photo Phantoms'.
Scale Models, May 1977, Lovelock AD and Long G., 'The Friendly Enemy' (527th TFTAS).
Tac Tanker Tales, Vol. 2 Issue 1 and 2, Weber, Dan, ' The 420th AREFS adventure in the Congo'.
Time, 20 March 1964, 'The 120 Mile Error' (Airborne Electronic Chicken, 10th TRW operations).